# COM101: HUMAN COMMUNICATION

## Department of Communication Studies
### *Ashland University*

### Fifth Edition

Cover image © Shutterstock, Inc.

www.kendallhunt.com
*Send all inquiries to*:
4050 Westmark Drive
Dubuque, IA 52004-1840

Published in the United States of America

# BRIEF CONTENTS

TEST 1    PARR 48/50    MALKI 36/50

# CONTENTS

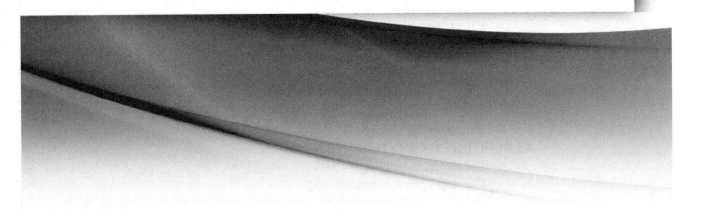

# COM101: HUMAN COMMUNICATION

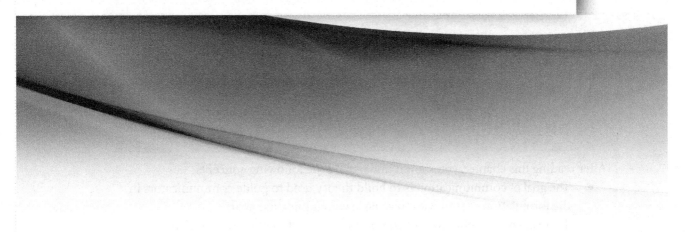

# CHAPTER 1

## What Is Communication?

## Chapter Objectives

After reading this chapter, you should understand the following concepts:

- The goal of communication is to build theory used to guide communicators in the formulation of strategies to achieve communication goals.
- There are many definitions of communication, but they share common characteristics: Communication is a process, messages are sent and received, participants interact in social contexts, and meaning is created and shared through symbols and behavior.
- The action model was the necessary first step in the evolution of communication models, but it has a weakness in that it lacks interaction.
- The interaction model includes the important aspect of feedback.
- The transactional model recognizes that communication is a process, it is irreversible, it means shared responsibility, and it occurs in context and culture.

# INTRODUCTION

"Oh, that's just a theory. It doesn't mean anything!"

Have you heard this before? There is a common misconception that a *theory* is the same thing as a "guess." A theory is a "shot from the hip," or it's a "Monday morning quarterback's" explanation of why his team won or lost on Sunday. Sometimes you hear people express doubt about "relativity" or "evolution" because they are "only theories," and not fact. Not true! A theory is not idle speculation unsupported by evidence that is spontaneously created or made up.

Theories are not guesses! Littlejohn states, "Any attempt to explain or represent an experience is a theory; an idea of how something happens."[1] Kerlinger says that a theory is "a set of interrelated constructs (concepts), definitions, and propositions that present a systematic view of phenomena by specifying relations among variables, with the purpose of explaining and predicting the phenomena."[2]

## WHAT IS THE NATURE OF COMMUNICATION THEORY?

Our definition is that a theory is *an attempt to describe, predict, and / or explain an experience or phenomenon.* The purpose of generating a theory is the attempt to *understand* something:
- Theory is a collection of statements or conceptual assumptions.
- It specifies the relationships among concepts or variables and provides a basis for predicting behavior of a phenomenon.
- It explains a phenomenon.

Here's an illustration from the distant past: Og the cave dweller comes out of his cave in the morning and sees the sun shining in the east. When Og visits the village well later in the day, he and his friends are able to *describe* what happened: "When I came out of my cave, I saw the bright light in the sky!" They can all try to agree on the description, and they will all know what happened.

Over the next several months, Og and his pals emerge from their caves every morning, and every morning they see the sun in the eastern sky. They also notice that the sun has moved to the western sky when they return to their caves in the evening. After several conversations at the village well, they discover or recognize that a *pattern* seems to exist in the behavior of the sun. In the morning, the bright light is over there. But in the evening, the bright light is on the other side. They

© 2008, JupiterImages Corporation.

Og the cave dweller systematically observes the environment.

set up an observational plan to see if their pattern holds up. In the mornings, when Og comes from his cave (which faces south), he looks to his left and he *expects* to see the sun. There it is! Eureka! The observations support the hypothesis (or informed assumption) that the sun will rise in the east! Og and his associates can now *predict* the behavior of the sun!

Og is attempting to build a theory. He is able to describe and predict, but he still comes up short because he does not understand *why* the sun behaves as it does. Og still has much uncertainty about the sun's behavior, and that makes him and all the rest of us humans uncomfortable. So we continue to study it. Now, please "fast forward" from this point several thousand years when, after gathering lots and lots of information, we were finally able to *explain* why the sun appears to rise in the east and set in the west.

Og and his buddies made some observations of phenomena and were able to describe it, then they noticed patterns in the phenomena and were able to predict its behavior. They might have even tried to explain the activity they observed, but they did not have enough knowledge to make a good explanation. The explanation came much later and is beyond the scope of this book. But you can go look it up!

**Empirical**
Describes knowledge claims that are based on observation of reality and are not merely subjective speculation based on the observer's perspective.

What they *did* do was create a partial theory, and that theory was based on empirical observation. Not bad for cave dwellers! *Empirical* means that knowledge claims are based on observations of reality (i.e., the real world) and are not merely subjective speculation based on the observer's perspective. The conclusions are based on *observed* evidence, which helps the observer remain more objective.[3] The cycle of study is repeated over and over: Observation is made, which leads to recognizing a pattern; attempts to predict and explain are made, which become basic theories; the theories help the observer create new hypotheses (predictions) about the behavior of the phenomenon; observation is made and the information analyzed in search of patterns; and those recognized patterns add to the basic theory.[4] As this cycle repeats itself, the body of theory becomes larger and more sophisticated, and the field of study matures.

Observation → Pattern Recognition → Theory → Hypotheses → Observation

The goal of any field of study, including communication, is to *build theory*. The body of communication theory is subsequently used to guide communicators in the formulation of strategies for achieving communication goals and to help communicators understand what skills are necessary for carrying out the strategies.

The purpose of this chapter is to help you understand the basic theory supporting human communication behavior. The skills and strategies necessary to accomplish your communication goals are derived from this theory. This chapter includes the following:
- A definition of communication
- An evolution of conceptions of communication
- A transactional model of communication
- A discussion of essential terms

# HOW IS COMMUNICATION DEFINED?

Defining communication is not quite as easy as it sounds because almost all people, even scholars, think they know what it is. We all communicate every day, so we all have an opinion. The problem is that nearly nobody agrees! Clevenger says that the term *communication* is one of the most "overworked terms in the English language."[5]

To try to make sense of the literally hundreds of different definitions, we will examine some significant attempts to define communication, and then we will draw out the commonalities in the attempt to build our own point of view. Here are some influential examples:
- An individual transmits stimuli to modify the behavior of other individuals.[6]
- Social interaction occurs through symbols and message systems.[7]
- A source transmits a message to receiver(s) with conscious intent to affect the latter's behavior.[8]
- "Senders and receivers of messages interact in given social contexts."[9]
- "Shared meaning through symbolic processes" is created.[10]
- There is mutual creation of shared meaning through the simultaneous interpretation and response to verbal and nonverbal behaviors in a specific context."[11]
- "Communication occurs when one person sends and receives messages that are distorted by noise, occur within a context, have some effect, and provide some opportunity for feedback."[12]

What do these definitions
have in common?
- Communication is a
  process.
- Messages are sent
  and received.
- Participants interact
  in social contexts.
- Meaning is created
  and shared through
  the use of symbols
  and behavior.

The perspective of this book is that *communication is a process in which participants create meaning by using symbols and behavior to send and receive messages within a social and cultural context.* This perspective will be expanded and explained in the remainder of this chapter.

# HOW HAVE THE CONCEPTIONS OF COMMUNICATION EVOLVED?

Now that we have a working definition of communication, let's examine where it came from. This section looks at classic models of communication spanning about 2,500 years. The goal of this section is to illustrate the evolution of the communication perspective taken by this book; to show you how we arrived at the point of view that influences every strategy and skill that we teach. We believe that if you understand why we teach it, you will be more motivated to learn and to use this point of view to plan and execute your own communication strategies!

# WHAT ARE THE MODELS OF COMMUNICATION?

You have seen and used a map many times. If you are looking for a particular street in your town, you pick up a map to find where the street is and to learn how to get there from where you are. A map is not your town, however, but a *representation* of your town. It's a picture or drawing that helps you understand the way your town is arranged. A *model* is the very same thing. But instead of representing a physical space, like a town, the model represents a process, or the way something happens.

As a map represents a place, a model represents a process.

The models discussed here represent three views of communication that have enjoyed popularity over the years. Those three views are action (or linear), interaction, and transaction. These models help illustrate and explain the current view of communication, the transactional perspective. Each will be discussed in the following pages.

© Stephen VanHorn, 2008, Shutterstock.

## The Action Model

Although many perspectives of communication contributed to what we are calling the action model, Aristotle and the *Shannon and Weaver models* had the most impact.

➤ **Shannon Weaver Model**
See Figure 1.1.

We'll start with *Aristotle*, a philosopher, scientist, and teacher who lived in ancient Greece. Educated by Plato and the son of a physician, he was trained as a biologist.[13] He was skilled at observing and describing, and at categorizing his observations.[14] Aristotle found himself interested in nearly all things that occupied the attention of the citizens of Athens, including the study of speaking.

➤ **Aristotle**
A philosopher, scientist, and teacher who lived in ancient Greece.

Ancient Athens was a democracy, and all citizens had the right and opportunity to influence public affairs and public policy. The more articulate citizens were able to affect events by persuading or influencing other citizens and law makers in public meetings. Because individual citizens had a voice, teachers of public speaking and persuasion were always in demand.

Aristotle's *Rhetoric* is a published collection of his teachings,[15] and it has been suggested that it is the "most important single work on persuasion ever written."[16] The focus of the *Rhetoric* is primarily on the speaker and the message. Some, but little, attention is paid to the audience. The philosophy is that a well-crafted message delivered by a credible speaker will have the desired effect with the audience. If Aristotle had a model of persuasion, the simple version would probably look something like this:

© 2008 JupiterImages Corporation.

Aristotle used his observation skills to study communication in ancient Greece.

> WELL-CRAFTED MESSAGE + CREDIBLE SOURCE = DESIRED EFFECT

Aristotle's contribution to communication would not have been this model. His contributions came in the form of instructions for how to use logic and emotions (*logos* and *pathos*) to craft a message, and how to establish and build credibility as a speaker or source of a message (*ethos*).

*ETHOS* ✱
*LOGOS*
*PATHOS*

For the second time in this chapter, please fast forward in time, but this time only about two thousand years. Stop when you get to the 1940s, and we'll take a look at **Claude Shannon** and **Warren Weaver**. Claude Shannon was a mathematician who worked at Bell Labs, and he was interested in ways to make more efficient use of telephone lines for the transmission of voices. He was not concerned about

**Source** A person.

**Message** Communication expressed in words or actions.

**Code** Language.

**Encoded** Describes messages created by a sender in a format that makes sense to the sender, in hopes that the messages will be understood in the same or similar way by the receiver.

**Transmitted** Describes messages or signals sent or passed on to communicate information.

**Channel** Sound waves created by the voice, or come via mediated signal.

A message in a bottle lacks the interaction we have in everyday conversations.

human communication, but he was very focused on electronic communication. Shannon teamed with Warren Weaver, a scientist and mathematician, to publish the *Mathematical Theory of Communication*. Shannon's focus was on the engineering aspects of the theory, while Weaver was more interested in the human and other implications. Communication scholars found this model to be very useful in helping them to explain *human* communication.[17]

The Shannon–Weaver model is consistent with Aristotle's point of view, and it extends it to include a transmitter, a channel, and a receiver. It also introduces the concept of *noise* to the explanation. The process is illustrated in Figure 1.1. The *source* (a person) initiates a *message* that is turned into a *code* (language), and the *encoded* message is sent (*transmitted*) through a *channel* (sound waves created by the voice, or some mediated signal). The *receiver decodes* the signal (turning it again into a message), which is sent to the *destination* (the other person). Noise is anything that can interfere with the signal. See Figure 1.1.

This model helps to understand human communication, but it has a significant shortcoming: it doesn't adequately capture the reality or the complexity of the process. It assumes that the participants in the process take on discrete speaker or listener roles, and that while one person speaks, the other person quietly listens with no response, until the speaker is finished. Then the roles are reversed. Then the roles are reversed again, and again and again, until the conversation is complete. *Human communication is arguably not that linear!* It is equivalent to placing a message in a bottle, throwing it into the sea, and waiting for it to reach the proper destination. The person (receiver) removes the message from the bottle, reads the message, writes a new message, places it back in the bottle, and throws it back into the sea. The model works, but it doesn't represent the way that we communicate in everyday conversations. It lacks *interaction*!

**FIGURE 1.1**

The Shannon–Weaver Mathematical Model

Information Source → Transmitter (Encoder) → Channel → Receiver (Decoder) → Destination

Message     Signal     Received Signal     Message

Noise Source

Courtesy of Ashland University

```
                            Message
SOURCE ─────────────────────────────────────────────▶ RECEIVER
                            Channel
```

FIGURE 1.2

Action Model

➤ **Receiver decodes**
The form in which a receiver understands a message or information; may or may not be similar to the understanding of the sender (see *Encoded*).

➤ **Destination**
Other person receiving a message.

➤ **Action model**
The fault is with the source.

As you consider the two models just discussed, you can see that they are primarily concerned with the source of the message and the content of the message itself. The focus is on the source and how he or she constructs and delivers the message. So a source that creates well-designed messages has done everything possible to ensure effective communication. Say the right thing and you will be successful! If something goes wrong, or if the source is not clearly understood by the potential receiver, the *action model* states that the fault is with the source. However, when everything goes well and the message is clearly understood, it is because the source crafted and sent a good-quality message. See Figure 1.2 for a depiction of the action model. The action model was the necessary first step in the evolution of the contemporary communication model.

## *The Interaction Model*

The *interaction model* remains linear, like the action model, but it begins to view the source and receiver as a team in the communication process.

➤ **Interaction model**
Remains linear, like the action model, but it begins to view the source and the receiver as a team in the communication process.

*Wilbur Schramm* introduced a model of communication that includes a notion of *interaction*.[18] The Schramm model does not consider the context or environment in which the communication takes place, and it does not explicitly treat codes (language) or noise. Although it is still very linear, it describes the dual roles played by the participants instead of viewing one as a source (speaker) and the other as a receiver (listener), and it makes a strong case for *interaction* among the participants. The flow of information can be seen as more ongoing or continuous, rather than a linear, back-and-forth type of flow. The conception of communication is emerging as a *process*. See Figure 1.3.

➤ **Wilbur Schramm**
Introduced a model of communication that includes a notion of *interaction*.

*David Berlo*, in *The Process of Communication*, began to discuss process and the complexity of communication.[19] This model fully includes the receiver, and it places importance on the *relationship* between the source and receiver. It also illustrates that the source and receiver are not just reacting to the environment or each other, but that each possesses individual differences based on knowledge and attitudes, and that each operates within a cultural and social system that influences meaning. Because we all have different knowledge and attitudes, we interpret or give meaning to messages in different ways. This makes human communication very complex!

➤ **David Berlo**
In The *Process of Communication*, began to discuss process and the complexity of communication.

FIGURE 1.3

Schramm's Model of
Communication

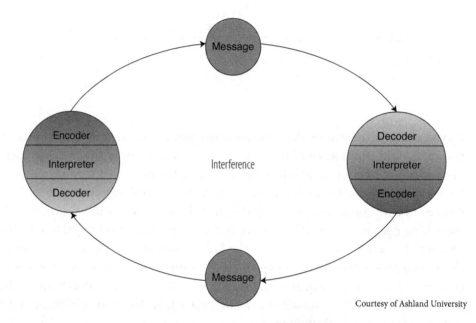

Courtesy of Ashland University

FIGURE 1.4

Berlo's SMCR Model of
Communication

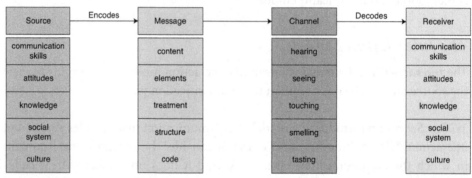

Courtesy of Ashland University

**Feedback**
Information that is routed
to the source, or fed back,
from the receiver.

Although it was not explicitly mentioned in the model (see Figure 1.4), Berlo discussed the notion of *feedback* in his book. Feedback is information that is routed to the source, or fed back, from the receiver. Berlo said, "Feedback provides the source with information concerning his success in accomplishing his objective. In doing this, it exerts control over future messages which the source encodes."[20]

Berlo completed the loop left unfinished by the Shannon–Weaver model. The source encodes a message, sent through a channel to a receiver, who decodes it and assigns meaning. The receiver then sends a message back to the source (feedback) indicating, among other things, that the message was understood. Even though this is still a linear model, we are getting closer to a model that begins to capture the nature of human communication. But it's not quite there yet!

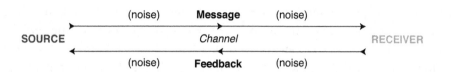

FIGURE 1.5

Interaction Model

These two models, and models like them, can be *summarized* in what we call the *interaction model* (see Figure 1.5). A source sends a message through a noise-filled channel to a receiver. The receiver responds to the source through feedback, which is a message sent by the receiver to the source through a noise-filled channel. The core of the interaction model is that the source is the originator and that the receiver creates feedback to that message. Like the action model, the interaction model implies that the process is linear; that is, communicators take turns being first a source then a receiver, and so on. The interaction model was the second step in the evolution of the contemporary communication model.

## *The Transactional Model*

More contemporary conceptions view communication as an ongoing process in which all participants send and receive messages simultaneously. All participants are both speakers *and* listeners.[21] "A person is giving feedback, talking, responding, acting, and reacting through a communication event."[22] The **transactional model** incorporates this point of view along with the notion that the creation of the meaning of a message is not the sole responsibility of the source or the receiver, but a responsibility that is shared among all participants in a communication situation or event.

> **Transactional model** Incorporates this view along with the notion that the creation of the meaning of a message is not the sole responsibility of the source or receiver, but a responsibility that is shared among all participants in a communication situation or event.

**PROPERTIES OF TRANSACTIONAL COMMUNICATION.** To get a clear view of the transactional model of communication, it is necessary to understand the important properties of communication. Properties include process, irreversibility, shared responsibility, context, and culture. These five properties are discussed in this section.

**Communication Is a Process.** Many conceptualizations of communication describe it as a process. The notion of *process* is not unique to communication; it comes to us from the literature of *theoretical physics*. A little closer to home, the notion of process and its relationship to human behavior can be found in *general systems theory*.[23] Although we use this term all the time, it's important to understand what the term *process* implies.

> **Process** Implies that communication is ongoing.

Process implies that communication is continuous and ongoing. It is *dynamic*: It never stops. Barnlund[24] says that a process has no beginning and no end. It constantly changes and evolves, new information and experience is added, and it becomes even more complex.[25] There is ongoing and constant mutual influence of the participants.[26] Participants are *constantly* sending and receiving verbal and nonverbal messages. You can try to take a "snapshot" of a single episode, and you can observe the date and time of its beginning and ending, but you can't say that this is where the communication began and ended. Heisenberg stated that to observe a process requires bringing it to a halt.[27] This gives us a fuzzy look at what is really happening, because stopping a process alters the process. So we have to do the best we can to observe, understand, and participate in communication events.

Consider, for example, a father asking his son to practice his saxophone. The father says, "Pete, please go to your room and practice your saxophone for 20 minutes." Pete (clearly annoyed) responds, "Come on, Dad! I'm right in the middle of this video game. Can't I do it later?" The father immediately gets angry and sends Pete to his room "to think about what he has done," followed by 20 minutes of saxophone practice.

The episode seems to be over, but we wonder why the young man was so annoyed at being asked to practice and why the father got angry so quickly. Could it be that this was only *one* installment in a series of episodes in which the father tries to get Pete to practice? Or could it be that Pete was having some difficulty with the saxophone that made him not want to practice? Or is there something else going on that we can't see in only this one episode? Will this episode affect future episodes?

The answer to the last question is yes! Communication is influenced by events that come before it, and it influences events that follow it.

**Communication Is Irreversible.** Messages are sent and received, and all participants give meaning to those messages as they happen. Once the behavior has occurred, it becomes part of history and can't be reversed. Have you ever said something that you wish you could take back? It doesn't matter if you meant it or not; once it's out there, you have to deal with it.

As mentioned in a previous section, the prior experience or history of the participants influences the meaning created in the current interaction. Even if you try to take something back or pretend it didn't happen, it still has influence in the current and future interactions. Occasionally, in a court case, an attorney or a witness will say something that the judge decides is inappropriate to the case, and he or she will instruct the jury to "disregard" the statement. Do you think the members of the jury are able to remove the statement from their memories? Have you ever heard that as a member of a jury? What did you do?

A friend of ours was asked the question that no married person wants to hear. While clothes shopping, the spouse asked, "Do these pants make me look fat?" Instead of pretending not to hear the question or saying an emphatic no, our friend said, "The pants are very nice, honey. It's your backside that makes you look fat!" For almost a whole minute, it seemed pretty funny. Multiple attempts to take back the comment failed. That communication episode affected the meaning of nearly every conversation they had for several months. *Communication is irreversible.* And you thought this book would have no practical advice!

**Communication Means Shared Responsibility.** Poor communication is not the fault of *one **participant*** in a conversation. If communication breaks down, you can't blame it on the "other guy." It is the fault of *all* the participants. The transactional perspective implies that it is the responsibility of all participants to cooperate to create a shared meaning. Even if a few of the participants are deficient in some communication skills, it is the responsibility of each person to adapt to the situation and ensure that everyone understands. Even the less capable have responsibilities: If they do not understand, they have the responsibility to ask the other participants to help them understand. *All participants cooperate to create meaning.*

**Communication Occurs in a Context.** The participants in the communication event affect or influence each other, and they are also affected and influenced by the context or environment in which the communication event occurs.

**Communication Occurs within Cultures.** Much like context, the participants are affected or influenced by the culture of which they are members and by the culture in which the communication event takes place.

SPECIFICS OF THE TRANSACTION MODEL. The evolution of communication theory through the action and interaction models has brought us to the current perspective, the transaction model. This book is based on the transaction model, and all of the communication strategies we suggest are based on the model and its properties.

➤ **Participant**
Person involved in communication. "Although the action and interaction models use the terms *source* and *receiver* or *speaker* and *listener*, we simply use the term **participant**... because all persons in communication events are simultaneously sending and receiving verbal and non-verbal message, the terms used in earlier models are no longer descriptive."

How does your culture affect communication?

© 2008 JupiterImages Corporation.

Wallace and others view the transactional perspective as *the joint creation of shared meaning through the simultaneous perception of verbal and nonverbal behaviors within a specific context.*[28] Although you are speaking or sending messages, you constantly receive and give meaning to information from the environment and from other participants. Similarly, while you are listening to another participant, you are sending nonverbal messages through eye contact, facial expressions, posture, and body movements. So we don't really take turns being the source and receiver as illustrated by the action and interaction models. Instead, we are constantly sending *and* receiving messages!

For example, a husband asks a wife if she minds if he plays golf on a Saturday afternoon. All the time he is asking the question, he is constantly scanning for every nonverbal clue to find out how she really feels. It might be her posture, or the way she looks at (or away from) him, or a particular facial expression, or some combination of everything that provides her response long before she speaks. Lots of information is being exchanged in this situation, which helps this couple create *and* share meaning.

Think about the first time you met your girlfriend's or boyfriend's parents. Think about your first date with somebody you were really interested in. Or consider meeting a potential client for a business deal. Doing business is important to both participants, so you both are very careful to gather all the available information to reduce uncertainty, become more comfortable, and formulate and confirm strategies for accomplishing communication goals. You use the information to create and share meaning!

How do you prepare for a meeting with a new business associate?

In the transaction model, *participants create shared meaning* by simultaneously sending and receiving verbal and nonverbal messages within a specific context. Please see Figure 1.6 for a depiction of the model. The transaction model is reflected and applied in every chapter of this book.

© Kiselev Andrey Valerevich, 2008. Shutterstock.

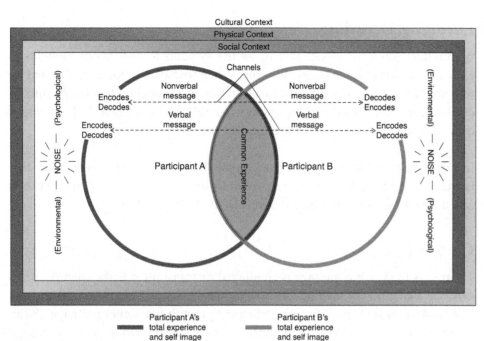

FIGURE 1.6

Transactional Model

# WHAT DO THE TERMS MEAN?

We know that you're tired of all the theory talk, but we have to define some terms so that we are all on the same page. All of these terms have been used in this chapter, but some have been used in different ways in the various models. This section will establish the way each term will be used throughout the book.

## *Communicators/Participants*

Although the action and interaction models use the terms *source* and *receiver* or *speaker* and *listener*, we will simply use the term participant. Because there is no exchange of speaker and listener roles, and because all persons in communication events are simultaneously sending and receiving verbal and nonverbal messages, the terms used in earlier models are no longer descriptive.

The message contains the content of the thought we wish to share with other participants.

## Encoding/Decoding

Communication is symbolic. That is, we use symbols to convey our thoughts to each other in the effort to create meaning. When we have a thought or idea that we want to share with others, we must first translate that thought into a set of symbols, or a language, that the other participants will be able to understand. This process of converting our thoughts to symbols is called encoding.

In turn, when we listen to or receive symbols/language, we have to translate that language into thoughts. That is, we give "meaning" to the symbols. This process is called decoding. Symbols are used to represent objects or ideas.

## Channel

The means by which a message is conducted or transmitted is the channel. Berlo says that a channel (or medium) is a *carrier* of messages.[29] As such, a channel can be sound waves that travel from a participant's mouth to another participant's ear. It can also be a form of sound amplification to reach a crowd of people in a large room. A channel can also be a radio or television signal, or a book or a newspaper that carries messages to millions of people. More recently, the Internet is a very popular channel for carrying messages to individuals or large groups of people.

## Noise

*Noise* is anything that interferes with or distorts the transmission of the signal. *Environmental noise* is interference with the signal as it moves from the source to the destination. This could take the form of sounds in the room that prevent the receiver from hearing the message; it could be static on a telephone line, or even a dropped call on a cellular phone. *Psychological noise* takes place inside the sender or receiver, such as misunderstanding or failing to remember what was heard.

## Context

Context can be viewed as physical or social. The *physical context* is made up of the space surrounding the communication event, or the place in which the communication event occurs. The context could be a classroom, a meeting room at work, a church, a physician's office, your house, your favorite "night spot," or about any other place you can imagine. The place in which the event takes place influences communication behaviors and the meanings attributed to them. How would your behavior change if you moved from your favorite night spot to a classroom? Would you behave the same way?

How does an event's context affect communication?

© 2008 JupiterImages Corporation.

The *social context* considers the nature of the event taking place in a physical context. The social expectations tied to particular events influence meaning attributed to communication. Even though you were still in a classroom, you would behave differently during an exam than during a group work session. You would behave differently in church during a funeral than celebrating a festive holiday, and you would certainly behave differently while playing bingo in the church basement!

## Culture

The *culture* in which the communication occurs and the native cultures of the participants can influence meaning. People belong to a variety of nations, traditions, groups, and organizations, each of which has its own point of view, values, and norms.[30] A culture is made up of the collective beliefs or principles on which a community or part of a community of people is based. These beliefs are often passed from generation to generation and provide a perspective through which the community makes sense of its experiences. The culture, then, provides a very powerful context or backdrop for communication events and has a profound influence on the meaning that participants create and share.

**Physical context** Made up of the space surrounding the communication event, of the place in which the communication event occurs.

**Social context** Considers the nature of the event taking place in the physical context.

**Culture** State in which the communication occurs and in which the native cultures of the participants can influence the meaning.

# CHAPTER SUMMARY

That's enough of the theory, at least for the moment. Let's get to the application! Keep in mind, however, that a solid understanding of the basics of the transactional model will provide a lot of help to you as you attempt to plan strategies and practice your skills to help you achieve your communication goals.

# KEY WORDS

*Action model* The fault is with the source.

*Aristotle* A philosopher, scientist, and teacher who lived in ancient Greece.

*Carrier* Means of sharing communication.

*Channel* Sound waves created by the voice, or come via mediated signal.

*Code* Language.

*Culture* State in which the communication occurs and in which the native cultures of the participants can influence the meaning.

*David Berlo* In *The Process of Communication*, began to discuss process and the complexity of communication.

*Destination* Other person receiving a message.

*Empirical* Describes knowledge claims that are based on observation of reality and are not merely subjective speculation based on the observer's perspective.

*Encoded* Describes messages created by a sender in a format that makes sense to the sender, in hopes that the messages will be understood in the same or similar way by the receiver.

*Environmental noise* Interference with the signal as it moves from the source to the destination.

*Feedback* Information that is routed to the source, or fed back, from the receiver.

*Interaction model* Remains linear, like the action model, but it begins to view the source and the receiver as a team in the communication process.

*Message* Communication expressed in words or actions.

*Noise* Anything that can interfere with a communication signal.

*Participant* Person involved in communication.

*Physical context* Made up of the space surrounding the communication event, of the place in which the communication event occurs.

*Process* Implies that communication is ongoing.

*Psychological noise* Takes place inside the sender or receiver, such as a misunderstanding or failing to remember what was heard.

*Receiver decodes* The form in which a receiver understands a message or information; may or may not be similar to the understanding of the sender (see *Encoded*).

*Shannon Weaver Model* (provide picture)

*Social context* Considers the nature of the event taking place in the physical context.

*Source* A person.

*Theory* An attempt to describe, predict, and/or explain an experience or phenomenon.

*Transactional model* Incorporates this view along with the notion that the creation of the meaning of a message is not the sole responsibility of the source or receiver, but a responsibility that is shared among all participants in a communication situation or event.

*Transmitted* Describes messages or signals sent or passed on to communicate information.

*Wilbur Schramm* Introduced a model of communication that includes a notion of *interaction*.

"Although the action and interaction models use the terms *source* and *receiver* or *speaker* and *listener*, we simply use the term **participant**... because all persons in communication events are simultaneously sending and receiving verbal and non-verbal message, the terms used in earlier models are no longer descriptive."

"The means by which a message is conducted or transmitted is the channel. Berlo says that a channel (or medium) is a carrier or messages"

"The **source** (a person) initiates a **message** that is turned into a **code** (language), and the **encoded** message is sent (**transmitted**) through a **channel** (sound waves created by the voice, or come mediated signal). The **receiver decodes** the signal (turning it into a message), which is sent to the **destination** (the other person). **Noise** is anything that can interfere with the signal."

# ENDNOTES

1. S. Littlejohn, *Theories of Human Communication* (Belmont, CA: Wadsworth, 1999), 2.
2. F. Kerlinger, *Foundations of Behavioral Research* (New York: Holt, Rinehart, and Winston, 1973), 9.
3. M. Polanyi, *Personal Knowledge* (Chicago: University of Chicago Press, 1958).
4. W. Wallace, *The Logic of Science in Sociology* (Chicago: Aldine, 1971).
5. T. Clevenger, "Can One Not Communicate? A Conflict of Models," *Communication Studies* 42 (1991), 351.
6. C. Hovland, I. Janis, and H. Kelley, *Communication and Persuasion* (New Haven, CT: Yale University Press, 1953).
7. G. Gerbner, "On Defining Communication: Still Another View," *Journal of Communication* 16 (1966), 99–103.
8. G. Miller, "On Defining Communication: Another Stab," *Journal of Communication* 16 (1966), 92.
9. K. Sereno and C.D. *Mortensen, Foundations of Communication Theory* (New York: Harper & Row, 1970), 5.
10. J. Makay, *Public Speaking: Theory into Practice* (Dubuque, IA: Kendall/Hunt, 2000), 9.
11. L. Hugenberg, S. Wallace, and D. Yoder, *Creating Competent Communication* (Dubuque, IA: Kendall/Hunt, 2003), 4.
12. J. DeVito, *Human Communication: The Basic Course* (Boston, Allyn & Bacon, 2006), 2.
13. J. Golden, G. Berquist, W. Coleman, and J. Sproule, *The Rhetoric of Western Thought, 8th ed.* (Dubuque, IA: Kendall/Hunt, 2003).
14. D. Stanton, and G. Berquist, "Aristotle's Rhetoric: Empiricism or Conjecture?" *Southern Speech Communication Journal* 41 (1975), 69–81.
15. L. Cooper, *The Rhetoric of Aristotle* (New York: Appleton-Century-Crofts, 1932).
16. Golden etal., 65.
17. C. Shannon, and W. Weaver, *The Mathematical Theory of Communication* (Urbana: University of Illinois Press, 1949). Also W. Weaver, "The Mathematics of Communication," in C.D. Mortensen (ed.), *Basic Readings in Communication Theory* (New York: Harper & Row, 1979).
18. W. Schramm, "How Communication Works," in W. Schramm, (ed.), *The Process and Effects of Communication* (Urbana: University of Illinois Press, 1954).

19. D. Berlo, *The Process of Communication* (New York: Holt, Rinehart, and Winston, 1960).
20. Ibid pp.111–112.
21. Barnlund, D. (1970). "A Transactional Model of Communication," in *Foundations of Communication Theory*, Sereno, K. and Mortensen, C. D. (eds.). New York: Harper & Row, 1970. Also P. Watzlawick, *How Real Is Real? Confusion, Disinformation, Communication: An Anecdotal Introduction to Communications Theory* (New York: Vintage, 1977).
22. M. Burgoon and M. Ruffner, *Human Communication.* (New York: Holt, Rinehart, & Winston, 1978), 9.
23. E. Lazlo, *The Systems View of the World: A Holistic Vision for Our Time* (New York: Hampton Press, 1996). Also L. von Bertalanffy, *General System Theory: Foundations, Development, Applications* (New York: Braziller, 1976).
24. Barnlund.
25. F. Dance, "Toward a Theory of Human Communication," In F. Dance (ed.), *Human Communication Theory: Original Essays* (New York: Holt, 1967).
26. K. Miller, *Communication Theories: Perspectives, Processes, and Contexts* (New York: McGraw-Hill, 2005).
27. W. Heisenberg, *The Physical Principles of Quantum Theory* (Chicago: University of Chicago Press, 1930).
28. S. Wallace, D. Yoder, L. Hugenberg, and C. Horvath, *Creating Competent Communication*, 5th ed. (Dubuque, IA: Kendall/Hunt, 2006).
29. Berlo.
30. Yoder, Hugenberg, and Wallace. *Creating Competent Communication.* (Dubuque, IA: Kendall/Hunt, 1993).

# REFERENCES

T. Newcomb, "An Approach to the Study of Communicative Acts," *Psychological review* 60 (1953), 393–404.

P. Watzlawick, J. Beavin, and D. Jackson, *Pragmatics of Human Communication* (New York: Norton, 1967).

# DEFINITIONS AND MODELS

Do you have all that? Communication is a process, messages are sent and received, meaning is created and shared, and all this happens in a social context. Okay, let's move on. No! Wait a minute! The point of this chapter is to show you how remarkably complicated the act of communication is. Most of us have been doing it for so long that we take it for granted. We say something, and people either get it or they don't. We blame them for the misunderstanding and we move on. Unfortunately, we may be at fault. (Don't you hate when that happens?) We have all been the victims of a misunderstanding or miscommunication. A friend tweets you a funny message but you take it the wrong way. You use a term that is perfectly clear to you but your instructor has no idea what you mean. An international student tries to translate an idea from her culture to make sense to an Ashland University student.

Communication is difficult to do well. That is why you are in this class.

# LESSON #1 IN COMMUNICATION STUDIES

### *There Is No* Perfect *in the Art of Communication.*

Every person is different. We each see the world differently. So when we try to talk to someone, we have to overcome the differences between us. Communication really is an art. Do you think there is a perfect painting or a perfect song? No, great paintings and songs speak to us and show us great beauty but humans are imperfect beings/artists. Paintings and music represent what we see or how we feel, but a portrait is not the person and a love song cannot say everything about the emotion of love. As a result, our art and our messages are also imperfect. The purpose of this course is to help us think about our communication in the hope that we can do it better. Better communicators are better friends, parents, employees, and people. Do you see how important this class is now?

The second problem we encounter as students of communication is this:

If everyone is different, how are we going to talk about communication? Think about it. You speak differently with your friends than you do with your parents. You might speak differently with a boyfriend/girlfriend than you do with your buddies. In fact, you probably speak a little differently with each of your friends. This means that every communication interaction is unique. Bob speaking with Mary is different than Jane speaking with Kahmal. And so on and so on.

To analyze and talk about communication we create **models** and **theories**. A **model** allows us to look at the **process** of communication. In this way, we can talk about all the things that must be present in an effective message. **Theories** have been given a bad name in recent years. Any idiot can create a theory. I believe that chicken soup causes cancer. You see, I knew a person who ate chicken soup and was diagnosed with cancer. Is it a theory: Yes. Is it a good theory: **No**! A scientific theory rises to a higher order of proof. Observation, testing, restatement, more testing, refinement; suddenly, the chicken soup statement is recognized as foolish.

Theories and models of communication will ground you in a better understanding of the research that has been conducted in the field of communication. The hope is that you will not only learn more about the communication process but you might become interested in the study of communication as well. There is some really interesting stuff here! Wait until you read about Verbal and Nonverbal Communication.

# CHAPTER 2

## What Is the Power of Verbal and Nonverbal Communication?

### Chapter Objectives

After reading this chapter, you should understand the following concepts:
- Language is a shared system of symbols and structures in organized patterns to express thoughts and feelings.
- Language is arbitrary, it changes over time, it consists of denotative and connotative meaning, and it is structured by rules.
- The semantic triangle, Sapir–Whorf hypothesis, and muted group theory are three models that help explain how meaning is created.
- Strategies for using language effectively involve using accurate and appropriate language, using unbiased language, and avoiding verbal distractions.
- We constantly send nonverbal messages that present an image of ourselves to others, so it important to be aware of what those messages are saying.

- Nonverbal communication is often ambiguous, continuous, unconscious, sometimes learned and intentional—and usually, more believed than verbal communication.
- Nonverbal messages perform six functions to create meaning: complementing, substituting, repeating, contradicting, regulating, and deceiving.
- Types of nonverbal communication include body movement, use of space, dress and appearance, and eye contact.

# INTRODUCTION

Using words to describe magic is like using a screwdriver to cut roast beef.
   —Tom Robbins, twentieth century American author
Better wise language than well-combed hair.
   —Icelandic Proverb
All credibility, all good conscience, all evidence of truth come only from the senses.
   —Friedrich Wilhelm Nietzsche, nineteenth century German philosopher
Eloquence is the power to translate a truth into language perfectly intelligible to the person to whom you speak.
   —Ralph Waldo Emerson, nineteenth century U.S. poet, essayist
Get in touch with the way the other person feels. Feelings are 55 percent body language, 38 percent tone and 7 percent words.
   —author unknown
The limits of my language means the limits of my world.
   —Ludwig Wittgenstein, twentieth century philosopher
The eyes are the windows to the soul.
   —Yousuf Karsh, twentieth century Canadian photographer
The difference between the right word and the almost right word is the difference between lightning and a lightning bug.
   —Mark Twain, nineteenth century American author
Dialogue should simply be a sound among other sounds, just something that comes out of the mouths of people whose eyes tell the story in visual terms.
   —Alfred Hitchcock, twentieth century film director

Through these quotations, you've just been exposed to the *power of verbal and nonverbal communication* to define our beliefs, expose our values, and share our experiences. The words that you use and the nonverbal behaviors that accompany them are critically important as you communicate, because they have the ability to clarify your ideas to others or to confuse them. In this chapter, you'll learn about verbal language and nonverbal communication, to discover how they are used to create shared meaning.

# WHAT IS LANGUAGE?

Verbal language and nonverbal communication are used to create shared meaning.

So what do we know about language? Linguists estimate that there are about 5,000 to 6,000 different languages spoken in the world today; about 200 languages have a million or more native speakers. Mandarin Chinese is the most common, followed by Hindi, English, Spanish, and Bengali.[1] However, as technology continues to shrink the communication world, English is becoming more dominant in mediated communication. According to Internet World Stats, which charts usage and population statistics, the top ten languages used in the Web are English (31% of all Internet users), Chinese (15.7%), Spanish (8.7%), Japanese (7.4%), and French and German (5% each).[2] English is one of the official languages of the United Nation, the International Olympic Committee, in academics and in the sciences.[3] English is also the language spoken by air traffic controllers worldwide. Yet the English that we speak in the United States is really a hybrid, using vocabulary taken from many sources, influenced by media, technology, and globalization. Let's consider what all of this means for you as you try to share meaning with others.

**Language** is a shared system of symbols structured in organized patterns to express thoughts and feelings. **Symbols** are arbitrary labels that we give to some idea or phenomenon. For example, the word *run* represents an action that we do, while *bottle* signifies a container for a liquid. Words are symbols, but not all symbols are words. Music, photographs, and logos are also symbols that stand for something else, as do nonverbal actions such as "OK," and "I don't know." However, in this section, we're going to focus on words as symbols. Note that the definition of language says that it's structured and shared. Languages have a **grammar** (syntax, a patterned set of rules that aid in meaning). You've learned grammar as you've been taught how to write, and it's become an unconscious part of your daily communication. Take, for example, this sentence:

The glokkish Vriks mounged oupily on the brangest Ildas.

Now, we can answer these questions:

Who did something? The Vriks mounged.
What kind of Vriks are they? Glokkish
How did they mounge? Oupily

On what did they mounge? The Ildas
What kind of Ildas are they? Brangest

You might have difficulty identifying noun, verb, adverb, and adjective, but because you know the grammar of the English language, you're still able to decipher what this sentence is telling you because of the pattern, even if the symbols themselves lack meaning for now. That leads to the next part of the definition: *symbols must be shared in order to be understood.* George Herbert Mead's Symbolic Interaction Theory asserts that meaning is **intersubjective**; that means that **meaning** *can exist only when people share common interpretations of the symbols they exchange.*[4] So if you were given a picture of Vriks and were told that these were ancient hill people of a particular region of the country, you'd have a start at meaning!

In order to get a grasp on language, this section will uncover basic principles about language, introduce to you a few theoretical perspectives, and then will suggest language strategies to enhance your communication.

English is the language spoken by airline pilots and air traffic controllers all over the world.

© 2008, JupiterImages.

# WHAT ARE THE BASIC PRINCIPLES OF LANGUAGE?

There are some basic principles of language. It is arbitrary, it changes over time, it consists of denotative and connotative meanings, and it is structured by rules. Let's look at these more closely.

## *Arbitrary*

"Language is arbitrary" means that *symbols do not have a one-to-one connection with what they represent.* What is the computer form that you use if you take a test? Is it a bubble sheet? A scantron? An opscan? Each of these names has no natural connection to that piece of paper, and it's likely that at different universities, it's called different names. Because language is arbitrary, people in groups agree on labels to use, creating private codes. That's why your organization might have specialized terms, why the military uses codes, and why your family uses nicknames that only they understand. The language that you create within that group creates group meaning and culture. The arbitrary element of language also adds to its ambiguity; meanings just aren't stable. To me, a test is the same as an exam; to you, a test might be less than an exam. If you say to me, "I'll call you later," how do I define the term *later*? We often fall into the trap of thinking that everyone understands us, but the reality is, it's an amazing thing that we share meaning at all!

## Changes over Time

Language *changes over time* in vocabulary, as well as syntax. New vocabulary is required for the latest inventions, for entertainment and leisure pursuits, for political use. In 2007, the top television buzzwords included *surge* and D'oh, while in 2006, they were *truthiness* and *wikiality*.[5] How many of those words play a role in your culture today? Words like *cell phones* and *Internet* didn't exist fifty years ago, for example. In addition, no two people use a language in exactly the same way. Teens and young adults often use different words and phrases than their parents. The vocabulary and phrases people use may depend on where they live, their age, education level, social status, and other factors. Through our interactions, we pick up new words and phases, and then we integrate them into our communication.

© 2008, JupiterImages.

How is your language different from your parents' and grandparents'?

## Consists of Denotative and Connotative Meanings

**Denotative meanings**, the literal, dictionary definitions, are precise and objective. **Connotative meanings** reflect your personal, subjective definitions. They add layers of experience and emotions to meaning. Elizabeth J. Natalle examined this dichotomy in a case study of urban music, examining how our language has evolved over the years to include more negative connotation regarding talk about women as compared to talk about men. Think about *chick, sweetie, sugar pie and old maid, versus stud, hunk, playboy*, and *bachelor*. Do you get a different image? Using a study of rap music, she attempted to clarify how urban music names a particular world, creates male community, and has implications for power and gendered relationships.[6]

A simpler way to consider denotative and connotative meanings is to examine the terms President Bush used to describe the terrorists who crashed the planes on Sept. 11, 2001. Bush's labels on that day in various locations began with "those folks who committed this act" (remarks by the president when he first heard that two planes crashed into World Trade Center)[7] to "those responsible for these cowardly acts" (remarks by the president upon arrival at Barksdale Air Force Base)[8] to "those who are behind these evil acts" and "the terrorists who committed these acts" (statement by the president in his address to the nation).[9] Consider how the connotative meaning shaped the image of the perpetrators.

David K. Berlo[10] provided several assumptions about meaning:

- Meanings are in people.
- Communication does not consist of the transmission of meanings, but of the transmission of messages.
- Meanings are not in the message; they are in the message users.
- Words do not mean at all; only people mean.
- People can have similar meanings only to the extent that they have had, or can anticipate having, similar experiences.
- Meanings are never fixed; as experience changes, so meanings change.
- No two people can have exactly the same meaning for anything.

These ideas echo the idea that when you use words, you need to be aware of the extent to which meaning is shared. For example, when an adoptive parent sees those "adopt a highway" locator signs, it's probable that that person sees something different than others might. "Adopt a" programs might be seen as confusing and misleading others about the term *adoption*. An adoptive parent might say that you don't adopt a road, a zoo animal, or a Cabbage Patch doll. Adoption is a means of family building, and it has a very subjective, emotional meaning.[11] To the town official who erected the sign, it's a representation of the good work being done by some group to keep the highway clean.

What does this sign's language mean to you?

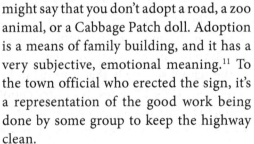

## *Structured by Rules*

As we understand and use the rules of language, we begin to share meaning. Think of rules as a shared understanding of what language means, as well as an understanding of what kind of language is appropriate in various contexts. Many of the rules you use weren't consciously learned; you gathered them from interactions with other people. Some, however, were learned aspects of your culture.

**Phonological rules** *regulate how words sound when you pronounce them.* They help us organize language. For instance, the word lead could be used to suggest a behavior that you do (you *lead* the group to show them the way) or a kind of toxic metallic element (*lead* paint in windows is harmful to children). Do you enjoy getting a *present*, or did you present one to someone else? Another example of phonological rules is demonstrated by your understanding of how letters sound when they're grouped in a particular way. Take for instance the letters *omb*. Now put a t in front of them, and you have *tomb*. Put a c in front, and it becomes *comb*. Put a b in front, and you have *bomb*. See how the sounds shift?

BASS

The way we make singular nouns plural is also phonological. It's not as simple as adding the letter s to the end of a word. The sound changes too: dog/dogs (sounds like a *z* at the end); cook/cooks (sounds like an ess); bus/buses (sounds like ess-*ez*). English has many inconsistent phonological rules like these, which makes making errors quite typical, especially for nonnative English speakers.

**Syntactical rules** *present the arrangement of a language, how the symbols are organized.* You saw that earlier in the "glokkish Vriks" example; you're usually unaware of the syntactical rules until they're violated. In English, we put adjectives prior to most nouns: I live in a red house. In French, you live in a house red (the adjective follows the noun).

You can count on a close friend for comfort when you have a problem.

© 2008, JupiterImages.

**Semantic rules** *govern the meaning of specific symbols.* Because words are abstractions, we need rules to tell us what they mean in particular situations. Take, for example, the headline, "School Needs to Be Aired." What does that mean? Is the school so smelly that it needs to be refreshed? Or are the needs of the school going to be broadcast or spoken in a public forum? Words can be interpreted in more than one way, and we need semantic rules to lead us to shared meaning. Although these three kinds of rules help us to pattern language, there are also rules that help us guide the entire communication event.[12]

**Regulative rules** *tell us when, how, where, and with whom we can talk about certain things*. You know when it's OK to interrupt someone; you know when turn-taking is expected. You may be enrolled in classes where you are expected to express your opinion; in other classes, you know to hold your tongue. How do you feel about public displays of affection? When is it OK to correct your boss? These regulative rules help us to maintain respect, reveal information about ourselves, and interact with others.

**Constitutive rules** *tell us how to "count" different kinds of communication*. These rules reveal what you feel is appropriate. You know that when someone waves or blows kisses, that person is showing affection or friendliness. You know what topics you can discuss with your parents, friends, teachers, co-workers, and strangers. You have rules that reveal your expectations for communication with different people; you expect your doctor to be informative and firm with advice, and you anticipate that your friend will compliment you and empathize. As we interact with others, we begin to grasp and use the rules. For instance, when you start a new job, you take in the rules on whom to talk with, how to talk with supervisors and co-workers, and what topics are appropriate, along with the mechanics of how to talk and the meaning of job-specific words. Interestingly enough, you might not even be aware of the rules until they're broken!

## HOW DO THEORISTS DESCRIBE LANGUAGE AND MEANING?

Can you picture a book, a pen, a laptop, and a horse? Your ability to conjure up these images means that you've been exposed to the symbols that represent them in the English language. How about the picture shown on the right? What do you see? If you said "keys," then that shows how you have acquired language; you've been taught that these things are associated with the symbol "keys." How are you able to do those connections? There are a great number of perspectives related to language, meaning, and symbols. In this section, you'll be exposed to three models that present varying perspectives on the way that meaning is created.

## Semantic Triangle

One of the models that demonstrate how words come to have meaning is the **semantic triangle**.[13] Ogden and Richards suggest that a major problem with communication is that we tend to treat *words* as if they were the *thing*. As a result, we confuse the symbol for the thing or object.

At the bottom right hand of the triangle is the **referent**, the thing that we want to communicate about that exists in reality. As we travel up the right side, we find the **reference(s)**, which consist of thoughts, experiences, and feelings about the referent. This is a causal connection; seeing the object results in those thoughts. Another causal connection exists as you travel down the left side of the triangle, to the *symbol*, or *word*. That's the label we apply to that referent.

The problem is that there is not a direct connection between a symbol and referent; it's an indirect connection, shown by the dotted line. According to this model, it's that indirect link between *referent* and *symbol* that creates the greatest potential for communication misunderstandings. We assume that others share our references, and we think that they must use the same label or symbol because of that shared state of being. A simple example should help.

A mom is teaching her son words by reading simple children's books—books about tools, farms, trucks, zoos, and dinosaurs. Usually, this reading activity happens on the front porch. One day, the mom sees the neighbor's cat sneaking up on her birdfeeders, and under her breath, she mutters something about the "stupid cat."

The next day, the toddler goes off to day care, and when mom comes to pick him up, she's met by the teacher. She laughingly tells how she was reading a book about animals that day, and when she got to the page with cute kittens on it, the little boy yelled out, "Stupid cat." The embarrassed mother just learned a lesson about the semantic triangle. For her, the referent (cat) evokes images of bird-murdering, allergy-causing felines (references). She creates the label "stupid cat." (symbol). When the boy sees a picture of one, he naturally thinks that is what those things are called. Unfortunately, that's not the universal name!

The Semantic Triangle—Ogden & Richards, 1923.

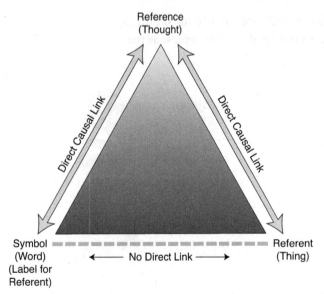

You can experience the same thing: If you tell others that you own a dog, what referent do you think they apply the label to? The semantic triangle is a practical tool that helps us to understand the relationship of referent, references, and symbol, *"BOAT"* or thing, thoughts, and word. It reminds us that one word doesn't necessarily evoke the same meaning in any two people.

## Sapir–Whorf Hypothesis

Another theoretical approach to language is the *Sapir–Whorf hypothesis*[14] (also *"SNOW"* known as the theory of linguistic relativity). According to this approach, your perception of reality is determined by your thought processes, and your thought processes are limited by your language. Therefore, language shapes reality. Your culture determines your language, which, in turn, determines the way that you categorize thoughts about the world and your experiences in it. If you don't have the words to describe or explain something, then you can't really know it or talk about it.

For example, researchers Linda Perry and Deborah Ballard-Reisch suggest that existing language does not represent the reality that biological sex comes in more forms than female and male, gender identities are not neatly ascribed to one's biological sex, and sexual orientation does not fit snugly into, "I like men, I like women, I like both, I like neither," choices. They also assert that evolving new language such as the word *gendex* (representing the dynamic interplay of a person's sexual identity, sex preference, sexual orientation, and gender identity) can work against biases and discrimination.[15] Another example is the concept of *bipolar disorder*. It used to be called *manic depressive*, and it refers to a mood disorder characterized by unusual shifts in a person's mood, energy, and ability to function.[16] But if you don't know what that illness is, you might just agree with a family member who says, "You're just going through a phase." The lack of language restricts our ability to perceive the world. Reality is embedded in your language.

The muted group theory suggests that language serves men better than women.

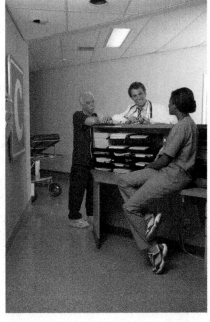

## Muted Group Theory

As these perspectives suggest, the *words* that you use are powerful. They have the ability to express attitudes and to represent values. Communication scholar Cheris Kramarae developed the *muted group theory* to suggest that power and status are connected, and because muted groups lack the power of appropriate language, they have no voice and receive little attention.[17] Kramarae noted, "The language of a particular culture does not serve all its speakers, for not all speakers contribute in an equal fashion to its formulation. Women (and members of other subordinate groups) are not as free or as able as men are to say what they wish, when and where they wish, because the words and the norms for their use have been formulated by the dominant group, men."[18] She asserts that language serves men better than women (and perhaps European Americans better than African Americans or other groups) because the European American men's experiences are named clearly in language, and the experiences of other groups (women, people with disabilities, and ethnic minorities) are not. Due to this problem with language, muted groups appear less articulate than men in public settings.

The task of muted groups is to conceptualize a thought and then scan the vocabulary that is suited to men's thinking for the best way to encode the idea. The term *sexual harassment* is an example. Although the act of harassment has existed for centuries, it wasn't until sex discrimination was prohibited by Title VII of the 1964 Civil Rights Act. It also took the Clarence Hill–Anita Thomas hearing in 1991 to make the term *gender discrimination* part of the popular dialogue, as the media focused attention on the workplace issue.

*CRITICAL*
*COMMUNICATION*

Because they are rendered inarticulate, muted groups are silenced in a variety of ways. Ridicule happens when the group's language is trivialized (men talk, women gab). Ritual creates dominance (the woman changes her name at the wedding ceremony but the man doesn't). Control happens as the media present some points of view and ignore others (we don't hear from the elderly or homeless). Harassment results from the control that men exert over public spaces (women get verbal threats couched as compliments when they walk down the streets). This theory affirms that as muted groups create more language to express their experiences and as all people come to have similar experiences, inequalities of language (and the power that comes with it) should change.

Each of these perspectives demonstrates how language impacts meaning. They show how we believe meaning comes into being, how we are limited by the language we possess, and how language wields power. By now, you should be sensitive to the many ways that you can miscommunicate, or at least communicate ineffectively through language choices. How can you become more sensitive to strategic language choices?

# HOW CAN I USE LANGUAGE EFFECTIVELY?

Communication scholar Julia T. Wood says that the single most important guideline is to engage in a **dual perspective**, recognizing another person's point of view and taking that into account as you communicate. Wood suggests that you should understand both your own and another's point of view and acknowledge each when you communicate.[19] You'll see that concept played out throughout this text; you need to consider your audience's beliefs, attitudes, and values as you create your message. Here are some strategic tips for effective language use to maintain that dual perspective.

## Use Accurate Language

Make sure you are using the term correctly, and if you're unsure if the audience will understand your meaning, define it. You'll learn about defining in the chapter on informative speaking. Remember, what makes perfect sense to you may be gobbledygook to me. When the doctor tells you that you have a rather large contusion, do you know what that is?

## Use Appropriate Language

It's important to use appropriate language for the occasion.

*Appropriate* means that the language you use is suitable for the context, for the audience, for the topic, and for you. Some occasions call for more formal language (proposals to a client), while others will let slang pass (texting a friend). Some audiences expect technical language, while others need simple terms. Off-color humor might work in certain instances and with specific groups, but you probably shouldn't choose to use it at a church gathering. You need to consider if your audience utilizes **regionalisms** (words or phrases that are specific to one part of the country) or **jargon** (specialized professional language) as you speak with them.

Your topic also can determine suitable language. Some topics call for lots of vivid language and imagery, while others are better suited to simplicity. If you are honoring your boss upon his retirement, then the topic probably calls for words that evoke appreciation and emotion. But if you're telling someone how to put together a computer table, then simple explanatory words are expected. Finally, you need to use words that are appropriate to you. You have developed your own style of language over the years; do you use the same words as your parents? Don't try to use words that just don't flow easily from your mind; it's not going to sound like you.

## 3  *Use Unbiased Language*

Biased language includes any language that defames a subgroup (women; people from specific ethnic, religious, or racial groups; people with disabilities) or eliminates them from consideration. Even if you would never think about using language that defames anyone else, you can fall into using language that more subtly discriminates. Sexist language is replete with this: We use the masculine pronoun (he, him) when we don't have a referent. So if you personify "the judge," "the executive," "the director," as male by using the pronoun *he*, you eliminate one whole subgroup from consideration.

The same holds true when you use the word *man* in occupational terms, when the job holders could be either male or female. Examples are fireman, policeman, garbage man, chairman; they're easily made nonsexist by saying firefighter, police officer, garbage collector, and chair or presiding officer. Finally, while the generic use of *man* (like in mankind) originally was used to denote both men and women, its meaning has become more specific to adult males. It's simple to change the word to be more inclusive: mankind becomes people or human beings; man-made becomes manufactured; the common man becomes the average person.

The *Associated Press Stylebook* has a lengthy entry on "disabled, handicapped, impaired" terminology, including when to use (and not to use) terms such as *blind, deaf, mute, wheelchair-user*, and so on. A separate entry on *retarded says* "mentally retarded" is the preferred term. The World Bank advises using *persons with disabilities* and *disabled people*, not handicapped.

Use appropriate labels when referring to sexual orientation. The terms *lesbians, gay men*, and *bisexuals* or *bisexual women and men* are preferred to the term homosexuals (because the emphasis on the latter is on sex, while the former all refer to the whole person, not just the sex partner he or she chooses). In general, try to find out what the people's preferences are, and be specific when applicable. For instance, if all the subjects are either Navajo or Cree, stating this is more accurate than calling them Native Americans.

# 4 *Avoid Verbal Distractions*

If you divert the audience from your intended meaning by using confusing words, your credibility will be lowered and your audience may become lost. The following are distractions:

- **Slang** *consists of words that are short-lived, arbitrarily changed, and often vulgar ideas.* Slang excludes people from a group. Internet slang was usually created to save keystrokes and consists of "u" for *you,* "r" for *are,* and "4" for *for.* Poker slang includes *dead man's hand* (two pair, aces, and eights); to *act* (make a play); and *going all in* (betting all of your chips on the hand). *Daggy* means out of fashion or uncool; *fives* means to reserve a seat.[20]

- **Cliches** *or* **trite words** *have been overused and lose power or impact.* The Unicorn Hunters of Lake Superior University keeps a list of banished words that is regularly updated. In 2007, it listed words such as combined celebrity names (*Brangelina and Tomcat*), *awesome* (because it no longer means majestic), and *undocumented alien* (just use the word *illegal*).[21]

- **Loaded words** *sound like they're describing, but they're actually revealing your attitude.* When speaking of abortion, consider the different image created by the terms *unborn child* or *fetus.* Are you *thrifty* but your friend is *cheap*? How about your brother; is he one of those *health-nuts* who is dedicated to the cult of marathoning? Colorful language is entertaining, but if it distorts the meaning or distracts the audience, then don't use it.

- **Empty words** *are overworked exaggerations.* They lose their strength because their meaning is exaggerated. How many products are advertised as *new and improved* or *supersized*? What exactly does that mean?

- **Derogatory language** *consists of words that are degrading or tasteless.* If you use degrading terms to refer to ethnic groups (Polack for a person of Polish descent; *Chink* for someone from China; *Spic* for an Italian) then you are guilty of verbal bigotry.

- **Equivocal words** *have more than one correct denotative meaning.* A famous example is of a nurse telling a patient that he "wouldn't be needing" the books he asked to be brought from home. Although she meant that he was going home that day and could read there, the patient took that to mean that he was near death and wouldn't have time to read. One time while evaluating a debate, an instructor encountered students arguing the issue of the legalization of marijuana. The side arguing for the legalization used the Bible, citing chapter and verse and asserting that God created the grass and said, "The grass is good." This sent the other side into a tailspin as they tried to refute the biblical passage. This simple equivocal use of the term grass lost the debate for the opposition!

## WHAT SHOULD YOU TAKE FROM THIS SECTION ON LANGUAGE?

Because our language is arbitrary and evolving, it's easy to be misunderstood. You can attempt to enhance shared meaning by remembering that language is a shared system of symbols; through language, you share ideas, articulate values, transmit information, reveal experiences, and maintain relationships. Language is essential to your ability to think and to operate within the many cultures (community of meaning) that you travel through. You should be sensitive to the words you choose as you attempt to connect with others. Now let's turn our attention to the other means by which you create meaning: your nonverbal communication behaviors.

## WHAT IS NONVERBAL COMMUNICATION?

Pretend you are hoarse and the doctor has told you not to speak at all for the next three days. Nor can you IM or text or do any other computer-related communication. How would you do the following?

- Let your friend know that you can't hear her. Or tell her that she's talking too loudly.
- Tell your lab partner that you want him to come where you are.
- Show the teacher that you don't know the answer to the question she just asked you.
- Let a child know that he needs to settle down; his play is getting too rough.
- Tell your significant other that you're not angry, and everything is OK.
- Express disappointment over a loss by your team, which always seems to lose the lead in the last two minutes.
- Signify that you're running late and have to leave.

How hard would it be to make yourself understood? What you've just attempted to do without verbal language is present a message nonverbally. We all constantly send nonverbal messages, giving our receivers all types of cues about ourselves. An awareness of nonverbal communication is important: your nonverbal behaviors present an image of yourself to those around you. They tell others how you want to relate to them, and they may reveal emotions or feelings that you either are trying to hide or simply can't express.

In the remainder of this chapter, you will be introduced to some of the elements of the study of nonverbal communication in the hopes of creating a greater awareness of these elements of the message. You will examine *definitions* of nonverbal communication, its *functions*, and *types* of nonverbal communication. Along the way, we will provide examples and illustrations to help you understand the applications of various nonverbal behaviors and how they can be used to help you interpret the messages of other people. You should also gain some insight into how to use nonverbal behaviors to enhance your own communication.

## WHAT IS THE NATURE OF NONVERBAL COMMUNICATION?

Although nonverbal communication is a complex system of behaviors and meanings, its basic definition *can be* fairly straightforward. Here are four definitions for comparison:

1. All types of communication that do not rely on words or other linguistic systems[22]
2. Any message other than written or spoken words that conveys meaning[23]
3. Anything in a message besides the words themselves[24]
4. Messages expressed by nonlinguistic means[25]

Taking these definitions and the body of related research into consideration, we propose a very simple definition: nonverbal communication is *all nonlinguistic aspects of communication.* That definition covers quite a lot of territory. Except for the actual words that we speak, *everything* else is classified as nonverbal communication. The way you move, the tone of your voice, the way you use your eyes, the way you occupy and use space, the way you dress, the shape of your body, your facial expressions, the way you smell, your hand gestures, and the way you pronounce (or mispronounce) words are all considered nonverbal communication. Some of these behaviors have meaning independent of language or other behaviors; others have meaning only when considered with what is said, the context and culture in which a communication event takes place, and the relationship between the communicators.

What can you say about her nonverbal communication?

Maybe you're getting a hint of the richness of nonverbal expression. Without any formal training, you already are able to interpret messages that others send nonverbally. Your skill level, however, may not be as strong as you think, so keep in mind the goal of increasing strategic communication as you continue. Researchers have also been

© mehmet alci, 2008, Shutterstock.

fascinated with the extent to which nonverbal communication impacts meaning, and their findings provide glimpses into the impact of nonverbals on shared meanings and culture. If nothing else, by the end of this section, you will discover that the study of nonverbal communication has come a long way since it was referred to only as *body language*!

# WHAT ARE THE CHARACTERISTICS OF NONVERBAL COMMUNICATION?

## *Ambiguous*

Most nonverbal behaviors have no generally accepted meaning. Instead, the connection between the behavior and its meaning is vague or *ambiguous*, leaving understanding open to various interpretations. The meaning we apply to words is fairly specific, but the meaning we give to nonverbal communication is nonspecific. The meanings you attribute to nonverbal behaviors are heavily dependent on the relationship between you and the others you're interacting with, the nature of the communication event, the content of the words that accompanies it, and the culture in which the event takes place. For example, consider the ubiquitous "thumbs up" hand gesture. In the United States it means, "OK" or "very good." In some eastern cultures, however, it is considered an insult and an obscene hand gesture. In Great Britain, Australia, and New Zealand, it could be a signal used by hitchhikers who are thumbing a lift; it could be an OK signal; it also could be an insult signal meaning "up yours" or "sit on this" when the thumb is jerked sharply upward. In Indonesia, the thumb gesture means

In the United States, a thumbs-up is appropriate for celebrating.

© Jason Stitt, 2008, Shutterstock.

"good job" in response to someone who has completed an excellent job, or "delicious" when great food is tasted. In another context, if you smile at a joke, that's understood in an entirely different way than if you do it after someone misses a chair and falls to the ground. A smile could also show affection, embarrassment, or even be used to hide pain or anger. As you can see, it is possible to find several meanings for the same nonverbal behavior, and it is possible to find several nonverbal behaviors that mean the same thing.[26]

## 2 Continuous

With verbal communication, if you stop speaking, listeners can't attribute any more meaning to your words. Nonverbal communication, by contrast, is so pervasive and complex that others can continue to gather meaning, even if you are doing absolutely nothing! The mere act of doing nothing can send a message; you might blush, stutter, wring your hands, or sweat unintentionally, causing others to react to you. You might not mean to send a message, but your lack of intention to communicate doesn't prevent other people from assigning meaning to your behavior. In addition, your appearance, the expression on your face, your posture, where (or if) you are seated, and how you use the space around you all provide information that is subject to interpretation by others.

What can you tell by this woman's expression?

## 3 Sometimes Unplanned and Unconscious

Nonverbal communication can be either unconscious or intentional, but most of our nonverbal behaviors are exhibited without much or any conscious thought. You rarely plan or think carefully about your nonverbal behaviors. When you are angry, it is naturally expressed on your face as well as elsewhere in your body. The same is true for how your voice changes when you're nervous, how your arms cross when you're feeling defensive, or how you scratch your head when you're unsure of something. These expressions and behaviors are rarely planned or structured; they just happen suddenly and without conscious thought.

## 4 Sometimes Learned and Intentional

Saying that some nonverbal behaviors are natural or occur without conscious thought doesn't mean that people are born with a *complete inventory* of instinctive nonverbal behaviors. Much of your nonverbal behavior is *learned* rather than instinctive or innate. You learn the "proper" way to sit or approach, how close to stand next to someone, how to look at others, how to use touch, all from your experiences and your culture. You have been taught their meaning through your experience in interactions with other people. As a result, you can structure some nonverbal behaviors to send intentional messages, such as disapproval when you shake your head from side to side or give a "high five" to show excitement. However, unlike the formal training you received in reading, writing, and speaking, you learned (and continue to learn) nonverbal communication in a much less formal and unceremonious way, and you use it in a much less precise way than spoken language. But *because* many of these behaviors are learned, you can actively work to improve your nonverbal skills. There is a debate as to whether unintentional nonverbal behaviors really count as communication. Since others incorporate their understanding of our nonverbals as part of shared meaning, we're going to say that intentional and unintentional nonverbals both are worth recognizing here.[27] Our position is that it's nearly impossible not to communicate nonverbally.

## *More Believable than Verbal*

5

Communication textbooks have been saying for years that, when verbal and nonverbal messages contradict each other, people typically believe the nonverbal message. Because nonverbal is more spontaneous and less conscious, we don't or can't manipulate it as easily as we can control verbal communication. When you were younger and your parents thought that you might be lying to them, they would say, "Look me in the eye and say that again." Your face was more believable to them than what you were saying verbally. Your nonverbal messages would tell them the truth. How could this be so?

Research suggests that between 65 percent and 93 percent of the meaning people attribute to messages comes from the nonverbal channel.[28] There is a small fudge factor in those percentages, however, because the Mehrabian and Ferris study assumed up to 93 percent of meaning came from nonverbal messages in situations *where no other background information* was available.[29] The reality is that many factors affect the meaning given to messages, including how familiar the communicators are with the language being spoken, cultural knowledge, and even individual differences in personality characteristics.[30]

Regardless of the exact percentage of meaning that comes from the verbal or nonverbal channels, we still appear to get more meaning from the nonverbal channel. Unless you are very good at controlling all your nonverbal behaviors, your parents can probably still know when you are not telling the truth.

# WHAT ARE THE FUNCTIONS OF NONVERBAL COMMUNICATION?

*Types* of nonverbal communication will be described a little later in the chapter, but you first need to understand what part nonverbals play in the communication process. Nonverbal communication performs six general functions that add information and insight to nonverbal messages to help us create meaning. Those functions are complementing, substituting, repeating, contradicting, regulating, and deceiving.

## Complementing Verbal Messages

If someone shakes your hand while saying "Congratulations" at your college graduation, the handshake gives added meaning to the verbal message. Gestures, tone of voice, facial expressions, and other nonverbal behaviors can clarify, reinforce, accent, or add to the meaning of verbal messages. For instance, if you are angry with a friend and are telling him off, pounding your hand into your fist would add depth to your meaning. These nonverbal behaviors are usually not consciously planned, but they are spontaneous reactions to the context and the verbal message.

## 2 Substituting for Verbal Messages

You can use a nonverbal message *in the place of* a verbal message. A substituting behavior can be a clear "stop" hand gesture; it can be nodding the head up and down to say yes; or it can be a shoulder shrug to indicate "I don't know." When you use this kind of gesture, you don't have to supply any verbal message for the meaning to be clear to others. However, keep in mind that your nonverbals may be interpreted differently, given what you have learned from your context and culture. As an example, someone in Japan might act in a controlled fashion, while someone from the Mideast might seem more emotional, even when both are feeling the same intensity of emotion. Your interpretation of those postures, without accompanying verbals, might lead you to the wrong conclusions.

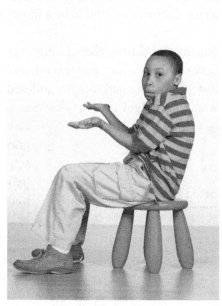

Nonverbal messages can substitute for verbal messages. What specific messages are being sent by the people in these photos?

© 2008, JupiterImages.

### 3 Repeating Verbal Messages

If a stranger on your college campus asks you for directions to the administration building, you might reply, "Carty Hall is two blocks south of here." While you are delivering the verbal message, you also *repeat* the message by pointing to the south. The gesture reinforces the meaning of the verbal message and provides a clear orientation to listeners who are unfamiliar with the campus.

### 4 Contradicting Verbal Messages

Nonverbal messages sometimes *contradict* the verbal message. It can be done by accident, such as when you say "turn right" but you point to the left. Or it could be done without thinking (unconsciously), such as when you have a sour expression on your face as you tell your former girlfriend how much you "really like" her new boyfriend. Finally, you could use planned nonverbal behaviors, such as a wink of the eye and a sarcastic tone of voice, to contradict the verbal message, "Nice hat!" A famous example of this contradiction happened in September 1960, when 70 million U.S. viewers tuned in to watch Senator John Kennedy of Massachusetts and Vice President Richard Nixon in the first-ever televised presidential debate. The so-called Great Debates were television's first attempt to offer voters a chance to see the presidential candidates "in person" and head to head. Nixon was more well known, since he had been on the political scene as senator and two-term vice president. He had made a career out of fighting communism right in the midst of the Cold War. Kennedy was a relative newcomer, having served only a brief and undistinguished time as senator; he had no foreign affairs experience. Expectations were low for Kennedy; there seemed to be a huge reputation disparity between them.

"The street you are looking for is about one mile to the east." Nonverbal messages repeat verbal messages.

During the debate, their points were fairly even. But it was the visual contrast between the two men that was astounding. Nixon had seriously injured his knee, had lost weight, and had recently suffered from the flu. When the first debate came, he was underweight and pasty looking, with a murky 5:00 shadow darkening his lower face. He wore a white, poorly fitting shirt and a gray suit that nearly blended into the background set, and he refused to wear make-up, even though he was advised to do so. Kennedy supplemented his tan with make-up, wore a dark suit, and had been coached on how to sit and where to look when he wasn't speaking. Kennedy's smooth delivery made him credible, because he came off as confident, vibrant, and poised. Nixon looked tired, pasty, and uncomfortable (he sweated heavily).

© 2008, JupiterImages.

Polls taken after the first debate showed that most people who listened to it on the radio felt that Nixon had won, while most who watched it on television declared Kennedy the victor. Those television viewers focused on what they saw, not what they heard.[31]

Contradictory messages can be difficult for others to interpret, so it's important to monitor your nonverbal behaviors. People have a tendency to prefer the meaning of the nonverbal message when it conflicts with the verbal, so when you say turn right, you should try to point to the right. Or if you don't want your former girlfriend to know how jealous you are of her new boyfriend, try to guard against making that sour face. Most adults, however, will interpret the "Nice hat" comment as sarcasm and clearly understand the message.

© 2008, JupiterImages.

Is there sarcasm detected in the "nice hat" comment?

## 5 Regulating the Flow of Communication

Nonverbal behaviors help us to control the verbal messages we're presenting. To prevent chaos when two are more people are engaged in conversation, we use a system of signals to indicate whose turn it is speak. Think about that. How do you know when it is appropriate for you to begin speaking in a group or in a classroom? When you're talking, no one is there saying, "Now, it's your turn." You might use tone of voice to indicate that you want to speak and silence to show that you're ready to yield the floor. If you don't want to be interrupted, you might not make eye contact with the potential interruptor. If you expect an answer, you might directly look at the other person.[32] You probably also use nonverbals to let others know that you're trying to control their talk. Have you ever started to put your computer or lecture materials away before the professor is done speaking? You use nonverbal behavior to indicate that you want to speak, that you are finished speaking, that you want to continue speaking, or that you do not want to speak at all. The nonverbal signals include tone of voice, posture, gestures, eye contact, and other behaviors.

## 6 Deceiving Listeners

Sometimes, your nonverbal behaviors are attempts to mislead somebody or hide the truth. This deception doesn't have to be malicious or mean. If you're a poker player, you might wear sunglasses in order to shield your eyes; pupils dilate when you're excited, and you want to keep that excitement close to your vest. Sometimes, you deceive to protect yourself or the other person, like when you pat someone on the back and say, "Everything will be all right," even when you know it won't.

There are many movies based on the premise that you can learn to nonverbally behave like someone you're not in order to deceive others. In *Tootsie* (1982), Dustin Hoffman becomes the female star of a television soap opera. Robin Williams stars as *Mrs. Doubtfire* (1993), dressing as a woman so he can see his children. In *The Birdcage* (1996), Robin Williams attempts to teach Nathan Lane how to do an exaggerated John Wayne walk to disguise his effeminate stroll. *Mulan* (1998) is a young woman wanting to fight the Huns in the place of her father, so she poses as a male to join the army. *Big Momma's House* (2000) stars Martin Lawrence, who plays an FBI agent who goes undercover and dresses as a heavy-set woman. In *White Chicks* (2004) Shawn Wayans and Marlon Wayans are sibling FBI agents who must protect two cruise line heiresses from a kidnapping plot. Finally, in *The Lord of the Rings: The Return of the King* (2004), Éowyn dresses as a soldier to be allowed to fight with the men.

A great deal of research on deception has practical implications. For instance, some occupations, such as lawyers and actors, require you to act differently than you might feel. Research has found that they are more successful at deception than the rest of the general population.[33] People who monitor themselves have been found to be more effective in hiding deception cues than are people who are not as self-aware.[34] Just think about the last time you told someone a "white lie." Were you a little nervous? How did you show that? Did the words come easily? Did you stammer or have to search for words? When you fib, you have to weigh the consequences of being caught versus the need to fib (telling a child that Santa or the Easter Bunny exists). You have to look and act sincere and believable, even though you're churning inside. If you can look composed and natural, then you are more likely to be a successful liar.[35] In fact, research tells us that people with a greater social skills repertoire and more communication competence will generally be more proficient, alert, confident, and expressive, and less fidgety, nervous and rigid, making them more skilled at deception than others.[36]

Now that you see the many roles that nonverbals can play in communication, let's turn from the functions to the categories of nonverbal communication.

# WHAT ARE THE TYPES OF NONVERBAL COMMUNICATION?

Although many types of behaviors can communicate, available space and the focus of this book limit our discussion of nonverbal communication to body movement (kinesics), the use of space (proxemics), dress and appearance, and eye contact (occulesics). Vocalics, or paralanguage (the use of the voice), is covered in the chapter on delivery.

## Body Movement/Kinesics

R. Birdwhistell first identified **kinesics**, or the study of our use of the body to communicate. It includes gestures, posture, facial expressions, and other body movements.[37] Five research themes have emerged in kinesics: the use of emblems, illustrators, regulators, affect displays, and adaptors. A brief look at all five themes will provide a good orientation to the complex ways that we can use our bodies to send messages.

EMBLEMS. An **emblem** is a nonverbal behavior that has a distinct verbal referent or even a denotative definition, and it is often used to send a specific message to others. The verbal referent is typically one or two words of a short phrase. For example, the "thumbs-up" hand gesture is listed in many dictionaries and is defined as a *gesture of approval*. There is a high level of agreement about the meaning of an emblem within cultures, but not usually across cultures.[38]

Most emblems are created with the hands, but we can create them in other ways. For example, a shoulder shrug suggests "I don't know," or a wrinkled nose indicates that "something stinks." But the emblems we are most familiar with are usually hand gestures. Try to make the gesture that goes with each of the following meanings:

- "Sit down beside me."
- "Follow me."
- "I can't hear you."
- "Be quiet!"
- "Shame on you!"

- "OK."
- "I promise."
- "What time is it?"
- "Good bye!"

In addition to everyday conversation, emblems are used by divers while under water, by police officers directing traffic, by construction workers, and by catchers, pitchers, and managers during baseball games. Don't forget the very familiar and more or less universal signal some people use to indicate displeasure with other drivers! Keep in mind, though, that the emblems you know are not always shared. The hand gesture we use for "come here," with the hand palm up with the index finger extending in and out three or four times, has a very different meaning in Latin America. It means that you are romantically interested in the person, and is considered a solicitation. Emblems can replace the verbal or reinforce it.

Police officers use emblems when directing traffic.

© Andrew Barker, 2008, Shutterstock.

**ILLUSTRATORS.** An **illustrator** is a gesture that is used *with* language to emphasize, stress, or repeat what is being said. It can be used to give directions, show the size or shape of something, and give clarification. Can you imagine trying to explain to a new parent how to "burp" a baby without using illustrators? Can you give directions to the campus library with your hands in your pockets? Sure you could, but the illustrators add much meaning and clarification to your directions or instructions; they help with that function of clarifying. In a study done several years ago, speakers were found to be more persuasive when they used illustrators than when they did not.[39] More recent research has even extended the importance of illustrators. Robert Krauss found that gestures do more than amplify or accent verbal communication. They also help people retrieve ideas and words, such as when you try to define a term with a spatial meaning such as underneath, next to, and above, which Krauss calls *lexical retrieval.* If not done to excess, "talking with your hands" can be a very good thing!

A common communication regulator is a turn-requesting signal.

**REGULATORS.** A **regulator** is a turn-taking signal that helps control the flow, the pace, and turn-taking in conversations, and you learned about their coordinating role earlier. If a group of people are talking and trying to share meaning, they

must take turns speaking, and taking turns requires cooperation among the communicators. To accomplish this cooperation, along with the content of the conversation, participants must also communicate about who will speak next and when that turn will begin. Regulators help us with this task.[40]

Weimann and Knapp and Argyle identified four categories of turn related signals in a typical conversation:[41]

1. *Turn requesting* signals: These are used by a nonspeaker to take the floor. Nonverbal regulators used to request a turn include rapid head nods, forward leaning posture, and increased eye contact with the speaker.
2. *Turn yielding* signals: The speaker uses these to give up the floor. Nonverbal regulators used to yield a turn include increased eye contact with a nonspeaker, leaning back from a forward posture, or a sudden end to gesturing used while speaking.

3. *Turn maintenance* signals: These are used by the speaker to keep the floor (i.e., continue speaking). Nonverbal signals used to keep the turn include speaking louder or faster (increasing volume or rate of speech), continuing to gesture, or avoiding eye contact with the person requesting the turn.

4. *Back channel* signals: Nonspeaker refuses a turn that has been offered by the speaker. Nonverbal signals used to refuse a turn include nodding the head and avoiding eye contact with the person exhibiting a turn-yielding signal.

D

AFFECT DISPLAYS. An **affect display** is a form of nonverbal behavior that expresses emotions. Although this behavior is most often associated with facial expressions, affect can also be expressed through posture and gestures. These behaviors cannot only express the type of emotion being experienced, but can also express the intensity of the emotion. A smile suggests that you are happy. A slumped-over posture and a scowl on your face can suggest that you are unhappy, while your clinched fists and tense muscles can communicate just *how* unhappy you might be.

The emotions communicated by your face and body can affect the way you are perceived by other people. People who smile spontaneously are often considered by others to be more likable and more approachable than people who do not smile or people who just pretend to smile.[42]

E

ADAPTORS. **Adaptors** are behaviors that can indicate our internal conditions or feelings to other people. We tend to use these behaviors when we become excited or anxious. Think about the kind of things that you do in communication situations when you feel nervous or excited. Do you scratch your head? Bite your nails? Play with your glasses? Rub your nose? You might not know, because most people are not aware of displaying these behaviors.

Can you make judgments about the nature and intensity of the emotions expressed on these faces?

What do these adaptors tell you about the internal feelings of the people in the photos?

© 2008, JupiterImages.

Adaptors are generally considered the least desirable type of nonverbal communication. Self-touching in this way could be a distraction to the audience, and it is often perceived as a sign of anxiety. One study found that deceivers bob their heads more often than people who tell the truth.[43] Cultural guidelines may prohibit these behaviors, too. Wriggling your nose or having a disgusted facial look to show that you're repulsed seems to have a universal meaning.[44]

However, in some cultures, people are socialized to mask emotional cues, and in others they're taught to emphasize them. Latin Americans will usually greet friends and relatives more personally than do Americans. Everyone hugs, including the men. Men usually also greet woman with *besitos*, meaning they touch cheeks while making a kissing noise with their lips. Women also greet other women with *besitos*. These little kisses are purely friendly and have no romantic meaning. Maslow and colleagues[45] suggested that the anxiety displayed by adaptors can be interpreted by other communicators as a sign of deception; you are anxious because you are not being honest with the others and you fear being discovered!

## Use of Space/Proxemics

The study of proxemics is typically divided into two applications: The use of personal space and how people claim and mark territory as their own. Most of us don't even think about the impact of space on our relationships, but research has shown that your use of space can influence shared meaning and impact your relationship. Knapp and Hall[46] found that our use of space can seriously affect our ability to achieve desired goals. Both applications can be used and managed by people to communicate fairly specific messages, and they can provide evidence to help us make judgments about the person using the space.

# PERSONAL DISTANCES

Hall recognized characteristic distances maintained between people in the U.S. culture, depending on their perceived relationships.[48] The distance categories are *intimate*, *personal*, *social*, and *public*.

| Type | Distance | Who Is Permitted/Context |
|---|---|---|
| Intimate Distance | touching to 18 inches | **Who**: Spouses and family members, boyfriends and girlfriends, and very close friends. **Context**: A date with your spouse. |
| Personal Distance | 18 inches to 4 feet | **Who**: Good friends and people you know well. **Context**: Having lunch with a good friend or co-worker. |
| Social Distance | 4 feet to 12 feet | **Who**: Business associates, teachers, and people you know but with whom you have a professional but less social relationship. **Context**: A business meeting, small group discussion, or an employment interview. |
| Public Distance | 12 feet and beyond | **Who**: A person you don't know; a stranger on the street. **Context**: Giving a presentation to a large group; walking downtown on a public sidewalk. |

A

© Andrejs Pidjass, 2008, Shutterstock.

B

© 2008, JupiterImages.

C

© 2008, JupiterImages.

D

© 2008, JupiterImages.

**PERSONAL SPACE.** When you consider the idea of personal space, think of a small amount of portable space that you carry around with you all the time. You control who is and who is not permitted inside of that space. Permission to enter that space is granted based on the relationship you have with that person, the context of the encounter, the culture in which you live, and your own personal preferences and tolerances. For example, you would be likely to allow business and professional colleagues to be reasonably close to you; you would allow good friends to be very close to you; and you would allow romantic partners to be closer still, even to the point of touching. In addition, you might allow people that you don't know to be very close to you in the appropriate context, like a crowded elevator or a busy airport.

When someone enters your space without permission, you can interpret it as a lack of courtesy, or even as a threat. You will feel uncomfortable, so you can either wait for the trespasser to move out of your space, or you can move away until you feel comfortable again.

The range of personal space varies across cultures. The box describes spaces typical to the culture in the United States. If you visit the United Kingdom, you will notice that these spaces are slightly expanded; that is, the British prefer just a bit more distance between people. By contrast, many Eastern cultures, including Asia and the Middle East, prefer a smaller distance. When these cultures meet, people from the United States often feel "crowded" by people from Asian cultures, while people from Japan might think that Americans are "cold" or "stand-offish" because of the increased interpersonal distances. As you can see, there is no shortage of opportunities for misunderstanding! Burgoon suggests that we want to stay near others, but we also want to maintain some distance—think about the dilemma this causes![47] Try to be sensitive to cultural norms when you assign meaning to the use of personal space.

Relationships affect the way we use space. Based on the use of space, describe the relationships in these photos. Be specific about the nonverbal clues that indicate the relationship.

(Photo credits: left, center, © 2008, JupiterImages, right, © Factoria singular fotografia, 2008, Shutterstock.)

B

**TERRITORIALITY.** We also have a tendency to claim space as our own. We have just looked at personal space, which is portable space that you carry around with you. Territory, by contrast, is not mobile; it stays in one place. You can think of territory as a kind of extension of you that is projected on to space or objects. Space that you occupy or control, and objects that belong to you or that you use regularly, are all important to you. If any person not authorized by you occupies that space or touches those objects, you feel violated and threatened. To help describe this kind of attachment to places and things, we turn to Altman, who classified territory into three categories: primary, secondary, and public.[49]

Sometimes we allow our personal space to be violated.

1

**Primary territory** is space or those items that you personally control. This includes personal items that only you would use, like your clothes and your toothbrush. It also includes the private spaces in your house like your bathroom and bedroom. Many people treat still other places as primary territory such as their car, their office at work, and even their refrigerator!

People mark their territory in many ways.

*2*

**Secondary territory** is not your private property. That is, it is not owned by you, but it is typically associated with you. Examples of secondary territory include the desk you always use in class, the seat you always sit in at the office conference table, your favorite fishing spot at the lake, or your usual table at the library.

*3*

**Public territory** is available to anyone, so any space that you try to claim is only temporary. You might define your space on the beach by using markers such as blankets, beach chairs, or umbrellas. Or you might spread out your books and notes at the library to claim space on a work table. Our use of the territory lasts as long as we are using it, or as long as other people respect our markers.[50]

Most of us pay little attention to these claims of space, and we probably don't even realize that we do it. However, these claims come clearly to our attention when they are violated. It seems like there is almost nothing worse than walking into the classroom on the day of the big exam to find someone else in your seat! Sure, any seat will work just as well, but that is *your* seat where you feel most comfortable and confident. We tend to feel violated whenever any unauthorized person uses our space or touches our stuff!

*4*

Lyman and Scott identified three levels of **intrusion of territory**: violation, invasion, and contamination.[51] A *violation* happens when your space or your stuff is used without your permission, like when a neighbor borrows one of your tools without asking first. An *invasion* occurs when an unauthorized person enters the territory that you have claimed with markers. They might move your books and notes at the library (while you were looking for a book) and take over your space at the table, or they could cut in front of you in a check-out line at the grocery store. Finally, a *contamination* occurs when space that you claim is used without your authorization, but your evidence of the use is not the presence of the user but objects left behind. For example, you arrive at your office in the morning to find cups and fast food wrappers on your desk. There is nobody in your office, but you know somebody *was* there, and he or she was eating at your desk. Territory that you claim as your own should not be used by anyone without your permission. How you respond to territory depends very much on who invaded the territory and why it was invaded, which you'll see explained in expectancy violations theory, which follows later in this chapter.

*3* ## Dress/Appearance

Your appearance, along with the way you dress, influences the way other people respond to you. In some situations, your appearance can be the primary factor that determines the response of others.[52] *Physical attractiveness*, as well as personal grooming and hygiene, weigh heavily on judgments that are made about you every day. If that's not enough pressure, along with protecting you from the environment and fulfilling cultural requirements for modesty, *clothing* is also a potent source of nonverbal information about you. Morris tells us that clothing sends continuous signals about us and who we think we are.[53] For example, watch the scene in the 1990 movie *Pretty Woman* when the character played by Julia Roberts first enters a "high-class" clothing store and is treated poorly by the staff. What about her appearance led to that treatment?

No one likes to have their territory violated.

Among other qualities, clothing can suggest social and economic status, education, level of success, or trustworthiness and character. Morris suggests that clothing can be a cultural display and one that communicates something special about the wearer.[54] People have a tendency to express certain values central to their belief systems that indicate the kind of people they perceive themselves to be. Katz tells us that we hold and express particular attitudes to satisfy this need and that those attitudes reflect a positive view of ourselves.[55] Clothing and appearance are consistent with this concept. For example, if you consider yourself to be the "artistic" type, or a successful business person, or a talented athlete, your clothing choices will likely reflect that self image.

Gordon etal., suggests that clothing fulfills a number of symbolic functions:[56]
- Traditional and religious ceremonies often involve specific clothing.
- Self-beautification (real or imagined) is often reflected in clothing.
- Clothing expresses cultural values regarding sexual identity and practice.
- Clothes differentiate roles and levels of authority.
- Clothing is used in the acquisition and display of status.

Think about the way you dress and why you make those clothing choices. What are you trying to say? Are you trying to fit in? Are you trying to identify yourself with a particular group? Are you trying to show respect for an occasion or person?

Clothing is not the only aspect of appearance to consider. Think of the other personal choices people make with tattoos, body art, and personal grooming. What are the impacts of blue hair, black nail colors, Mohawks or dreadlocks, multiple piercing and colorful tattoos? You have the right to communicate about yourself in any way you want, but remember that if you go against cultural norms, you may be creating perceptual barriers that impede communication. Your appearance is a prime

© 2008, JupiterImages.

© Ronald Sumners, 2008, Shutterstock.

How could her tattoos impact others' perceptions?

source of information that others use to make judgments about you. Try to use some care when making choices about how you should look in particular situations. You can always maintain your individuality, but you should also dress to show respect for the occasion and the people that you will be coming into contact with. If you have to give a presentation for a business group, for example, you can show your respect for the group by dressing in more formal attire. Wearing jeans with ripped out knees may say a lot about who you think you are, but wearing the suit for the business group also communicates who you think you are. You are someone who combines your own needs with a respect for the needs of other people!

4

## Eye Movement/Occulesics

In many Western cultures, including the United States, making **eye contact** with another person is considered a sign of sincerity, caring, honesty, and sometimes power or status.[57] Pearson found that men sometimes use eye contact to challenge others and to assert themselves.[58] Women tend to hold eye contact more than men, regardless of the sex of the person that they're interacting with.[59] Some Eastern cultures view eye contact with others as an impolite invasion of privacy and they especially disapprove of eye contact with a person of higher status. In another study, it was found that inner-city African-American persuaders look continually at the listener, and African-American listeners tend to look away from the persuader most of the time. The opposite is true of middle-class Whites; as persuaders, they look only occasionally at the listener, and White listeners look continuously at the persuader. This could explain why the two groups could have incorrect inferences about the amount of interest the other has when they communicate.[60]

We consider the use of eye contact to be an essential tool for achieving communication goals. In U.S. culture, how does it make you feel when someone will not make eye contact with you? Do you trust this person? Do you suspect his or her motives?

Eye contact helps us communicate in at least four ways: It can open a channel of communication, demonstrate concern, gather feedback, and moderate anxiety.[61]

A

OPEN A COMMUNICATION CHANNEL. You can let others know that you would like to communicate with them by simply looking at them. A brief moment of eye contact can open a channel of communication and make other messages possible.

B

**DEMONSTRATE CONCERN.** Engaging other people in eye contact during conversations shows a concern for them, as well as your commitment that they understand your message. In addition, eye contact can be used to communicate liking and attraction.

C

**GATHER FEEDBACK.** If you would like information about what other people are thinking, take a look at their eyes. You won't be able to read thoughts, but you can certainly find clues to indicate that they are listening, that they understand the message, and perhaps that they care about what you are saying. The old adage that speakers should look at the back wall of the room when giving a public speech is pretty bad advice; you will miss out on critical information about the frame of mind of audience members, as well as other feedback essential to achieving your goals.

© Dmitriy Shironosov, 2008, Shutterstock.

D

**MODERATE ANXIETY.** When speakers get nervous or anxious during a public presentation, they have a tendency to avoid eye contact with the listeners by either looking at the floor, the back wall of the room, or at their notes. As they continue to stare at the floor, anxiety (fear of unknown outcomes) continues to build. Occasionally, but rarely, anxiety can build to the point at which it completely takes over, and the speaker freezes. You can avoid this scenario through *careful preparation* for the event, and by allowing the listeners to provide you with support. By *establishing eye contact* with members of your audience, you will see listeners smiling at you or expressing support with their posture, head nods, or other behaviors. Not looking at the audience or conversational partners removes your opportunity to get or give supportive feedback. When others notice your anxiety, they usually want to help you. Look at the audience, feel the support and try to relax, and then refocus on your communication goals.

By making eye contact with others, you can find clues about their level of understanding and interest.

## HOW DOES THEORY DESCRIBE NONVERBAL BEHAVIOR'S IMPACT ON RELATIONSHIPS?

Have you ever played elevator games with strangers? You know, you enter an empty elevator and take the "power position" by the buttons. At the next floor, someone enters and either asks you to push the button for a floor or reaches in front of you to select a floor and then retreats to the opposite corner away from you. There's no further talk or eye contact. The next person who enters does the same thing, finding a corner. Everyone faces the doors, anticipates its opening, watching the

EVT
THEORY

numbers change as if by magic. If others enter, their volume drops to a hush, or they stop talking until they leave. Now, have you ever tried *this*? Get on an elevator and keep walking until you face the back wall. After all, that's how you entered, right? Go stand right next to the power person, real close. Keep talking real loud. Sit down on your backpack or luggage. What do you think will happen? How will others react to you?

One theory that attempts to explain the influence of nonverbal communication on meaning and relationships is **expectancy violations** theory. Judee Burgoon said that "nonverbal cues are an inherent and essential part of message creation (production) and interpretation (processing)."[62] Expectancy violations theory (EVT) suggests that we hold expectations about the nonverbal behavior of others. It asserts that when communicative norms are violated, the violation may be perceived either favorably or unfavorably, depending on the perception that the receiver has of the violator. Burgoon's early writing on EVT integrated Hall's ideas on personal space (which you read about earlier) as a core aspect of the theory.[63] EVT says that our *expectancies* are the thoughts and behaviors anticipated when we interact with another.

We have expectations of how others ought to think and behave. Levine says that these expectancies are a result of social norms, stereotypes, and your own personal idiosyncrasies, and these expectancies cause us to interact with others.[64] We have both preinteractional and interactional expectations. *Preinteractional* expectations are made up of the skills and knowledge you bring to an interaction; *interactional expectations* are your skills and knowledge that let you carry out the interaction.

Another basic idea of EVT is that we learn our expectations from our cultures: You've learned what kind of touching is appropriate with whom, how to greet a stranger, and where to stand in relationship with another, for example.

Finally, EVT says that we make predictions about others based on their nonverbal behavior. So how does this work? Let's say you're standing in line at the grocery store, and the person in front of you looks at what you're about to buy and then makes eye contact with you. At first, you might be uncomfortable, thinking that the person is judging you by the way she is eyeing your groceries. If she then gives you a warm smile and points to her big pile containing the same things, you might feel a bit more comfortable. You've made predictions based on nonverbal behavior: The person is not threatening or judging you negatively.

But EVT is about *violations* of our expectations. Burgoon says that when people deviate from expectations, that deviation is judged based on the other's ability to reward us. A reward could be something as simple as a smile, friendliness, or acknowledgment of competence. This potential to reward is called *communicator reward valence*, which is the interactants' ability to reward or punish and the positive and negative characteristics they have. Someone in power, like your professor for instance, may have more communicator reward valence than a stranger, because the professor has the power of grades and probably has more credibility for you. If someone violates our expectations, these deviations cause *arousal*, an increased attention to the deviation.[65] Cognitive arousal is mental awareness of the deviation; physical arousal involves physiological heightening. For instance, if a person stares at you, you might wonder why he's doing that (cognitive arousal) or you might start to sweat (physical arousal). Once arousal happens, threats occur. Your *threat threshold* is the tolerance you have for deviations; how threatened do you feel? Maybe you don't mind if another person stands too close; maybe you can't put up with someone staring at you. The size of your threat threshold is based on how you view the person who is deviating from your expectations; what is that other's communicator reward valence? Then you add in the *violation valence*, which consists of your positive or negative value placed towards the deviations from your expectations.

When someone violates one of your expectations (for instance, he touches you when you didn't expect it), you interpret the meaning of that violation and decide if you like it or not. If you don't like it, then the violation valence is negative; if the surprise was pleasant (even though you didn't expect it), then the violation valence is positive. The theory predicts that if a violation is ambiguous, then

On an interview, you want to be positively evaluated.

the communicator reward valence will influence how you interpret and evaluate the violation. If the person is someone you like, then you'll positively evaluate his violation; if you don't like him, then you'll negatively evaluate his violation. Take a simple example of how someone is dressed. On an interview, there are certain expectations of how you should look. If you go in wearing jeans and a t-shirt and the company wants its workers to wear suits, then you've violated expectancies. It's pretty likely that you don't have any power here, or any way to reward the company for hiring you. Thus, the interviewer will evaluate you negatively, feeling aroused that

© iofoto, 2008, Shutterstock.

you didn't understand such a basic concept like appropriate attire. However, what if you are a highly sought-after, uniquely imaginative individual that the company has been pursuing? Your violation of the dress code might be seen positively; you're bold and creative, just like they thought. EVT is an interesting theory that focuses on what we expect nonverbally in conversations, as well as suggesting what happens when our expectations aren't met. It's very practical in applications across many contexts.

## WHAT ARE THE KEY POINTS TO REMEMBER ABOUT NONVERBAL COMMUNICATION?

Nonverbal communication is a complex combination of behaviors that form a source of information used by other people to make sense of messages that you send. Even though much of your nonverbal behavior is spontaneous and unconscious, you should realize that it contributes a significant percentage of the meaning that people attribute to your messages. As such, you should try as hard as you can to be a good self-monitor and pay close attention to your nonverbal behaviors. However, nonverbal behavior is also a source of information for you. It can help you to more accurately interpret the communication of others, so pay attention!

Be careful to not overgeneralize the meanings of particular nonverbal cues. The specific meaning of any nonverbal behavior is typically dependent on multiple factors, including (but not limited to) culture, the relationship between the people communicating, the specific communication context, and individual characteristics of the participants. You wouldn't want others to make stereotypical assumptions about your behavior, so make sure that you don't make those same assumptions about the behavior of others. Gather as much information as possible before reaching conclusions. Sometimes a touch is just a touch!

## CHAPTER SUMMARY

Verbal and nonverbal communication are powerful, critically important elements in the creation of shared meaning, because they have the ability to clarify your ideas to others or to confuse them. It's not always easy to use language or nonverbal behavior correctly, because both are arbitrary and ambiguous. The relationship that words or movements have with ideas is not based on a concrete characteristic; instead, you are relying on the ability of the audience to associate your symbols with their cognitions (beliefs, attitudes, and values). You've been exposed to some theoretical explanations of how these attempts to create meaning work in our lives.

We interpret language and nonverbal communication because of our particular culture, which provides a frame of reference on how to assign meaning. In order to be a competent communicator, you need to remain aware that your words aren't always understood as you mean them to be and that your nonverbal behavior can supplement or contradict those words. The next chapters will let you put those meanings into action!

## KEY WORDS

*Adaptors*
*Affect display*
*Clichés*
*Connotative meanings*
*Constitutive rules*
*Denotative meanings*
*Derogatory language*
*Dual perspective*
*Emblem*
*Empty words*
*Equivocal words*
*Expectancy violations*
*Eye contact*
*Grammar*
*Illustrator*
*Intersubjective*
*Intrusion of territory*
*Jargon*
*Kinesics*
*Language*
*Loaded words*
*Meaning*
*Personal space*
*Phonological rules*
*Primary territory*
*Public territory*
*Reference*
*Referent*
*Regionalisms*
*Regulative rules*
*Regulator*
*Secondary territory*

*Semantic rules*
*Semantic triangle*
*Slang*
*Symbols*
*Syntactical rules*
*Theory*
*Trite words*

# ENDNOTES

1. Language and Culture, Introduction, http://anthro.palomar.edu/language/language_1.htm.
2. "Internet World Users by Language," Internet World Stats, http://www.internetworldstats.com/stats7.htm (accessed Sept. 22, 2007).
3. In 1997, the Science Citation Index reported that 95 percent of its articles were written in English, even though only half of them came from authors in English-speaking countries. David Graddol, "The Future of English?" (digital edition), http://www.britishcouncil.org/de/learning-elt-future.pdf (accessed Sep. 22, 2007).
4. G.H. Mead, *Mind, Self and Society; From the Standpoint of a Social Behaviorist* (Chicago: University of Chicago Press, 1934).
5. "Top Television Buzzwords of 2007," The Global Language Monitor. http://www.languagemonitor.com/wst_pagell.html (accessed Sept. 22, 2007).
6. E. Natalle, with J.L. Flippen, "Urban Music: Gendered Language in Rapping," in Philip Backlund and M.R. Williams (ed.) *Readings in Gender Communication* (Belmont, CA: Wadsworth-Thompson, 2004), 140–149.
7. "Remarks by the President after Two Planes Crashed into World Trade Center," http://www.whitehouse.gov/news/releases/2001/09/20010911.html (accessed Sept. 22, 2007).
8. "Remarks by the President Upon Arrival at Barksdale Air Force Base," http://www.whitehouse.gov/news/releases/2001/09/20010911-1.html (accessed Sept. 22, 2007).
9. "Statement by the President in His Address to the Nation," http://www.whitehouse.gov/news/releases/2001/09/20010911-16.html (accessed Sept. 22, 2007).
10. D. Berlo, *The Process of Communication* (New York, Holt, Rinehart and Winston Inc., 1960).
11. "Adopt-a Confusion" Perspectives Press, http://www.perspectivespress.com/pjadopta.html (accessed Sept. 22, 2007).
12. Cronen, Pearce, and Snavely 1979. Vernon E. Cronen, W. Barnett Pearce, and Lonna Snavely (1979). "A Theory of Rule Structure and Forms of Episodes, and a Study of Unwanted Repetitive Patterns (URPs)," pp.225–240 in Dan Nimmo, ed. Communication Yearbook III. Edison, NJ: Transaction Books.

13. C.K. Ogden and I.A. Richards, *The Meaning of Meaning*, 8th ed. (New York, Harcourt, Brace & World, 1923), 9–12.
14. S. Trenholm, *Thinking through Communication* (Boston: Allyn and Bacon, 2000), 87.
15. L.A.M. Perry and D. Ballard-Reisch, "There's a Rainbow in the Closet," in Philip Backlund and M.R. Williams (ed.), *Readings in Gender Communication* (Belmont, CA: Wadsworth-Thompson, 2004), 17–34.
16. Bipolar.com http://www.bipolar.com/ (accessed May 1, 2008).
17. C. Kramarae, *Women and Men Speaking: Frameworks for Analysis* (Rowley, MA: Newbury House, 1981), 1.
18. Ibid.
19. J.T. Wood. *Communication in Our Lives*, 4th ed. (Belmont, CA: Thompson Wadsworth, 2006), 137.
20. Urban dictionary http://www.urbandictionary.com/ (accessed Sept. 12, 2007).
21. Lake Superior State University, "List of Banished Words," http://stuft.vox.com/library/post/lakesuperior-state-university-2007-list-of-banished-words.html (accessed Sept. 12, 2007).
22. M. Orbe and C. Bruess, *Contemporary Issues in Interpersonal Communication* (Los Angeles: Roxbury, 2005).
23. D. O'Hair, G. Friedrich, and L. Dixon, *Strategic Communication in Business and the Professions* (Boston: Houghton Mifflin, 2005).
24. K. Adams and G. Galanes, *Communicating in Groups: Applications and Skills* (Boston: McGraw-Hill, 2006).
25. R. Adler, L. Rosenfeld, and R. Proctor, *Interplay: The Process of Interpersonal Communication* (New York: Oxford University Press, 2004).
26. J. Burgoon and A. Bacue, "Nonverbal Communication Skills," in J. Greene and B. Burleson (eds.), *Handbook of Communication and Social Interaction Skills* (Mahwah, NJ: Lawrence Erlbaum, 2003).
27. F. Manusov, "Perceiving Nonverbal Messages: Effects of Immidiacy and Encoded Intent on Receiver Judgements," *Western Journal of Speech Communication* 55 (Summer 1991), 235–253. Also M. Knapp and Hall, *Nonverbal Communication in Human Interaction,* 6th ed. (2005).
28. R.L. Birdwhistell, "Background to Kinesics." *Etc.* 13, (1955), 10–18.
29. A. Mehrabian and S. Ferris, "Inference of Attitudes from Nonverbal Communication in Two Channels," *Journal of Consulting Psychology* 31 (1967), 248–252.
30. J. Shapiro, "Responsivity to Facial and Linguistic Cues," *Journal of Communication*, 18 (1968), 11–17. Also L. Vande Creek and J. Watkins, "Responses to incongruent verbal and nonverbal emotional cues," *Journal of Communication*, 22 (1972), 311–316; and D. Solomon and F. Ali, "Influence of Verbal Content and Intonation on Meaning Attributions of First-and-Second-Language Speakers," *Journal of Social Psychology*, 95 (1975), 3–8.
31. "The Kennedy-Nixon Presidential Debates, 1960," The Museum of Broadcast Communications, http://www.museum.tv/archives/etv/k/htmlk/kennedy-nixon/kennedy-nixon.htm (accessed May 1, 2008).

32. K. Drummond and R. Hopper, "Acknowledgment Tokens in Series," *Communication Reports* 6, (1993), 47–53.

33. R. Riggio and H. Freeman,"Individual Differences and Cues to Deception," *Journal of Personality and Social Psyhchology* 45 (1983), 899–915.

34. J. Burgoon, D. Buller, L. Guerrero, and C. Feldman, "Interpersonal Deception: VI, Effects on Preinteractinal and International Factors on Deceiver and Observer Perceptions of Deception Success," *Communication Studies,* 45 (1994), 263–280.

35. A. Vrij, K. Edward, K. Roberts, and R. Bull, (2002). Detecting deceit via analysis of verbal and nonverbal behavior. *Journal of Nonverbal Behavior* 24, 239–263.

36. Burgoon etal.

37. R. Birdwhistell, *Kinesics and Context* (Philadelphia: University of Pennsylvania Press, 1970).

38. P. Ekman, "Movements with Precise Meanings," *Journal of Communication* 26 (1976), 14–26.

39. A. Mehrabian and M. Williams, "Nonverbal Concomitants of Perceived and Intended Persuasiveness," *Journal of Personality and Social Psychology* 13 (1969), 37–58.

40. G. Savage (1978). Endings and beginnings: Turn taking and the small group in Wall, V. (ed.), Small Group Communication: Selected Readings (Columbus, OH: Collegiate).

41. J. Weimann and M. Knapp, "Turn Taking and Conversations," *Journal of Communication* 25 (1975), 75–92. Also M. Argyle, *Bodily Communication* (New York: International Universities Press, 1975).

42. G. Gladstone and G. Parker, "When You're Smiling, Does the Whole World Smile for You?" *Australasian Psychiatry* 10 (2002), 144–146.

43. W. Donaghy and B.F. Dooley, "Head Movement, Gender, and Deceptive Communication," Communication Reports 7 (1994), 67–75.

44. J. Martin and T. Nakayama, *Intercultural Communication in Contexts* (New York: McGraw Hill, 2000).

45. C. Maslow, K. Yoselson, and H. London, "Persuasiveness of Confidence Expressed via Language and Body Language," *British Journal of Social and Clinical Psychology*, 10 (1971), 234–240.

46. Knapp and Hall, 2005.

47. J. Burgoon, "A Communication Model of Personal Space Violations: Explication and an Initial Test," *Human Communication Research*, 4 (1978), 129–142. Also J. Burgoon, "Nonverbal Signals," in M. Knapp and G. Miller (eds.), *Handbook of Interpersonal Communication* (Thousand Oaks, CA: Sage, 1994); and J. Burgoon, "Spatial Relationships in Small Groups," in R. Cathcart, L. Samovar, and L. Heaman, *Small Group Communication: Theory and Practice* (Madison, WI: Brown, 1996).

48. E.T. Hall, *The Silent Language* (Garden City, NY: Doubleday, 1959); and E.T. Hall, "A System for the Notation of Proxemic Behavior," *American Anthropologist*, 65 (1963), 1003–1026.

49. I. Altman, *The Environment and Social Behavior* (Monterey, CA: Brooks Cole, 1975).

50. L. Malandro, L. Barker, and D. Barker, *Nonverbal Communication* (New York: Random House, 1989).

51. S. Lyman and M. Scott, "Territoriality: A Neglected Sociological Dimension," *Social Problems* 15 (1967), 236–249.

52. M. Knapp, *Essentials of Nonverbal Communication* (New York: Holt, Rinehart & Winston, 1992).

53. D. Morris, *Manwatching: A Field Guide to Human Behavior* (New York: Harry N. Abrams, 1977).

54. Ibid.

55. D. Katz, "The Functional Approach to the Study of Attitudes," *Public Opinion Quarterly* 24 (1960), 163–204.

56. W. Gordon, C. Teagler, and D. Infante, "Women's Clothing as Predictors of Dress at Work, Job Satisfaction, and Career Advancement," *Southern States Speech Communication Journal* 47 (1982), 422–434.

57. P. Andersen, *Nonverbal Communication: Forms and Functions* (Mountain View, CA: Mayfield, 1999). Also D. Leathers, *Successful Nonverbal Communication: Principles and Applications*, 3rd ed. (Boston: Allyn and Bacon, 1997).

58. J. Pearson, *Gender and Communication* (Dubuque, IA: William C. Brown, 1985).

59. J. Wood, *Gendered Lives: Communication, Gender, and Culture*, 5th ed. (Belmont, CA: Wadsworth, 2002), 141.

60. S. Rosenberg, S. Kahn, and T. Tran, "Creating a Political Image: Shaping Appearance and Manipulating the Vote," *Political Behavior* 13 (1991), 347.

61. S. Wallace, D. Yoder, L. Hugenberg, and C. Horvath, *Creating Competent Communication: Interviewing.* (Dubuque, IA: Kendall/Hunt Publishing, 2006).

62. Burgoon, 1994.

63. Burgoon, 1978.

64. T.R. Levine, L. Anders, J. Banas, K. Baum, K. Endo, A. Hu, and C. Wong, "Norms, Expectations, and Deception: A Norm Violation Model of Veracity Judgments," *Communication Monographs* 67 (2000), 123–137.

65. Burgoon, 1978. P. 133

# REFERENCES

D. Berlo (1960). *The Process of Communication*. New York, Holt, Rinehart and Winston Inc.

S. Campo, K.A. Cameron, D. Brossard, and M. Frazer (2004) "Social norms and expectancy violations theories: Assessing the effectiveness of health communication campaigns." Communication Monographs 71, 448–470

P. Ekman and W. Friesen (1975). *Unmasking the face*. Englewood Cliffs, NJ: Prentice-Hall.

P. Ekman and W. Friesen (1969). The repertoire of nonverbal behavior: Categories, origins, usage, and coding. *Semiotica*, 1, 49–98.

R. Gass and J. Seiter (2003). *Persuasion, social influence, and compliance gaining*. Boston: Allyn & Bacon.

D. Graddol (2000). The Future of English? (digital edition). http://www.britishcouncil.org/de/learning-elt-future.pdf

J. Hornick (1992). Tactile stimulation and consumer response. *Journal of consumer research*, 19, 449–458.

L. Howells and S. Becker (1962). Seating arrangement as leadership emergence. *Journal of abnormal and social psychology*, 64, 148–150.

D. Kaufman and J. Mahoney (1999). The effect of waitress touch on alcohol consumption in dyads. *Journal of social psychology, 139,* 261–267.

C. Kramarae (1981), Women and men speaking: Frameworks for analysis. Rowley, MA: Newbury house.

R.M. Krauss and U. Hadar (1999). The role of speech-related arm/hand gestures in word retrieval. In, R. Campbell & L. Messing (Eds.), Gesture, speech, and sign (pp.93–116). Oxford: Oxford University Press.

E. Morsella and R.M. Krauss (in press). The role of gestures in spatial working memory and speech. American Journal of Psychology. http://www.columbia.edu/cu/psychology/commlab/publications.html (retrieved Sept. 28, 2007)

G.H. Mead (1934). *Mind, self and society; From the standpoint of a social behaviorist*. Chicago: University of Chicago press.

E. Natalle and J. Flippen (2004). Urban Music: Gendered language in Rapping. In Backlund, P., and Williams, M. (ed) Readings in Gender Communication. Belmont, CA: Wadsworth-Thompson. 140–149.

C.K. Ogden and I.A. Richards (1923). *The Meaning of Meaning*. New York, Harcourt, Brace & World, Inc., 9–12.

L. Perry and D. Ballard-Reisch (2004). There's a Rainbow in the closet. In Backlund, P., & Williams, M. (ed.). *Readings in Gender Communication*, Belmont, CA: Wadsworth-Thompson, 2004, 17–34.

S. Rosenberg, S. Kahn, and T. Tran (1991). "Creating a political image: Shaping appearance and manipulating the vote." Political Behavior 13, 345–367 P. 347

G. Savage (1978). Endings and beginnings: Turn taking and the small group. In Wall, V. (ed). *Small group communication: Selected readings*. Columbus: Collegiate.

F. Strodtbeck and L. Hook (1961). The social dimensions of a twelve man jury table. *Sociometry*, 24, 297–415.

G. Trager (1958). Paralanguage: A first approximation. *Studies in linguistics*, 13, 1–12.

S. Trenholm (2000). *Thinking through Communication*. Boston: Allyn and Bacon.

J. Wood (2006). *Communication in Our Lives, Fourth Ed*. Belmont, CA: Thompson Wadsworth, 2006.

# VERBAL AND NONVERBAL COMMUNICATION

Was anyone else confused by the Icelandic proverb at the beginning of this chapter? "Better wise language than uncombed hair." I clearly do not relate to Icelandic wisdom. Were they trying to say: "You should speak well rather than worry about looking good?"

One of the themes of this chapter is **sharing**. In the process of communication we try to share meaning. Our world is getting more complicated all the time. The authors of this chapter state there are over 5,000 languages on the planet. That means there are at least 5,000 ways to say "boy," "girl," and "Yes, we should live in peace." Some cultures have several words for the one thing. The Aleuts (Eskimos) reportedly have several words for snow. (I do not speak Aleut.) There is crunchy snow, wet snow, etc., etc. When you live in a snowcovered land, you create different words for different kinds of snow. We create new words all the time to express new ideas and define new things. Do you think your grandparents googled answers? Or did they have to look up information in a book? (Gasp!)

Then we add the channel of nonverbal communication to the verbal channel, and things get even more complex. Have you ever seen someone who looks like they are lying? A child tells a parent, "I didn't take the last cookie." But they are looking away, avoiding eye contact, searching for the right words. They have *guilty* written all over their face. Adults exhibit many of the same characteristics when we want to avoid the truth. Yet we are amazingly good at deciphering combinations of verbal and nonverbal messages that we see simultaneously. Next, we want to consider the context for these messages in different relationships.

# CHAPTER 3

## Interpersonal Communication

Whether texting, talking, or tweeting, the most common form of communication you will do in your life is interpersonal communication.[1] Up to this point you have learned all about the theory of communication. You have defined it, seen models of it, and dissected it into verbal, nonverbal, and listening. You have even explored the inner workings of perception. Now it's time to look at the ways we actually use communication.

This course was designed to give you insight (and practice) into the three major ways people use communication: giving speeches (formal or informal), working in small groups (like campus clubs and committees), and the thing you will do most in your life, interpersonal communication (or talking with others one-on-one). Yes, you may be asked to speak in front of a group some day or present a report for your job. Yes, committees are unavoidable and it's unlikely that you will always be working with people you agree with or like. The reality is that you will deal with the day-to-day, face-to-face, and let us not forget the ever-popular electronic versions, referred to as computer-mediated communication

(CMC) within the communication field, with individuals in all aspects of your life. The fact is that we use interpersonal communication to connect with others and keep those connections going through the good times and the bad. Sometimes we stay connected for decades, other times we need to find ways to "disconnect." There's an old 1960s song titled "Breakin' Up Is Hard to Do." Maybe we can make connecting—or disconnecting—a little easier for you, or at least make it so you don't feel so alone in your misery.

So, what is interpersonal communication? Let's spend some time focusing on how we do what we do, why we do it, and why it sometimes goes terribly wrong. In this chapter we look at *interpersonal communication* in terms of four basic questions:

> **Interpersonal communication**
> Interaction based on sharing of emotions, ideas, or information, usually face to face.

1. What is interpersonal communication?
2. How do needs and attraction impact interpersonal communication?
3. How do we accomplish interpersonal communication?
4. How do we keep interpersonal communication going (or get out of it, if desired)?

## WHAT IS INTERPERSONAL COMMUNICATION?

There are two basic ways to define interpersonal communication. The simplest way is by counting the number of people. If there is only one person we call it *intrapersonal communication*. Once you add a second person it becomes *interpersonal communication*. Most scholars agree that the addition of a third person shifts things into *small-group communication*.

FIGURE 3.1

Impersonal
Communication

| Impersonal Communication | | Interpersonal Communication |
|---|---|---|
| Role-based | | Individualized |
| General | | Specific |
| Highly scripted | | Unique |
| I-It | I-You | I-Thou |

But merely counting heads misses many of the complexities of defining interpersonal communication. We are all aware of the vast difference in interactions between ordering food at McDonalds and a long, heart-to-heart talk with a close friend. So there must be more to defining interpersonal communication than just numbers. One way to distinguish these differences is to add the notion of *impersonal communication* to our discussion. Think about all the one-on-one interactions you have in a day and try to rank them on the following continuum.

Think of the left side of the continuum as those interactions that are very general, usually based on a role being played or a task being accomplished. This would easily cover your McDonalds encounter. You are the customer, and they are the employee. Your desire is to order your food and have it served quickly and accurately. There is an expected script ("Do you want fries with that?") for both roles, and if the interaction goes well, all parties move on to the next task (you eat the food, and they serve the next customer) with little thought.

Think of the right side of the continuum as those interactions that are very specific and individualized. These are the people who know you best. They know your moods, your body language; they even know your past. They are probably your BFFs, your family members, and possibly that "one true love." Each encounter

with these people is unique. Sometimes you provide support for one another and other times you simply enjoy each other's company. The scripts are loosely defined (although one classic indication of these close encounters is the "secret language" you share: the code words, nicknames, and phrases that only your best friends or family members understand).

Of course, any continuum leaves room in the middle. In this case,

**Impersonal communication** Interaction based on societal roles, usually transactional.

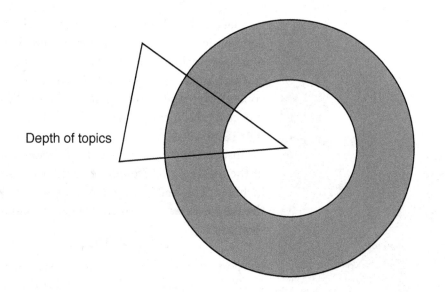

FIGURE 3.2

Social Penetration
Theory Image

Depth of topics

you have many acquaintances and friends that fall somewhere in between the ends of the continuum. The philosopher Martin Buber[2] had language to describe these differences. He referred to the range in terms of: "I–It," "I–You," and "I–Thou." I–It matches the Impersonal end of the continuum, and the I–Thou aligns with the Interpersonal end. What Buber's language adds is a category for the middle range of the Impersonal–Interpersonal continuum. The I–You refers to those acquaintances that go beyond the role-based, superficial level, but do not reach the fully personal level of the I–Thou.

*Social Penetration Theory*[3] would have us trade in the continuum for nesting circles. In this case, the closest relationships are shown in the innermost circle. Others are represented by the varying degrees of closeness for each outer circle. For this theory, issues of the encounter's **depth** and **breadth** are key factors. For those persons on the outer rim, a wide range of topics might be discussed, but the depth to which they go is minimal. Chatting about the weather is a classic example. For the innermost circle, those dearest to you, the range of topics may have narrowed over time, but the depth to which you will reveal your thoughts and feelings goes deep. That classic heart-to-heart talk mentioned above clearly fits this category.

Defining **relational communication** is the final aspect needed for our understanding of interpersonal communication. It is important to note that when we use the term *relationship* or *relational* in this text, we are not only talking about the romantic, makes-you-feel-all-tingly-inside thing. Relational communication refers to any type of relationship: work, family, school, the guy who delivers your pizza at 2 a.m., etc.

> **Social penetration theory** Process by which communication between persons or groups deepens through longer, closer, or more comfortable discussion.
>
> **Depth** Measure or degree or intimacy in communication.
>
> **Breadth** Measure or degree of range of information shared in communication.

©2013 by Heider Almeida, Shutterstock, Inc.

In fact, the basis of defining relational communication stems from the notion that all messages include two levels of meaning: the **content-level** and the **relational-level**.[4] The content level meaning of any message is the "what" aspect of the message: What does the message mean? However, to figure out what a message means, you must also look at the relational level of the message, the "context" aspect. This aspect includes: who said it, to whom they said it, why they said it, where and when they said it, and how they said it. ~~SARCASM~~

If I go to the local bar and order a screwdriver, I will be surprised if the server brings me a Sears Craftsman tool. On the other hand, if the electrician asks you for a screwdriver while he is working on your wiring and you bring him a vodka and orange juice, he may or may not be appreciative, but certainly he will be surprised. The content-level of the word *screwdriver* in and of itself cannot provide enough information for anyone to attribute correct meaning. We are constantly deciphering the content-level of any message based on the relational-level or message context, including the sender, the receiver, the setting, etc.

Interpersonal communication occurs in specific relational contexts. As two individuals work to share their ideas through verbal and nonverbal messages, they are, in turn, developing relationships. In fact, you know well that some of those impersonal, role-based encounters you have had in your life have continued long enough to develop into acquaintances that become good friends, that quite possibly end up as best buddies. As the relational level of a message develops, so does the relationship. That is how you develop those secret code words, nicknames, and phrases. Spoken outside that particular relational context, their meanings are changed.

*DEFINED* →

For the purposes of this book, *interpersonal communication* will be defined as interactions between two people that vary in depth, breath, and quality to create a variety of relational encounters.

FLOYD SONG

# HOW DO NEEDS AND ATTRACTION IMPACT INTERPERSONAL COMMUNICATION?

Both individual human needs and issues of attraction between people have great impact on the ways we communicate interpersonally. They motivate our behavior and help define our relationships.

## *Needs*

Most communication scholars look to research on human needs to begin understanding why we ever started communicating with others. Beyond its basic functional purposes, like "Hey, Mac, a sabertooth tiger is about to eat you," human interactions have contributed to deeper and ever-more-important connections between people over the ages. But why did these connections come about? What did we need interpersonal communication for? Abraham Maslow,[5] the best-known scholar on the subject of needs, created an inverted pyramid to demonstrate what he called a *hierarchy of needs*. According to Maslow, we have basic needs of air, food, water, shelter, and sex. (Yes, sex is a basic need directly connected to our survival; our need to procreate; turns out it is just one of our basic biological needs playing itself out on a college campus). So, back to Maslow... (I know it is hard to focus on this reading when we were just talking about sex, but do your best.) Maslow believed that once you covered all the basics on the bottom of the pyramid, you now had energy to move on to other things, like "belonging."

Alfred Schutz,[6] another well-known scholar on the topic of needs laid out a simple (but much less popular) set of reasons why we need human relationships. Much like Maslow's second tier, Schulz believed that people have three basic needs with regard to interpersonal interactions: inclusion, affection, and control.

Everyone has a desire for *inclusion*, to be a part of something. Think back to your very first moments on this campus. I don't mean your campus visits when you were still in high school. Fast-forward to the point where your parents and friends drove away and left you here alone. Do you remember anything about how that moment felt? What did you do first? Where did you go? Did you immediately turn to your phone as a way to connect virtually with another person? Even "virtual inclusion" counts. With whom did you eat your first meal in convo? Was it your new roommate? Was it someone from across the hall? Some of you may have come to AU with a few friends from high school. Maybe you were even rooming with one of them. In that case, you were not as alone as you might have been. Some of you were a part of some campus organizations like the football team or the band. In that case, you probably came to campus early and you had a built-in network of upper-class students to instantly connect with. The fact is that experts know how vulnerable people feel in those moments when they are yanked away from the places where they belong and dropped into a new, unfamiliar environment. Feeling "a part of" or included somewhere is a vital human need. The first day of college is one of those rare times when you may get a glimpse of just how important that need is. To help you find new friends, campus activity boards across the nation work diligently to plan activities those first few days of college. Some of you may have been connected with your new roommate on Facebook or by email before you ever came to campus. That is not a coincidence. That is careful planning on the part of student life administrators. They want you to feel included as soon as possible, and they will go to extreme measures to ensure that it happens. They are aware of the research showing that student satisfaction with their college experience depends largely on the satisfaction students have with their campus relationships.

That first day you may have been a tad desperate. You may have gone to convo with anyone who would make eye contact and say a few words. Compared to that first meal, do you still eat with the same people? Do you still sit in the same place in convo? If you were one of the lucky ones (the band members and football players), you were guided and mentored by the older students in that group, so you may well still be doing what you did with the people you did it with. But, if you were on your own trying to navigate this new territory, there is a good chance you are no longer hanging out with that person you first befriended, and your seat choice (while always the same now) may have changed drastically. Schultz would say that is due to our second primary need: *affection*. At first you just sought out a warm body, but now that you have been here a while you can be more particular. You probably find yourself continuing to hang around the people who are nice to you.

Schutz would add one more piece to the puzzle. He would say that your journey to make friends here at AU is driven by your need for *control*. Everyone desires some level of predictability in their life. You want to know that the people you sit with in convo day after day will treat you the same basic way each day. You want to know that your circle of friends will act a certain way or think a certain way. It isn't controlling in a negative sense, but more a way to create a world that is familiar to you and comfortable. In fact, later in this chapter as we discuss conflict, you may notice that a common source of relational turbulence comes from people changing their behavior or attitudes. We humans hate change, especially change that disturbs the balance of our relationships.

Along with our individual needs, there are factors of attraction influencing our interpersonal encounters.

CREATE SLIDE(s)
↓

## Attraction

People become attracted to a variety of things. We might be attracted to the color of an individual's eyes. Someone might be drawn to a person who matches their intellect and wit, or the fact that another human being on the planet actually owns the same rare album from an obscure musical group. Sometimes the hotty sitting next to you in class might be attractive to you. The reasons for attractions break into three categories: *physical attraction*, *situational attraction*, and *similar interests*.

©2013 by Diego Cervo, Shutterstock, Inc.

**PHYSICAL ATTRACTION.** If you think back to Maslow and his hierarchy, you will remember that sex was one of the basic needs all humans' experience. Is it any wonder that physical attraction is usually the primary factor in early relationships? Each culture establishes its own parameters of beauty, and those messages are sent to children at an early age through the media, family messages, their community, and even the toys they play with. The Barbie doll has been a "blond bombshell" since her origination in 1961, and no matter how many brown-haired friends she has in her doll network, children learn from a young age that blonds do have more fun… and more boyfriends. Based on societal notions of beauty, we tune into others around us and seek out those who possess the most beauty traits. Physical fitness levels, body shape and size, hair and eye color, as well as issues of grooming and cleanliness, factor into the purely physical attraction between individuals.

> **Physical attraction**
> Attraction based on a person's appearance (looks).
>
> **Situational attraction**
> Attraction based on interaction in a specific event or setting.

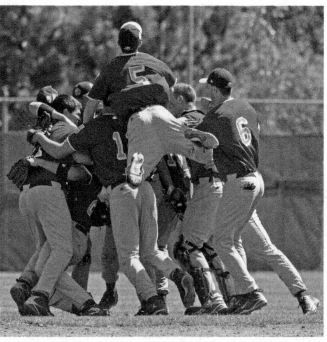
©2013 by Jamie Roach, Shutterstock, Inc.

**SITUATIONAL ATTRACTION:** Some friendships stem from the situational convenience of proximity. If you find yourself spending time with the people you work with, have classes with, or share hobbies with, you may not realize how much of the friendship is based on the mere fact that you are around that person much of the day. In fact, only time will tell if the friends you make based on physical proximity and frequent encounters will last beyond the convenience of those current situations. Once you find yourself in different classes, a new dorm floor, or away from an old hobby, you will figure out which people you truly want to seek out (as a friendship of choice) and which people you lose interest in once the circumstances that brought you together have passed.

➤ Similar interests
Enjoyment or engagement in, or curiosity about, similar things.

**SIMILAR INTERESTS:** Initially the physical features are the predominant factor in making connections, but even as children we learned that beauty is skin deep. While much of life's pleasures may be found in surface-level attraction, for most people there needs to be something of substance wrapped up in that beautiful skin. You may just as easily be drawn to individuals based on common hobbies and interests. People who work in theatre tend to be drawn to other theatrical types. Athletes share the common bond of teamwork and that camaraderie can build life-long friendships.

# HOW DO WE ACCOMPLISH INTERPERSONAL COMMUNICATION?

There are many types of relationships: family, friends, work, romantic. Some you are born into, some you are placed into, and others you seek out. Some are face-to-face and others are online. We make sense of our relationships in the form of a story, "The story of us," as the song lyrics put it. As with any good story, all of our relationships have beginnings, middles, and ends. While there is always a "Once upon a time," we don't all get to the "happily ever after."

**FIGURE 3.3**

Model of Relationships

➤ Models of relationships
Forms and paths of communication and interaction.
Levinger, Knapp & Vangelisti, Rawlings all show the continuum of relationships from greeting to termination with varying degrees of detail.

|  | | Levinger | Knapp & Vangelisti | Rawlins |
|---|---|---|---|---|
| **Beginnings** | | Acquaintance | Initiating | Role-limited |
| | | | Experimenting | Friendly relations |
| | | Build-up | Intensifying | Moving toward friendships |
| | | | Integrating | Nascent friendships |
| **Middles** | | Continuation | Bonding | Stabilized friendships |
| | | | Differentiating | Waning friendships |
| | | Deterioration | Circumscribing | |
| | | | Avoiding | |
| | | | Stagnating | |
| **Ends** | | Endings | Terminating | |

Scholars have identified common stages that most relationships go through as they develop and solidify. Many of these stages have been articulated in the shape of models that map out relationship progression. No one model is able to accommodate all the intricacies of relationship development and decline, but a few have become recognizable standards in the communication field.

One of the earliest attempts to illustrate relationship stages was Levinger's[7] simplistic ABCDE model. While missing many significant details, it did capture the essence of relationship stages clearly and succinctly. Others, most notably Knapp,[8] have built more complex models featuring the types of communication one displays during the stages of relational change. Rawlins[9] contributed by developing a model featuring stages that are unique to friendships.

Models are not perfect and no one model can capture all the details of human relations. In an effort to be clear, each model leaves many basic assumptions unstated. One of those assumptions is that no one is obligated to stay on the path. People move at their own speed, jump off the track at varying times, and often never reach stages of relationship disintegration. Only death is inevitable. Beyond that, each individual will move through his or her relationships in unique ways. Flawed as they are, models do give us language and ideas to help frame our perceptions of relationships. They categorize and compartmentalize relationship movement in useful ways.

Each model describes the beginning differently, but all try to capture the spirit of those first moments, the early days when relationships are hardly even called "relationships." In that first encounter, far more is unknown than known. With every new encounter lies the potential for a sustaining relationship. The reality is that a very small percentage, maybe as few as 1 percent, of our initial interactions goes much beyond the initial engagement. We meet new people every day, at the doctor's office, holding a door for us, in the grocery store checkout line. Have you ever stopped to think about all the potential relationships you dismiss with little thought? You might chat about the weather, an upcoming holiday, or the length of the line

you are standing in, but few encounters go beyond that superficial level of interactions. In any encounter, we humans have an intense need to know and understand as much as we can. We do not handle uncertainty well. It makes us nervous, causes confusion, and throws off our equilibrium. ***Uncertainty reduction theory***[10] tells us that we will do whatever we can to reduce uncertainty and discover where we are and with whom we are talking. In fact, many people gravitate toward the places and people they know, in part to avoid uncertainty. Others are more comfortable with new people and new situations. Reducing that uncertainty helps us make sense of the encounter and better predict what comes next.

The models show ways in which we can move beyond initial movements to learn more about the people we are around. The world of social media provides new ways to gather basic information about a person and interact.[11] Through Facebook we can see what music they like, what school they attend, and quite literally what they "Like." In early conversations we can experiment or "try on" a relationship, by asking questions about background, activities, and interests. Each new piece of information allows us to decide whether to proceed with the relationship or abandon the cause.

One of the best ways to increase the comfort level of both people is through self-disclosure. Relationships develop almost exclusively through the sharing of ideas, opinions, and details of our lives. We call this level of personal sharing *self-disclosure*. Once the interaction moves beyond surface-level talk about weather, hometowns, and "what's your major?" people gradually share more personal information. The more you share of yourself with another person, the more the relationship has the potential to grow. Most people have an expectation of what is called ***reciprocity*** when they self-disclose.[12] There is an unwritten rule that any time someone shares something about themself, the recipient will respond by sharing their information too. In most well-developing relationships this is certainly the case. However, people have varying levels of comfort when it comes to disclosing personal information.

**➤ Uncertainty Reduction Theory**
Refers to the idea that people require information about other parties prior to initial communication between parties, to reduce uncertainty or nerves and form reasonable expectations in communication.

**➤ Reciprocity**
Engagement and mutual interest in communication beyond passive delivery or acceptance of a message.

FIGURE 3.4

Johari Window

| | Known to me | Unknown to me |
|---|---|---|
| **Known to others** | Open | Blind |
| **Unknown to others** | Hidden | Unknown |

Joseph Luft and Harry Ingham[13] created a famous image called the *Johari Window* to display four possible categories of information between two people.

➤ **Johari Window**
A measurement technique to improve communication and self-perception by determining qualities or attitudes known to self, known to others, unknown to self, and unknown to others.

Information shared openly between two people fits into the Open quadrant. Our secrets belong in the Hidden. Less prominent, but there nonetheless, is information others know about us, but we cannot see ourselves. These are the things to which we are Blind. One sign of true friendship is the ability to point out the good and bad features of which our friends may be unaware. These may be as superficial as the piece of food stuck between their teeth or as intimate as their personal flaws. The Unknown category can only be known through sustained and long-term relationships. But, there has been more than one instance of romance, unknown to both parties for years, developing between longtime friends.

We all can envision our key relationships in terms of the Johari Window. It is yet another way to describe the Impersonal-Interpersonal continuum. In fact, it is a key explanation of those variations of connectedness. In our lives, we know whom we can trust enough to tell our secrets. We know when it is socially appropriate and personally beneficial to keep quiet. We also know that the lines dividing these quadrants are fluid and even changing. The high school confidant to whom you once bared your soul may have grown distant over time. Your parents, who you swore as a teen would never understand your secrets, may have become (once again) your best friends.

Whether they are based on work relationships, friendships, family, or romance, the more we self-disclose and learn to trust individuals with the parts of us we have kept secret, the more the relationship will grow. As we spend more time together, we intensify the relationship. One line of research documents key moments, called *turning points*,[14] as a way to see the progression of closeness. The classic "first 'I love you'" and "first kiss" are clear examples of a turning point. There are many other little ways in which we mark the intensity of the relationships. The first time you take someone home to meet your family, the first fight you have … and survive, the first vacation you take together; all of these moments demonstrate new levels of closeness between friends and romantic partners.

As trust builds, lives become increasingly interwoven, social circles overlap, and "coupledness" is publicly evident. This is clearly seen in romance. Couples mark their connection by holding hands, wearing the other person's clothing, or leaving personal belongings in their partner's living space. Friends can publicly mark their relationships too. We all know those inseparable friends who are rarely seen without the other. They take the same classes, work at the same job, go to the same parties, and eat at the same dining table.

Increasing levels of trust, commitment, and planning for the future move relationships into what Knapp refers to as "bonding." Marriage is the undisputable example for romantic relationships. We have fewer ways to publicly mark the bonding stage for friendships. College friends who become roommates when they graduate might be one exception. Brides and grooms publicly mark friendships with their choices of a best man or maid-of-honor. Designation of "godparents" also functions as a way to clearly demonstrate closeness between friends.

## HOW DO WE KEEP IT GOING/GET OUT OF IT?

All relationships experience some level of disturbance at some time. *Relational maintenance*[15] research acknowledges the importance of studying how people weather these momentary disruptions and reconnect into a new level of comfort and security. Looking at the models, you could get the impression that "what goes up must come down." However, much of the relational work that occurs in daily life is more about maintaining the relationship. All relationships have growing pains of one sort or another. One useful model that attempts to capture the ever changing levels of connectedness is ***Conville's Helical Model.***[16] Built on the metaphor of a spiral, he shows the cyclic progression we go through as we move from periods of security to times of alienation. These cycles parallel a back-and-forth movement between Knapp's earlier *integration* and *differentiation* stages. Ultimately, the model reassures us that even in times of distance, there is hope of a return to stabilization and security.

**Conville's Helical Model**
Theory that relational communication is continuously developing and that development, via communication, cannot be reversed.

**FIGURE 3.5**

Helical Model

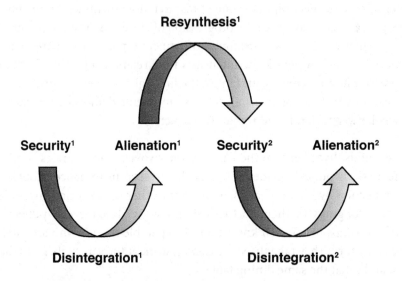

FIGURE 3.6

Dialectic Tensions

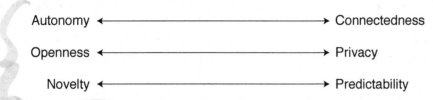

Autonomy ←——————————→ Connectedness

Openness ←——————————→ Privacy

Novelty ←——————————→ Predictability

One example of issues that can cause problems in all types of relationships is referred to as **Dialectic Tensions**.[17] People have differing needs for things like personal space and privacy. Baxter and Montgomery found several sets of opposing needs that cover the basic differences.

Even though some individuals may have higher needs for autonomy (alone time), their partners might have a higher need for togetherness. You might want to spend time alone, while your friend or romantic partner wants to spend every waking hour together. These opposing needs can create relationship tensions if unattended. Neither end of the continuum is better or worse, but perceptions of what is appropriate behavior varies greatly. Some individuals are more private, disclosing less personal information. Others disclose high levels of information and see disclosure as a primary indicator of affection and intimacy. Equally frustrating are the differing needs for planned and predictable behavior, as opposed to last-minute, spontaneous choices. The person needing more novelty might break up with someone because he or she is seen as "boring." The person needing more predictability might resent the lack of planning and ability to depend on consistent behavior from their partner. Depending on the level of needs, the tensions between individuals can mount. Think of it like rubber bands being stretched in opposite directions. Left unattended the band will snap, and so too will the bond between humans.

Several coping techniques have been identified. Relational partners can make alternating choices of whose needs will be met. Or they might decide that in certain situations, one person's needs will prevail, while in other situations the opposite need will be chosen. Sometimes partners give up their own needs entirely for the sake of the relationship. An attempt at reframing the opposing needs is an option that could bring a resolution for all parties.

Conflict is an inevitable part of all relationships. The introduction of problems, disagreements, and tension can actually be seen as a positive part of relational maintenance, depending on how that conflict is managed. Conflict introduces a dialog on issues of disagreement in order to facilitate change. ***Conflict management strategies*** have sometimes been characterized in two dimensions: cooperation and

**Conflict management strategies**
Continuum of cooperation and assertiveness.

assertiveness. The image below shows a two-dimensional chart with **cooperation** and **assertiveness** on two axes. Ranking a person's willingness to cooperate with his or her partner (from high to low) and his or her need to assert individual desires (from high to low) sets forth five possible conflict management strategies.[18]

Each of the five possible configurations has benefits and drawbacks given particular conflict situations. In an ideal world, everyone would have all of their needs met in harmonious *collaboration.* That storybook way of settling conflicts is rare and takes a great deal of time and discussion. It is highly cooperative and highly assertive, and unfortunately, highly unlikely. Most people support such resolutions to their conflict in theory more than in practice. It is more likely that a range of other strategies will be employed during conflict negotiations. Those who are low in both cooperation and assertiveness tend to **avoid** conflict. This choice might have advantages when engaging in the situation that is not worth the time or energy (or could result in some level of danger). However, avoiding conflicts leads to no productive change and can prolong the inevitable. On the opposite end of the cooperation continuum, those who "give in" and yield to the wishes of others may do so for strategic relational reasons. If the conflict is less important than the relationship, *accommodation* works well. On the other hand, if a person always sacrifices his or her needs, it can lead to resentment and unhealthy relationships. *Competition,* which is seen as a positive attribute in our culture, does allow an

> **Collaboration**
> Mutual communication in working toward an end goal, product, or resolution.
>
> **Accommodation**
> The adjustment of communication (language, gesture, vocal pattern) to adapt to the needs of others.
>
> **Competition**
> Strategy of communication in which a party desires to be "right," to "win," or to gain esteem.

**FIGURE 3.7**

Conflict Management Strategies

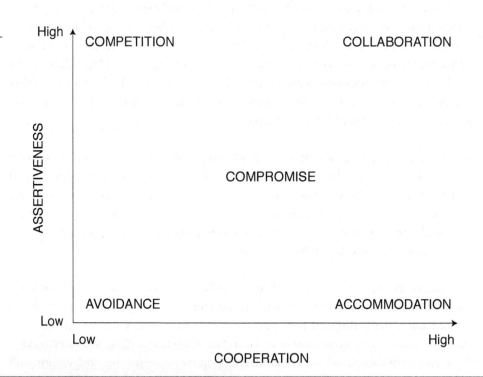

individual to get his or her needs met. However, that success might come at the detriment of the relationship. As with many "majority rule" decisions made in our culture, a common middle ground is ***compromise.*** While neither party may be completely satisfied with the result, all parties may be willing to live with the decision. Relationship characteristics vary in degrees of power, status, gender, and culture. Each brings with it unique expectations of social appropriateness when it comes to conflict. Partners who navigate the ups and downs of conflict effectively can use each incident as a way to grow.

> **Compromise**
> Strategy of communication in which the end goal is a mutual acceptance of ideas, terms, or transactional detail.

*Social Exchange Theory*[19] has been proposed as a way to imagine the internal debate we may have as we navigate the course of relational maintenance. We are constantly measuring the costs and rewards of the relationship to decide whether we want to keep working toward a sustained connection. If there is more work involved (costs) to stay together than the benefits we reap (rewards), we might decide to enter the stages of relationship dissolution. There are probably as many ways to define relational costs as there are people in the world. Each person must make her or his own judgment on the worth of continuation. Some reasons for leaving relationships are more complicated and sensitive than others. A wide range of dysfunctional interactions within relationships, including both physical and mental abuse, have been studied under the category of the **dark side of interpersonal communication**. In such cases, the costs can weigh even more heavily on the individuals involved.[20]

> **Social Exchange Theory**
> Refers to communication based on the idea that relationships are formed or grow through an analysis of the costs or benefits to the involved parties.

Regardless of the reasons, individuals often decide not to continue in a relationship. While we see this most clearly in romance, even friends can have a falling out and family members are not above "cutting someone out of the will." Knapp's model of relationship stages, shown earlier in the chapter, indicates the progression of movement in relationship deterioration. This can involve varying periods of **stagnation**, *avoidance*, and backing away referred to as **circumscribing**. Friendships might wane, according to Rawlins model, but those endings are often less measurable.

> **Avoidance**
> Purposeful refusal or strong reluctance to participate in communication that involves unfamiliar language or behavior.

Duck proposed a different set of stages to describe communication behaviors during relationship termination.[21] Originally, there were five steps, but later a sixth step was added to the model to allow for a resurrection of the relationship.[22]

Intrapsychic
Dyadic
Social
Grave Dressing
Resurrection

FIGURE 3.8

Duck's Model

➤ **Duck's model of relationships**
A theory of relationship dissolution that implies relationships end through one or more of four models: pre-existing doom (poor compatibility from initial stage of relationship); mechanical failure (poor communication or interactions in relationship that are never improved or resolved); process loss (relationships do not build on foundations to reach their potential); sudden death (violations of trust or reveal of new information in relationship).

When a final breakdown occurs and an individual decides to end a relationship, there is a complex set of stages still needed. People enter into an **intrapsychic** level (intrapersonal) where an internal dialogue occurs. Only when they move to a **dyadic** (interpersonal) level do they actually talk with their partner about the decision. Once a decision is made, the news has to be shared publically in the **social** phase. Just as with all losses in life, the pair also goes through a **grave dressing** (like a postmortem) process to transition to the next chapter in their lives. The added sixth stage is one we have all experienced first- or secondhand. With any termination there exists the possibility of **resurrection**. In some instances there could be many such declines that lead to rebirth of the relationship. The potential for reconnection makes it difficult to play the role of "supporting friend" when your BFF breaks up with her boyfriend. The social and grave dressing phases are necessary, but from an outsider's viewpoint, they are also sometimes difficult to navigate. The adage "Be careful what you say, it may come back to haunt you" applies appropriately here, as some supportive friends may well know.

Most people say there are only two things in life that are unavoidable: taxes and death. As you can see from this chapter, we might easily add interpersonal communication to this list. However unavoidable it may be, understanding what it is, how our needs and attractions impact it, how we accomplish it, and how we keep it going (or end it, depending on the circumstances) brings awareness that can enhance our relationships in significant and productive ways.

## KEY WORDS

*Accommodation* The adjustment of communication (language, gesture, vocal pattern) to adapt to the needs of others.

*Avoidance* Purposeful refusal or strong reluctance to participate in communication that involves unfamiliar language or behavior.

*Breadth* Measure or degree of range of information shared in communication.

*Collaboration* Mutual communication in working toward an end goal, product, or resolution.

*Competition* Strategy of communication in which a party desires to be "right," to "win," or to gain esteem.

*Compromise* Strategy of communication in which the end goal is a mutual acceptance of ideas, terms, or transactional detail.

*Conflict management strategies* Continuum of cooperation and assertiveness.

*Conville's Helical Model* Theory that relational communication is continuously developing and that development, via communication, cannot be reversed.

*Depth* Measure or degree or intimacy in communication.

*Duck's model of relationships* A theory of relationship dissolution that implies relationships end through one or more of four models: pre-existing doom (poor compatibility from initial stage of relationship); mechanical failure (poor communication or interactions in relationship that are never improved or resolved); process loss (relationships do not build on foundations to reach their potential); sudden death (violations of trust or reveal of new information in relationship).

*Impersonal communication* Interaction based on societal roles, usually transactional.

*Interpersonal communication* Interaction based on sharing of emotions, ideas, or information, usually face to face.

*Johari Window* A measurement technique to improve communication and self-perception by determining qualities or attitudes known to self, known to others, unknown to self, and unknown to others.

*Models of relationships* Forms and paths of communication and interaction. Levinger, Knapp & Vangelisti, Rawlings all show the continuum of relationships from greeting to termination with varying degrees of detail

*Physical attraction* Attraction based on a person's appearance (looks).

*Reciprocity* Engagement and mutual interest in communication beyond passive delivery or acceptance of a message.

**Similar interests** Enjoyment or engagement in, or curiosity about, similar things.

*Situational attraction* Attraction based on interaction in a specific event or setting.

*Social Exchange Theory* Refers to communication based on the idea that relationships are formed or grow through an analysis of the costs or benefits to the involved parties.

*Social penetration theory* Process by which communication between persons or groups deepens through longer, closer, or more comfortable discussion.

*Uncertainty Reduction Theory* Refers to the idea that people require information about other parties prior to initial communication between parties, to reduce uncertainty or nerves and form reasonable expectations in communication.

# ENDNOTES

1. Extensive material can be found in both Knapp, M. L., & Daly, J. A. (Eds.) (2011). *Handbook of Interpersonal Communication.* (4th ed.). Thousand Oaks, CA: SAGE; Canary, D., & Dainton. M. (Eds.) (2003). *Maintaining Relationships through Communication: Relational, Contextual, and Cultural Variations. Mahwah, NJ: Lawrence Erlbaum.*

2. Buber, M. (1970). *I and thou.* New York: Scribner. (Original work published 1936)

3. Altman, L,. & Taylor, D. A. (1973). *Social Penetration: The Development of Interpersonal Relationships.* New York: Holt, Rinehart & Winston.

4. Watzlawick, P., Beavin, J. H., & Jackson, D. D. (2011). *Pragmatics of Human Communication.* New York: W. W. Norton

5. Maslow, A. H. (1943). A Theory of Human Motivation. *Psychological Review,* 50, 370–396.

6. Schutz, W. C. (1958). FIRO: *A Three-Dimensional Theory of Interpersonal Behavior.* New York: Holt, Rinehart & Winston.

7. Levinger, G., & Raush, H. (Eds). (1977). *Perspectives on the Meaning of Intimacy.* Amherst MA: University of Massachusetts Press.

8. Knapp, M. L., & Vangelisti, A. L. (2006) *Interpersonal Communication and Human Relationships* (6th ed.) Boston: Allyn and Bacon; Avtgis, T. A., West. D. V., & Anderson, T. L. (1998). Relationship Stages: An Inductive Analysis Identifying Cognitive, Affective, and Behavioral Dimensions of Knapp's Relational Stages Model. *Communication Research Reports,* 15(3), 280–287.

9. Rawling, W. K. (1992). *Friendship Matters: Communication Dialectics in the Life Course.* New York: Aldine de Gruyer; Rawlins, W. K. (2008). *The Compass of Friendship: Narrative, Identities and Dialogues.* Thousand Oaks, CA: SAGE.

10. Berger, C. R., & Calabrese. R. J. (1975). Some Explorations in Initial Interaction and Beyond Toward a Developmental Theory of Interpersonal Communication. *Human Communication,* 1, 99–112.

11. Antheunis, M. L., Schouten, A. P., Valkenburg, P. M., & Peter, J. (2012). Interactive Uncertainty Reduction Strategies and Verbal Affection in Computer-Mediated Communication. *Communication Research,* 39(6) 757–780; Gibbs, J. L., Ellison, N. B., & Lai, C. (2011). First Comes Love, Then Comes Google: An Investigation of Uncertainty Reduction Strategies and Self-Disclosure in Online Dating. *Communication Research,* 38(1) 70–100.

12. Gouldner, A.W. (1960). The Norm of Reciprocity: A Preliminary Statement. *American Sociological Review*, 25, 161–178.

13. Luft, J. (1970). *Group Processes: An Introduction to Group Dynamics.* (2nd ed.). Palo Alto: CA National Press Books; Wheeless, L. R. (1978). A Follow-Up Study of the Relationships among Trust, Disclosure, and Interpersonal Solidarity. *Human Communication*, 4, 143–145.

14. Baxter, L. A., & Bullis, C. (1986). Turning Points in Developing Relationships. *Human Communication*, 12, 469–493.

15. Canary, D. J., & Stafford, L. (Eds). (1994). *Communication and Relational Maintenance.* San Diego, CA: Academic Press.

16. Conville, R. L. (1991). *Relational Transitions: The Evolution of Personal Relationships.* Westport, CT: Praeger.

17. Baxter, L. A., & Montgomery, B. M. (1996). *Relating: Dialogues and dialectics.* New York: Guilford Press.

18. Wilmot, W., & Hocker, J. L. (2010). *Interpersonal conflict.* (8th ed). New York: McGraw Hill.

19. Thibaut. J. W., & Kelley, H. H. (1959). *The Social Psychology of Groups.* New York; Wiley.

20. Spitzberg, B. H., & Cupach, W. R. (Eds.) (2007). *The Dark Side of Interpersonal Communication* (2nd Ed.). Mahwah, NJ: Lawrence Erlbaum.; Cupach, W. R., & Spitzberg, B. H. (Eds.) (2010). The Dark Side of Close Relationship (2nd Ed.). New York: Routledge.

21. Duck, S. W. (Ed.) (1992). *Personal Relationships 4: Dissolving Personal Relationships.* London: Academic Press.

22. Rollie, S. S., & Duck, S. W. (2006). Stage Theories of Martial Breakdowns. In J. H. Harvbey & M. A. Fine (Eds.). *Handbook of Divorce and Dissolution of Romantic Relationships* (pp. 176-193). Mahwah, NJ: Lawrence Erlbaum.

# INTERPERSONAL COMMUNICATION

In some ways, this is what this unit is all about: **relationships**. Humans are social animals; our lives are enriched by family and friends. There is an old saying in Communication: "You cannot **start** a relationship without communication. You cannot **maintain** a relationship without communication. It is even difficult to **end** a relationship without communication." When we try to start a relationship, we put ourselves at risk. You open up to someone, you are **self-disclosing**. The risk in this action is if the person rejects the invitation, he is not only rejecting the message, he is rejecting you. (**You** didn't really want to go out with him anyway.)

If you were successful at starting a relationship, now you have to maintain it. Friends share information and stories and do more than text each other. Have you ever seen two people grow apart? They lose interest in each other and stop sharing information about their lives. Friendships and marriages dissolve when partners stop talking to each other.

There is one other interesting point in this chapter along these same lines. **Conflict** is a natural part of all relationships. Now, we don't mean fistfights and wrestling. Everyone is unique and has her own experiences and **connotative** definitions. If two people see the world in different ways, there will be disagreements. In healthy relationships, people can learn from these conflicts. You can teach me something new. I can teach you, or we may discover a new idea by compromising. (If only politicians and countries would learn this lesson, we would all be better off.) A healthy body requires exercise. A good mind needs new information and challenges. It should be no surprise that a good relationship also requires a little work.

In the next chapter, we discuss two of the tools for a healthy relationship: understanding **perception** and learning to **listen**.

# CHAPTER 4

## Perception and Listening
## Do You Hear What I Hear?

### Chapter Objectives

After reading this chapter, you should understand the following concepts:

- Explain the reason humans are limited in their capacity to process information
- Distinguish between the three key perception processes
- Define the primary selectivity processes
- Describe the factors that affect the selective exposure, selective attention and selective retention processes
- Demonstrate an understanding of social identity theory

- Explain schemata and the types of information that it typically includes
- Describe the four schemata that we use to interpret communication events
- Define attribution theory and distinguish between internal and external attributions
- Explain covariation theory and the three types of information used to interpret people's behavior
- Define self-serving bias and explain how it is problematic
- Describe the fundamental attribution error
- Discuss three factors that influence our perceptions
- Distinguish between hearing and listening processes
- Identify the seven steps to effective listening
- Recall the four listening styles and identify the focus of each
- Explain the four motivations to listen and recall a potential pitfall of each
- Recognize the six common listening misbehaviors

In the *Friends* episode "The One Where Ross and Rachel Take a Break," Ross becomes frustrated by Rachel's enthusiasm for her new job. To make matters worse, Ross has also been acting jealous over Rachel's relationship with her boss, Mark. Ross tries to explain to Rachel that he wants to have a relationship with her, that he is tired of always getting her answering machine and having dates cancelled because of her work. The situation becomes a bit heated when Rachel sarcastically asks Ross if he wants her to quit her job so she can be his girlfriend full-time, with no other obligations. Rachel gets very frustrated and tells Ross that they can't keep arguing about the same thing over and over again.

© Elena Kouptsova-Vasic, 2007, Shutterstock.

Finally, Rachel suggests that maybe they should take a break. Ross understands that to mean a moment to cool off and calm down; maybe do something that will take their minds off the problem. Rachel has something else in mind: a break from the relationship.

## CHAPTER OVERVIEW

Just like Ross and Rachel, we have all encountered situations in relationships where our perceptions have caused us to interpret messages differently than they were intended. Ross perceived Rachel's request to take a "break" to mean that she needed a temporary time-out from their discussion. In Rachel's mind, the meaning of the word "break" was much different.

Imagine a world where we could completely eliminate misunderstandings between roommates, co-workers, relationship partners, parents, children, teachers, and students. Could such a world ever exist? In this chapter we explore the reasons our messages are sometimes partially interpreted, completely misinterpreted, or even ignored by others. Two processes that play a key role in how we send and receive messages in our relationships are perception and listening. In the first part of this chapter we examine the process of perception, paying special attention to the relationship between elements of perception and their relationship to interpersonal communication. We will then turn our attention to the process of listening and how it impacts our interpersonal relationships. Can you recall a time when someone accused you of not listening? Perhaps you *heard* what the person said but did not really *listen* to what they were saying. In the second part of this chapter we will distinguish between the terms *hearing* and *listening*, and advance a number of ways to improve listening, an extremely important, yet often neglected, communication skill.

Perception and listening are so closely intertwined that it is difficult to discuss one without addressing the other. As we form relationships, our perception impacts how we view the other person as well as how we interpret their messages and behaviors. In the opening scenario Ross perceived his relationship with Rachel to be solid. Rachel, on the other hand, perceived the relationship to be on rocky ground due to Ross' jealous behavior. It is not at all unusual for two people to perceive the same relationship in very different ways. Now consider the role that perception plays on your ability to listen. It should come as no surprise that if our perception differs, our listening skills will also differ. In fact, interpretation is a common factor present in both of the processes of perception and of listening. When Rachel commented that they needed a "break," Ross' perception of their relationship caused him to listen and interpret her message in a way that was very different from what Rachel intended. If you watch reality television shows such as *Survivor* or *Big Brother*, you see numerous examples of the link between perception and listening. Since these programs involve strategy, many of the players plant "seeds of doubt" in the minds of their competitors with the hope that it impairs their perception and ability to listen and interpret messages from others. Often, the winning contestant is the player who has succeeded in impairing the perception and listening skills of the competitors.

Our hope is that once you gain a better understanding of the relationship between these two concepts, you will gain a better understanding of why individuals view relationships, people, behaviors, and messages in different ways. An awareness of the impact of perception and listening in our relationships will increase the accuracy of our interpersonal communication. Let us first focus on the primary perceptual processes and examine the relationship between perception and interpersonal communication.

# PERCEPTION AND INTERPERSONAL COMMUNICATION

Perception can be best described as the lens through which we view the world. Just as your view of color would be altered if you were to wear a pair of glasses with blue lenses, our *perception* impacts our view of people, events, and behaviors. One definition of perception is that it is the process of selecting, organizing and interpreting sensory information into a coherent or lucid depiction of the world around us (Klopf 1995). Stated more simply, perception is essentially how we interpret and assign meaning to others' behaviors and messages based on our background and past experiences. The word "experience" is important in understanding the overall process of perception. Consider the role that perception has played in your college experience. Perhaps you enjoy writing and have kept a personal journal. If your English professor assigned daily journal entries in her class, you might tell others that the class was one of the most enjoyable ones you have ever taken. Based on your experience—and your love for writing and journaling—you perceived the class to be easy and enjoyable, and you looked forward to communicating with your professor during her office hours to discuss how you could improve on your writing. But suppose there is another student who has struggled with writing throughout his academic career. He might report to others that the teacher was difficult to talk with and that her assignments were unfair. Based on his perception, their conversations during office hours may have been full of criticism and confusion, and he may describe the instructor as being "uncaring" and an "impossible perfectionist." Since each student brought a unique background and set of experiences to the class, the resulting perceptions of the teacher and class were very different.

> **Perception**
> The process of selecting, organizing, and interpreting sensory information into a coherent or lucid depiction of the world around us.

Chances are that you have learned about perception in other classes, such as psychology or sociology. Researchers from a wide range of academic fields study perceptual processes. While psychologists conducted much of the initial research in the area of perception, communication scholars have focused specifically on the impact of perception on the meanings assigned to messages. From a communication perspective, perception is important because we often define ourselves based

Have you ever felt over-whelmed at work?

on our perceptions of how others see us. Recall our discussion in Chapter Two of reflected appraisal (or looking glass self) which explains how we form impressions of ourselves based on how we think others see us. If people respond favorably toward us, we may feel more self-assured and communicate in a more confident manner. Our perception also causes us to form impressions of others which impacts how we communicate with them. How would you feel if you approached one of your classmates at a party and she ignored you? Chances are you would perceive her to be rude and would avoid subsequent interactions with her when you see her in class or on campus. But take a moment to consider the factors that might have influenced your perception. Perhaps you, or maybe even your classmate, were nervous because you have not been to many parties on campus. Maybe your classmate did not recognize you due to the fact that there are many people in the class. There are a number of factors that could alter the perception each of you has of the interaction at the party. All of our interpersonal interactions are influenced by the perceptions we form of ourselves and others. In order to fully grasp the importance of perception, let us examine how we break down bits of information from our environment and form perceptions of ourselves and others.

Lyrics from a song made popular by the group The Police illustrate a common problem most of us have experienced in our lifetime—being inundated with too much information. Have you ever felt overwhelmed because it seemed as though your professor disseminated too much information in one lecture? Or have you experienced problems at work because your manager gave you too many instructions, tasks or responsibilities at once? Perhaps you have returned to your apartment after being away for a few days only to find that your inbox is overflowing with email and your answering machine is filled with messages. If any of these situations seem familiar to you, you are not alone. On any given day, we encounter literally thousands of stimuli that bombard our senses and compete for our attention.

Social psychologist Robert Cialdini (2001) notes that we live in an extremely complicated society which he describes as "easily the most rapidly moving and complex that has ever existed on this planet" (7). Cialdini (2001) further states that we cannot analyze all aspects of our environment because "we haven't the time, energy or capacity for it" (7). If it is not possible to process and recall everything we see, hear, taste, touch, or smell, then how do we make sense of the world around us?

The way humans manage all of the stimuli encountered in the environment is to limit the amount and type of information taken in. This elimination process often occurs at a subconscious level. Thus, on any given day, we put limits on what we choose to see, hear, taste, touch, or smell. Because of the innate limitations in our ability to process information, humans are often described as *limited capacity processors*. Stated simply, we consciously and subconsciously make choices about the amount and type of stimuli we perceive. Think of a time when you were so focused on your homework that when your mother commented on how loud you were playing your music, you thought, "Wow, I can't even really hear it." To fully understand how people make sense of their environment, we need to take a closer look at three key perceptual processes: selection, organization and interpretation.

## Selection

The first perception process is *selection*. While you might not always be consciously aware of the process of selection, we are continually making choices about the amount and type of information that we choose to notice. Remember our earlier discussion about our ability to be limited capacity processors? It is virtually impossible to pay attention to all the things we could possibly sense at any given time. These limitations in our ability to assimilate and interpret information prevent us from "taking it all in" and so we must select certain messages or stimuli over others. These selections we make are often done in a purposeful rather than random manner (Klopf 1995). Three primary selectivity processes which impact our perception include selective exposure, selective attention, and selective retention. The next sections provide an overview of each of these processes and discuss variables that affect them.

*Selective exposure* refers to the choice to subject oneself to certain stimuli. Choices regarding which messages and stimuli you will subject yourself to are made each day. You choose whether to expose yourself to the messages being sent by advertisers and newscasters when you decide whether to turn on your television or radio each morning. You choose whether to subject yourself to the messages left on your answering machine or via email. Often the choice to engage in selective exposure is based on our

It's your choice to watch television and subject yourself to shows and advertising.

© Philip Date, 2007, Shutterstock.

**Limited-capacity processors** Systems of information retention with fixed and limited ability to store, process, and understand that information.

"Because of the innate limitations in our ability to process information, humans are often described as **limited-capacity processors**. Stated simply, we consciously and subconsciously make choices about the amount and type of stimuli we perceive."

**Selection** First perception process.

**Selective exposure** Refers to the choice to subject oneself to certain stimuli.

desire to seek information or stimuli that is comfortable or familiar to us. Culture plays a key role in determining what messages or stimuli we choose to expose ourselves to and those which we avoid. Consider the fact that some people avoid communicating with those from other cultural backgrounds. They engage in selective exposure by avoiding conversations with people from different cultures. Individuals may focus on the obvious differences of race or ethnicity and assume that they do not have anything in common with people who are so dissimilar. The choice to avoid communication may cause individuals to miss learning about all the beliefs and interests that are shared. According to Fischer and his colleagues (2005), we are most likely to seek out information consistent with our beliefs, values, and attitudes and to avoid information that is viewed as inconsistent. Our propensity to seek out certain types of information and avoid others is referred to as a *biased information search* (Fischer et al. 2005). While we might not consciously be aware of this process, each day we selectively choose to associate with particular individuals or groups of people and attend to certain types of messages in a variety of contexts. Perhaps today you chose to attend your communication class rather than going out to eat lunch with a friend. The decision to attend your communication class is yet another example of selective exposure.

There are a number of factors that affect selective exposure including, among others: proximity, utility, and reinforcement. Not surprisingly, we are most likely to selectively expose ourselves to messages that are nearby, or close in proximity. In fact, *proximity* is the number one predictor of whether we will develop a relationship with another person (Katz and Hill 1958). Consider the relationships that you formed with those who attended your high school. Proximity impacted your ability to selectively expose yourself to those in the same school and form relationships. While the Internet has changed the way we communicate and form relationships, most people still find it difficult to form relationships and communicate with those who are not physically close to them. Second, we are most likely to expose ourselves to messages that we perceive as being useful. *Utility* refers to the perception that particular messages are immediately useful; these messages have a much greater chance of being selected than those that are not seen as useful (McCroskey and Richmond 1996). Expecting an important message from your parents will influence your choice to selectively expose yourself to your email messages. If there are several messages in your inbox, a message from friend or family member is more likely to be viewed than one from the Department of Student Services at your university. Finally, most people expose themselves to messages that are consistent with their views, or *reinforce*, their attitudes and beliefs (Fischer et al. 2005). Thus, if you are strongly opposed to the death penalty, you will probably not attend a lecture delivered by a professor advocating capital punishment for convicted murderers.

**➤ Biased information search**
Our propensity to seek out certain types of information and avoid others.

**➤ Proximity**
Limited distance, or nearness, between two or more things or people.

**➤ Utility**
Measure of satisfaction, usefulness, or purpose derived from an object or experience.

**➤ Reinforce**
To provide or create a stimulus that strengthens or encourages the likelihood of repetition of action or emotional response.

Once we have made the decision to place ourselves in a position to physically receive a message, we then focus on certain aspects or elements of the message. *Selective attention* refers to the decision to pay attention to certain stimuli while simultaneously ignoring others. Factors which affect selective attention often include the novelty, size, and concreteness of the stimuli. *Novelty* refers to the tendency to pay attention to stimuli that are novel, new, or different. Novel aspects are more likely to capture our attention than those with which we are familiar. For example, we tend to notice a friend's new hairstyle almost immediately. In the *Friends* episode discussed at the beginning of the chapter, Rachel became more aware of and paid closer attention to changes in Ross' behavior. Previously, he had been secure and confident in their relationship, but as Rachel became more focused on her career, his messages communicated a new jealousy. Another factor that affects selective attention is the *size,* or magnitude, of the stimuli. We are more likely to pay attention to large items, objects, or people. It probably is not completely by chance that most Chief Executive Officers in U.S. companies are at least six feet tall and that virtually every U.S. President elected since 1900 has been the taller of the two candidates. Finally, we are more likely to pay attention to information that is **concrete**, or well-defined, than to information which is perceived as abstract or ambiguous. Individuals have an easier time attending to messages that are clear and straightforward. For example, if a manager tells an employee to "change her attitude and behavior," but does not provide specific or concrete information about how or why the attitude or behavior is problematic, the employee is likely to ignore this message (McCroskey and Richmond 1996).

> **Selective attention**
> Refers to the choice to engage with or respond only to certain stimuli when several stimuli are presented at the same time.

> **Novelty**
> Quality of an object, person, or experience being new, different, uncommon, or rare.

> **Size**
> Measurement of an object or grouping of objects, usually in relation to other objects or groupings.

Once the decision has been made to expose and attend to stimuli, the final stage in the selectivity process involves **selective retention**, which refers to the choice to save or delete information from one's long term memory. Two factors affecting the propensity to retain information include primacy and recency effects, and utility. Researchers have identified a range of variables which affect an individual's ability to retain information. When studying the type of information people are most likely to retain, researchers note that arguments delivered first (**primacy**) and last (**recency**) in a persuasive presentation are more likely to be recalled and to be more persuasive (Gass and Seiter 2003). As we form relationships, we are often concerned with the first or last impression that we

What kind of an impression do you try to make in a job interview?

© Marcin Balcerzak, 2007,Shutterstock.

make. It has been estimated that we form our initial impression of others during the first three to five seconds. Recall the last job interview that you attended. Careful attention was paid to your clothing and appearance to ensure that you would make a positive first impression that the interviewer would remember. However, if you tripped and spilled the contents of your portfolio as you exited the interview, the recency of the last impression may be imprinted on the interviewer's memory. A second important factor related to retention is utility, or usefulness. Almost all of us have heard the phrase, "use it or lose it." Essentially what this phrase implies is that if we do not apply the information we obtain, we may not retain it later. For example, many of you might have received training in cardiopulmonary resuscitation (CPR) at one time in your life. But if one of your classmates needed CPR, would you remember the steps? The same principle is true of the information and skills discussed in this text. It is our hope that by providing you with examples of concepts and information, you will see the usefulness of the strategies and become more effective in your interpersonal interactions with others.

## Organization

Once we have selected information, or stimuli, we then begin the process of placing it into categories in order to make sense of it. **Organization** "refers to our need to place the perceived characteristics of something into the whole to which it seems to belong" (Klopf 1995, 51). Organization is the process by which we take the stimuli and make sense of it so that it is meaningful to us. Remember the earlier example of the classmate who ignored you at a party? Some of the stimuli that caused you to form your perception included her lack of eye contact and her failure to reciprocate your greeting. In the organization process, you take each of these stimuli (eye contact and lack of communication) and put them together to form an impression.

One theory that is useful in understanding how individuals organize information in meaningful ways is constructivism. Kelly (1970) developed the theory of **constructivism** to explain the process we use to organize and interpret experiences by applying cognitive structures labeled schemata. **Schemata** are "organized clusters of knowledge and information about particular topics" (Hockenbury and Hockenbury 2006, 265). Another way to describe schemata is as mental filing cabinets with several drawers used to help organize and process information. Schemata are the results of one's experiences and, therefore, are dynamic and often changing as we encounter new relationships and life experiences. Suppose your first romantic relationship was a disaster. The initial schema you formed to organize information about romantic relationships (which may have been obtained from television shows or movies) was likely altered to include this negative experience you encountered. But suppose your next romantic partner is incredibly thoughtful and romantic. New information is incorporated to your schema that now enables you to evaluate various aspects of romantic relationships based on both the positive and negative experiences you encountered in the past. Thus, we apply schemata to make sense of our communication experiences. More specifically, we apply four different types of schemata to interpret interpersonal encounters: prototypes, personal constructs, stereotypes, and scripts (Fiske and Taylor 1984; Kelley 1972; Reeder 1985).

Have you ever thought of your ideal romantic partner? What would he or she be like? **Prototypes** are knowledge structures which represent the most common attributes of a phenomenon. These structures are used to help organize stimuli and influence our interactions with others (Fehr and Russell 1991). Prototypes provide us with a "benchmark" that is the standard used to evaluate and categorize other examples that fall into the same category. Recall your initial encounter with someone you dated recently. It is very likely that you evaluated this individual's behaviors based on whether this person fit your "prototypical," or best, example of a relationship partner. If you were to make a list of the characteristics you desire in the "ideal" romantic partner, these preconceived ideas and expectations represent your prototype and affect how you will perceive each potential romantic partner encountered in the future. Research by Fehr and Russell (1991) supports the idea that we have prototypes about love and friendship. They conducted six different studies in an attempt to identify participants' prototypical examples of different types of love (e.g., maternal love, paternal love, friendship love, sisterly love, puppy love, infatuation, and so on) and the factors associated with love. Characteristics such as caring, helping, establishing a bond, sharing, feeling free to talk, demonstrating respect, and exhibiting closeness were all associated with perceptions of love. In a related study, Fehr (2004) examined prototypical examples of interactions which led to greater perceived intimacy in same-sex friendships. Fehr (2004) found that interaction patterns which involved increased levels of self-disclosure and emotional support were perceived by friends as being more prototypical of expectations for intimacy than other types of practical support. Prototype theory is extremely useful in shedding light on how we organize our thoughts about interpersonal communication and relationships.

A second type of schemata is **personal constructs** which Kelly (1955; 1970; 1991) describes as bipolar dimensions of meaning used to predict and evaluate how people behave. Personal constructs have also been described as the "mental yardsticks" that we use to assess people and social situations. Several examples of

Personal constructs serve to help you evaluate others and influence your interactions.

© Yuri Arcurs, 2007, Shutterstock.

personal constructs include: responsible-irresponsible, assertive-unassertive, friendly-unfriendly, intelligent-unintelligent, and forthright-guarded. Personal constructs serve as another means of evaluating others and simultaneously influence how we approach interactions. For example, if you label your co-worker as "friendly" you may smile more at this person and share more personal information than you would with another co-worker labeled as "unfriendly." Raskin (2002) notes that we monitor our personal constructs closely and keep track of how accurately they predict life circumstances. When necessary, we revise them when we perceive them as unreliable. We tend to define situations and people based on the personal constructs that we use regularly. Thus, it is possible that we might not be aware of qualities some people possess or situations that we do not access regularly (Raskin 2002).

The third type of schema we use to help us organize information is stereotypes. **Stereotypes** are impressions and expectations based on one's knowledge or beliefs about a specific group of people which are then applied to all individuals who are members of that group. Stereotypes greatly influence the way messages are perceived. Some researchers argue that stereotypes are often activated automatically when an individual observes a member of a group or category (Carlston 1992) and we are likely to predict how that person will behave. For example, Hamilton and Sherman (1994) note that individuals' perceptions of different racial and ethnic groups are often "planted in early childhood by influential adults in their lives" (3). Influential individuals, such as family members, and the media play an important role in shaping how we define others and how we view the world.

Why do we categorize people, events, and objects? As mentioned previously, we are limited in our ability to process the sheer number of stimuli bombarding us at any given time. Thus, we identify ways to categorize and organize stimuli to enhance "cognitive efficiency," or to make information more manageable. A second explanation for our tendency to stereotype as described by Hamilton and Sherman (1994) is "categorization as self-enhancement" (6). Simply stated, we tend to evaluate those groups to which we belong more favorably than groups to which we do not belong. Recall the groups you associated with in high school. If you were a member of the student council, you may have viewed members as being strong leaders and very organized. Students who were not members of the student council may have created their own schema for

If you're on a sports team, you may identify more closely with other athletes.

© PhotoCreate, 2007, Shutterstock.

evaluating its members—they may have labeled them as being "powerhungry," or aggressive. **Social identity theory** offers an explanation for our tendency to evaluate in-groups more positively than out-groups. According to social identity theory, an individual's self-esteem is often connected to membership or association with social groups (Hamilton and Sherman 1994; Turner 1987). In an effort to maintain a positive identity, we may overemphasize or accentuate differences between in-groups and out-groups.

Can placing people into groups or categories based on particular traits or characteristics be problematic? Absolutely! For example, individuals are often categorized based on whether they have some type of physical or mental disability. Braithwaite and her colleagues found that people without disabilities often assume that individuals with physical disabilities are helpless, while this is certainly not the case (Braithwaite and Harter 2000). They conducted a number of interviews with persons with physical disabilities and found that they often received a great deal of either unwanted or unsolicited help from persons without disabilities. This example illustrates the problem of inaccurately categorizing people. In this case, persons without disabilities inaccurately categorized persons with disabilities as helpless or needy, resulting in inappropriate "helping" behavior. Suggestions for managing these interactions more appropriately will be addressed in Chapter Thirteen when we discuss interpersonal communication in health-related contexts.

People form stereotypes about individuals based on race, culture, sex, sexual orientation, age, education, intelligence, and affiliations, among other characteristics. It is crucial that we realize that stereotypes are formed as a result of our perceptions of others and, as a result, can be accurate or inaccurate. When inaccurate or inflexible stereotypes are applied to individuals, they often divide rather than unite people. Is it possible to resist the temptation to stereotype or categorize people? While the research on changing stereotypes is not extensive, much of it is promising. Stereotyping is a normal tendency. Our desire to reduce our level of uncertainty about people and situations leads us into the stereotype "trap." We are uncomfortable in situations where we have little or no information about others, and our initial tendency is to open our schematic files in an attempt to locate any information that will help us figure out how to communicate. For example, one of the authors of your textbook is a native of West Virginia. Throughout her life, she has encountered stereotypes of people from West Virginia. When she lived in California, one of her college roommates commented, "You're nothing at all what I expected someone from West Virginia to be like!" When asked to describe her expectations, the roommate described some very negative stereotypes. The two became best friends and discovered that even though one was from Texas and the other was from West

Virginia, they had more in common than they thought. If you have never communicated with a person from another culture, your first tendency may be to recall any information associated with the person's culture that you have read about or seen on television. Regardless of whether this information is accurate or inaccurate, it is often used as a "guide" for our expectations and communication. The key to overcoming the negative outcomes of stereotyping is to remain open-minded and flexible. While your tendency may be to look for something to help organize and make sense of stimuli, remember that the information used to form the stereotype may be incorrect. Fortunately, there is a growing body of scholarship which suggests that the stereotypes people form can be modified over time (Hamilton and Sherman 1994).

The last type of schema we use to organize is scripts. According to Abelson (1982), **scripts** are knowledge structures that guide and influence how we process information. Abelson (1982) describes scripts as an "organized bundle of expectations about an event sequence" (134). Simply stated, we adhere to a number of different scripts throughout a day, scripts that tell us what to do and say, as well as *how* to do and say it. Very often we never notice how scripted our day-to-day interactions are until someone deviates from the expected script. A comedian makes reference to the potential embarrassment caused by scripts in his description of an encounter he had when exiting a taxi cab at the airport.

> **Taxi Driver:** Thanks! Have a nice flight!
>
> **Comedian:** You too! *(then, realizing that the taxi driver is not flying)* I mean, the next time you fly somewhere.

Another scenario, a casual conversation between two co-workers at the copy machine in the workplace, illustrates the relevance of scripts to our day-to-day functioning.

> **Dominique:** Hi Anthony!
>
> **Anthony:** Hey Dominique, how are you?
>
> **Dominique:** Not so good. My arthritis is acting up and it's making it impossible for me to get any work done on this report that is due at noon. Then my son's school just called to say he's not feeling well, and I can't get a hold of my sister to go pick him up at school. It's just been one thing after another.
>
> **Anthony:** *(looking at his watch)* Wow, I didn't realize it was so late! Um, yeah, well, hey, nice talking to you. I've got to go!

Did Anthony respond appropriately to Dominique's explicit description of how she was feeling? Can you explain why Anthony had to go? **Script theory** explains Anthony's reaction to Dominique's description of her arthritis and problems with child care. According to script theory, we often interact with others in a way that could be described as "automatic" or even "mindless." Because we have repeated experience with these scripts, we are able to adhere to them in a manner described as "mindless," meaning that we are not consciously aware of the fact that we are following a script. Essentially, we rely on scripts to tell us how to proceed in situations and what to say. We enter into situations that we have been in before with a specific set of expectations and, when individuals violate our expectations by not adhering to the script, we are not sure what to do. From an interpersonal communication perspective, we use scripts to determine how to proceed during social interaction and form perceptions of others based on whether or not they are following the "script."

## *Interpretation*

After we have selected and organized information, the final step in the perception process involves interpretation. **Interpretation** is the subjective process of making sense of our perceptions. The interpretation process is described as highly subjective because individuals' interpretations of communication events vary extensively and are influenced by a wide range of factors. The following sections serve as an overview of the dominant theory used to explain how people interpret information, discuss errors in interpretive processes, and identify factors that influence the ways we interpret information.

The dominant theory that explains how people explain their own and others' behavior is known as **attribution theory** (Heider 1958; Kelley 1967; 1971). This theory is also known as naïve psychology because people often try to connect observable behavior to unobservable causes (Littlejohn 1983). Can you recall a time when you have tried to explain a friend's unusual behavior? Perhaps she was supposed to phone you at a scheduled time, and the call never came. You may try to explain her lack of communication by theorizing that she overslept, the car broke down, or she had a fight with a significant other. All of these are causes that you have not directly observed, but they are

Maybe you visualize your friend standing by her broken-down car as a reason she didn't call you

© Bartosz Ostrowski, 2007, Shutterstock.

used as potential explanations for the friend's behavior. Attribution theory is commonly applied to interpret the reasons for our own actions as well as the actions of others. According to Heider (1958) there are three basic assumptions to attribution theory: (1) that it is natural for people to attempt to establish the causes of their own and others' behavior, (2) that people assign causes for behavior systematically, and (3) that the attribution impacts the perceiver's feelings and subsequent behavior. Thus, the causes assigned to peoples' behaviors play a significant role in determining reactions to interpreted behaviors.

According to attribution theory, people assign causes to behaviors in a fairly systematic way and typically use different types of information to make these decisions. Generally, when individuals attempt to explain behaviors, they will choose among three different explanations: the situation, unintentionality or chance, and intentionality or dispositions (Heider 1958). A person's behavior may be best explained by considering the situation and how this factor may have influenced behavior. Situational factors are often referred to as **external attributions**. For example, perhaps you are normally talkative and outgoing when in social situations. However, you go to a party with some friends and see your former relationship partner with a new "love" interest. Because you still have feelings for this person, this situation is upsetting to you, and you spend the evening moping and avoiding conversations. Hence, your behavior at the party could be best explained by situational or external attributions. The second factor typically used to explain behavior is unintentionality or chance, which refers to one's inability to predict whether the behaviors will be consistent in the future (Kelsey et al. 2004). For example, someone may guess several answers on a difficult test and then claim that they may or may not be able to replicate their test performance again in the future. The third factor, **intentionality**, or disposition, is also referred to as an internal attribution. **Internal attributions** are typically described as being stable or persistent and often refer to behaviors that are likely to be exhibited repeatedly across a variety of contexts (Heider 1958). If your friend Sally acts quiet and reserved in almost all situations, then you would explain her quiet and reserved demeanor at your birthday party based on internal attributions or personality traits. When attempting to explain her behavior, you might say "Sally is just that way," or tell others that she is normally very shy.

Harold Kelley (1973) also developed a prominent theory of attribution which attempts to explain how we formulate perceptions of others. Kelley's **covariation theory** states that we decide whether peoples' behavior is based on either internal or external factors by using three different and important types of information: distinctiveness, consensus, and consistency. In order to apply Kelley's covariation principle, we must have multiple observations of individuals to accurately explain their behavior. **Distinctiveness** refers to whether or not a person typically behaves the same way with the target, or receiver, of the behavior. When distinctiveness is high, we tend to attribute others' behavior to external causes. When distinctiveness is low, we tend to attribute others' behavior to internal causes. For example, if Professor Munhall is always pleasant and helpful toward all students, he would be exhibiting low levels of distinctiveness. In this situation, Dr. Munhall's behavior would be attributed to internal factors (e.g., he is such a caring teacher). Suppose one minute Professor Munhall snaps at Alan during class and the next minute he responds calmly to Marcus' request for clarification. In this situation, his behavior would be described as highly distinctive since he does not normally behave this way toward students. External factors would be used to explain his highly distinctive behavior (e.g., he had a bad day).

The second type of information used to attribute causes to behaviors is consistency. **Consistency** refers to whether an individual behaves the same way across contexts and at various times. For example, would the person behave the same way regardless of whether she was at a party, at work, at school, or at a bar? It is important to keep in mind that the key element here is the context or situation. When an individual acts in a highly consistent manner, we tend to attribute the individual's behavior to internal rather than external causes. Very often, we ask whether the behavior is unique or consistent in the particular context. If your friend Kaia is always loud and outgoing in social situations, and you observe her acting this way at a party, you would explain her behavior based on internal rather than external factors. That is, Kaia acted in a loud, outgoing manner because this is the way she typically behaves with most individuals and in most situations (high consistency). Conversely, if Kaia was quiet, shy, and withdrawn at the same party, you might explain her behavior by saying that the party must not have been fun (external factor) because she was acting differently than the expected behavior in social situations (low consistency).

The final factor, **consensus**, considers whether the behavior is unique to the individual or if they are behaving in the way that would be typically expected of others. We say that consensus is high when a person acts the same way that others would behave. Recall our example from the beginning of the chapter. Did Ross behave in a way that was similar to the way Joey, Chandler, or several other men would respond? The key element in this factor is the actor, or source of behavior, (as opposed to the context, which is the focus of consistency). When consensus is high, we attribute peoples' behavior to external rather than internal factors. For example, the majority of Americans say that they do not enjoy giving speeches and typically experience anxiety prior to and during the event (high consensus). Thus, we attribute Jay's speech anxiety to external (everyone is nervous about public speaking) rather than internal factors. But suppose Jay actually looks forward to the prospect of public speaking. When someone actually enjoys giving speeches (low consensus), we might explain this person's unique behavior by saying this person is highly confident and self-assured (internal factors).

Not surprisingly, we often evaluate and explain our *own* behavior using standards that are very different from those used to evaluate and explain the behavior of *others*. The two most common attribution errors people make are known as the self-serving bias and the fundamental attribution error. The **self-serving bias** states that we tend to manufacture, or construct, attributions which best serve our own self-interests (Hamachek 1992). For example, when we excel in school or sports, we often explain our success based on internal factors or causes. We might think "I am smart" or "I am an incredible athlete," both of which are internal attributions. The self-serving bias provides us with a viable explanation for the sources of student motivation in the classroom. Research by Gorham and her colleagues (1992) indicates that students view motivation in school as a student-owned trait or characteristic. Thus, when a student feels motivated to do well in school, he or she credits this intention to do well on internal rather than external factors. On the other hand, when a student feels unmotivated, or is unwilling to work hard in school, he or she is more likely to attribute the cause of this lack of motivation to the teacher's behavior (external attributions—the teacher did not explain the assignment clearly) rather than to the self (internal attributions). Why do we avoid taking responsibility for our poor performance, mistakes, or shortcomings? One explanation for attributing our failures to external causes is to save face. While our tendency to protect our own self-image is understandable, it is important to realize that these distorted perceptions of self are problematic. Falsely taking credit for accomplishments and blaming others (or circumstances) for our failures can lead to distorted self-images and inaccurate representations of ourselves during social interaction (Hamacheck, 1992).

The next question to ask is whether we attribute others' failures and successes to external or internal factors? A second common attribution error often made during the interpretation stage of perception is the **fundamental attribution error**. When attempting to explain others' negative behaviors, we tend to overestimate the internal factors or causes and underestimate the external factors or causes. Conversely, when attempting to explain our *own* mistakes or shortcomings, we tend to overestimate the external causes and underestimate the internal causes. For example, if you are driving to school and see someone speeding by you, you might say to your friend, "What a reckless driver," (internal attribution). However, if you are speeding down the same road the next day and that same friend asks you why you are in such a rush, you might respond, "I am late for work," or "I need to get a parking space," both of which are external attributions. Kelsey and her colleagues (2004) recently used attribution theory to investigate the explanations students provided for their college instructors' classroom "misbehaviors." Examples of teacher misbehaviors include boring lectures, unfair grading, and providing too much information. The researchers found that students were more likely to attribute their teachers' inappropriate classroom behaviors to internal causes (e.g., he doesn't care about teaching) rather than to external causes (e.g., she's had a bad day). It is important to understand and acknowledge that while the way we make sense of our own and others' behaviors is less than perfect, it greatly affects how we interact with others. To improve the way we select, organize, and interpret information, it is also essential to consider our individual differences and how these differences impact our perception.

# INDIVIDUAL DIFFERENCES AND PERCEPTIONS

While there are numerous factors that affect the way we perceive information, in this section we focus on three widely researched and acknowledged variables related to perception. Three variables that have been identified by scholars as impacting perception are sex, age, and culture. We begin our discussion by considering how sex differences affect perception and communication.

Do you think men and women view the world differently? Deborah Tannen, a noted gender scholar and linguist, would answer this question with an unequivocal "Yes!" Tannen (1986; 1990; 1994) notes that men and women hold different worldviews and philosophies regarding how they are expected to act in society which evolve from early interactions with family members, peers, and society. Tannen and other gender scholars (see, for example, Wood 1999) assert that men and women are socialized differently and, as a result, develop different perceptions of the world and their place within it. For example, women often perceive the world as a place to connect and form bonds with others. Men, on the other hand, view the world as a place to assert their independence and autonomy. These differences in perceptions affect the ways that men and women approach social interactions. Tannen says that women often engage in **rapport talk** which is analogous to small talk or phatic communication, while men often exhibit **report talk** which involves discussions about facts, events, and solutions. The following scenario illustrates the difference between rapport and report talk.

> *Elyse and Dave got a flat tire during their drive to work. As they discuss the event with colleagues, Elyse explains various details associated with the tire episode when speaking with her friends. "It was horrible! We were driving down the freeway when all of the sudden we heard a 'thump-thump' under the car. Of course, today would be the day that we left the cell phone at home on the table! Didn't you get a flat tire about a month ago, Janelle?"*

Typically, other females respond by sharing their similar stories and experiences. Dave, on the other hand, would provide the details of the morning's event differently.

> *"We got a flat tire on Interstate 270 this morning. We didn't have a cell phone, but the car behind us pulled over and let me use their phone to call AAA."*

It is important to note that not all men and women communicate this way. However, because men and women may see the world differently, it affects how they perceive themselves and others and ultimately impacts their interpersonal communication.

A second frequently studied variable that affects perceptions is age. Recall the last time you engaged in a conversation with older relatives, friends, or co-workers. Did you notice any differences in your perspectives on various issues? One student recently shared an example of a conversation held with her mother that illustrated the impact of age on perceptual differences. Because this female student does not like to cook or clean, her mother told her that "No man will want to marry her!" The daughter argued her "case" by explaining to her mother that times have changed and that women and men today often share domestic responsibilities in the home. This conversation between mother and daughter illustrates how age and experience impacts our perceptions. As we grow older, we tend to build on our diverse life experiences and our perceptions often change or, in some cases, become more firmly ingrained. Some research indicates that older individuals possess more consistent and stable attitudes and are more difficult to persuade (Alwin and Krosnick 1991). Other findings suggest that as people age they become more cognitively sophisticated and are better able to see the world from others' perspectives (Bartsch and London 2000). Thus, it is important to consider how age affects both our own and others' perceptions.

Finally, culture affects our perceptions of the world and simultaneously influences our communication with others. In Chapter Ten we discuss the impact of cultural differences on perceptions and interpersonal communication in greater detail. However, it is important to restate the powerful impact culture can have on our perceptions. One reason for examining cultural differences is to learn more about how socialization in different cultures affects peoples' perceptions and behavior. For example, researchers often study perceptual and behavioral differences in individualistic and collectivistic cultures. Collectivistic cultures emphasize group harmony and concern for others. An example of a collectivistic culture is found in China. Individualistic cultures, as found in the United States, tend to value individual rights, independence, and autonomy. Members of collectivistic cultures view the world much differently than individuals from highly individualistic cultures. There are numerous research examples which illustrate the difference between individualistic and collectivistic cultural beliefs, attitudes, behaviors, and values. One interesting study explored Chinese and U.S. managerial differences in attempts to influence employees (Yukl, Fu, and McDonald 2003). According to Yukl and his colleagues, "the cross-cultural differences in rated effectiveness of tactics were consistent with cultural values and traditions" (Yukl, Fu, and McDonald 2003, 68). Chinese managers rated informal strategies and strategies that emphasized personal relations as more effective than traditional Western strategies which emphasize being direct and task oriented. Swiss and American managers perceived more direct task-oriented tactics as being more effective than informal strategies and strategies that emphasized personal relations. In another study, Miller (1984) examined the impact of culture on the fundamental attribution error. She asked children and adults in India and the U.S. to provide possible explanations for pro-social (e.g., helping someone paint their house) and anti-social behaviors (e.g., engaging in aggressive behavior). Miller's findings provide valuable insight into how factors such as age and culture impact our perception. Children in both cultures offered similar attributions for the behaviors. However, adults in the U.S. were more likely than their Indian counterparts to explain events by attributing them to individual traits. Adults from India, on the other hand, focused on situational or contextual causes as possible explanations for behaviors. It is important to remember that most of us hold more favorable perceptions of the groups we belong to than those to which we do not belong. Thus, we should be cognizant of our tendency to be favorably disposed towards people, ideas, beliefs, and concepts from our culture and our inclination to be more critical of people, ideas, and concepts from other cultural perspectives.

# THE LINK BETWEEN PERCEPTION AND LISTENING

By now you have a more sophisticated understanding of why some information is selected over others, how information is organized, and how messages are interpreted. Additionally, we have provided you with some information about common attribution errors that individuals make and variables that affect the process of perception. To further understand the potential implications of perception, we must consider how our different perspectives of people and messages influence and are influenced by listening. At the beginning of this chapter, we pointed out that perception and listening are closely related to one another. Our perception of others impacts both our ability and our desire to listen in social interactions.

In the *Friends* episode "The One the Morning After" Ross tries to explain to Rachel his reasons for sleeping with another woman on the same night that Rachel suggested that they take a "break" from their relationship. Ross pleads with Rachel to work through it. He tells her he can't even think of what his life would be like without her; without everything she is to him. Rachel just can't get beyond what Ross did to betray her. She tells him that he has become a completely different person to her, now that she's seen that he is capable of hurting her. Rachel believes there will never be anything he can say or do that will change the way she feels about him now.

Because her perception of Ross' commitment to their relationship has changed, so has Rachel's ability to listen to the messages he attempts to communicate. As we listen to messages communicated by others, new information is provided that may cause us to change existing perceptions or perhaps even form new ones. Listening is an essential part of effective interpersonal communication. Yet it is often understudied and underemphasized in communication courses. In the next section we make a distinction between hearing and listening, offer strategies to enhance your own listening skills, and describe the various listening styles employed by individuals.

## Listening

Marge, it takes two to lie. One to lie and one to listen.

—Homer Simpson

The most basic of all human needs is the need to understand and be understood. The best way to understand people is to listen to them.

—Ralph Nichols

Listening, not imitation, may be the sincerest form of flattery.

—Dr. Joyce Brothers

These quotations illustrate the power and functions of listening in the communication process. Listening is a key element for acquiring information and developing and sustaining our relationships. Yet, communication practitioners often refer to listening as the "forgotten" communication skill. The fact that listening skills are often neglected or undervalued is surprising since most people engage in listening more than any other type of communication activity. For example, college students report that up to 50 percent of their time is spent listening, compared to speaking (20 percent), reading (6 percent), and writing (8 percent) (Janusik and Wolvin 2006). While colleges often require classes which emphasize competence in writing and speaking, few highlight listening as an important communication skill.

When we engage in effective listening behaviors we communicate a message that we comprehend and care about what the speaker has to say. Recall a time when you attempted to communicate with a friend or family member, only to receive a distracted response of "Yeah. Uh-huh. Mm-hmm." The lack of active listening behavior is extremely frustrating. A lack of awareness of ineffective listening behaviors has potential negative implications for both personal and professional relationships. Our goal in focusing on this topic is twofold: to assist you in understanding the listening process and to shed some light on how your own behaviors may be interpreted by others. Our hope is that after completing this chapter you will be able to evaluate your own listening skills and to implement some of our suggestions.

As stated earlier, individuals typically spend more time listening during their lifetime than any other communication activity. For many of you, this chapter will be the only formal training in appropriate and effective listening skills you will ever have. The implications of effective listening span a variety of interpersonal contexts. In the health care setting, Wanzer and her colleagues (2004) found that patients who perceived their physicians to employ effective listening skills were more satisfied with their doctor and the care provided. Research has also identified a link between one's career success and effective listening skills. Employers report that listening is a top skill sought in hiring new employees, and it plays a significant role in evaluations for promotion and incentives (AICPA 2006). As we begin our discussion of effective listening skills, it is important that we first distinguish between the concepts of "hearing" and "listening."

> Gina was cooking dinner for Joni one evening after a long day at work. As she stirred the pasta sauce on the stove, she sighed, "I just don't understand why my manager doesn't see what's happening with our latest project. Half of the team is running around clueless, and I keep getting left with their messes to clean up."
>
> Joni gave a half-hearted response while scanning her emails on her laptop. "Uh-huh," she said without breaking eye contact with the computer screen.
>
> Gina stopped cooking and scolded Joni, "You never listen when I try to tell you about my day at work!"
>
> Joni was shocked, "What do you mean? I heard every word you said!"
>
> Gina countered, "Prove it! What did I just say?"
>
> Joni dropped her head and apologized, realizing that while she had heard Gina talking, she hadn't really listened to a word she said.

Have you ever been involved in a situation similar to the one described above? Perhaps you have been the one who has heard the words but did not listen to what was being said. Perhaps one of the most common mistakes made in the listening process is making the assumption that hearing is the same as listening. In fact, listening and hearing are two distinct processes. **Hearing** involves the physical process of sound waves traveling into the ear canal, vibrating the ear drum and eventually sending signals to the brain. Although we often hear messages, we do not necessarily attend to them. This explains why you might be sitting in your room right now reading this text and hearing an air conditioner turn on, birds chirping outside, or friends yelling in the hallway. But while your brain has processed these sound waves, you may not have necessarily been listening for these stimuli. **Listening** not only involves the physical process of hearing, but it also involves the psychological

TABLE 4.1

Daily Average Hours Devoted to Communication Activities

| Communication Activities | Total Number of Hours | Approximate Percentage of Time |
|---|---|---|
| Writing | 1.82 | 8 |
| Reading | 1.40 | 6 |
| Speaking | 4.83 | 20 |
| Listening* | 5.80 | 24 |
| Television* | 2.12 | 9 |
| Radio* | .86 | 4 |
| CD/Tapes* | 1.32 | 5 |
| Phone* | 1.87 | 8 |
| Email | 1.33 | 6 |
| Internet | 2.73 | 11 |
| **Total Listening Hours** | **11.97** | **50** |

Items marked with an * represent those activities which focus primarily on listening.

How can you keep your-self from daydreaming during a long lecture?

© Anita, 2007, Shutterstock.

process of attending to the stimuli, creating meaning and responding. Listening is often described as a dynamic and ongoing process in which individuals physically receive a message, employ cognitive processes to attribute meaning to the message, and provide verbal and/or non-verbal feedback to the source.

As you reflect on this definition, it should become quite apparent that listening is a highly complex process. First, listening is dynamic because it is an ongoing activity that requires an individual to be active and engaged. Unlike hearing, listening requires an individual to be mindful and aware of one's surroundings. After we physically receive the sound waves and hear the message, the next step involves employing cognitive processing to attribute meaning to the information that was received. Hopefully the steps involved in this cognitive process are familiar to you. They include: selection, organization, and interpretation. Do you recall our earlier discussion of these stages as part of the perception process? These same elements are involved in listening. We are selective in the information we expose ourselves to and attend to in the perception process; the same is true in listening. We select what sounds and messages we will listen to and which we will ignore. Have you ever encountered a mother who can carry on a phone conversation and never become distracted while children are screaming and playing in the background? The mother has selected what sounds to focus her attention on in the listening process—she has selected the message that is being received via the telephone. Just as we organize stimuli during the perception process, information is also organized as a part of the listening process. Finally, we must interpret information and assign a meaning to what we have heard while listening. The relationship between perception and listening should be even clearer—the similarities between both processes are nearly identical. The final stage of the listening process involves formulating a response, or feedback, to send to the source via verbal and/or nonverbal channels. Examples of verbal feedback may include, "You look sad," "Tell me more," or "What do you plan to do?" Some examples of nonverbal responses could include nodding your head, making eye contact, or even giving a hug.

To help you remember some of the key strategies involved in effective listening, remember the following acronym: **BIG EARS**. Each of these strategies is discussed in the paragraphs that follow.

**BE OPEN TO THE MESSAGE.** Listening is difficult enough to begin with, but when we fail to prepare ourselves to receive messages, it becomes even more so. Effective listening requires you to employ effective nonverbal listening behaviors, control message overload, and manage your preoccupations and other distractions.

First, we need to be aware of our nonverbal listening behaviors. The next time you are sitting in class listening to a lecture, take a moment and consider the role your nonverbal behaviors play in the listening process. Do you look like you are open to

TABLE 4.2

Key Strategies for Effective Listening (BIG EARS)

| B | Be open and receptive to the message |
|---|---|
| I | Interpret the message |
| G | Give feedback |
| E | Engage in dual perspective |
| A | Adapt your listening style |
| R | Reduce noise |
| S | Store the message |

receiving messages? Maintaining an open body position, engaging in eye contact, and responding to the lecture by nodding your head are all examples of nonverbal behaviors that communicate a willingness to listen.

Next, focus on ways to manage the multiple sources of information that are competing for your attention. Remember our discussion of perception and the role of selective attention and exposure? Effective listening behaviors require you to dedicate your attention to a particular message. The next time you are tempted to watch *Grey's Anatomy* while carrying on a phone conversation with your mother, think twice. One of the sources will ultimately win out over the other—will it be the television show or your mother?

Finally, identify ways to manage the multiple preoccupations and distractions that can impair your ability to listen. Look beyond superficial factors that may be hindering your ability to focus on the message. While a professor's distracting delivery style or prehistoric clothing choices may cause your attention to focus away from the lecture being delivered, these are not excuses to disregard the source's message. Remain focused on the content of the message. On average, Americans speak at a rate of 125 words per minute. However, the human brain can process more than 450 words per minute (Hilliard and Palmer 2003) and we can think at a rate of 1000–3000 words per minute (Hilliard and Palmer 2003). So what happens with all that extra time? Often we daydream or we become bored because our brain can work faster than the speaker can talk. Therefore, it is important to dedicate yourself to relating the information to existing information that you already know. While this can be challenging at times, chances are that it will prove to be extremely useful. Ask yourself questions during a conversation or lecture such as, "How will this information benefit me?" or "How will this information benefit my relationship with the source?" Being open to receiving messages is the first step to ensuring an effective listening experience.

**INTERPRETING THE MESSAGE.** Interpretation refers to the cognitive processes involved in listening. Recall our discussion of the role of interpretation in perception. We pointed out that associations are often made between stimuli and things with which we are already familiar. Interpretation is also a key element in listening, and in verifying that the meaning we assigned to the message is close to that which was intended by the source. Some strategies to assist in interpretation of messages include asking questions, soliciting feedback, and requesting clarification. These

✗ PARAPHRASIN

strategies will help you interpret the source's message more accurately. Consider the following interaction between Maya and Raj:

**Maya:** I hate biology.

**Raj:** Why?

**Maya:** Well, I guess I don't hate it, but I am upset I did poorly on the first exam.

**Raj:** Why did you do poorly?

**Maya:** Because I studied the wrong chapters.

**Raj:** So, do you dislike the material?

**Maya:** Well, no, I actually enjoy the teacher and the book.

**Raj:** So, you like biology but you are upset you studied the wrong material?

**Maya:** Yes, I actually like the course; I am just mad because I know I could have received an A if I had studied the right material.

Because Raj asked Maya to provide additional information to help clarify why she hated biology he was able to interpret Maya's situation more clearly. In fact, it changed the meaning of the message entirely. Maya's initial message was that she hated biology and it turns out that she actually enjoys biology. Raj was able to accurately interpret the message because he asked questions and solicited feedback. But soliciting feedback is not the only element involved in listening. **Paraphrasing** is another useful strategy for clarifying meaning and ensuring that you have accurately interpreted a message. Paraphrasing involves restating a message in your own words to see if the meaning you assigned was similar to that which was intended. But this is still not enough. Effective listening also requires you to provide the source with feedback to communicate that you have both received and understood the message.

What kinds of positive-feedback show that you are interested and listening?

© Phil Date, 2007, Shutterstock.

**GIVE FEEDBACK.** Feedback serves many purposes in the listening process. By providing feedback to the source, we are confirming that we received the message and were able to interpret and assign meaning to what was being communicated.

Feedback can be either positive or negative and communicate its own message. Positive feedback includes verbal and nonverbal behaviors that encourage the speaker to continue communicating. Examples of **positive feedback** include eye contact, nods, and comments such as, "I see," and "Please continue." **Negative feedback** is often discouraging to a source. Examples of negative feedback would be disconfirming verbal comments such as "You are over-reacting" or "I don't know why you get so upset," or negative nonverbal responses such as avoidance of eye contact, maintaining a closed body position (e.g., crossed arms), or meaningless vocalizations such as "Um-hmm." Positive feedback communicates interest and empathy for the speaker, whereas negative feedback often results in feelings of defensiveness.

**ENGAGE IN DUAL-PERSPECTIVE TAKING.** **Dual-perspective taking**, or empathy, refers to the attempt to see things from the other person's point of view. The concept of empathy has been a primary focus of the listening process required of social workers and counselors. Norton (1978) explains this by theorizing that all people are part of two systems—a larger societal system and a more immediate personal system. While it is often possible to gain insight into an individual's societal system, truly understanding someone's personal system is often a more difficult task. Consider the phrase, "Put yourself in another person's shoes." Do you think it is possible to truly put yourself in another person's shoes? This would require us to be able to tap into their unique background and experiences in order to perceive things exactly as they do. But is this ever really possible? Our position is that it is not. This may help explain why we find it difficult to respond to a friend who is going through a difficult break-up. Our initial response may be to respond with a statement like, "I know exactly how you feel. I've been through dozens of broken relationships." But this is not necessarily the best response. There is a unique history to your friend's relationship that you can never truly understand. While you cannot fully put yourself in her shoes, you can communicate empathy by attempting to see

Empathetic listening requires an attempt to see things from your friend's point of view.

© Galina Barskaya, 2007,Shutterstock.

things from her point of view. Reaching into their "field of experience" (as discussed in Chapter One) and trying to understand the framework which they use to interpret the world can influence your ability to effectively listen. Dual-perspective taking requires a receiver to adapt his listening style to accommodate a variety of situations.

**ADAPT YOUR LISTENING STYLE.** Effective communicators are flexible in their communication style and find it easy to adjust both their speaking and listening styles, based on the unique demands of the receiver, the material, or the situation. Duran (1983) defines communicative adaptability as a cognitive and behavioral "ability to perceive socio-interpersonal relationships and adapt one's interaction goals and behaviors accordingly" (320). Duran and Kelly (1988) developed the Communicative Adaptability Scale. Their scale suggests we can adapt our communication in six different ways which include: social composure (feeling relaxed in social situations), social experience (enjoying and participating socially), social confirmation (maintaining the other's social image), appropriate disclosures (adapting one's disclosures appropriately to the intimacy level of the exchange), articulation (using appropriate syntax and grammar), and wit (using humor to diffuse social tension). You can determine the extent to which you are adaptable on these six dimensions by completing the Communication Adaptability Scale at http://cart.rmcdenver.com/instruments/communicative_adaptability.pdf.

**REDUCE NOISE.** Noise refers to anything that interferes with the reception of a message. Recall the various types of noise that were discussed in Chapter One: physical, psychological, and physiological noise. Our job as listeners is to focus on ways to reduce the noise that interferes with the reception of messages.

Oftentimes, this is easier said than done. While we are able to control some forms of physical noise that interfere with listening (e.g., cell phones or radios), other types of physical noise may be more difficult to manage (e.g., a neighbor mowing her yard). Obviously, the less noise there is, the better our chances of effectively receiving the message. Reducing psychological and physiological noise may be more difficult. Sometimes it is difficult to listen to a professor's lecture knowing that you have a big midterm exam in the class that follows, and gnawing hunger pains that begin during your 11:00 a.m. class can impair listening as well. Consider ways to manage these potential distractions and maximize listening potential—be prepared for that exam, be sure to eat something before leaving for class. Planning ahead for potential distractions to listening can ultimately assist you in receiving a message that you can store in memory for future reference.

**STORE THE MESSAGE.** A final strategy in the listening process involves storing what we have received for later reference. This process involves three stages: remembering, retention, and recall. Have you ever been impressed with a doctor or a professor because they remembered, retained, and recalled your name? This is not an easy task. Nichols (1961) demonstrated that immediately after listening to a ten-minute lecture, students were only able to remember about fifty percent of what they heard. As time passes, so does our ability to remember. Nichols' study suggested that after two weeks, most listeners were only able to remember about twenty-five percent of what they had heard. The following are strategies that can be used to enhance message retention.

1.  Form associations between the message and something you already know.
2.  Create a visual image of the information you want to remember.

3. Create a story about what you want to remember to create links between ideas. *Suppose your mother asks you to go to the store to pick up soda, laundry detergent and paper cups. You can enhance your ability to remember the information by creating a story which links the ideas such as, "Sam dropped a paper cup full of soda on her jeans and now they need to be put in the laundry machine."*
4. Create acronyms by using the beginning letters of a list of words to assist your recall. BIG EARS is an example of this tool.
5. Rhyme or create a rhythm to organize information. Creating a song or rhyme that is unusual or humorous typically helps trigger recall.

## *Listening Styles*

Reflecting on your own interpersonal relationships, did you ever notice that individuals have different listening styles? Or perhaps you have noticed that an individual's listening style changed when the topic changed. Have you considered your own listening style and how it may change with the person or topic? For example, with our friends we might pay more attention to their feelings and when we listen to co-workers we may be more focused on the content of the message. Research has identified four predominant listening styles (Watson, Barker, and Weaver 1995). **Listening style** is defined as a set of "attitudes, beliefs, and predispositions about the how, where, when, who, and what of the information reception and encoding process" (Watson, Barker, and Weaver 1995, 2). This suggests that we tend to focus our listening. We may pay more attention to a person's feelings, the structure or content, or particular delivery elements, such as time. The four listening styles are people-oriented, action-oriented, content-oriented, and time-oriented. There is no optimal listening style. Different situations call for different styles. However, it is important to understand your predominate listening style. Let us take a closer look at each of these listening styles.

PEOPLE-ORIENTED. First, **people-oriented** listeners seek common interests with the speaker and are highly responsive. They are interested in the speaker's feelings and emotions. Research shows a positive relationship between the people-oriented listening style and conversational sensitivity (Cheseboro 1999). This makes sense since people-oriented listeners try to understand the speakers' perspective and therefore are more sensitive to their emotional needs. They are quick to notice slight fluctuations in tone and mood. For example, they may comment, "You really look upset," or "You smile every time you say her name." Although you must consider the individual and the situation, this style may work best when we are communicating with our friends or family about sensitive issues.

ACTION-ORIENTED. An **action-oriented** listener prefers error-free and concise messages. They get easily frustrated with speakers who do not clearly articulate their message in a straightforward manner. They tend to steer speakers to be organized and timely in their message delivery. They grow impatient with disorganized speakers that use ambiguous descriptions or provide unrelated details. For example, an action-oriented listener may use the phrase "Get to the point," when the speaker is telling a lengthy story or may interrupt a speaker and say, "So. . . . what did you do?" The action-oriented listening style may work best when there is little time for extra details and decisions need to be made quickly.

CONTENT-ORIENTED. Unlike the people-oriented listener, the **content- oriented** listener focuses on the details of the message. They pick up on the facts of the story and analyze it from a critical perspective. They decipher between credible and non-credible information and ask direct questions. They try to understand the message from several perspectives. For example, they may say, "Did you ever think they did that because . . ." or "Another way to think about the situation is . . ." Because they analyze the speaker's content with a critical eye, the speaker may feel reluctant to share information because they do not want to hear alternative perspectives. Additionally, they may feel intimidated by the criticalness of content-oriented listeners since they are engaged by challenging and intellectual discussion. The content- oriented listening style works best in serious situations that call for vital  decision-making.

TIME-ORIENTED. Finally, **time-oriented** listeners are particularly interested in brief interactions with others. They direct the length of the conversation by suggesting, "I only have a minute," or they send leave taking cues (such as walking away or looking at the clock) when they believe the speaker is taking up too much of their time. This type of listening is essential when time is a limited commodity. Usually, time is precious in the workplace. A day can be eaten up by clients, co-workers, supervisors, and other individuals needing our attention. Time-oriented individuals protect their time by expressing to others how much effort they will devote to their cause.

## Gender and Cultural Differences in Listening Styles

Some researchers suggest there are gender differences when it comes to listening styles. In the mid-1980s, Booth-Butterfield reported that "males tend to hear the facts while females are more aware of the mood of the communication" (1984, 39). Just about twenty years later, researchers' findings were  consistent in indicating that men score themselves higher on the content-oriented listening style and women score themselves higher on the people- oriented listening style (Sargent and Weaver 2003). In addition, Kiewitz and Weaver III (1997) found that when comparing young adults from three  different countries, Germans preferred the action style, Israelis preferred the content style, and Americans preferred the people and time styles.

Although no listening style is best, it is imperative to understand your own listening style and to recognize the listening styles of others. Depending on the situation and the goals in communicating, you may need to adjust your listening style. In addition, recognizing the listening style in others will help direct your responding messages. For example, if you notice your boss is engaging in action-oriented listening style, you may want to produce a clearly articulated message. He may become irritated if you include miscellaneous information or use confusing vocabulary.

## Motivation to Listen and Potential Pitfalls

When we do anything, we have some kind of motivation, or purpose. Sometimes this motivation is driven by our goals, dreams, and interests. Other times motivation may be a result of guilt, responsibility, or shame. Consider your motive for attending school. Perhaps you are a student because you have set a goal to graduate or maybe you are motivated out of a sense of responsibility to your parents. Either way, motivation drives behavior. Have you ever considered your motivation for listening? Researchers have identified five listening motivations (Wolvin and Coakley 1988). Certain motivations for listening lend themselves to particular listening barriers. Therefore, let us examine each of these motivations independently and offer potential pitfalls for each. Table 4.3 presents some guidelines for effective listening.

TABLE 4.3

Guidelines for Effective Listening

| Effective listeners do their best to avoid these behaviors: |
| --- |
| 1. Calling the subject uninteresting |
| 2. Criticizing the speaker and/or delivery |
| 3. Getting overstimulated |
| 4. Listening only for facts (bottom line) |
| 5. Not taking notes or outlining everything |
| 6. Faking attention |
| 7. Tolerating or creating distractions |
| 8. Tuning out difficult material |
| 9. Letting emotional words block the message |
| 10. Wasting the time difference between speed of speech and speed of thought |

Source: Nichols, R. G., and L. A. Stevens. 1957. Are you listening? New York: McGraw-Hill.

DISCRIMINATE LISTENING. First, we may listen for the purpose of discriminating. The purpose of **discriminate listening** is to help us understand the meaning of the message. In certain situations we want to discriminate between what is fact and what is an opinion. Or perhaps we try to discriminate between what is an emotionally-based argument and what is a logicallybased argument. One example of a situation in which we might engage in discriminate listening is in the workplace when we attentively listen to how a co-worker responds to our new recommendation. Here we are trying to determine if they agree or disagree with us. Another example is engaging in listening in the classroom when the teacher suggests that portions of the lecture will be on the exam. In this example, we are discriminating between what the teacher believes is important material for the exam and what is not going to be on the exam. Furthermore, we tend to use discriminate listening when we are trying to determine whether someone is lying to us.

**Potential Pitfall.** Often when we are trying to discriminate between messages, we selectively listen to certain stimuli while ignoring others. For example, if someone does not maintain eye contact with us, we may jump to conclusions regarding her trustworthiness. If discrimination is your motivation, it is important to keep an open mind and attend to the entire message.

APPRECIATIVE LISTENING. Another motivation we have for listening is **appreciative listening**. The purpose of appreciative listening is for the pure enjoyment of listening to the stimuli. This may be listening to your favorite tunes on your iPod, attending the opera, a musical or the movies, or listening to the sounds of the waves crashing on the shore.

**Potential Pitfall.** With appreciative listening it is important to be proactive. In order to be successful in appreciative listening you must *decrease noise.* You can do this by controlling distractions. For example, turn off your cell phone. Sometimes you can even choose your physical environment. If you are going to the movies, you can choose a particular seat away from potentially "loud" patrons. Or you may choose to go to the movies with a partner that will not inhibit your pleasure-seeking experience by talking or asking questions throughout.

COMPREHENSIVE LISTENING. We also may be motivated to listen in order to grasp new information. **Comprehensive listening** involves mindfully receiving and remembering new information. When our boss is informing us of our new job duties or a friend is telling you when they need to be picked up at the airport we are engaging in comprehensive listening. Our goal is to accurately understand the new information and be able to retain it.

**Potential Pitfall.** Often there are several messages that the speaker is sending and it is the job of the listener to determine which messages are the most important. With comprehensive listening it is critical to *recognize the main ideas and identify supportive details.* If you are unsure, *seek feedback or paraphrase the message.* For example, you may ask, "So you are flying Southwest and you need me to pick you up at baggage claim at 10:00 p.m., correct?"

EVALUATIVE LISTENING. When our motivation goes beyond comprehending messages to judging messages we are engaging in evaluative listening. **Evaluative listening** involves critically assessing messages. This occurs when a salesperson is trying to persuade us to buy a product or when we listen to political speeches. We are evaluating the credibility and competency of the speaker and the message. Our goal here is to create opinions and sound judgments regarding people and information.

**Potential Pitfall.** Prejudices and biases may interfere with our listening ability when we are motivated to listen for evaluative purposes. For example, individuals who identify with a particular political party are quick to judge the messages of an individual representing an alternative party. It is important to *be aware of your own preconceived notions* and not let that impede on your ability to effectively interpret the speaker's message.

EMPATHETIC LISTENING. The last motivation to listen is for empathetic reasons. The purpose of **empathetic** (or therapeutic) **listening** is to help others. For example, we may meet up with our friends to discuss their most recent romantic episodes or we may help our family members make tough financial decisions. Our goal is to provide a supportive ear and assist in uncovering alternative perspectives. Often, just by listening our friends will identify their own issues or our family members will uncover their own solutions to their problems. Other times, they may ask for suggestions or recommendations.

**Potential Pitfall.** It is critical to distinguish if the speaker indeed wants you to be an active participant in offering solutions or if he wants you "just to listen." Sometimes we assume that solutions are being sought, but what is really wanted is someone to act as a "sounding board."

## *Common Listening Misbehaviors*

There can be severe consequences when we choose not to listen effectively. One study found that the second most frequently occurring mistake made by education leaders deals with poor interpersonal communication skills and that the most frequent example given for this type of mistake was *failure to listen* (Bulach, Pickett, and Booth

1998). The perception that we are not listening may be because we lack appropriate eye contact with the speaker, we appear preoccupied or distracted with other issues, or because we do not provide the appropriate feedback. When we send these signals, the speaker interprets our behavior as not caring. This can damage internal and external business relationships. These behaviors can have severe consequences. Another study examined the top five reasons why principals lost their jobs (Davis 1997). The results of this study found that the most frequently cited response by superintendents focused on failure to communicate in ways that build positive relationships. The results of this study can be applied to situations outside of the educational setting. So, how do people communicate in ways that do not build positive relationships? This section will identify the six common listening misbehaviors.

PSEUDO-LISTENING. **Pseudo-listening** is when we are pretending to listen. We look like we are listening by nodding our head or providing eye contact, but we are faking our attention. This is a self-centered approach to listening. Let us be honest, when we are pseudo-listening we are not "fooling" anyone. We are not able to ask appropriate questions and we are not able to provide proper feedback.

MONOPOLIZING. Listeners that engage in **monopolizing** take the focus off the speaker and redirect the conversation and attention to themselves. Often, monopolizers interrupt the speaker to try to "one up" the speaker. They may try to top his story by saying "That reminds me . . ." or "You think that is bad–let me tell you what happened to me. . . ."

DISCONFIRMING. Listeners that deny the feelings of the speaker are sending disconfirming messages. Recall our discussion in Chapter Four regarding the implication of sending disconfirming messages. Examples of disconfirming messages include: "You shouldn't feel bad . . ." or "Don't cry . . . there is no need to cry." This misbehavior discourages the source to continue speaking and decreases perceptions of empathy.

DEFENSIVE LISTENING. An individual who engages in **defensive listening** perceives a threatening environment. Defensive communication has been defined as "that behavior which occurs when an individual perceives threat or anticipates threat in the group" (Gibb 1961, 141). Defensiveness includes "how he appears to others, how he may seem favorable, how he may win, dominate, impress, or escape punishment, and/or how he may avoid or mitigate a perceived or anticipated threat" (141). In other words, defensiveness is a process of saving "face." The issue of face is associated with people's desire to display a positive public image (Goffman 1967). An example of defensive listening is, "Don't look at me, I did not tell you to do that. . . ."

SELECTIVE LISTENING.  Selective **listening happens** when a listener focuses only on parts of the message. She takes parts of the message that she agrees with (or does not agree with) and responds to those particular parts. We reduce cognitive dissonance or psychological discomfort, screening out messages that we do not agree with, to remain cognitively "stable." For example, if we recently bought a new SUV, we may choose not to pay attention to messages suggesting that SUV's are not environmentally sound. We would, however, choose to pay attention to messages that suggest SUV vehicles rated higher on safety tests.

AMBUSHING.  Ambushers will listen for information that they can use to attack the speaker. They are selectively and strategically listening for messages that they can use against the speaker. Often ambushers interrupt the speaker. They do not allow the speaker to complete his thought and jump to conclusions. Ambushers make assumptions and get ahead of the speaker by finishing his sentences. They are self-motivated and lack dual perspective.

# CHAPTER SUMMARY

In this chapter, we explained the perception process: selecting information, organizing information and interpreting information. Additionally, we identified and explained factors related to each of the three primary selectivity processes. At this point, you should have a more detailed understanding of why certain messages or information gets selected over others. We also learned more about the four types of schema that affect interpersonal communication. Once information has been selected and organized, the final step is interpretation. The primary theory that explains how we make sense of our own behavior and that of others is attribution theory. The way that we make sense of our own and others' behavior is quite different and flawed. In the final sections we discussed the two primary attribution errors as well as factors that affect our interpretation process.

In the last section of this chapter, we explained the difference between hearing and listening. Remember, listening refers to the dynamic process in which individuals physically hear a message, employ cognitive processes to attribute meaning to the message, and provide verbal and/or nonverbal feedback to the source. Afterwards, we identified the seven steps to effective listening by using the acronym BIG EARS: Be open to the message, Interpret the message, Give positive feedback, Engage in dual perspective, Adapt your listening style, Reduce noise, and Store the message. Not only is it important to increase your listening skills, it is also crucial to recognize different listening styles. We discussed four different types of listening styles:

people-oriented, action-oriented, content-oriented, and time-oriented. Then we explained why people are motivated to listen. Four motivations to listen are to discriminate, appreciate, comprehend, and evaluate. By identifying potential pitfalls for each motivation, our hope is that you can adapt your communication to the message recipient and also be aware of your own shortcomings. Finally, we recognized six common listening misbehaviors including: pseudo-listening, disconfirming, defensive listening, monopolizing, selective listening, and ambushing.

# EXERCISES

## *Activity #1: "Chatter Matters"*

Youngsters are encouraged to become little chatterboxes to promote better communication skills. Children aged three to five at Hardwick Primary School, Stockton, will receive a Chatter Matters bag each week, containing a game, book, toy, and CD designed to improve their talking, listening, and reading. Teacher Linda Whitwell said each week the children will swap bags, so they get to use a number of different devices to develop their talents. She said: "The children will be taking the bags home each week, so we are hoping to encourage parents to work with their children to improve their reading, writing, and speaking ability. It will be something fun and different for everyone to use, and hopefully it will have the desired affect." (p. 6). *This excerpt was taken from "The Northern Echo" on February 22, 2006.*

**Discussion Questions:**
1. What are some advantages of this endeavor?
2. What might be some limitations?
3. If you were coordinating "Chatter Matters," what would you emphasize?

From *The Northern Echo*, February 22, 2006. Reprinted with permission.

## *Activity #2: Practice Responding*

Complete the conversation below using the prompts in parentheses.
Sample: Erica: I am really sad.

      You: *What's the matter?* (Probe to find out more.)

1. Erica: My mom just called and she sounded awful.
   You: _____ (Probe to get an example.)
2. Erica: She said that my dad is leaving her.
   You: _____ (Paraphrase what Erica just said.)
3. Erica: Well, they have not been getting along lately.
   You: _____ (Probe to find out more.)

4. Erica: I noticed they were fighting more often over Thanksgiving.
   You: _____ (Empathize with Erica.)
5. Erica: Yeah. I am totally miserable.

## Activity #3: Listening Responses

Identify which listening responses are positive and which are negative by placing a "P" or an "N" on the line before the response.

_____ There is no reason to get upset.
_____ This happens to everyone.
_____ Can you give me an example? / What do you mean?
_____ Don't feel bad.
_____ So you're not getting along? / Do you mean you're arguing a lot?
_____ You're tougher than this.
_____ Snap out of it.
_____ What makes you think that? Tell me more.
_____ You must be really upset. That's terrible.
_____ She is not worth it.
_____ Get over it.
_____ It's not that bad.

## Activity #4: Listening Is Work: Willingness to Listen

Often, it is not a lack of skill that makes someone a poor listener; rather it is a lack of effort on the listener's part (Richmond and Hickson 2001). Determine the extent to which you do or do not make an effort to listen to speakers by completing the Willingness to Listen Measure. This measure tells you how well you listen in public speaking situations and can be found at http://www.jamescmccroskey.com/measures/wtlisten.htm.

## KEY WORDS

**Biased information search** Our propensity to seek out certain types of information and avoid others.

**Limited-capacity processors** Systems of information retention with fixed and limited ability to store, process, and understand that information.

"Because of the innate limitations in our ability to process information, humans are often described as **limited-capacity processors.** Stated simply, we consciously and subconsciously make choices about the amount and type of stimuli we perceive."

**Novelty** Quality of an object, person, or experience being new, different, uncommon, or rare.

**Perception** The process of selecting, organizing, and interpreting sensory information into a coherent or lucid depiction of the world around us.

**Proximity** Limited distance, or nearness, between two or more things or people.

**Reinforce** To provide or create a stimulus that strengthens or encourages the likelihood of repetition of action or emotional response.

**Selection** First perception process.

**Selective attention** Refers to the choice to engage with or respond only to certain stimuli when several stimuli are presented at the same time.

**Selective exposure** Refers to the choice to subject oneself to certain stimuli.

**Size** Measurement of an object or grouping of objects, usually in relation to other objects or groupings.

**Utility** Measure of satisfaction, usefulness, or purpose derived from an object or experience.

# REFERENCES

Abelson, R. P. 1982. Three modes of attitude-behavior consistency. In M. P. Zanna, E. T. Higgins, and C. P. Herman (Eds.), *Consistency in social behavior: The Ontario symposium* (Vol. 2, 131–146). Hillsdale, NJ: Lawrence Erlbaum Associates.

AICPA. 2006. *Highlighted Responses from the Association for Accounting marketing survey: Creating the Future Agenda for the Profession—Managing Partner Perspective.* Retrieved December 22, 2006, from *http://www.aicpa.org/pubs/ tpcpa/feb2001/ hilight.htm.*

Alwin, D. F., and J. A. Krosnick. 1991. Aging, cohorts, and the stability of sociopolitical orientations over the lifespan. *American Journal of Sociology, 97,* 169–195.

Bartsch, K., and K. London. 2000. Children's use of state information in selecting persuasive arguments. *Developmental Psychology, 36*, 352–365.

Booth-Butterfield, M. 1984. She hears . . . he hears; What they hear and why. *Personnel Journal, 63*, 36–43.

Braithwaite, D. O., and L. M. Harter. 2000. Communication and the management of dialectical tensions in the personal relationships of people with disabilities. In D. O. Braithwaite and T. L. Thompson (Eds.), *Handbook of communication and people with disabilities*. Mahwah, NJ: Lawrence Erlbaum Associates.

Bulach, C., W. Pickett, and D. Boothe. 1998. *Mistakes educational leaders make*. ERIC Digest, 122. ERIC Clearinghouse on Educational Management, Eugene, OR.

Carlston, D. E. 1992. Impression formation and the modular mind: The associated systems theory. In L. L. Martin and A. T. Tesser (Eds.), *The construction of social justice* (pp. 301–341).

Chesebro, J. L. 1999. The relationship between listening and styles and conversational sensitivity. *Communication Research Reports, 16*, 233–238.

Cialdini, R. B. 2001. *Influence: Science and practice*. Boston, MA: Allyn and Bacon.

Davis, S. H. 1997. The principal's paradox: Remaining secure in precarious position. *NASSP Bulletin, 81*, 592, 73–80.

Duran, R. L. 1983. Communicative adaptability: A measure of social communicative competence. *Communication Quarterly, 31*, 320–326.

Duran, R. L., and L. Kelly. 1988. An investigation into the cognitive domain of competence II: The relationship between communicative competence and interaction involvement. *Communication Research Reports, 5*, 91–96.

Fehr, B. 2004. Intimacy expectations in same-sex friendships: A prototype interaction-pattern model. *Journal of personality and social psychology, 86*, 265–284.

Fehr, B., and J. A. Russell. 1991. The concept of love viewed from a prototype perspective. *Journal of Personality and Social Psychology, 60*, 425–438.

Fischer, P., E. Jonas, D. Frey, and S. Schulz-Hardt. 2005. Selective exposure to information: The impact of information limits. *European Journal of Social Psychology, 35*, 469–492.

Fiske, S. T., and S. E. Taylor. 1984. *Social cognition*. Reading, MA: Addison-Wesley.

Gass, R. H., and J. S. Seiter. 2003. *Persuasion, social influence and compliance gaining*. Boston, MA: Allyn and Bacon.

Gibb, J. R. 1961. Defensive communication. *Journal of Communication, 11*, 141–149.

Goffman, E. 1967. *Interaction ritual: Essays on face-to-face behavior*. New York: Pantheon Books.

Gorham, J., and D. M. Christophel. 1992. Students' perceptions of teacher behaviors as motivating and demotivating factors in college classes. *Communication Quarterly, 40*, 239–252.

Hilliard, B., and J. Palmer. 2003. Networking like a pro!: 20 tips on turning the contracts you get into the connections you need. Agito Consulting.

Hamachek, D. 1992. *Encounters with the self (3rd ed.)*. Fort Worth, TX: Harcourt Brace Jovanovich.

Hamilton, D. L., and J. W. Sherman. 1994. Stereotypes. In R. Wyer and T. Srull (Eds.), *Handbook of social cognition (2nd ed.)*. (1–68). Hillsdale, NJ: Lawrence Erlbaum.

Heider, F. 1958. Attitudes and cognitive organization. *Journal of Psychology, 21,* 107–112.

Hockberg, J. E. 1978. *Perception (2nd ed)*. Englewood Cliffs, NJ: Prentice Hall.

Hockenbury, D. H., and S. E. Hockenbury. 2006. *Psychology (4th ed.)*. New York, NY: Worth Publishers.

Janusik, L. A., and A. D. Wolvin. 2006. *24 hours in a day: A listening update to the time studies.* Paper presented at the meeting of the International Listening Association, Salem, OR.

Katz, A. M., and R. Hill. 1958. Residential propinquity and marital selection: A review of theory, method, and fact. *Marriage and Family Living, 20,* 27–35.

Kelley, H. H. 1967. Attribution theory in social psychology. In D. Levine (Ed.), *Nebraska Symposium on Motivation* (Vol. A5, p. 192–238). Lincoln: University of Nebraska Press.

———. 1971. *Attribution in social interaction.* Morristown, NJ: General Learning Press.

———. 1972. Causal schemata and the attribution process. In E. E. Jones, D. E. Kanouse, H. H. Kelley, R. E. Nisbett, S. Valins, and B. Weiner (Eds.), *Attribution: Perceiving the causes of behavior* (151–174). Morristown, NJ: General Learning Press.

———. 1973. The process of causal attribution. *American Psychologist, 28,* 107–128.

Kelly, G. A. 1970. A brief introduction to personal construct psychology. In D. Bannister (Ed.), *Perspectives in personal construct psychology* (1–30). San Diego: Academic Press.

———. 1991. *The psychology of personal constructs: Vol. 1. A theory of personality.* London: Routledge. (Original work published in 1955.)

Kelsey, D. M., P. Kearney, T. G. Plax, T. H. Allen, and K. J. Ritter. 2004. College students' attributions of teacher misbehaviors. *Communication Education, 53,* 40–55.

Kiewitz, C., and J. B. Weaver III. 1997. Cultural differences in listening style preferences: A comparison of young adults in Germany, Israel and the United States. *International Journal of Public Opinion Research, 9,* 233–247.

Klopf, D. 1995. *Intercultural encounters: The fundamentals of intercultural communication.* Englewood, CA: Morton.

Littlejohn, S. W. 1983. *Theories of human communication.* Belmont, CA: Wadsworth.

McCroskey, J. C., and V. A. Richmond. 1996. *Fundamentals of human communication.* Prospect Heights, Illinois: Waveland Press.

Miller, J. 1984. Culture and the development of everyday social explanation. *Journal of Personality and Social Psychology, 49,* 961–978.

Nichols, R. G. 1961. Do we know how to listen? Practical helps in a modern age. *Speech Teacher, 10,* 118–128.

Norton, D. 1978. *The dual perspective.* New York: Council on Social Work Education.

Raskin, J. D. 2002. Constructivism in psychology: Personal construct psychology, radical constructivism, and social constructivism. In J. D. Raskin and S. K. Bridges (Eds.), *Studies in meaning: Exploring constructivist psychology (1–25).* New York: Pace University Press.

Reeder, G. D. 1985. Implicit relations between disposition and behavior: Effects on dispositional attribution. In J. H. Harvey and G. Weary (Eds.), *Attribution: Basic issues and application* (87–116). New York: Academic Press.

Richmond, V. P., and M. Hickson, III. 2001. *Going public: A practical guide to public talk.* Boston: Allyn & Bacon.

Sargent, S. L., and J. B. Weaver III. 2003. Listening styles: Sex differences in perceptions of self and others. *International Journal of Listening, 17,* 5–18.

Tannen, D. 1986. *That's not what I meant.* New York: Ballantine Books.

———. 1990. *You just don't understand: Women and men in conversation.* New York: Ballantine Books.

———. 1994. *Gender and discourse.* New York: Oxford University Press.

Turner, J. C. 1987. *Rediscovering the social group: A self-categorization theory.* New York: Basil Blackwell.

Wanzer, M. B., M. Booth-Butterfield, and M. K. Gruber. 2004. Perceptions of health care providers' communication: Relationships between patient-centered communication and satisfaction. *Health Communication, 16,* 363–384.

Watson, K. W., L. L. Barker, and J. B. Weaver Ill. 1995. The listening styles profile (LSP-16): Development and validation of an instrument to assess four listening styles. *International Journal of Listening, 9,* 1–13.

Wolvin, A. D., and C. G. Coakley. 1988. Listening. Dubuque, IA: William C. Brown, Publishers.

Wood, J. T. 1999. *Gendered lives: Communication, gender, and culture* (3rd ed.). Belmont, CA: Wadsworth Publishing Co.

Yukl, G., P. P. Fu, and R. McDonald. 2003. Cross cultural differences in perceived effectiveness of influence tactics for initiating or resisting change. *Applied Psychology: An International Review, 52,* 68–82.

# PERCEPTION AND LISTENING

When I was a kid, **Big Ears** was an insult. (I will save the stories of my child- hood trauma for another time.) We are not good listeners. I say: We are not good listeners. We have more distractions in our lives than any people in his- tory. There are more messages, thoughts, and useless information bombard- ing us than ever before.

Have you ever watched a modern student write a paper? The computer screen is on. A word processing program is operating and Facebook is on another screen, music is playing, and friends are walking by talking and inter- rupting. Oh, and of course, the ever-present phone is open on the desk in anticipation of a text or call. OMG! Whassup? LOL.

Our messages and our attention spans are getting shorter. Some people call it mul- titasking but research indicates that the brain works better when it focuses on one thing. We are losing the abilities to concentrate and to listen. Businesses hold semi- nars to teach employees how to listen. Communication professionals hold work- shops to teach nurses, doctors, and police officers how to listen more effectively. Clearly, business professionals must under- stand the information being commu- nicated to them and be able to effectively translate this material to others. Do our friends and families deserve any less? Relationships are lost when people do not lis- ten to each other. Everyone needs to work on their **perception** and **listening skills**.

# CHAPTER 5

## Development of Self and Individual Differences Just Me, Myself, and I

### Chapter Objectives

After reading this chapter, you should understand the following concepts:
- Define the term self and explain why it is viewed as a complex process
- Define the term self-complexity and explain the benefits of high self-complexity
- Explain the three components of the self-system and discuss how each component affects interpersonal communication
- Discuss the development of the self with special emphasis on the individuals and groups of individuals that play important roles in the development of the self

- Explain attachment theory, including the three attachment styles that affect the way individuals view the self and others
- State the importance of direct definitions and identity scripts
- Discuss the significance of the self-fulfilling prophecy and social comparison processes for identity formation
- State the difference between state and trait approaches in studying communication
- Define communication apprehension and discuss its effects
- Discuss the way communication apprehension is typically measured and identify treatment options for individuals scoring high in communication apprehension
- Define willingness to communicate and distinguish it from communication apprehension
- Define and give examples of the two forms of destructive aggression
- Explain why some individuals are verbally aggressive
- Define and give examples of two forms of constructive aggression
- Define humor orientation
- Define affective orientation

# CHAPTER OVERVIEW

In an excerpt from a song by the 1980s rock band, The Talking Heads, the burning question "How did I get here?" is raised. Most of us, at one time in our lives, have asked the same question. Another profound question, "Who am I?" fixates our culture. It is asked in song lyrics from rock groups and Broadway alike, from No Doubt, Alanis Morisette, Will Smith, Elvis Presley, Seal, and the Smashing Pumpkins to the musical *Les Miserables*. The Talking Heads added another concern "How did I get to be this way?" The theme song of television's most popular show is "Who Are You?" and *CSI* and similar programs involve the audience in the weekly unraveling of someone's identity, seeking answers from his interactions with others. The preoccupying search for self is this chapter's concern. In the first half of this chapter we address these questions by discussing the process of identity formation. Special emphasis will be placed on the role that interpersonal communication and relationships play in this process. A definition of the term self is provided, along with an overview of relevant terms used to describe and explain various aspects of the self. Next, a detailed description of the development of the self is presented, with special attention given to those individuals and processes considered essential to identity formation.

© amygala imagery, 2007, Shutterstock.

In the second part of this chapter, we examine the impact of individual differences on interpersonal communication. When communication researchers want to learn more about the impact of individual differences on social interaction, they often turn their attention to communication-based personality traits. According to communication researcher John Daly (2002), "the greatest proportion of articles in our journals have explored topics directly or indirectly related to personality" (133). To learn more about how people differ in their communication patterns, we define the term personality, distinguish between trait and *state approaches* to interpersonal communication research, and provide explanations of a number of different communication based personality traits. While there are many traits that influence our communication with others, we focus on several that have been researched extensively. These have been identified as predispositions that can either hinder or facilitate communication with others. "Everyone thinks of changing the world, but no one thinks of changing himself," wrote Leo Tolstoy. By looking within instead of outwardly, we can choose to improve our ability to communicate.

> ➤ **State approach**
> An approach to studying communication behaviors that involves examining how individuals communicate in a particular situation or context.

## DEFINITION OF SELF

While individuals use the term self frequently and with relative ease, it is quite challenging for researchers to offer a single consistent definition for the term (Baumeister 1998). The *self* has been defined as a psychological entity consisting of "an organized set of beliefs, feelings, and behaviors" (Tesser, Wood, and Stapel 2002, 10). Another way of understanding the self is as a complex system made up of a variety of interdependent elements that attain self-organization (Vallacher and Nowak 2000). In attempting to explain the self, theorists often emphasize the origins of self, noting that it emerges through communication and established relationships with others and is constantly developing and evolving (Epstein 1973; Park and Waters 1988). Take a moment to consider how your self-perceptions have changed over the years. Are you the same person you were five, ten, or fifteen years ago? You have probably changed and matured a great deal over the years and see yourself as being quite different from when you were younger. Thus, one's perception of self is often described as a process because it evolves and is largely determined by ongoing communication with significant others. This idea is further validated by social psychologist Arthur Aron (2003) who says, "What we are and what we see ourselves as being seems to be constantly under construction and reconstruction, with the architects and remodeling contractors largely being those with whom we have close interactions" (Aron 2003, 443). In later sections of this chapter we explore the specific individuals and processes that exert the greatest influence in shaping our self-perceptions.

> ➤ **Self**
> A psychological entity consisting of "an organized set of beliefs, feelings, and behaviors."

The self is also recognized as <u>highly complex and multidimensional.</u> Researchers agree that there are numerous dimensions, or aspects, of the self that make up one overall perception of the self. While we might think of ourselves as relatively uncomplicated individuals, most of us are highly complex and can assume a variety of roles. For example, on any given day, you may assume the roles of student, employee, daughter, sister, friend, teammate, roommate, or resident comedian. This example illustrates how individuals vary in their ***self-complexity*** or number of self-aspects, also known as subselves. Individuals possessing higher levels of self-complexity reap a number of personal benefits. What does it mean to possess higher levels of selfcomplexity? Referring back to the example of the student, if she views her multiple roles (sister, teammate, friend, etc.) as separate or unique, and at the same time has encountered a number of life experiences associated with those roles, then she probably has a greater number of non-overlapping selfaspects, or higher self-complexity. On the other hand, a woman who views herself only in two closely-related roles, e.g., teammate and student, and has limited life experiences associated with these roles, will probably have fewer self-aspects, or lower self-complexity.

**⇒ Self-complexity**
Defined by the number of self-aspects or sub-selves a person possesses.

How does one benefit from higher levels of self-complexity? Individuals with higher self-complexity may be less prone to having mood fluctuations (Linville 1985) and may cope better with stress (Koch and Shepperd 2004). When individuals report lower self-complexity they are more likely to experience negative affect in response to a negative life event than someone who reports higher self-complexity. Individuals with lower self-complexity may not be able to separate the limited roles they assume and may experience what researchers call "spill over." Thus, a student athlete who has a bad game may not be able to separate her experience on the soccer field ("me as soccer player") from her experience in the classroom ("me as a student") and the negative affect from the soccer game will expand, or spill over, to other self-aspects (Koch and Shepperd 2004). The student athlete has a bad game, does not study for her chemistry exam because she is still angry about her performance on the field and, as a result, fails her chemistry test the next day.

How could her performance on the soccer field affect other aspects of this girl's day?

Higher self-complexity may actually act as a buffer for people by allowing them to mentally separate themselves from painful life events (Linville 1987). Furthermore, the buffer effect has direct interpersonal, or relational, implications. The buffer effect was observed for those higher in selfcomplexity faced with relationship dissolution. Individuals

© Robert J. Beyers II, 2007.Shutterstock.

higher in self-complexity thought about the relationship less and were less upset about their relationships ending than individuals lower in self-complexity (Linville 1987). Familiar fictional characters demonstrate instances of high and low self-complexity following relationship disengagement. For instance, *Gilmore Girls'* Rory Gilmore, whose roles of daughter, granddaughter, friend, and student are emphasized more heavily than that of girlfriend, dealt with the end of relationships with various boyfriends by spending more time with her mother and friends, and by increasing her involvement at school. These actions served as a buffer for Rory, which kept relationship concerns from dominating her thoughts or actions. In contrast, the popular show *The O.C.* exhibited the character Marissa Cooper, who fell into alcoholism and depression after her own breakup with central character Ryan Atwood. Marissa allowed the role of romantic relationship, which she found self-defining, to affect all other aspects of her self. While typically not as extreme as these two situations, instances of lower selfcomplexity, compared to high, are more likely to produce negative effects.

## *Importance of Studying the Process of Identity Formation*

Why should interpersonal communication scholars study aspects of the self and the process of self development? Similar to other frequently studied concepts, research and perspectives on the self are vast and vary greatly (see, for example, Tesser, Felson, and Suls 2000; Tesser et al. 2002). There are a number of terms related to self in the literature and definitions for them are often inconsistent, making it difficult to integrate and interpret research on the self (Houck and Spegman 1999). But, before we can engage in a meaningful discussion of the self and related processes, we need to offer clear definitions of terms such as *self-concept*, *self-esteem*, and *self-regulation*. We also need to highlight distinctions between key terms and concepts. In addition, if we want to understand how and why individuals vary in attitudes, beliefs, values, mannerisms, security, psychological states, etc., we need to take a closer look at both how and why people perceive themselves in a particular way. Exploring the communicative and relational processes that affect the development of the self either positively or negatively is important because it helps us to understand who we are and why we are this way. Once we understand differences in how individuals develop a sense of self as well as the processes associated with the development of a more positive self-perception, we can train individuals to interact more competently with those around them. As Houck and Spegman (1999) argue, "Given its manifestation of social competence, the development of the self is of fundamental importance not only to the well-being of individuals, but also to the well-being of others with whom they associate" (2).

**Self-concept**
A cognitive construct that is a "descriptive reference to the self, or a definition of the nature and beliefs about the self's qualities."

**Self-esteem**
Subjective perception of one's self-worth, or the value one places on the self.

**Self-regulation**
The capacity to exercise choice and initiation.

There are three constructs related to the self that typically emerge in discussions about the self and developmental processes. These three specific aspects of the self are: self-concept, or cognitions about the self; self-esteem, or affective information related to the self; and autonomy/self-initiative, or self-regulation, processes. In order to better understand the self-system and its related components, it is important to define and distinguish between these related constructs. In this chapter, we present a detailed definition of each of these three components, offer examples of related terms used to discuss each of these key areas, and provide a brief overview of the importance of these concepts to interpersonal communication and relationships.

## The Self System

Terms such as self-concept, self-esteem, self-schema, and self-regulation are used in dialogues about the self and identity development. Some of these terms have been used interchangeably and yet, as we will see, they are very different constructs.

SELF-CONCEPT/COGNITIONS ABOUT THE SELF. One term that often emerges in discussions about the self is self-concept. Houck and Spegman describe the self-concept as a cognitive construct which is a "descriptive reference to the self, or a definition of the nature and beliefs about the self's qualities" (Houck and Spegman 1999, 2). While there are a variety of other terms used when describing the self (self-cognition, self-image, self-schema, and self-understanding), self-concept is used most frequently. In the most basic sense, self-concept refers to what someone knows about himself.

Social psychologists and sociologists argue that people possess multiple perceptions of the self-concept, or different personas (Bargh, McKenna, and Fitzsimons 2002). For example, Goffman (1959) and Jung (1953) draw distinctions between a *"public" self*, or the self that we project during social interaction, and an *"inner" self* that we keep private and that may reflect how we really feel about ourselves. The public self is described as our "actual" self-concept while the inner self is presented as our "true" self. Psychologists note that individuals often project an actual self in public that is quite different from their true self. Individuals may not present their true selves for a variety of reasons. One reason could be the fear of evaluation from others. Or, in some instances, an individual may not yet fully know or understand his or her true self.

One place where individuals may feel more comfortable expressing their true selves is on the Internet (Bargh et al. 2002). According to researchers, the anonymity of the Internet gives people the chance to assume different personas and genders and to express aspects of themselves "without fear of disapproval

**➤ Public self**
The self we project during social interaction.

**➤ Inner self**
The self we keep private and that may reflect how we really feel about ourselves.

"TRUE SELF"

Why do you think some-people find it easier to express their "true" selves over the Internet?

and sanctions by those in their real-life social circle" (Bargh et al. 2002). Two different experiments were performed that used a reaction time task to access college students' perceptions of their true and actual selves. Researchers found that the true self-concept was more readily recalled during Internet interactions while the actual self was more accessible during face-to-face interactions. In a third related experiment, college students were randomly assigned to interact, either via the Internet or face-to-face. Students assigned to the Internet had an easier time expressing their true selves to their partners than those assigned to the face-to-face condition. If individuals feel more comfortable expressing their true selves during Internet exchanges, they are then more likely to establish relationships with individuals they meet on the Internet (McKenna, Green, and Gleason 2002). This research may provide some explanation for the fact that more individuals are using the Internet to establish romantic and platonic relationships.

An individual's self-concept influences how one views or interprets social interaction, and at the same time it regulates one's involvement in the interaction. Suppose the student council president is asked to speak to the superintendent of schools to discuss student views on proposed schedule changes. Her self-confidence in her role as a student leader causes her to assert herself in the interaction and offer suggestions for an alternative plan. Research on the relationship between self-concept and interpersonal processes has explored the effects of self-concept on social perception, the relationship between self-concept and selection of interaction partners, strategies individuals use to mold and interpret communication with others, and how individuals respond to feedback that is not consistent with their self-concept. Three of these areas of research—the relationship between self-concept and social perception, self-concept and partner choice, and self-concept and interaction strategies—are particularly interesting and relevant to understanding how and why our self-concept affects our communication with others.

Much of the research on the relationship between self-concept and social perception concludes that people are likely to view others as relatively similar to themselves (Markus and Wurf 1987). When you interact with your friends, family members, and co-workers, you perceive them to be more similar than dissimilar to you in attitudes, beliefs, values, goals, and behaviors. From an interpersonal communication perspective, similarity is an important variable that affects our interactions with others and, when used strategically as an affinity-seeking behavior, can potentially increase liking between interactants (Bell and Daly 1984).

The way one sees or defines one's self also affects both the choice of relationship partners and subsequent behavior in those relationships (Markus and Wurf 1987). Research on the relationship between self-perception and relationship satisfaction indicates that individuals report greater relationship satisfaction when they choose partners that validate views of themselves (Schlenker 1984; Swann 1985). In other words, individuals attempt to find a relationship partner who expresses similar or consistent views with their ideal or desired self. Much of the research on the role of the self in social interaction has examined the process of impression management during interpersonal encounters (Markus and Wurf 1987). Not surprisingly, individuals work diligently to present a particular image of themselves to both external (Goffman 1959) and internal audiences (Greenwald and Breckler 1985). Using impression management techniques consciously and effectively is linked to heightened self-awareness (Schlenker 1985). While we may not always be aware of our impression management efforts, our day-to-day choice of dress, hairstyle, choice of words, and artifacts are selected strategically to project a specific desired image of ourselves to those around us. Think about the choices you make when deciding what to wear and how to style your hair in various social situations. It is highly likely that impression management played a role in your decisions.

SELF-ESTEEM/AFFECT ABOUT THE SELF. Another term used frequently when discussing the self is self-esteem, defined as the subjective perception of one's self-worth, or the value one places on the self (Houck and Spegman 1999). There are a number of related evaluative terms associated with self-esteem that include: self-affect, self-worth, and self-evaluation. All of these terms illustrate the evaluative nature of this concept with individuals typically experiencing either positive or negative feelings about themselves or their behavior. Self-esteem can be measured objectively, unlike self-concept. Research indicates that individuals typically vary in their reported levels of self-esteem. Those reporting higher levels of self-esteem feel more favorable about themselves and their behaviors than individuals with lower self-esteem.

According to researchers, self-esteem has become a "household" term today. Teachers, parents, therapists, coaches, and individuals that communicate regularly with children and have the potential to affect a child's self-esteem have been encouraged to focus on ways to help children see themselves more favorably (for

How can a teacher influence a child's self-esteem?

an overview of this research, see Baumeister, Campbell, Krueger, and Vohs 2003). The previously held assumption driving these efforts was that individuals with higher self-esteem would experience a number of positive benefits and outcomes. More recently, Baumeister and his colleagues examined the extensive research on self-esteem with special attention on the relationship between self-esteem and performance, interpersonal success, happiness, and lifestyle choices (for an overview of this research, see Baumeister et al. 2003). The findings from their extensive research were unexpected. Surprisingly, there was only a modest relationship between perceptions of self-esteem and school performance. Why? According to social psychologists, high self-esteem does not necessarily cause higher performance in school. Instead, researchers suspect that solid academic performance in school actually leads to higher self-esteem. When researchers investigated efforts to boost students' self-esteem, students did not improve in school and sometimes even performed at lower levels.

Similar to findings reported in the educational context, researchers concluded that occupational success may boost self-esteem rather than self-esteem leading to greater success in the workplace. The conclusions in this area are mixed, at best, with some research illustrating a positive relationship between self-esteem and occupational success and other research contradicting these findings (Baumeister et al. 2003). By this point, you might be asking yourself, "Are there any meaningful educational or occupational advantages associated with higher levels of self-esteem?" There *are* benefits to possessing higher self-esteem; they are just not as extensive as researchers initially estimated. For example, individuals with higher self-esteem seem to be more tenacious than those with low self-esteem. Social psychologists conclude that self-esteem may help individuals continue working on a task even after they failed initially (Baumeister et al. 2003).

What is the relationship between self-esteem and interpersonal communication and relationship success? Individuals self-reporting higher self-esteem typically indicate that they are well-liked and attractive, have better relationships, and make more positive impressions on others than those reporting lower levels of self-esteem. However, when researchers further investigated whether high self-esteem individuals were perceived this way by others using objective measures, the results were disconfirmed. The researchers further explain this finding by noting that while "narcissists are charming at first," they tend to eventually alienate those around them by communicating in ways that are perceived by others as inappropriate and ineffective (Baumeister et al. 2003, 1). The connection between self-esteem and the quality of romantic and platonic relationships is small to moderate, at best (Aron 2003). Some research indicates that there is a small consistent relationship between self-esteem and marital satisfaction and success over time (see, for example, Aube and Koestner 1992; Karney and Bradbury 1995). Based on research conducted thus far, couples' reported self-esteem does not appear to be a major predictor of marital satisfaction or persistence.

Rewarding children for good behavior gives them a boost in self-esteem.

However, in addition to tenaciousness, there are some additional recognized benefits of having higher self-esteem. For example, higher self-esteem has been linked to feelings of happiness. Individuals reporting higher self-esteem are generally happier folks than individuals selfreporting lower self-esteem and are probably less likely to be depressed. Lower self-esteem has been repeatedly linked to greater incidence of depression under certain situations or circumstances. While it is disappointing to find that programs and initiatives created to boost individuals' self-esteem were generally ineffective in doing so, it is important to emphasize specific communication patterns that might be beneficial in helping others formulate positive self-impressions. Baumeister and his colleagues (2003) note that instead of giving children "indiscriminate praise" which may lead to excessive narcissism, parents and educators should focus on "using praise to boost self-esteem as a reward for socially desirable behavior and self-improvement" (1).

As you can imagine, there is a great deal of information available on how to boost one's self-esteem in order to avoid depression, increase tenaciousness, and relate more effectively to others. Perceptions of one's self-esteem can change over time because of significant life experiences. There are numerous websites, books, workshops, and even computer games available for individuals who want to address problems with low self-esteem. See table 5.1 for an example of the type of information currently available to help individuals combat self-esteem problems.

**TABLE 5.1**

Ways to Boost Your Self-Esteem

| | |
|---|---|
| 1. | *Think back to when you tackled a task for the very first time.* <br> Trying something for the first time can be a daunting experience. The next time you feel under-confident, recall the first time you tried something new— and succeeded! This will help you to overcome your fears. |
| 2. | *Do something you have been putting aside.* <br> Once you complete this task, it will help you feel as though you can follow through on something. |
| 3. | *Work on your ability to relax.* <br> There are a number of different ways to reduce anxiety and stress in your life. Consider taking exercise classes, meditating, or involving yourself in something that helps you relax. |
| 4. | *Recall all of your accomplishments.* <br> Take a minute to reflect on all of the times you have succeeded at doing something that you set out to do (e.g., passing your driver's test, passing exams, putting money away for vacation). |

Adapted from an article that appears on the Uncommon Knowledge website www.self-confidence.co.uk/self/esteem/tips.

## Research Brief: Playing Computer Games May Boost Self-Esteem

Mark Baldwin, a psychologist at McGill University in Montreal, argues that computer games offer another less conventional and interesting way to boost one's self-esteem. While these games are not recommended for individuals with seriousself-esteem problems, Baldwin and his team of researchers found that the game shelped people feel better about themselves and their relationships by focusing on the positive, not the negative (Dye 2004). Visit *http://abcnews.go.com/Technology/story?id=99532&page=1* to read the entire article.

SELF-REGULATION. The third and final component of the self-system, self-regulation, is occasionally referred to in literature as self-determination, independence, self-assertion, self-control, or internalization. Self-regulation is regarded by some as a highly significant component of human existence (Bargh and Chartrand 1999). Why is self-regulation so important? Because **self-regulation**, defined as "the capacity to exercise choice and initiation" (Houck and Spegman 1999, 3), allows us to pursue and engage in goaldirected activity. It is important to study the process of self-regulation in order to understand how and why individuals are motivated and make choices. Research in this area examines aspects of initiative, motivation, and decision-making in relation to morality and developing a conscience. It also sets out to discover why some individuals are motivated to achieve goals and others are not. The significant process of self-regulation can occur at either a conscious or a subconscious level (Bargh and Chartrand 1999). You probably exert self-regulation, whether you are aware of the process or not.

What is the relationship between self-regulation and interpersonal communication and relationships? Baumeister and Vohs (2003) offer several examples of how the process of self-regulation is related to interpersonal communication and relationships. Problems such as interpersonal violence between relationship partners and extradyadic sexual relations are obviously linked in some way to failures in self-regulation. Self-regulation is closely related to successful maintenance of close romantic relationships (Baumeister and Vohs 2003). Related research by Finkel and Campbell (2001) indicated that individuals reporting higher levels of self-regulation were more likely to exhibit accommodating behaviors in their romantic relationships. Not surprisingly, most individuals prefer being in relationships with partners that are accommodating, or willing to compromise, to meet each other's needs.

The extent to which one communicates effectively and appropriately with others is also linked to self-regulation or initiative. Recall from Chapter One our discussion of Spitzberg and Cupach's (1984) model of communication competence and its three components. This model advances the significance of motivation or initiative in communicating effectively with others. While individuals may posses the skills and knowledge necessary for communicating effectively, if they are not motivated to do so, they will not enact the appropriate behavior. Thus, the process of self-regulation directly affects our communication abilities and the quality of interpersonal relationships.

Now that we understand the three main components of the self-system and their relationship to interpersonal communication, we move on to the discussion of the development of self. Two important questions to consider are: Which individuals or groups of individuals are most influential in forming or shaping our self-perceptions? And why? Exploring these questions in much greater detail will help to answer the questions: Who am I? And how did I become this way?

## Interpersonal Communication and the Development of Self

Most scholars agree that the self emerges and develops through communication with those to whom we are close (see, for example, Aron 2003). What exactly does this mean? This statement implies that, as infants, we do not possess a sense of self, but that one develops through our interactions with significant others (Cooley 1902; Mead 1934). Cooley (1902) was the first to advance "the **looking glass self**" metaphor

A child who feels secure in the family environment will naturally expect positive peer relationships.

which describes the impact of interpersonal communication on the development of self. Researchers (Felson 1989) extended the concept of looking glass self to include the term *reflected appraisal*, referring to the tendency to view ourselves based on the appraisals of others. Who are these significant others that affect our self-perceptions? Researchers have generally studied the influence of family and other significant individuals such as peers and relationship partners as they affect the development of self. We review the importance of interpersonal communication with family, peers, and significant others as it relates to the construction and reconstruction of the self over time.

**Reflected appraisal/looking glass self**
A metaphor that describes the impact of interpersonal communication on the development of self.

**Attachment theory**
A theory that attempts to explain the strong bond children form with the parent caregiver and the stress which results from separation from one another.

**Secure**
An attachment characterized by intense feelings of intimacy, emotional security, and physical safety when the infant is in the presence of another.

**Anxious-avoidant**
Attachment style resulting from trauma or neglect from parents.

FAMILY. Family plays a significant role in the development of one's identity. One theory that has received a great deal of attention from researchers studying the process of identity development is *attachment theory*. John Bowlby (1969, 1973) developed **attachment theory** in an attempt to explain the strong bond children form with the primary caregiver and the stress which results from separation from one another. Communication plays a pivotal role in creating the security associated with this attachment. Other theorists have expanded on the original theory advanced by Bowlby (1969) and typically recognize three different types of attachment relationships—*secure, anxious-avoidant*, and *anxious-ambivalent* (Ainsworth, Blehar, Waters, and Wall 1978).

When the primary caregiver behaves in a loving, supportive, and nurturing way towards her child, the child is likely to develop a secure attachment. A **secure** attachment is often "characterized by intense feelings of intimacy, emotional security, and physical safety when the infant is in the presence of the attachment figure" (Peluso, Peluso, White, and Kern 2004, 140). Because children raised in a secure environment typically have a history of responsive and supportive caretaking from their caregivers (Ainsworth et al. 1978), these experiences lead the children to believe that others will act in a supportive and caring way as well. Children who develop secure attachment styles are confident in their interpersonal relationships with their peers (Park and Waters 1988). Why is this the case? Bowlby (1973) and others (see, for example, Sroufe 1988) hold that children's first exposure to relationships is in the family context and that this experience helps them formulate expectations for subsequent relationships. Secure children, whose previous relationship experiences are generally positive, expect people in future encounters

© Losevsky Pavel, 2007, Shutterstock.

to act similarly, and therefore behave accordingly. Some research indicates that secure children recreate communication patterns and practices they experienced with their primary caregivers when interacting with peers, ultimately leading to more positive peer relationships (Sroufe 1988).

🔖 **Anxious-ambivalent** An attachment style resulting from inconsistent and irregular treatment from parents.

Conversely, individuals experiencing an insecure or anxious-avoidant attachment relationship with their primary caregiver often report trauma or neglect from their parents and exhibit significant developmental deficits (Peluso et al. 2004). Mothers of children who develop this attachment style act emotionally distant and rejecting, behaving with anger towards their children. Not surprisingly, this style of parenting can have long-term negative psychological and relational effects on individuals (Peluso et al. 2004). Unlike secure children, insecure children experience difficulty in forming relationships with others. Working from Bowlby's original theory (1973), insecure children, whose previous relationship experiences were negative, often develop a more negative "working model" of relationships and recreate negative communication patterns among peers. Some research supports this premise, with insecure children behaving more negatively and aggressively toward both known and unknown peers than secure children (Lieberman 1977; Sroufe 1988).

The third attachment style, labeled anxious-ambivalent, develops as a result of inconsistent and irregular treatment from parents (Ainsworth et al. 1978). Compared to secure children, those with anxious-ambivalent attachment styles experience more developmental delays, exhibit an unusual amount of conflict and confusion associated with their relationship with the primary caregiver, and are more accident prone (Ainsworth et al. 1978; Lieberman and Pawl 1988; Sroufe 1988). Both the anxious-avoidant and anxious-ambivalent attachment styles are problematic because children typically internalize perceptions of the self that are negative, which affect subsequent relationships with peers and romantic partners (Park and Waters 1988).

Communication with family members also affects how we define ourselves. Many of you have probably heard your parents describe your talents, personality traits, or other attributes in detail to other family members, friends, or even total strangers. **Direct definitions** are descriptions, or labels, families assign to its members that affect the way we see and define ourselves (Wood 2001). A child whose nickname is "slugger" may perceive herself to be an outstanding softball player. Consider the impact that the nickname "trouble" would have on a child's perception. Most of us can recall the way our family members referred to us and it is likely that many of these references were internalized. Researchers point out the significance of direct definitions by recognizing that positive labels can enhance our self-esteem while negative ones can have potentially deleterious effects on our self-perceptions (Wood 2001).

When you reflect back on your childhood, can you recall sayings or phrases that were repeated in your family? How about, "money does not grow on trees," "people who live in glass houses should not throw stones," "remember the golden rule," or "a family that prays together stays together?" Do any of these sayings sound familiar to you? Can you generate a list of phrases that were repeated in your family? These sayings are all examples of *identity scripts,* or rules for living and relating to one another in family contexts. Identity scripts help individuals to define who they are and how to relate to others (Berne 1964; Harris 1969). These phrases, which most have probably heard more than once, influence the way we relate to others and also our self-perceptions.

➤ **Identity scripts**
Rules for living and relating to one another in family contexts.

➤ **Attachment security hypothesis**
A hypothesis that states that individuals are attracted to and seek out peers and relationship partners who can provide them with a sense of security.

Have you ever compared your talents to those of your friends?

**PEER RELATIONSHIPS.** While family relationships are important and clearly affect the development of the self, other relationships, such as peers, also play a significant role in identity development (Park and Waters 1988). The *attachment security hypothesis,* based on Bowlby's (1973) work, states that individuals are attracted to and seek out peers and relationship partners that can provide them with a sense of security. Not surprisingly, peers, like parents, can also provide a sense of security and social support for one another. Some research indicates that attachment related functions are eventually transferred from parents to peers over time (Surra, Gray, Cottle, Boettcher 2004).

© paulaphoto, 2007, Shutterstock.

Research by Meeus and Dekovic (1995) supports the significance of peer relationships later in life and indicates that peers, to a certain extent, are even more influential than parents in the identity development of adolescents. According to researchers, as young children age and mature they also begin the process of separation and individuation from their parents. Children begin to socialize more frequently with their peers, and to protest when they are separated from them. They begin to discover that most of their peer interactions are characterized by qualities such as equality and symmetry. Peer relationships, which tend to be more egalitarian, soon become more important than parental relationships and tend to influence child-parent relationship expectations. As children grow and mature, they expect to form new relationships with their parents, also based on symmetry and equality. When these relationships do not progress as expected, adolescents become frustrated and perhaps even more bonded with their peers (Meeus and Dekovic 1995). While initially researchers suspected that peers were only influential in certain areas of identity formation, research by Meeus and Dekovic (1995) illustrates the impact of peers on the formation of relational, educational, and occupational identity. Not surprisingly, best friends exerted the greatest influence on one's development of relational identity while peers or colleagues exerted the greatest influence on occupational and educational identities.

Peer relationships are also important in defining the self because individuals often use peers as a means of personal assessment. It is not unusual for individuals to compare themselves to others to determine whether they are smart, attractive, athletic or successful. When individuals compare themselves to others in order to determine their abilities, strengths and weaknesses, they are engaging in the process of social comparison. Leon Festinger (1954) developed *social comparison theory.* This theory suggests that most individuals have a basic need, or drive, to evaluate and compare themselves to those around them. Festinger holds that one of the only ways of validating an evaluation of oneself is to find out if similar others agree with it (Tesser 2003). Thus, if a student wants to evaluate his ability in school, he will typically compare his abilities to those of his fellow similar classmates. How many of you immediately consult with your peers after receiving a test or paper grade?

**Social comparison theory**
A theory that suggests that most individuals have a basic need, or drive, to evaluate and compare themselves to those around them.

Another way that relationships with others affect the development of self is through a phenomenon called *behavioral confirmation,* or self-fulfilling prophecy (Aron 2003). Aron (2003) defines *self-fulfilling prophecy* as a process in which people act to conform to the expectations of others (see, for example, Darley and Fazio 1980). One of the classic studies that illustrated self-fulfilling prophecy was conducted in the classroom with teachers who were randomly informed that their students were academic overachievers. Academic performances improved significantly for those average students whose teachers were told that they were high achievers. Why did the students improve academically? Because the teachers communicated with the students as if they were overachievers, the students internalized these perspectives and acted accordingly (Snyder, Tanke, and Berscheid 1977). Researchers also found that previous relationship experiences can influence our expectations of new relationship partners' behaviors (see, for example, Andersen and Berensen 2001). Thus, if an individual experienced problems in previous relationships, he or she may expect similar negative experiences in the future and may circuitously contribute to how the relationship progresses.

**Behavioral confirmation/self-fulfilling prophecy**
Process in which people act to conform to the expectations of others.

Your intimate relationships have a major influence on how you view yourself.

**Relationship Partners.** Over time, the bond formed between partners in a romantic relationship is sure to affect the development of the self. One particularly interesting study provides further support for this statement. Researchers found that married couples come to look more alike over extended periods of time. Zajonc and his colleagues (1987) found students were more successful in matching pictures of couples married twenty-five years compared with pictures of the same couples, newly married.

Intimate relationships are also important to the development of the self because they influence how positively or negatively one views oneself (Aron 2003). Some recent research indicates that getting married and having children can actually increase an individual's feelings of selfworth (Shackelford 2001).

> **Similarity hypothesis**
> A hypothesis that states that we are most attracted to individuals who exhibit an attachment style similar to our own.

According to the *similarity hypothesis*, also related to Bowlby's research on attachment theory, we are most attracted to individuals that exhibit an attachment style similar to our own (Surra et al. 2004). Not surprisingly, researchers found that college students with secure attachment styles were more attracted to relationship partners that had also developed this attachment style. As the similarity hypothesis would predict, anxious-attachment individuals were also more likely to date anxious-attachment partners and to report being satisfied with these relationships (Surra et al. 2004). This research indicates that we often seek out individuals with similar attachment styles that also verify our perceptions of self-worth.

Relationships with family members, peers, and significant others affect the way we define ourselves and influence our evaluative perceptions of the self. Another way that we define ourselves, and simultaneously distinguish ourselves from others, is by describing our predominant personality traits.

In the second part of this chapter, we explore some of the ways people differ in how they communicate with others. While individual differences such as age, culture, ethnicity/race, sex/gender, and cognitive traits certainly affect the way we communicate. with others, interpersonal researchers have turned their attention to the powerful role that communication-based predispositions play in making sense of social phenomena (Daly 2002). In the next sections we discuss: (1) the impact of individual differences on social interaction, (2) differences between state and *trait approaches* to research, and (3) a number of personality traits that affect our communication with others. Because students are often interested in finding their scores on the communication-based personality instruments, we have included ways to measure many of the traits discussed in the chapter.

**Trait approach**
An approach to studying communication behaviors that attempts to identify enduring, or consistent, ways that people behave.

# THE IMPACT OF INDIVIDUAL DIFFERENCES ON SOCIAL INTERACTION

Most of us have interacted with someone we might label "difficult" because of his or her communication behaviors. It is not unusual for students to share stories of the "difficult" or "less-than-popular" roommate who lives with them. This roommate is often described as difficult because he acts in a consistently problematic manner or manages regularly to offend others. Not surprisingly, this roommate's poor behavior not only impacts all of the housemates, but also affects relationship partners, friends, classmates and neighbors that must hear about and interact with the difficult roommate. A number of authors have written books about dealing with difficult people (see, for example, Keating 1984). Dealing with difficult personality types is an important and relevant topic for a number of reasons: (1) we all have to deal with difficult people, whether at home, school, or work, (2) we might be one of those "difficult people" because we have communication challenges linked to our personality, and (3) asking an individual to completely change his or her personality is unreasonable and can damage relationships. Social psychologist John Gottman (1999) describes *perpetual conflict* as disagreements between relationship partners that are often directly related to personality issues. This type of conflict is pervasive and not easily fixed because it often involves fighting over matters that cannot be easily resolved, like differences in couples' personality traits. It is very frustrating when someone tells you, matter-of-factly, to "completely change your personality" in order to become a better relationship partner. We know that this unproductive criticism is an unreasonable request.

**Perpetual conflict**
Disagreements between relationship partners that are often directly related to personality issues.

When someone asks you repeatedly to change the same aspect of your personality, e.g., to talk more or to talk less, it is likely that this person is requesting a change in a personality trait. Much of the communication research conducted to date has adopted a trait approach to studying personality differences, which is quite different from a state approach.

# A COMPARISON OF TRAIT AND STATE APPROACHES TO RESEARCH

When communication researchers investigate differences in communication behaviors, they clarify whether they are studying these behaviors from either a trait or a state approach. When they adopt a state approach to studying communication behaviors, they examine how individuals communicate in a particular situation or context. For example, an interpersonal communication researcher might examine how individuals feel right before they ask someone out on a date. Researchers might measure an individual's state anxiety to determine if this affects his or her ability to advance a request for a date. Thus, when researchers adopt a state approach to communication research they examine situationally specific responses (Daly and Bippus 1998).

When researchers adopt a **trait approach**, they attempt to identify enduring, or consistent, ways that people behave. If a researcher adopts a trait approach to studying communication behaviors, it means that he is interested in examining how individuals interact the majority of the time. Guilford (1959) defines a trait as "any distinguishable, relatively enduring way in which one individual differs from another" (6). Daly and Bippus (1998) identify several conclusions about traits: (1) they define ways in which people differ, (2) they can be broad or narrow in focus, (3) some address social characteristics while others emphasize cognitively-oriented variables, and (4) some can be measured using questionnaires while others are recognized by observing behaviors. Daly and Bippus comment on the distinction between state and trait approaches in research by stating, "The differences between trait and state are, in actuality, primarily differences in emphasis. Personality scholars tend to emphasize the trait over the state" (2).

Why are communication scholars so interested in studying personality traits? Communication scholars study traits because they are related to communication variables in a number of different ways. For example, in the following sections of this chapter we will learn about individuals who are highly apprehensive about communicating with others. These individuals are described as having trait-CA (*Communication Apprehension*) because they are consistently apprehensive about communication with others. Explained another way, high CA individuals tend to exhibit high levels of apprehension across a wide range of situations and with varied persons. Not surprisingly, research indicates that these individuals tend to exhibit a variety of behavioral disruptions when forced to interact with others (Allen and Bourhis 1996). This example illustrates the relationship between a trait (CA) and communication variables (behavioral disruptions, stuttering, pauses, etc.).

> **Communication apprehension (CA)** An individual's level of fear or anxiety about either real or anticipated communication with another person or persons.

Because our *personality*, or predisposition to behave a certain way, is an important and relatively enduring part of how we see and define ourselves, interpersonal communication researchers are naturally interested in learning more about the impact of individual differences on social interaction. In addition, most researchers argue that communication behaviors linked to personality differences are explained, at least in part, by social learning; that is, we learn how to communicate by observing and imitating those around us. While a number of communication scholars have argued that one's genetic background best explains his or her personality predispositions (Beatty, McCroskey and Heisel 1998), it is still important to consider both explanations.

© Yuri Arcurs, 2007, Shutterstock.

**Personality**
Predisposition to behave a certain way.

Finally, by learning more about how individuals with specific personality traits approach social interaction, we can advance some predictive generalizations about how they interact and plan our own behaviors accordingly. You might ask, why do communication researchers not just study self-concept? Unlike one's self-concept, which is subjective and could change from moment to moment, one's personality is relatively stable and consistent over time. For example, if you complete one of the communication-based personality measures in this chapter today and then complete the same one a year from now, it is very likely that your scores will be highly similar or even the same. Learning more about communication behaviors that are trait-based helps researchers understand the impact of individual differences across different contexts. In the remaining sections of this chapter, we review research that adopts a trait or personality approach to studying differences in communication behaviors.

How is your communication affected by those around you?

# COMMUNICATION APPREHENSION AND WILLINGNESS TO COMMUNICATE

In John Maxwell's (2002) book, *The Seventeen Essential Qualities of a Team Player*, he emphasizes communication as one of the most important skills needed for succeeding in teams. Other essential skills included in his list are adaptability, collaboration, enthusiasm, and the ability to establish relationships with team members. Not surprisingly, all of these qualities also require strong

Highly apprehensive individuals are more stressed and lonely than those who are low in communication apprehension.

communication skills. Maxwell and countless other authors from a variety of academic and professional fields emphasize the relationship between communication skills and success at work. Throughout our own textbook we continually emphasize the link between communication and relationship stability and professional success. However, what if you are not comfortable communicating with others? If you or someone you know often avoids talking in most situations and with most people, it is likely that this individual would score high in communication apprehension and low in willingness to communicate. In the following sections, we examine these two related communication-based personality traits. For each communicationbased personality trait we provide a general overview of the construct, describe ways to reliably measure the trait, and discuss research on the link between the personality trait and communication behaviors. Because high levels of communication apprehension can be extremely debilitating for individuals, treatment options are also discussed.

Approximately one in five individuals in the United States is considered high in communication apprehension (McCroskey 2006). For highly apprehensive individuals, even anticipated communication with others evokes a significant amount of stress and psychological discomfort (McCroskey, Daly, and Sorensen 1976). James McCroskey (1977) conducted the seminal research in this area and defines **communication apprehension** as an "individual's level of fear or anxiety with either real or anticipated communication with another person or persons" (78). Communication apprehension (CA) can be measured in a variety of ways, but is frequently assessed using the Personal Report of Communication Apprehension (PRCA) developed by McCroskey (1978). The PRCA is a twenty-four-item five point Likert-type measure that assesses individuals' communication apprehension in general, as well as across four different areas: public, small group, meeting, and interpersonal/dyadic situations (see Applications at the end of this chapter). Individuals scoring high on the PRCA are generally quite anxious about communicating with others and will attempt to avoid interaction. Highly apprehensive individuals are less communicatively competent, less disclosive, and are more stressed and lonely than individuals low in communication apprehension (Miczo 2004; Zakahi and Duran 1985). Highly apprehensive college students are more likely to be considered "at risk" in college settings (Lippert, Titsworth, and Hunt 2005) and are less likely to emerge as leaders in work groups (Limon and La France 2005).

*Willingness to communicate* (WTC) is similar to communication apprehension because it also taps into an individual's propensity to avoid or approach communication with others. The willingness to communicate construct does not assess fear or anxiety, only one's tendency to approach or avoid communication in varied situations and with varied persons. McCroskey and Richmond (1987) coined the term willingness to communicate (WTC) and describe this construct as a person's tendency to initiate communication with others (McCroskey and Richmond 1998). WTC is further described as a "personality-based, trait-like predisposition which is relatively consistent across a variety of communication contexts and types of receivers" (McCroskey and Richmond 1987, 134). WTC can be measured via the WTC scale, which is a twenty-item measure that assesses an individual's willingness to interact with different individuals in different situations (see Applications section at the end of this chapter). Individuals completing the WTC scale indicate the percent of time they would choose to communicate in public, during a meeting, within a group, in a dyad, with a stranger, and in situations with acquaintances. For example, individuals are asked to indicate how often they would "talk with a service station attendant" or "talk with a physician." When individuals consistently indicate that they would not want to talk in most of the contexts listed, they are described as low in WTC. Conversely, individuals who indicate that they are willing to interact with others in a wide range of contexts are described as high in WTC.

> **Willingness to communicate**
> A construct that assesses one's tendency to approach or avoid communication in varied situations and with varied persons.

Not surprisingly, highly apprehensive individuals are more likely to be low in WTC. Richmond and Roach (1992) summarize a significant body of research on the benefits and drawbacks for employees described as quiet, or low in WTC. First, they identify several positive factors associated with lower WTC. For example, individuals reporting lower WTC are typically less likely to initiate or perpetuate gossip and are also less likely to emerge as "squeaky wheels" within the organization. In addition, quiet individuals are less likely to take long breaks, unlike their more social high WTC counterparts. Finally, individuals with lower WTC are more likely to be discreet than more talkative individuals. Thus, organizations do not have to worry as much about quiet individuals sharing corporate secrets or new developments.

While there are some benefits of employing quiet individuals, Richmond and Roach (1992) note that, in general, quiet employees "are considered at risk in an organizational setting" for various reasons (Richmond and Roach 1992). More often than not, quiet individuals are perceived as less competent and intelligent because they do not contribute to discussions or share their accomplishments with others. Consequently, quiet employees are often mislabeled as incompetent and lacking business savvy. Research indicates that we tend to formulate negative impressions of employees who are quiet and, as a result, they are often less likely to get interviewed or considered for promotions. In research by Daly, Richmond, and Leth (1979), it was found that when individuals were described as quiet or shy in recommendation letters, they were less likely to be granted interviews than highly verbal individuals. Unfortunately, low WTC individuals may be more likely to experience the "last hired" and "first fired" syndrome than their high WTC counterparts (Richmond and Roach 1992).

What can be done to help individuals who are either high in CA or low in WTC? There is a significant amount of research that has identified treatment options for high CA individuals. Communication apprehension can be treated with methods similar to other types of phobias and neurotic anxieties (Berger, McCroskey, and Richmond 1984). According to McCroskey and his associates (1984), high levels of CA can be overcome or managed by applying three widely accepted treatment options. If these treatment options are not available, "there are other options available for individuals in the absence of these more formal treatments" (153). The three primary treatment options available for individuals high in communication apprehension are systematic desensitization, cognitive modification, and skills training.

**Systematic desensitization**
A type of behavior modification derived from learning theory that is used to treat individuals with high levels of CA.

**Cognitive modification**
A method of managing high levels of CA—the rationale for which is that people have learned to think negatively about themselves and how they communicate—that involves teaching the individual to think positively about him- or herself.

**Skills training**
A method of managing high levels of CA that involves taking courses to help an individual learn to communicate more effectively.

One of the most effective means of treating high levels of CA is *systematic desensitization* (SD), a type of behavior modification derived from learning theory. Eighty to ninety percent of individuals who use systematic desensitization eliminate completely their high level or fear or anxiety. The basic premise behind systematic desensitization is that anxiety related to communication is learned and, as such, can be unlearned. *Cognitive modification*, also based on learning theory, is the second method of managing high levels of CA. "The underlying rationale for this treatment is that people have learned to think negatively about themselves, in this case, how they communicate, and can be taught to think positively" (Berger et al. 1984). The third and least successful way to treat high levels of CA is skills training. Skills training, when used as the sole method, is typically considered the least effective method for treating high levels of CA. Communication *skills training* might involve taking courses to help individuals learn to communicate more effectively. For example, individuals may take public speaking courses to improve their ability to design and deliver speeches. Experts recommend that persons with high levels of communication apprehension first employ systematic desensitization or cognitive modification as a means of reducing their anxiety and then participate in skills training courses to help manage deficient communication skills. Whether you or someone you know is highly apprehensive about communication, it is important to note that the tendency to fear communication can be treated successfully.

# AGGRESSIVE BEHAVIOR

Infante (1987a) recognizes a behavior as aggressive when it "applies force... symbolically in order, minimally to dominate and perhaps damage, or maximally to defeat and perhaps destroy the locus of attack" (58). He further explains that there are two types of aggressive behavior; he labels them destructive and constructive. *Destructive forms of aggression* are those that can potentially damage individual's self-esteem or, to use Infante's words "destroy the locus of attack." Two widely recognized types of destructive aggression are hostility and verbal aggression.

## *Hostility*

*Hostility* is defined as "using symbols (verbal or nonverbal) to express irritability, negativism, resentment, and suspicion" (Infante 1988, 7). When someone expresses hostility, he or she might say, "I am so angry I did not get chosen for the lacrosse team and I blame the selection committee!" Individuals presenting hostile personalities generally devalue the worth and motives of others, are highly suspicious of others, feel in opposition with those around them, and often feel a desire to inflict harm or see others harmed (Smith 1994). One way to measure hostility is to use Cook-Medley Hostility Scale (Cook and Medley 1954) which is one of the most commonly used means of assessing trait hostility and appears to have construct, predictive, and discriminant validity (Huebner, Nemeroff, and Davis 2005; Pope, Smith, and Rhodewalt 1990). Sample items on the hostility measure are "I think most people will lie to get ahead," and "It is safer to trust nobody." Individuals completing the hostility measure indicate the extent to which they either agree or disagree with the statements using a five-point Likert scale.

Needless to say, feeling consistently hostile toward others affects the way one views the world and impacts relationships with others. Hostile individuals tend to be quite unhappy individuals who are more likely to report depression and lower self-esteem (Kopper and Epperson 1996). From a communication perspective, researchers try to accurately identify people or communication situations that evoke feelings of hostility in order to better understand this construct. If we can identify the types of situations or people that cause others to feel hostile, perhaps we can make attempts to modify or improve these situations. Recent research by Chory-Assad and Paulsel (2004) examined the relationship between students' perceptions of justice in college classrooms and student aggression and hostility toward their instructors. As expected, when students felt instructors were not fair in regard to course policies, scheduling, testing, amount of work, etc., they were more likely to feel hostile toward their teachers. Now that we know that perceptions of injustice in

> **Destructive forms of aggression**
> Forms of aggression that can potentially damage an individual's self-esteem or, in Infante's words, "destroy the locus of attack."

> **Hostility**
> Use of symbols (verbal or nonverbal) to express irritability, negativism, resentment, and suspicion.

Verbally aggressive attacks can permanently damage relationships.

college classrooms leads to greater hostility in students, we can make recommendations on how to alter these situations and to reduce hostile reactions.

Hostile individuals are more likely to experience problems in committed romantic relationships. Rogge (2006) and his colleagues examined communication, hostility, and neuroticism as predictors of marital stability and found that couples were less likely to stay together when spouses reported higher levels of hostility and neuroticism. The researchers noted that while communication skills distinguished those who were married-satisfied and those who were married-unsatisfied, they did not always predict marital dissolution. It is important to note that hostility and neuroticism "contribute to a rapid, early decline in marital functioning" (Rogge et al. 2006, 146). In addition, an inability to empathize with relationship partners and manage conflict in a productive way may negatively impact future chances at relationship success. From an interpersonal communication perspective, it is important to determine the kinds of behaviors that elicit feelings of hostility from others, to then reduce or eliminate those behaviors, and to attempt to repair the damaged relationship using relationship maintenance strategies.

## Verbal Aggression

Another personality trait labeled difficult, or problematic, during face-to-face encounters is verbal aggression. When individuals lack the ability to effectively argue, they often resort to verbally aggressive communication. Wigley (1998) describes *verbal aggressiveness* as the tendency to attack the self-concept of an individual instead of addressing the other person's arguments. Dominic Infante (1987; 1995) identified a wide range of messages that verbally aggressive communicators use. For example, verbally aggressive communicators may resort to character attacks, competence attacks, background attacks, physical appearance attacks, maledictions, teasing, swearing, ridiculing, threatening, and nonverbal emblems. On occasion, they might also use blame, personality attacks, commands, global rejection, negative comparison, and sexual harassment in their attempts to hurt others. As Wigley (1998) notes, "there seems to be no shortage of ways to cause other people to feel badly about themselves" (192).

**⇒ Verbal aggressiveness**
The tendency to attack the self-concept of an individual instead of addressing the other person's arguments.

Infante and Wigley (1986) developed the Verbal Aggressiveness Scale, which is a twenty item self-report personality test that asks people to indicate whether they are verbally aggressive in their interactions (found in Applications at the end of this chapter). Infante and Wigley were aware of the fact that people might not self-report their use of aggression. With this in mind, the researchers designed items on the measure to make it seem like they approved of aggressive messages. The researchers developed the Verbal Aggressiveness instrument to learn more about the behavior of people who were verbally aggressive.

For those of us who have ever interacted with someone who is highly verbally aggressive, one of the more common questions is why this person acts this way. There are a number of viable explanations for why some individuals possess trait verbal aggressiveness. Individuals may be verbally aggressive because they learned this behavior from others. Thus, social learning, or modeling effects explain why verbally aggressive parents have children that also become verbally aggressive. Another explanation for this trait is that verbally aggressive individuals lack the ability to argue effectively and, as a result, are more likely to become frustrated during arguments. The inability to defend one's position is frustrating and often causes the highly aggressive person to lash out at others. In this case, trait levels of verbal aggression are linked to argument skill deficiency (ASD). Researchers note that if verbal aggression is linked to ASD, then one way to combat this problem is to train individuals in effective argumentation (Wigley 1998).

There are a number of significant negative consequences for individuals who regularly communicate in verbally aggressive ways. Verbally aggressive individuals are more likely to use a variety of antisocial behaviors and, as a result, are less liked (Myers and Johnson 2003). Research by Infante, Riddle, Horvath, and Tumlin (1992) compared individuals who were high and low in verbal aggressiveness to determine how often they used different verbally aggressive messages, how hurtful they perceived these messages to be, and their reasons for using verbally aggressive messages. Individuals who were high in verbal aggressiveness were more likely to use a wide range of verbally aggressive messages (e.g., competence attacks, teasing, and nonverbal emblems). High verbal aggressives were less likely than low verbal aggressives to perceive threats, competence attacks, and physical appearance attacks as hurtful. When high verbal aggressives were asked to explain their behavior, they stated that they were angry, did not like the target, were taught to be aggressive, were in a bad mood, or were just being humorous. Wanzer and her colleagues (1995) found that verbally aggressive individuals are less socially attractive and more likely to target others in humor attempts than to target themselves. Their inappropriate use of humor may explain why acquaintances rate them as less socially attractive.

College students scoring high in verbal aggressiveness were more likely to be considered academically at risk in college settings than students scoring low in verbal aggressiveness (Lippert et al. 2005). Lippert and his colleagues (2005) call for more research to understand why verbally aggressive college students are more academically at risk. They suspect that verbally aggressive students' inappropriate classroom behavior may lead to negative evaluations from teachers and peers. Consistently negative experiences in the classroom may contribute to verbally aggressive students' at risk status.

What can be done to help high aggressives? From a communication perspective, it is important to recognize when we are being verbally aggressive with others and to attempt to eliminate these behaviors. Recognize that when you communicate in a verbally aggressive way, others may model your behavior. Have you ever had a younger sibling mimic your verbal or nonverbal messages? There is a substantial amount of research on this trait and the potentially negative effects of high amounts of verbal aggression on relationships in married (Infante, Chandler, and Rudd 1989), family (Bayer and Cegala 1992), and organizational contexts (Infante and Gorden 1991). If you are predisposed to using verbal aggression, enroll in courses that might help you improve your ability to argue. One of the most widely recognized ways to address or treat verbal aggression is to train individuals who are skill deficient in argumentation to defend their positions more effectively.

Next, we turn our attention to several communication-based personality traits that may help individuals communicate more effectively during social interaction. More specifically, we examine argumentativeness, assertiveness, humor orientation, and affective orientation.

# CONSTRUCTIVE AGGRESSIVE BEHAVIOR

**Constructive forms of aggression** Forms of aggression that are more active than passive, that help us achieve our communication goals and do not involve personal attacks.

Argumentativeness and assertiveness are described by Infante as *constructive forms of aggression*. Both of these behaviors are considered constructive forms of aggression because they are more active than passive, help us achieve our communication goals, and do not involve personal attacks (Rancer 1998). For some individuals, arguing with friends, colleagues, or family members is considered enjoyable and challenging. For others, arguing leads to hurt feelings, confusion, or even anger.

## Argumentativeness

According to Rancer, individuals vary extensively in their perceptions of argumentative behavior. Infante and Rancer (1982) define *argumentativeness* as "a generally stable trait which predisposes individuals in communication situations to advocate positions on controversial issues and to attack verbally the positions which other people hold on these issues" (72). When individuals are argumentative, they attack issues and positions. When individuals are verbally aggressive, they attack others by using competence or character attacks, or possibly even swearing. When someone exhibits high levels of argumentativeness, they are able to both advocate and defend positions on controversial issues. Infante and Rancer (1982) developed the Argumentativeness Scale, which is a twenty-item Likert-type scale that asks people to record how they feel about responding to controversial issues. Ten items on the scale assess motivation to approach argumentative situations and ten items assess motivation to avoid argumentative situations (see Applications section at the end of this chapter).

> **Argumentativeness**
> A generally stable trait that predisposes individuals in communication situations to advocate positions on controversial issues and to verbally attack the positions other people hold on these issues.

There are a number of benefits associated with argumentativeness. Highly argumentative individuals are more effective in their attempts to persuade others. They employ a wider range of persuasion and social influence tactics and tend to be more tenacious in their persuasion attempts (Boster and Levine 1988). Highly argumentative individuals are more resistant to compliance attempts from others and generate more counterarguments in response to persuasive encounters (Infante 1981; Kazoleas 1993). Argumentative individuals are viewed as more credible and competent communicators who are also more interested in communicating with others (Infante 1981; 1985). More recently, research by Limon and La France (2005) explored communicator traits associated with leadership emergence in work groups. As predicted by their hypotheses, college student participants low in CA and high in argumentativeness were more likely to emerge as leaders in work groups than students high in CA and low in argumentativeness. These findings illustrate the significance of this communication skill as it relates to one's potential to become a leader.

As mentioned previously, the inability to argue effectively is extremely problematic for individuals and for relationships. Research by Andonian and Droge (1992) linked males' reported verbal aggressiveness to date rape, which is an especially aggressive form of interpersonal behavior. They found that males' tendency to report acceptance of date rape myths, e.g., females might say no to sexual intercourse but really mean yes, was positively related to verbal aggressiveness and negatively related to argumentativeness. Again, this study, like others, emphasizes the constructive nature of argumentativeness and the destructive nature of verbal aggression. Similarly, in the organizational setting, the best conditions for organizational communication are when managers and employees are both high in argumentativeness and low in verbal aggression (Infante and Gorden 1987; 1989). Research on the benefits of argumentativeness in organizational contexts supports the notion of ***independent-mindedness***, which refers to the extent to which employees can openly express their own opinions at work (Rancer 1998). The research on the benefits of argumentativeness in different contexts illustrates the significance of this skill.

**Independent-mindedness**
The extent to which employees can openly express their own opinions at work.

Can we train individuals to argue more constructively? A number of programs have achieved successful results in training individuals to improve their ability to argue effectively. Anderson, Schultz, and Staley (1987) implemented cognitive training in argument and conflict management to encourage individuals to argue with one another. For individuals who are low in argumentativeness, this can be a daunting task. The researchers were pleased that they were able to see results from females who were low in argumentativeness. This study, as well as others, indicates that individuals can be trained to argue more effectively.

## Assertiveness

**Assertiveness**
The capability to defend one's own rights and wishes while still respecting and acknowledging the rights of others.

How can assertive behavior contribute to individual success?

Another form of constructive aggression is ***assertiveness***, which is defined as the capability to defend your own rights and wishes while still respecting and acknowledging the rights of others. When individuals act in an assertive

© Yuri Arcurs, 2007, Shutterstock.

way, they stand up for themselves and are able to initiate, maintain, and terminate conversations to reach interpersonal goals (Richmond and Martin 1998). One way to measure assertiveness is by using the Socio-Communicative Orientation Scale developed by Richmond and McCroskey (1990). This measure includes ten assertiveness items and ten responsiveness items. Individuals are asked to report how accurately the items apply to them when they communicate with others. Some examples of assertive characteristics include: defends own beliefs, independent, and forceful. Individuals use Likert-type responses to indicate whether they strongly agree or strongly disagree that these characteristics apply to them (see the Applications section at the end of this chapter).

There are innumerable benefits associated with the assertiveness trait. By acting in an assertive manner, individuals are able to defend themselves, establish relationships, and take advantage of opportunities. Richmond and Martin (1998) note that assertive communication is more beneficial than aggressive communication and can lead to "long-term effectiveness while maintaining good relationships with others" (136). Assertive individuals are perceived as more confident and self-assured and often rated as more effective teachers and managers than unassertive individuals. When it comes to practicing safe sex, sexually assertive males are more likely than unassertive males to use condoms to protect themselves (Noar, Morokoff, and Redding 2002). Researchers say that increasing sexual assertiveness in males may lead to long-term increases in safer sexual behaviors (Noar et al. 2002).

## *Humor Orientation*

Booth-Butterfield and Booth-Butterfield (1991) developed the concept of *humor orientation* and define it as the extent to which people use humor as well as their self-perceived appropriateness of humor production. Humor orientation (HO) can be measured using the Humor Orientation Scale (found in the Applications section at the end of this chapter), which is a seventeenitem questionnaire that assesses how often people use humor in their day-to-day communication and how effective they are at enacting humorous messages. When developing the HO measure, M. Booth-Butterfield and S. Booth-Butterfield (1991) examined the different types of humorous communication behaviors people used when they were attempting to be funny. They found that individuals scoring higher on the HO measure (also called high HO's) accessed more categories of humorous communication behaviors such as nonverbal techniques, language, expressivity, and impersonation. Persons who enacted humor frequently and effectively perceived themselves as funny, and utilized a variety of humorous communication behaviors across diverse situations. Wanzer, Booth-Butterfield, and Booth-Butterfield (1995) later confirmed that high humor-oriented people were perceived by others as funnier than low HO's when telling jokes. Thus, being humorous is not simply in the eye of the high HO.

> **Humor orientation**
> The extent to which people use humor as well as their self-perceived appropriateness of humor production.

There appear to be a variety of intrapersonal and interpersonal benefits associated with the humor orientation trait. For example, high HO's are typically less lonely (Wanzer et al. 1996a), are more adaptable in their communication with others, have greater concern for eliciting positive impressions from others, and are more affectively oriented, i.e., are more likely to use their emotions to guide their communication decisions (Wanzer et. al. 1995). Honeycutt and Brown (1998) found that traditional marital types, which usually report the highest levels of marital satisfaction (Fitzpatrick 1988), were also higher in HO than other types.

When managers are perceived as more humor-oriented by their employees, they are also viewed as more likable and effective (Rizzo, Wanzer, and Booth-Butterfield

Humor can add more than just laughs to the work environment.

1999). Not surprisingly, there are a number of benefits for teachers who use humor effectively in the classroom. For example, students report learning more from instructors perceived as humor-oriented (Wanzer and Frymier 1999) and also report engaging in more frequent communication outside of class with humor-oriented teachers (Aylor and Opplinger 2003).

More recently, researchers have examined whether high humor-oriented individuals are more likely than low humor-oriented individuals to use humor to cope with stress and whether they benefit from this "built in" coping mechanism (Booth-Butterfield, Booth-Butterfield, and Wanzer 2006; 2005). In two different, yet similar studies, employed participants reported their HO, whether they used humor to cope with stressful situations, coping efficacy, and job satisfaction. The researchers speculated that individuals employed in highly stressful jobs, such as nursing, would: (1) benefit from the ability to cope using humor, and (2) would vary in this ability based on HO scores (Wanzer et al. 2005). Nurses who reported higher HO were more likely than low HO nurses to use humor to cope with stressful work situations and to perceive their coping strategies as effective (higher coping efficacy). In addition, humor-oriented nurses reported greater coping efficacy, leading to higher job satisfaction. Researchers found the same relationships between HO, coping and job satisfaction in a similar study of employed college students (Booth-Butterfield, Booth- Butterfield, and Wanzer 2006). These studies illustrate how humor can help individuals cope with difficult or stressful situations.

Can we train people to use humor more appropriately and effectively? Perhaps. We know that people often participate in improv classes and classes on stand-up comedy to improve their ability to deliver humorous messages. It seems likely that if people understand why certain messages are universally perceived as funny, they could be trained to improve their ability to deliver humorous messages with greater success. For now, researchers who study humor and the effects of humor recommend that individuals avoid using any type of humor based on stereotypes, or humor viewed as racist, sexist, ageist, or homophobic. Individuals need to be aware of audience characteristics that influence the way humorous content is interpreted and make attempts to use humor that is innocuous. For example, individuals who want to incorporate more humor into their day-to-day communication may use more self-disparaging humor, making certain not to overuse this type of humor as it may damage one's credibility.

## Affective Orientation

*Affective orientation* refers to the extent to which individuals are aware of their own emotional states and use them when making behavioral decisions (Booth-Butterfield and Booth-Butterfield 1990). Individuals described as affectively oriented tend to be quite aware of their affective states and consult them before acting. Conversely, individuals described as low in affective orientation tend to be relatively unaware of their emotions and tend to reject their emotions as useful (Booth-Butterfield and Booth-Butterfield 1998). Affective Orientation (AO) can be measured via the Affective Orientation (AO15) Scale which is a fifteen-item instrument used to assess the extent to which individuals are aware of and consult their affective states and can be found in the Applications section at the end of this chapter. The revised fifteen-item measure "offers a more definitionally focused and concise operationalization of AO, exhibits minimal gender differences in mean scores and it is psychometrically more sound than the original AO scale" (Booth-Butterfield and Booth-Butterfield 1998, 180).

What kind of campaign might work to persuade this individual to quit smoking?

>= **Affective orientation**
The extent to which individuals are aware of their own emotional states and use them when making behavioral decisions.

What are some of the benefits and/or drawbacks of higher AO? Individuals that exhibit higher levels of AO tend to be more nonverbally sensitive and better at providing comfort to others (Booth-Butterfield and Andrighetti 1993; Dolin and Booth-Butterfield 1993). Interestingly, individuals with higher AO also tend to utilize humor more frequently than lower AO individuals (Wanzer et al. 1995). The researchers suspect that higher AO individuals might use humor as one method of treating or managing negative affective states. From a relationship perspective, higher AO individuals tend to be more romantic and idealistic in their beliefs about intimate relationships (Booth-Butterfield and Booth-Butterfield 1994). More recent research on AO has examined the relationship between this trait and health behaviors. Specifically, researchers have been examining the relationships between AO and specific health practices such as smoking. Higher AO individuals are more likely to smoke than low AO's (Booth-Butterfield and Booth-Butterfield 1998). These findings are important and can be used to formulate successful persuasive campaigns. For example, the researchers note that since smokers are more affectively oriented, persuasive prevention campaigns should generate negative affective states (e.g., fear) and then connect them in some way to smoking (Booth-Butterfield and Booth-Butterfield 1998).

Individuals may reap a variety of personal and interpersonal benefits when they exhibit higher levels of argumentativeness, assertiveness, humor orientation, and affective orientation. While these traits are not the only ones that have proven to be beneficial for sources (e.g., cognitive complexity), they are studied frequently, and can be assessed via self-report instruments, and are linked to other positive traits and characteristics.

## CHAPTER SUMMARY

The goal of this chapter was to help you learn more about the complex, evolving, and multidimensional nature of the self. To learn more about who we are and why we act a certain way, we explored the role of interpersonal communication and relationships in identity formation. Communication with family members, peers, and relationship partners influences how we see ourselves and how we relate to others. Our personality differences also affect the way we relate to others. In this chapter we discussed differences between state and trait approaches to studying personality and the connection between personality traits and communication behaviors. Communication based personality traits such as CA, WTC, hostility, verbal aggression, argumentativeness, assertiveness, humor orientation, and affective orientation were discussed in this chapter. Some of the behaviors associated with these communication traits can be problematic for both sources and receivers. We hope that after reading this chapter you now have a better understanding of these traits and how some can either hinder or facilitate our communication with others.

## APPLICATIONS

### *Discussion Questions*

A. Write about or discuss in small groups the person/persons that were most influential in your life. What other individuals play a role in the process of identity formation that were not identified in this chapter?

B. Visit several websites that offer suggestions for improving one's self-esteem. Critique these websites based on the following criteria: (1) Quality and quantity of information presented, (2) Inclusion of a discussion of both the pros and cons of high and low self-esteem, (3) Credentials of the individuals posting these sites, and (4) Ease of navigation of these sites. Based on your analysis of these sites, would you use these sites or send friends to these sites for information?

C. Complete one or more of the following personality measures and score them:
- Personal Report of Communication Apprehension http://www.hawaii. edu/gened/oc/PRCA-24.pdf
- Verbal Aggressiveness Scale http://commfaculty.fullerton.edu/rgass/335%20 Fall2001/Aggressiveness%20Scale.htm
- Argumentativeness Scale http://commfaculty.fullerton.edu/rgass/argume-ntativeness_scale1.htm
- Assertiveness-Responsiveness Measure http://www.as.wvu.edu/~richmond/ measures/sociocommunicative.pdf
- Humor Orientation Scale http://healthyinfluence.com/wordpress/2009/07/17/ the-humor-orientation-scale-original-17-item-version/
- Affective Orientation Scale http://www.as.wvu.edu/~mbb/ao21.htm

Recruit a friend that knows you quite well to complete the measure based on how the friend perceives your communication behaviors. Next, draw comparisons between self and other reports of the communication-based personality assessments. After examining the self and other reports closely, write about the following: (1) Are there similarities in the self and other reports, (2) Are there differences in the self and other reports, (3) Are these scores valid—do they accurately explain your communication tendencies, (4) After completing these assessments, do you feel it is necessary to change any aspect of communication behaviors? Why or why not?

# ACTIVITIES

## *Willingness to Communicate Scale (WTC)*

Below are twenty situations in which a person might or might not choose to communicate. Presume you have completely free choice. Indicate the percentage of times you would choose to communicate in each type of situation. Indicate in the space at the left what percent of the time you would choose to communicate.

0=never, 100=always

|        |     |                                                    |
|--------|-----|----------------------------------------------------|
| _____ | 1.  | Talk with a service station attendant.             |
| _____ | 2.  | Talk with a physician.                             |
| _____ | 3.  | Present a talk to a group of strangers.            |
| _____ | 4.  | Talk with an acquaintance while standing in line.  |
| _____ | 5.  | Talk with a salesperson in a store.                |
| _____ | 6.  | Talk in a large meeting of friends.                |
| _____ | 7.  | Talk with a police officer.                        |
| _____ | 8.  | Talk in a small group of strangers.                |
| _____ | 9.  | Talk with a friend while standing in line.         |

Source: Richmond, V. P. and J. C. McCroskey. 1995. Communication: Apprehension, avoidance, and effectiveness. (4th ed.). Scottsdale, AZ: Gorsuch Scarisbrick.

|       | 10. | Talk with a waiter/waitress in a restaurant. |
|-------|-----|----------------------------------------------|
|       | 11. | Talk in a large meeting of acquaintances. |
|       | 12. | Talk with a stranger while standing in line. |
|       | 13. | Talk with a secretary. |
|       | 14. | Present a talk to a group of friends. |
|       | 15. | Talk in a small group of acquaintances. |
|       | 16. | Talk with a garbage collector. |
|       | 17. | Talk in a large meeting of strangers. |
|       | 18. | Talk with a spouse (or girl/boyfriend) |
|       | 19. | Talk in a small group of friends. |
|       | 20. | Present a talk to a group of acquaintances. |

SCORING: To calculate the total WTC score follow these steps:

Step 1: Add scores for items 3, 8, 12, and 17; then divide by 4.

Step 2: Add scores for items 4, 11, 15, and 20; then divide by 4.

Step 3: Add scores for items 6, 9, 14, and 19; then divide by 4.

Step 4: Add the final scores from steps 1, 2, and 3; then divide by 3.

>82 High overall WTC

<52 Low overall WTC

*Affective orientation* The extent to which individuals are aware of their own emotional states and use them when making behavioral decisions.

*Anxious-ambivalent* An attachment style resulting from inconsistent and irregular treatment from parents.

*Anxious-avoidant* Attachment style resulting from trauma or neglect from parents.

*Argumentativeness* A generally stable trait that predisposes individuals in communication situations to advocate positions on controversial issues and to verbally attack the positions other people hold on these issues.

*Assertiveness* The capability to defend one's own rights and wishes while still respecting and acknowledging the rights of others.

*Attachment security hypothesis* A hypothesis that states that individuals are attracted to and seek out peers and relationship partners who can provide them with a sense of security.

*Attachment theory* A theory that attempts to explain the strong bond children form with the parent caregiver and the stress which results from separation from one another.

*Behavioral confirmation/self-fulfilling prophecy* Process in which people act to conform to the expectations of others.

*Cognitive modification* A method of managing high levels of CA—the rationale for which is that people have learned to think negatively about themselves and how they communicate—that involves teaching the individual to think positively about him- or herself.

*Communication apprehension (CA)* An individual's level of fear or anxiety about either real or anticipated communication with another person or persons.

*Constructive forms of aggression* Forms of aggression that are more active than passive, that help us achieve our communication goals and do not involve personal attacks.

*Destructive forms of aggression* Forms of aggression that can potentially damage an individual's self-esteem or, in Infante's words, "destroy the locus of attack."

*Hostility* Use of symbols (verbal or nonverbal) to express irritability, negativism, resentment, and suspicion.

*Humor orientation* The extent to which people use humor as well as their self-perceived appropriateness of humor production.

*Identity scripts* Rules for living and relating to one another in family contexts.

*Independent-mindedness* The extent to which employees can openly express their own opinions at work.

*Inner self* The self we keep private and that may reflect how we really feel about ourselves.

*Perpetual conflict* Disagreements between relationship partners that are often directly related to personality issues.

*Personality* Predisposition to behave a certain way.

*Public self* The self we project during social interaction.

*Reflected appraisal/looking glass self* A metaphor that describes the impact of interpersonal communication on the development of self.

*Secure* An attachment characterized by intense feelings of intimacy, emotional security, and physical safety when the infant is in the presence of another.

*Self-complexity* Defined by the number of self-aspects or sub-selves a person possesses.

*Self-concept* A cognitive construct that is a "descriptive reference to the self, or a definition of the nature and beliefs about the self's qualities."

*Self-esteem* Subjective perception of one's self-worth, or the value one places on the self.

*Self-regulation* The capacity to exercise choice and initiation.

*Self* A psychological entity consisting of "an organized set of beliefs, feelings, and behaviors."

*Similarity hypothesis* A hypothesis that states that we are most attracted to individuals who exhibit an attachment style similar to our own.

*Skills training* A method of managing high levels of CA that involves taking courses to help an individual learn to communicate more effectively.

*Social comparison theory* A theory that suggests that most individuals have a basic need, or drive, to evaluate and compare themselves to those around them.

*State approach* An approach to studying communication behaviors that involves examining how individuals communicate in a particular situation or context.

*Systematic desensitization* A type of behavior modification derived from learning theory that is used to treat individuals with high levels of CA.

*Trait approach* An approach to studying communication behaviors that attempts to identify enduring, or consistent, ways that people behave.

*Verbal aggressiveness* The tendency to attack the self-concept of an individual instead of addressing the other person's arguments.

*Willingness to communicate* A construct that assesses one's tendency to approach or avoid communication in varied situations and with varied persons.

# REFERENCES

Ainsworth, M.D.S., M.C. Blehar, E. Waters, and S. Wall. 1978. *Patterns of attachment: A psychological study of the strange situation.* Hillsdale, NJ: Erlbaum.

Allen, M., and J. Bourhis. 1996. The relationship of communication apprehension to communication behavior: A meta-analysis. *Communication Quarterly, 44,* 214–226.

Andersen, S.M., and K. Berensen. 2001. Perceiving, feeling, and wanting: Motivation and affect deriving from significant other representations and transference. In J.P. Forgas, K.D. Williams, and L. Wheeler (Eds.), *The social mind: Cognitive and motivational aspects of interpersonal behavior* (231–256). New York: Cambridge University Press.

Anderson, J., B. Schultz, and C. Courtney Staley. 1987. Training in argumentativeness: New hope for nonassertive women. *Women's Studies in Communication, 10,* 58–66.

Andonian, K.K., and D. Droge. 1992. *Verbal aggressiveness and sexual violence in dating relationships: An exploratory study of antecedents of date rape.* Paper presented at the annual meeting of the Speech Communication Association, Chicago, IL.

Aron, A. 2003. Self and close relationships. In M.R. Leary and J.P. Tangney (Eds.), *Handbook of self and identity.* New York: The Guilford Press.

Aube, J., and R. Koestner. 1992. Gender characteristics and adjustment: A longitudinal study. *Journal of Personality and Social Psychology, 70,* 535–551.

Aylor, B., and P. Opplinger. 2003. Out-of-class communication and student perceptions of instructor humor orientation and socio-communicative style. *Communication Education, 52,* 122–134.

Bandura, A. 1986. *Social foundations of thought and action.* New York: Prentice Hall.

Bargh, J.A., and T.L. Chartrand. 1999. The unbearable automaticity of being. *American Psychologist, 54,* 462–479.

Bargh, J.A., K. McKenna, and G.M. Fitzsimons. 2002. Can you see the real me? Activation and expression of the *"true self"* on the Internet. *Journal of Social Issues, 58,* 33–48.

Baumeister, R.F. 1998. The self. In D. Gilbert, S.T. Fiske, and G. Lindzey (Eds.), *The Handbook of social psychology* (680–740). New York: Oxford Press.

Baumeister, R.F., and K.D. Vohs. 2003. Self-regulation and the executive function of the self. In M.R. Leary and J.P. Tangney (Eds.), *Handbook of self and identity.* New York: The Guilford Press.

Baumeister, R.F., J.D. Campbell, J.I. Krueger, and K. Vohs. 2003. Does high self-esteem cause better performance, interpersonal success, happiness or healthier lifestyles? *Psychological Science in the Public Interest, 4,* 1–44.

Bayer, C.L., and D.J. Cegala. 1992. Trait verbal aggressiveness and argumentativeness: Relations with parenting style. *Western Journal of Communication, 56,* 301–310.

Beatty, M.J., J.C. McCroskey, and A.D. Heisel. 1998. Communication apprehension as temperamental expression: A communibiological perspective. *Communication Monographs, 65,* 197–219.

Bell, R.A., and J.A. Daly. 1984. The affinity-seeking function of *communication. Communication Monographs, 49,* 91–115.

Berger, B.A., J.C. McCroskey, and V.A. Richmond. 1984. Communication apprehension and shyness. In W.N. Tinally and R.S. Beardsley (Eds.), *Communication in pharmacy practice: A practical guide for students and practitioners* (128–158). Philadelphia, PA: Lea & Febiger.

Berne, E. 1964. *Games people play.* New York: Grove.

Booth-Butterfield, M., and A. Andrighetti. 1993. *The role of affective orientation and nonverbal sensitivity in the interpretation of communication in acquaintance rape.* Paper presented at the annual convention of the Eastern Communication Association, New Haven, CT.

Booth-Butterfield, M., and S. Booth-Butterfield. 1990. Conceptualizing affect as information in communication production. *Human Communication Research, 16,* 451–476.

———. 1991. Individual differences in the communication of humorous messages. *Southern Communication Journal, 56,* 32–40.

———. 1994. The affective orientation to communication: Conceptual and empirical distinctions. *Communication Quarterly, 42,* 331–344.

———. 1996. Using your emotions: Improving the measurement of affective orientation. *Communication Research Reports, 13,* 157–163.

———. 1998. Emotionality and affective orientation (171–190). In McCroskey et al. (Eds.), *Communication and personality.* Cresskill, NJ: Hampton Press.

Booth-Butterfield, M., S. Booth-Butterfield, and M.B. Wanzer. 2006. Funny students cope better: Patterns of humor enactment and coping effectiveness. *Communication Quarterly.* (In Press)

Boster, F.J., and T. Levine. 1988. Individual differences and compliance-gaining message selection: The effects of verbal aggressiveness, argumentativeness, dogmatism, and negativism. *Communication Research Reports, 5,* 114–119.

Bowlby, J. 1969. *Attachment and loss: Vol. 1. Attachment.* New York: Basic Books.

———. 1973. *Attachment and loss: Vol. 3. Loss, sadness, and depression.* New York: Basic Books.

Chory-Assad, R.M., and M. Paulsel. 2004. Classroom justice: Student aggression and resistance as reactions to perceived unfairness. *Communication Education, 53,* 253–273.

Cook, W.W., and D.M. Medley. 1954. Proposed hostility and pharisaic-virtue scales for the MMPI. *Journal of Applied Psychology, 38*, 414–418.

Cooley, C.H. 1902. *Human nature and the social order*. New York: Scribner's.

Daly, J.A. 2002. Personality and interpersonal communication. In Knapp and Daly (Eds.), *Handbook of interpersonal communication* (133–180). Thousand Oaks, CA: Sage Publications.

Daly, J.A. and A.M. Bippus. 1998. Personality and interpersonal communication: Issues and directions. In McCroskey etal. (Eds.), *Communication and personality* (1–40). Cresskill, NJ: Hampton Press.

Daly, J.A., V.P. Richmond, and S. Leth. 1979. Social communicative anxiety and the personnel selection process: Testing the similarity effect in selection decisions. *Human Communication Research, 6*, 18–32.

Darley, J.M., and R.H. Fazio. 1980. Expectancy confirmation processes arising in the social interaction sequence. *American Psychologist, 35*, 867–881.

Dolin, D., and M. Booth-Butterfield. 1993. Reach out and touch someone: Analysis of nonverbal comforting responses. *Communication Quarterly, 41*, 383–393.

Dye, L. 2004. Researchers design games to boost self-esteem. Retrieved on 12/20/2006 from *abcnews.go.com/Technology/print?id*.

Epstein, S. 1973. The self-concept revisited: Or a theory of a theory. *American Psychologist, 28*, 404–416.

Felson, R.B. 1989. Parents and reflected appraisal process: A longitudinal analysis. *Journal of Personality and Social Psychology, 56*, 965–971.

Festinger, L. 1954. A theory of social comparison processes. *Human Relations, 7*, 117–140.

Finkel, E.J., and W.K. Campbell. 2001. Self-control and accommodation in close relationships: An interdependence analysis. *Journal of Personality and Social Psychology, 81*, 263–271.

Fitzpatrick, M.A. 1988. *Between husbands and wives: Communication in marriage*. Newbury Park, CA: Sage.

Goffman, E. 1959. *The presentation of self in everyday life*. Garden City, NY: Doubleday.

Gottman, J.M. 1999. *The marriage clinic: A scientific based marital therapy*. New York: Norton.

Greenwald, A.G., and S.J. Breckler. 1985. To whom is the self presented? In B.R. Schlenker (Ed.), *The self and social life* (126–145). New York: McGraw-Hill.

Guilford, J.P. 1959. *Personality*. New York: McGraw-Hill.

Harris, T. 1969. *I'm OK, you're OK*. New York: Harper & Row.

Honeycutt, J., and R. Brown. 1998. Did you hear the one about?: Typological and spousal differences in the planning of jokes and sense of humor in marriage. *Communication Quarterly, 46*, 342–352.

Houck, G.M., and A.M. Spegman. 1999. The development of self: Theoretical understandings and conceptual underpinnings. *Infants and Young Children, 12,* 1–16.

Huebner, D.M., C.J. Nemeroff, and M.C. Davis. 2005. Do hostility and neuroticism confound associations between perceived discrimination and depressive symptoms? *Journal of Social and Clinical Psychology, 24,* 723–740.

Infante, D.A. 1981. Trait argumentativeness as a predictor of communicative behavior in situations requiring argument. *Central States Speech Journal, 32,* 265–272.

———. 1985. Inducing women to be more argumentative: Source credibility effects. *Journal of Applied Communication Research, 13,* 33–44.

———. 1987. Aggressiveness. In J.C. McCroskey and J.A. Daly (Eds.), *Personality and interpersonal communication* (157–192). Newbury Park, CA: Sage.

———. 1988. *Arguing constructively.* Prospect Heights, Illinois: Waveland Press.

———. 1995. Teaching students to understand and control verbal aggression. *Communication Education, 44,* 51–63.

Infante, D.A., and W.I. Gorden. 1987. Superior and subordinate communication profiles: Implications for independent-mindedness and upward effectiveness. *Central States Speech Journal, 38,* 73–80.

———. 1989. Argumentativeness and affirming communicator style as predictors of satisfaction/dissatisfaction with subordinates. *Communication Quarterly, 37,* 81–90.

———. 1991. How employees see the boss: Test of an argumentative and affirming model of superiors' communicative behavior. *Western Journal of Speech Communication, 55,* 294–304.

Infante, D.A., and A.S. Rancer. 1982. A conceptualization and measure of argumentativeness. *Journal of Personality Assessment, 46,* 72–80.

Infante, D.A., B.L. Riddle, C.L. Horvath, and S.A. Tumlin. 1992. Verbal aggressiveness: Messages and reasons. *Communication Quarterly, 40,* 116–126.

Infante, D.A., and C.J. Wigley. 1986. Verbal aggressiveness: An interpersonal model and measure. *Communication Monographs, 53,* 61–69.

Infante, D.A., T.A. Chandler, and J.E. Rudd. 1989. Test of an argumentative skill deficiency model of interspousal violence. *Communication Monographs, 56,* 163–177.

Jung, C.G. 1953. *Psychological reflections.* New York: Harper and Row.

Karney, B.R., and T.N. Bradbury. 1995. The longitudinal course of marital quality and stability: A review of theory, methods, and research. *Psychological Bulletin, 118,* 3–34.

Kazoleas, D. 1993. The impact of argumentativeness on resistance to persuasion. *Human Communication Research, 20,* 118–137.

Keating, C. 1984. *Dealing with difficult people: How you can come out on top in personality conflicts*. New York: Paulist Press.

Koch, E.J., and J.A. Shepperd. 2004. Is self-complexity linked to better coping? A review of the literature. *Journal of Personality, 72*, 727–760.

Kopper, B.A., and D.L. Epperson. 1996. The experience and expression of anger: Relationships with gender, role socialization, depression and mental health functioning. *Journal of Counseling Psychology, 43*, 158–165.

Lieberman, A.F. 1977. Preschooler's competence with a peer: Relations with attachment and peer experience. *Child Development, 48*, 1277–1287.

Lieberman, A.F., and J.H. Pawl. 1988. Clinical applications of attachment theory. In J. Belsky and T. Nezworski (Eds.), *Clinical implications of attachment* (327–351). Hillsdale, NJ: Erlbaum.

Limon, S.M., and B.H. LaFrance. 2005. Communication traits and leadership emergence: Examining the impact of argumentativeness, communication apprehension and verbal aggressiveness in work groups. *Southern Communication Journal, 70*, 123–133.

Linville, P.W. 1985. Self-complexity and affective extremity: Don't put all your eggs in one cognitive basket. *Social Cognition, 3*, 94–120.

———. 1987. Self-complexity as a cognitive buffer against stress-related illness and depression. *Journal of Personality and Social Psychology, 52*, 663–676.

Lippert, L.R., B.S. Titsworth, and S.K. Hunt. 2005. The ecology of academic risk: Relationships between communication apprehension, verbal aggression, supportive communication, and students' academic risk. *Communication Studies, 56*, 1–21.

Markus, H., and E. Wurf. 1987. The dynamic self-concept: A social psychological perspective. *Annual Review of Psychology, 38*, 299–337.

Maxwell, J.C. 2002. *The seventeen essential qualities of a team player*. Nashville, TN: Thomas Nelson Publishers.

McCroskey, J.C. 1977. Oral communication apprehension: A summary of recent theory and research. *Human Communication Research, 4*, 78–96.

———. 1978. Validity of the PRCA as an index of oral communication apprehension. *Communication Monographs, 45*, 192–203.

McCroskey, J.C. 2006. Personal communication with the author.

McCroskey, J.C., and M.J. Beatty. 1984. Communication apprehension and accumulated communication state anxiety experiences: A research note. *Communication Monographs, 51*, 79–84.

McCroskey, J.C., J.A. Daly, and G.A. Sorensen. 1976. Personality correlates of communication apprehension. *Human Communication Research, 2*, 376–380.

———. 1995. Correlates of compulsive communication: Quantitative and qualitative characteristics. *Communication Quarterly, 43*, 39–52.

———. 1998. Willingness to communicate. In McCroskey et al. (Eds.), *Communication and personality* (119–132). Cresskill, NJ: Hampton Press.

McCroskey, J.C., and V.P. Richmond. 1987. Willingness to communicate. In J.C. McCroskey and J.A. Daly (Eds.), *Personality and interpersonal communication* (129–156). Newbury Park, CA: Sage.

McKenna, K.Y.A., A.S. Green, and M.E.J. Gleason. 2002. Relationship formation on the Internet: What's the big attraction? *Journal of Social Issues, 58*, 9–31.

Mead, G.H. 1934. *Mind, self, and society*. Chicago: University of Chicago Press.

Meeus, W., and M. Dekovic. 1995. Identity development, parental and peer support in adolescence: Results of a national Dutch survey. *Adolescence, 30*, 931–945.

Mizco, N. 2004. Humor ability, unwillingness to communicate, loneliness, and perceived stress: Testing a security theory. *Communication Studies, 55*, 209–226.

Myers, S.A., and A.D. Johnson. 2003. Verbal aggression and liking in interpersonal relationships. *Communication Research Reports, 20*, 90–96.

Noar, S.M., P.J. Morokoff, and C.A. Redding. 2002. Sexual assertiveness in heterosexually active men: A test of three samples. *AIDS Education and Prevention, 14*, 330–342.

Park, K.A., and E. Waters. 1988. Traits and relationships in developmental perspective. In S. Duck (Ed.) *Handbook of personal relationships: Theory, research, and interventions* (161–176). Chichester: John Wiley & Sons Ltd.

Peluso, P.R., J.P. Peluso, J.F. White, and R.M. Kern. 2004. A comparison of attachment theory and individual psychology: A review of the literature. *Journal of Counseling and Development, 82*, 139–145.

Pope, M.K., T.W. Smith, and F. Rhodewalt. 1990. Cognitive, behavioral and affective correlates of the Cook and Medley Hostility Scale. *Journal of Personality Assessment, 54*, 501–514.

Rancer, A.S. 1998. Argumentativeness. In McCroskey et al. (Eds.), *Communication and personality* (149–170). Cresskill, NJ: Hampton Press.

Richmond, V.P., and D.K. Roach. 1992. Willingness to communicate and employee success in U.S. organizations. *Journal of Applied Communication*, 95–115.

Richmond, V.P., and J.C. McCroskey. 1990. Reliability and separation of factors on the assertiveness-responsiveness measure. *Psychological Reports, 67*, 449–450.

Richmond, V.P., and M.M. Martin. 1998. Sociocommunicative style and sociocommunicative orientation. In McCroskey et al. (Eds.), *Communication and personality*. Hampton Press: Cresskill, NJ.

Rizzo, B., M.B. Wanzer, and M. Booth-Butterfield. 1999. Individual differences in managers' use of humor: Subordinate perceptions of managers' humor orientation, effectiveness, and humor behaviors. *Communication Research Reports, 16*, 370–376.

Rogge, R.D., T.N. Bradbury, K. Halweg, J. Engl, and F. Thurmaier. 2006. Predicting marital distress and dissolution: Refining the two-factor hypothesis. *Journal of Family Psychology, 20,* 156–159.

Schlenker, B. 1984. Identities, identifications and relationships. In V. Derlega (Ed.), *Communication, intimacy and close relationships.* New York: Academic Press.

———. 1985. Identity and self-identification. In B.R. Schlenker (Ed.), *The self and social life* (65–99). New York: McGraw-Hill.

Self-Improvement. (n.d.). Retrieved September 29, 2005, from *http://www.mygoals. com/content/self-improvement.html.*

Shackelford, T.K. 2001. Self-esteem in marriage. *Personality and Individual Differences, 30,* 371–391.

Smith, T.W. 1994. Concepts and methods in the study of anger, hostility, and health. In A.W. Siegman and T.W. Smith (Eds.), *Anger, hostility, and the heart* (23–42). Hillsdale, NJ: Erlbaum.

Snyder, M., E.D. Tanke, and E. Berscheid. 1977. Social perception and interpersonal behavior: The self-fulfilling nature of social stereotypes. *Journal of Personality and Social Psychology, 35,* 656–666.

Spitzberg, B.H. and W.R. Cupach. 1984. *Interpersonal communication competence.* Newbury Park, CA: Sage.

Sroufe, L.A. 1988. The role of infant-caregiver attachment in development. In J. Belsky and T. Nezworski (Eds.), *Clinical implications of attachment* (18–38). Hillsdale, NJ: Erlbaum.

Surra, C.A., C.R. Gray, N. Cottle, and T.M. Boettcher. 2004. Research on mate selection and premarital relationships: What do we really know? In A.L. Vangelisti (Ed.), *Handbook of family communication* (53–82). Mahwah, NJ: Lawrence Erlbaum.

Swann, W.R. 1985. The self as architect of social reality. In B.R. Schlenker (Ed.), *The self and social life* (100–126). New York: McGraw-Hill.

Tesser, A. 2003. Self-evaluation. In M.R. Leary and J.P. Tangney (Eds.), *Handbook of self and identity.* New York: The Guilford Press.

Tesser A., J.V. Wood, and D.A. Stapel. 2002. Introduction: An emphasis on motivation. In A. Tesser, D.A. Stapel, and J.V. Wood (Eds.), *Self and motivation: Emerging psychological perspectives* (3–11). Washington, DC: American Psychological Association.

Tesser, A., R.B. Felson, and J.M. Suls (Eds.). 2000. *Psychological perspectives on self and identity.* Washington, DC: American Psychological Association.

Vallacher, R.R., and A. Nowak. 2000. Landscapes of self-reflection: Mapping the peaks and valleys of personal assessment. In A. Tesser, R.B. Felson, and J.M. Suls (Eds.), *Psychological perspectives on self and identity* (35–65). Washington, DC: American Psychological Association.

Wanzer, M.B., and A.B. Frymier. 1999. The relationship between student perceptions of instructor humor and student's reports of learning. *Communication Education, 48,* 48–62.

Wanzer, M.B., M. Booth-Butterfield, and S. Booth-Butterfield. 1995. The funny people: A source orientation to the communication of humor. *Communication Quarterly, 43,* 142–154.

———. 1996. Are funny people popular? An examination of humor orientation, verbal aggressiveness, and social attraction. *Communication Quarterly, 44,* 42–52.

———. 2005. "If we didn't use humor, we'd cry:" Humorous coping communication in health care settings. *Journal* of *Health Communication, 10,* 105–125.

Wigley, C.J. 1998. Verbal aggressiveness. In McCroskey et al. (Eds.), *Communication and personality* (191–214). Cresskill, NJ: Hampton Press.

Wood, J.T. 2001. *Interpersonal communication: Everyday encounters. (3rd ed.)* Belmont, CA: Wadsworth Publishing Company.

Zajonc, R.B., R.K. Adelmann, S.B. Murphy, and R.N. Niedenthal. 1987. Convergence in the appearance of spouses. *Motivation and Emotion, 11,* 335–346.

Zakahi, W.R., and R.L. Duran. 1985. Loneliness, communication competence, and communication apprehension: Extension and replication. *Communication Quarterly, 33,* 50–60.

# SELF—IDENTITY

Who are you? It is a simple question. You have been answering it since you were able to talk. My name is David. On the other hand, this is one of the most difficult and important questions that we will face throughout our lives.

Who are you now? How do you feel about yourself? Are you happy, successful, comfortable? Are there things you would like to change about yourself? College is a time when many people define themselves for the first time. You are away from home. You are no longer the child of Homer and Marge Simpson. You are you. You can dye your hair purple and call yourself Raoul (at least until the next break when you return home). **Self-identity** and **selfesteem** are two of the most critical components of communication. If you feel good about yourself, you are likely to take a few chances and open up to people. On the other hand, if you are having a bad hair day, you are less likely to ask out that cute guy in your biology class. How you see yourself and how you define yourself can shift from day to day or even hour to hour. A professor tells you that you have written a really good paper. The most wonderful person in the world tells you that he loves you. Because you are brilliant and lovable, you feel really good about yourself and are likely to risk talking to someone new.

Unfortunately, a bad paper or a rejection from a significant other can have the opposite effect. Who are you is and will remain a fundamental question in the process of communication. The next chapter complicates matters even further by exploring your cyber-self and cyber-communication.

# CHAPTER 6

## From Face-to-Face to Cyberspace
## Forming Relationships Online*

### Chapter Objectives

After reading this chapter, you should understand the following concepts:

- Discuss how relationships developed prior to the Internet
- Explain how the evolution of the Internet has changed the way people develop interpersonal relationships
- Discuss factors of online attraction
- Explain the differences between face-to-face and computer mediated communication
- Identify the benefits and drawbacks of forming relationships via CMC
- Identify and explain the two factors individuals should consider when forming online relationships
- Identify cues that may indicate deception in online communication

# CHAPTER OVERVIEW

The process of initiating relationships has evolved. Online social networks such as Facebook and MySpace have created opportunities for individuals to research other people and decide whether they want to pursue a relationship. Even dating practices have changed over the last few years. No longer do we have to count on friends to introduce us to someone they think is perfect for us or to frequent singles bars to look for love. Thanks to the Internet, we can find our perfect mate by posting a list of personal interests or by completing online personality profiles and allowing sites such as eHarmony and match.com to find a match.

Examples of the connection between Computer Mediated Communication (CMC) and relationship development are identified and discussed throughout this book. In Chapter Six we discussed the role of CMC in the initiating stages of relationship development. In Chapter Seven, we discussed how CMC is used to help us maintain relationships. In this chapter, we focus exclusively on research, theories, and constructs related to CMC and relationship development processes. In addition, we take a much closer look at how the use of this medium has altered interpersonal communication and the process of relationship development.

Online dating is one of the many ways in which people use online communication to build and sustain relationships. While mediated matchmaking is not necessarily a new phenomenon (Ellison, Heino, and Gibbs 2006) it certainly has changed and increased in popularity. Ellison and her colleagues describe the evolution of

© Franz Pfluegl, 2007, Shutterstock.

A significant number of single people turn to the Internet to find their "perfect match."

© Yuri Arcurs, 2007, Shutterstock.

mediated matchmaking and note that as early as the mid-nineteenth century, singles placed ads in the newspaper to find a perfect mate (Ellison, Heino, and Gibbs 2006). Decades later, in the 1980s, singles used video dating services to meet potential mates. Today, a significant percentage of single persons turn to the Internet to help them find their "perfect match" (Lenhart and Madden 2006a). Nearly thirty-seven percent of single people state that they have visited Internet dating sites in the pursuit of romance.

Interpersonal scholars Mark Knapp and John Daly (2002) encourage researchers to study CMC because of its impact on face-to-face communication and relationship development processes. As we have stated throughout this text, communication competence is essential to building and maintaining effective relationships. Individuals require knowledge, skill, and motivation to communicate effectively and establish rewarding relationships. The same is true in the context of online communication.

This chapter addresses competent online communication by providing an overview of existing research on CMC that explains why online communication has become so prevalent and how to use it effectively and appropriately to establish relationships. The prospect of forming interpersonal relationships through CMC poses a multitude of questions. Will these relationships be similar to those formed via face-to-face interaction? What are the positive and negative aspects of forming a relationship through CMC? What are some suggestions for establishing successful online relationships? How has the Internet altered the way people establish, maintain and terminate relationships? In the first section of this chapter, we briefly discuss the methods used in the past in developing interpersonal relationships. Next, we focus on positive and negative aspects of interpersonal relationships formed through CMC. In the final section, we offer suggestions for using CMC as a means of developing interpersonal relationships.

Since the early 1990s, communication scholars have written about how online relationships are developed and maintained (see, specifically, Wildermuth 2001; Rumbough 2001; Parks and Roberts 1998; Parks and Floyd 1996; Walther 1996;

Walther 1995; Walther, Anderson, and Park 1994; Walther 1993; Walther 1992; Walther and Burgoon 1992). However, communication researchers are not the only ones studying the development of online relationships. Researchers from academic fields such as computer science, behavioral science, psychology, sociology, and business have written about the impact of CMC on social interaction (see, for example, Nie 2001; Conley and Bierman 1999; Capulet 1998; Gwinnell 1998; Tanner 1994). At the end of 2004, more than an estimated 945 million people worldwide were participating in some form of online communication (Cyber Atlas 2005), and that number continues to increase. In fact, due to the prevalence of CMC, Steve Jacobs, cofounder of Apple Computer, made the recommendation that "personal computers be renamed 'interpersonal computers'" (Adler and Towne 2003, 20).

To better understand the how and why of relationships initiated and maintained online, let us first look at some comparisons between relationships that form via face-to-face communication (hereafter referred to as FTF) and those that form through CMC.

# METHODS OF DEVELOPING INTERPERSONAL RELATIONSHIPS

In previous chapters, we have explored the ways in which individuals initiate, maintain, and terminate all types of relationships. It is important to note that the majority of the research conducted to discover how and why people come together and grow apart in relationships was in FTF contexts. Because we know that the communication situation, or context, greatly affects how messages are sent and received, it is important to consider how communication and relationship development processes may differ when individuals use CMC as a primary means of interaction. Before we identify the differences between FTF and CMC, let us examine some of the ways relationships began prior to the introduction of CMC.

# ESTABLISHING RELATIONSHIPS: BEFORE THE INTERNET

Take a minute and imagine how your relationships with friends and family members would change if you did not have access to the Internet or a cellular phone. Would it be possible to establish and maintain relationships with others without this technology? Of course, it would be possible! But prior to the introduction of these technological advancements, the ways people communicated in relationships were

How would your personal relationships change if you couldn't use a cell phone?

© Leah-Anne Thompson, 2007, Shutterstock.

**Social networking**
The process of connecting with others to form different types of relationships.

very different. In the following sections, we discuss some of the different methods individuals used to establish and maintain their relationships prior to the development of the Internet.

## Family and Community

Stated simply, *social networking* refers to the process of connecting with others to form different types of relationships. Before the Industrial Revolution in 1760, families functioned as independent economic units and served as the primary source of social networking for most individuals. People relied almost exclusively on FTF interactions with others in their community as the primary means of establishing relationships. The family played a significant role in the socialization of its members and was most likely to interact with other families that lived in close proximity. During this era, many relationships initially formed due to convenience. Relationships also developed through family members' involvement in church activities or arrangements made among families and friends (Rogers 1997).

## Advances in Transportation

The Industrial Revolution, which occurred from 1760–1830, transformed the family and resulted in drastic changes in social network systems. Advances in transportation such as the rail system and automobiles increased options for the formation of interpersonal relationships. Individuals could now leave their hometowns and travel across the country to establish relationships with people hundreds of miles away. As society became more mobile, individuals were no longer restricted geographically in their choices of relationship partners. Individuals could establish and even maintain long distance relationships with greater ease (Rogers 1997).

## Letter Writing and Telephone Use

Prior to the invention of the telephone, writing letters was the primary means of establishing and maintaining interpersonal relationships. Written correspondence provided a method of remaining faceless and allowed intimacy with a reduced amount of risk (Pratt etal. 1999). The number of couples who fell in love through written correspondence peaked during World War II as women began to write to soldiers overseas. Gwinell (1998) points out the significance of letter writing by noting that it served as a means of helping individuals with similar backgrounds communicate across greater geographic distances. While letter writing was an important means of communicating with friends, relatives, and relationship partners, the feedback from receivers was limited to textual information only and the rate of receiving feedback was extremely slow.

The telephone, created in 1876, drastically altered the way individuals communicated with one another on a day-to-day basis. Unlike letter writing, the telephone allowed individuals to send verbal and nonverbal messages and the feedback was immediate. Today we use cellular phones that provide us with the ability to communicate with virtually anyone, anywhere, and anytime! While cellular phones offer the convenience of being able to communicate with our friends, family, and significant others, they also can be a source of frustration and annoyance. In a recent *20/20* survey, eighty-seven percent of Americans indicated experiencing rude cell phone behavior that included people talking on cell phones in public places in loud voices (Cohen and Langer 2006).

## Singles Clubs

During the last few decades, individuals have flocked to bars and singles clubs in order to meet the "right person." Not only has the singles scene replaced the family's influence on interpersonal relationships, but Rogers (1997) also contends, "The singles scene replaced the church social as one of the chief places to meet a member of the opposite sex" (1). Many agree that even today bars and clubs remain a common place to meet people (DeGol 2003). Think about how relationship initiation is portrayed in many television shows. Aside from on *Seventh Heaven*, no relationships are forming at church socials. Rather, Dr. McDreamy and Meredith Grey begin their relationship over drinks at the local bar in *Grey's Anatomy*, and the main characters in sitcoms such as *How I Met Your Mother* and 30 Rock vainly attempt to forge connections with other singles at bars or clubs.

## Mediated Matchmaking

While mediated matchmaking "is certainly not a new phenomenon" (Ellison, Heino, and Gibbs 2006, 416) it has evolved and, more recently, has increased in popularity. Ellison and her colleagues describe the evolution of mediated matchmaking and note that as early as the mid-nineteenth century, singles placed ads in the newspaper to find a perfect mate (Ellison, Heino, and Gibbs 2006; Schaefer 2003). Later, in the 1980s, singles used video dating services to meet potential mates (Woll and Cosby 1987; Woll and Young 1989).

During the late 1970s and early 80s, some individuals used dating services to help them find the perfect match (Jedlicka 1981). These singles agencies typically advertised in magazines and promised to match individuals using sophisticated computer technology. Singles using these services typically paid between fifteen and thirty dollars and then completed a questionnaire that asked for a variety of information such as physical appearance, race, age, religion, and hobbies. Once individuals submitted this information to the agency, they were matched with someone who scored similarly or who was deemed a good match. Jedlicka (1981) notes that "the computer's ability to evaluate and suggest alternatives is limited" (374). At the time, research on this type of mediated matchmaking was significant because it illustrated both the potential and limitations of computers as a means of social networking in the early 1980s.

With advances in technology, individuals have been able to increase the ways in which individuals establish and maintain their relationships. While many of the communication channels and forms of social networking mentioned in this section are still used, the arrival of the Internet has had a significant impact on the way we communicate with one another and the methods used to develop and maintain our relationships.

Have any of your current relationships been established through email?

# ESTABLISHING RELATIONSHIPS: THE INTERNET ERA

© Juriah Mosin, 2007, Shutterstock.

The birth of the Internet in the late 1960s resulted in electronic mail, or email. Originally, researchers used email to correspond with one another, but this technology rapidly moved beyond the research setting and became available for the general population (Lerner Productions 2003). For example, from 1995 to 1998, the number of people using email increased by fifty percent and by the year 2000, seventy-eight percent of the people online reported using the Internet specifically for email. This statistic is staggering—nearly three-fourths of online users depend on the medium to communicate via email (Boneva, Kraut, and Frohlich 2001).

Because of its popularity and immediacy, email has evolved into a common form of CMC. In fact, many of today's interpersonal relationships are established through email. Friendships form in MySpace or Facebook communities instead of at local community socials and events. Romantic relationships form because of connections made through Match.com or Yahoo! Personals as opposed to meeting at church socials or in high school classes. As Pratt and his co-authors (1999) have contended, the use of CMC as a form of correspondence in interpersonal relationships is merely the natural evolution of interpersonal relationships beyond face-to-face interaction.

In today's world, people can video conference with colleagues and clients across the globe.

The Internet has become one of the most rapidly growing technologies in the world. In 1997, over 50 million people utilized Internet services and almost half of them described the Internet as an "indispensable" part of their day-to-day lives (Miller and Clemente 1997). Although defining the Internet as "indispensable" may seem extreme, this medium has certainly added convenience to communication. With the click of a mouse, individuals can access a multitude of services from email to stock quotes. One can simply go to eBay to purchase a car, a rare collector's issue of *Sports Illustrated*, or the latest Fendi purse that has sold out in all the stores. Co-workers can easily access databases from all over the world or have a video conference with a client on the other side of the globe. In fact, research has suggested that the Internet is replacing other more traditional media (La Ferle, Edwards, and Lee 2002; Althaus and Tewksbury 2000; Johnson and Kaye 1999).

With all of these services, it seems logical that people turn to the Internet as a source of social networking. Today, a significant percentage of single persons are turning to the Internet to help them find their "perfect match" (Lenhart and Madden 2006a). Nearly thirty-seven percent of single people state that they have visited Internet dating sites in the pursuit of romance (Lenhart and Madden 2006b). Specifically, some people choose to use the Internet as a source for seeking out and developing interpersonal relationships. Yet many romantic partners are reluctant to admit to others that they met online. Why does this stigma of online romance exist? Individuals may be reluctant to admit meeting a relationship partner online because the use of CMC as a means of establishing relationships continues to be somewhat of an anomaly. Because many individuals meet their relationships partners through FTF encounters, using CMC to establish relationships is often regarded as nontraditional (Emmers-Sommer 2005) or somewhat unusual. However, we speculate that meeting partners online will be viewed differently over time as more singles use Internet services to "shop" for the ideal mate. After all, individuals use the Internet to shop for everything from cars to clothes online (Conley and Bierman 1999), why not "shop" for relationship partners as well?

## *Online Dating*

Technological advancements such as cell phones and computers have certainly altered the way we communicate with others during the initial stages of relationship development. Recall our discussion of "silent dating" practices in Chapter Six. With the advent of cell phones, individuals can now send multiple text messages first to gauge whether the other party is interested in furthering the relationship. Today, individuals that are interested in establishing a relationship will often "text" and "IM" one another prior to advancing to that first phone call or going on that first date.

It is also more common today for individuals to use CMC to meet, maintain, and terminate romantic relationships. As interpersonal relationships form because of connections made via the Internet, numerous online dating sites assist people in their search for similar relationship partners. Recall our earlier discussion of the role that similarity plays in deciding whether to initiate a relationship with someone. In cyberspace, the search for similarities in age, cultural background, sexual orientation, religion, educational level, interests, and likes and dislikes is easier. Many sites, such as eHarmony, Match.com, or Yahoo! Personals provide users with the opportunity to enter preferences for a variety of demographic categories. Some sites have even targeted specific audiences: silversingles.com for seniors; eSPIN-the-Bottle for tweens and older; Jdate for singles of the Jewish faith, and a few off-the-garden-path varieties, including gothicmatch.com and several variations thereof. Books such as *The Complete Idiot's Guide to Online Dating and Relating* (Swartz 2000) offer popular Internet sites that fulfill a variety of interpersonal needs and requirements. Many of these sites are increasing in popularity when it comes to initiating relationships because they provide more information than can be included in a written personal ad and they allow people to correspond anonymously for longer periods of time (Scharlott and Christ 1995). Consider the popularity of the online dating service, match.com. The website was created in 1995 and advances "a simple mission: to take the lottery out of love" (www.match.com). The creators of this website boast that use of their site has resulted in over 250,000 marriages per year! With over 15 million members, match.com offers a significant amount of choices in potential relationship partners. Individuals simply log on to the site and begin viewing portraits and reading descriptive information about the members of this online community. If members are uncomfortable posting personal information, they can use the alternative online dating service known as chemistry.com. Individuals choosing to use this online dating service allow others to do the "searching and matching for them."

As the demand for online dating websites increases, the services offered by these sites have become more sophisticated and now cater more specifically to users' needs. If a person is concerned about the honesty of a potential date, there are even sites such as true.com that conduct background checks on its members. Criminal background investigations and public record screenings are conducted to ensure that members are not married and are free of criminal charges. If an online dater is still uneasy about a potential date, sites such as truedater.com allow him to read reviews posted by others who have met the potential date through a dating website. Truedater.com claims to provide an objective review of how honestly someone has portrayed himself in his online profile by allowing others to comment on experiences with the person.

The convenience of CMC can help family members stay in touch more often.

Individuals also use CMC to maintain their relationships. As mentioned in Chapter Seven, individuals send emails and use IM (instant messenger) to correspond regularly with friends, family members, and relationship partners. One of the most frequently used relationship maintenance strategies, labeled "mediated communication," involves the use of computers to stay in touch with significant others and sustain the quality of the relationship.

Not surprisingly, CMC can also be used to terminate relationships with significant others. Individuals can use the Internet to learn more about how to end a relationship and they can use email and Instant Messenger (IM) as a means of terminating the relationship. For example, individuals can use Positively Passionate Inc. (www.positively.biz), an Internet break-up service, to end an unwanted relationship. For $200 this company will call or send an email to your partner and terminate the relationship for you. This website also offers a variety of relationship-related information and services.

## Online Social Networks

Just as online dating sites have gained in popularity, so have online social networking sites. Online social networking sites provide people with a place to come together to identify and discuss common interests or causes. The network expands as users add or invite "friends" to the site. Currently, some of the more popular social networking sites are MySpace, Facebook, and Xanga. For those who wish to share audio or video files, sites such as YouTube and Flickr provide a forum for distributing personal recordings to online friends. Children with Internet savvy visit sites such as clubpenguin.com, which allow them to chat with other children

There are Internet sites available for children to chat with other kids from all over the country.

from around the country. While the social aspects of these sites have broadened our opportunities for forming friendships with those who may live thousands of miles away, there are also new "uses" for these sites.

Not only are Harry Potter and Rolling Stones fans seeking one another in online social networks, marketers, scammers, predators, and even journalists are reviewing these sites to gain information about individuals. A 2006 study conducted by Purdue University found that many employers report using online social networks for background checks of potential employees. Nearly thirty-five percent of the employers surveyed reported that they use search engines such as Google to locate information on potential hires, thirteen percent check social networking sites such as Facebook and MySpace, and an additional fifteen percent search for personal blogs posted on the Internet.

As the number of people forming relationships via online dating sites and social networking sites increases, so does the need to understand the appeal of these sites for connecting individuals.

## WHAT ATTRACTS PEOPLE TO ONE ANOTHER ONLINE?

When answering the question "What attracts people to one another online?" we discover qualities and characteristics that are similar to those that attract us to others in FTF relationships. Physical attractiveness and social attractiveness are still paramount. Recall our discussion of the importance of physical and social attractiveness in Chapter Six. If you have ever glanced at an online profile, you probably noticed that most individuals highlight their physical characteristics. A unique aspect of initiating relationships online is that individuals also spotlight factors of social attractiveness in their list of desired qualities in a potential mate. Background, attitude, and demographic similarities—information that often requires extensive small talk on a first date—can easily be determined by browsing an online profile.

Earlier in the text, we discussed the importance of self-disclosure in achieving intimacy in relationships. **Self-disclosure** involves divulging personal information to another individual and is usually delivered through face-to-face or computer-mediated channels. Consider the rate at which self-disclosure occurs in FTF relationships compared to CMC. When scholars compare FTF with online relationship development processes, they note quite significant differences. Walther (1996) advances a *hyperpersonal model of CMC*, noting that online communication often facilitates relationship development and perceptions of intimacy. Walther further explains his hyperpersonal model of CMC based on the following factors:

**hyperpersonal model of CMC** Online communication that often facilitates relationship development and perceptions of intimacy.

1.  *The sender's ability to construct a specific and desired image of him/herself.* The sender can create an image that reflects an "ideal" versus the "real" self if he or she chooses. Unlike in FTF interactions where physical flaws or idiosyncratic personality traits may be readily apparent, a person's weaknesses are not on display or are often omitted from the personal description in computer-mediated contexts.

2.  *The sender's ability to alter any message content prior to sending them.* The sender can create messages, review them, and then alter them as needed when using computer-mediated channels of communication. This process may improve the quality of the information exchanged and elicit more favorable responses from receivers.

3.  *The receiver's propensity to create positive impressions of the partner.* Because the sender has created an ideal or desired image and has carefully monitored and edited the information exchanged, the receiver is likely to form more favorable impressions via CMC than through FTF contexts.

4.  *The increased depth and breadth of self-disclosure exchanged between the relationship partners.* Similar to FTF interactions, if the initial exchanges between individuals are positive, this leads to increased disclosure. In CMC the rate at which individuals exchange private information tends to be much faster than in FTF contexts (Walther 1996; Anderson and Emmers-Sommer 2006).

Walther (1996; 1997) and other scholars agree that greater levels of intimacy can be established through CMC than in similar types of FTF interactions. Follow-up research has substantiated this claim, noting that intimate relationships often develop in computer-mediated contexts faster than in FTF contexts because of the higher frequency of interaction (Hian, Chuan, Trevor, and Detenber 2004).

If you are one of the millions of students who have created an online social profile on a site such as MySpace, think about how much personal information you have disclosed on the Internet. A twenty-year old woman named Sami posted one profile on MySpace.com. Sami is a college graduate and is employed as a dental assistant. She enjoys wakeboarding, jet skiing, and going to the mall to hang out with her friends. She has a countdown on her profile that informs us how soon the day of her wedding to David will arrive. In case we might question how she and David feel about one another, she posts a video clip of the two of them locked in a passionate embrace. For those of us who want to know her likes and dislikes, Sami posts a survey that details this information. We know how many tattoos and piercings she has and that she is right-handed. After only five minutes, we learn Sami's full name, birth date, and hometown, her weight, her eye color, her weaknesses and goals, how many CDs she owns, where she wants to visit abroad, and that she wants to have children. We also know what high school and college she attended and where she works. Sami also blogs her daily itinerary as well as her current "mood" status, and everyone can learn where she and her friends will be on Friday night. In less than ten minutes, you may know more about Sami than you know about classmates you have known since first grade! As you can see from this example, individuals tend to open up in the online environment more quickly than they do in FTF interactions. Information that one might typically keep "private" until a friendship or romantic relationship develops is posted on a site for the entire world to see. What are the benefits of this online disclosure? It has made it easier for people to "cut to the chase" in identifying similarities. A simple glance at an online profile allows us to determine whether we have anything in common with the other person.

What are some of the pitfalls associated with Internet disclosure? Perhaps the biggest concern with online disclosure of information is safety. Not surprisingly, people differ in the amount and type of information they disclose on these Internet sites. In a 2006 study of 487 teenagers who reported having an online profile posted on a site, gender differences emerged when comparing the types of information boys and girls disclosed online. See the findings at http://www.pewinterest.org/. Select "teens", then search for Privacy and Online Social Networks. Select article: Online Privacy: What Teens Share and Restrict in an Online Environment.

Boys and girls were similar in their willingness to share first names, school names, or IM screen names. However, females indicated a tendency to post more photos (both of themselves and of their friends) than males, while boys were more likely to post videos or to reveal their hometowns and last names in their online profile. Thus, there appears to be subtle gender differences in the type of information disclosed online.

## *How Do FTF and CMC Differ?*

Now that we have examined the transformation in relationship development because of the introduction of the Internet, let us focus on the distinctions between FTF and CMC and how these differences affect relationship development. Table 6.1 highlights the distinctions between these two forms of communication.

TABLE 6.1

Comparisons of FTF and CMC Qualities

| Qualities | Face-to-Face (FTF) | Computer-Mediated Communication (CMC) |
|-----------|--------------------|----------------------------------------|
| Level of communication activity | Active | Passive (lurking, viewing) Active (source of message) |
| Nonverbal cues | Real | Artificial |
| Language style | Elaborate and more formal | Restricted and less formal |
| Synchronicity | Synchronous | Asynchronous and synchronous |
| Richness of interaction | High | Low |
| Social presence | High | Low |

**LEVEL OF COMMUNICATION ACTIVITY.** The vast majority of our FTF interactions require us to be active participants in a conversation. Of course, there are times when someone may engage in **passive** communication behaviors (e.g., responding "uh-huh" to a question while watching a game on television), but our physical presence typically requires us to be engaged in an interaction. In the CMC environment, the level of *communication activity* can range from active to passive. Active participation occurs when one sends an instant message (IM) to a friend or posts a response to an online chat room. Examples of passive activity are often less obvious and include "lurking," or viewing posts made on a discussion board or chat forum without responding. Since there are often several people engaged in chat room discussions, many who are unknown to the "regulars" participating in the online conversation, this passive behavior often goes unnoticed. This behavior is in stark contrast to social expectations in the FTF environment. If one were to stand by and listen in on a conversation without responding, others would perceive the behavior as strange or threatening. The person that was not participating in the conversation would probably be asked if he or she had something to contribute.

**NONVERBAL CUES.** In cyberspace, the rules for nonverbal communication are drastically different from the rules in face-to-face interactions. One theory developed to explain the absence of nonverbal cues in online interactions is *reduced social cues theory* (Sproull and Kiesler 1986). According to this theory, humans depend on social cues such as a person's appearance, attire, facial expressions, and gestures to help interpret received messages.

© Romanchuck Dimitry, 2007, Shutterstock.

> **Active vs. passive communication activity** Active communication requires involvement between the two or more participants, with prompted questions and answers and implied mutual interest in communication. Passive communication involves less engagement between participants, including potential avoidance of expression in one or both participants.

> "The vast majority of our face-to-face interactions require us to be **active** participants in a conversations. Of course, there are times when someone may engage in **passive** communication behaviors, but our physical presence typically requires us to be engaged in an interaction."

> **Reduced social cues theory** Explains the absence of nonverbal cues in online interactions.

> Passive behavior online often goes unnoticed by active participants.

Many of the social cues that we depend on in FTF interactions are absent in CMC. One look at another person's face reveals a myriad of cues about the mood or intent of a message. During FTF interactions, we often check to see whether the other person is smiling, whether he or she looks confused, or if the person is focused on the message. The absence of cues makes the process of managing and interpreting online interactions much more difficult. As a result, alternative forms of nonverbal cues compensate for the lack of social cues: Emoticons are used to communicate emotion, capital letters are used to indicate the severity of the message, and acronyms or abbreviations are inserted in messages to indicate a playful or informal tone. Examples of these artificially created nonverbal cues are included in Table 6.2.

TABLE 6.2

Examples of CMC Nonverbal Cues

| Emoticons | Smiling | ☺ or :-) |
|---|---|---|
| | Bad hair day | &:-) |
| | Laughing | :-D |
| | Kissing | :-* |
| | Giving a rose | @-}— |
| Capital Letters | I WISH YOU WOULD STOP POSTING MESSAGES TO MY BULLETIN BOARD! | |
| Acronyms | AWHFY | Are we having fun yet? |
| | ROTFL | Rolling on the floor laughing |
| | CYAL8R | See you later |
| | EMFJI | Excuse me for jumping in |
| | HAK | Hug and kiss |

**Flaming**
Aggressive attacks made against another person.

**Detachment**
Voluntary or involuntary inability to form attachments or emotional connections.

"Another consequence of reduced social cues is the tendency for **detachment**."

Several outcomes are associated with the reduction in social cues. Because we cannot see the expressions or responses of others in the online world, the social norms and constraints that typically guide our behavior are modified. In essence, our interpersonal behavior becomes "deregulated." In the absence of cues, people have a greater tendency to use "flaming" in their online communication. *Flaming* refers to aggressive attacks made against another person. An example of flaming would be the excessive use of capital letters in an attempt to scold a person. Another consequence of reduced social cues is the tendency for *detachment*. In CMC environments, participants may perceive themselves to be less connected to the conversation. As a result, a person may exit a chat room discussion abruptly and without warning or they may deliberately ignore attempts by others to communicate. In an FTF conversation, most people would make some indication of their intention to leave a conversation rather than simply walking away.

**LANGUAGE STYLE.** Think about the last email you sent to a close friend or family member. Chances are the style of language was less formal than language typically used in your FTF conversations. Due to the tedious nature of typing, it is often easier to take "short cuts" when composing written messages. As a result, our CMC messages are often more **informal** in terms of language style compared to the more elaborate and **formal** nature of FTF messages. For example, one friend might say to the other, "Are you okay? You seem to be upset about something," in an FTF conversation. If the same interaction occurred via email or text message, the interaction might look more like this: "RUOK? U seem 2B upset…" For some Internet users, this informal language style has found its way into their written communication. Some faculty members report that students who engage in frequent online communication tend to use poor grammar in their academic writing. Lee (2002) points out that teachers are frustrated by student papers that include shortened words, improper capitalization and punctuation, and the erratic use of characters such as & and @.

© Galina Barskaya, 2007, Shutterstock.

In FTF interactions, one look at someone's face can tell you how that person is reacting to your message.

**Informal vs. formal language style** Informal language style is casual and/or intimate, while formal language style adheres to societal and grammatical rules and/or boundaries.

"As a result, our CMC messages are often more **informal** in terms of language style compared to the more elaborate and **formal** nature of FTF messages."

**SYNCHRONICITY.** Another notable distinction between FTF and CMC interactions involves the synchronicity, or the rate at which responses occur in the exchange of messages. In FTF interactions, the sending and receiving of messages is *synchronous*, or occurs in real time, or simultaneously. At the same time a source sends a message, feedback cues are being received to help interpret the receiver's response. When you ask a friend to comment on your outfit, and you notice an odd look on his face while you are asking the question, feedback is being received while the message is being communicated. The source and the receiver are sending cues to one another simultaneously, thus synchronous communication occurs. Online environments can provide opportunities for synchronous communication in forums such as chat rooms or via instant messaging. The expectation is that once a message is received, an immediate response will be provided.

**Synchronous** Occurs in real time, or simultaneously.

*Asynchronous* communication involves a time lapse between when a message is received and when a response is made. Asynchronous CMC messages are typically in the form of emails or discussion board postings. We do not expect a friend to respond immediately to an email that we send and often several days may pass between the time when someone posts a message to an online discussion board and others post responses.

**Asynchronous** Involves a time lapse between when a message is received and when a response is made.

RICHNESS OF INTERACTION. *Media richness theory* (Daft and Lengel 1984) describes the capability of a communication channel to convey a variety of cues. By information richness, or media richness, we refer to the channel's level of synchrony, the availability of social cues, the ability to use natural language (as opposed to text or symbols), and the ability to convey emotions using the channel. As CMC lacks social cues and nonverbal expressions and uses text language instead of natural language, it is typically judged as being "less rich" on the media richness continuum although it spans across varying levels of richness. Emails are low in richness due to the lack of nonverbal cues. However, suppose you were to have a conversation with a friend using a web camera attached to your computer. The camera allows you to observe a number of your friend's nonverbal cues and increases the level of media richness.

© Supri Suharjoto, 2007, Shutterstock.

FTF interactions are the richest communication channel on the continuum. Recall some of the cues you received in the last conversation you had with your best friend. Not only did you receive the actual words of the message, you could also sense the mood through tone of voice, facial expressions, and posture.

SOCIAL PRESENCE. Short, Williams, and Christie (1976) created *social presence theory* to describe the perceived psychological closeness that occurs during a FTF interaction. Earlier chapters have discussed the concept of immediacy. Social presence focuses on the immediacy that occurs when we communicate with others. In a FTF conversation, there are numerous cues that cause us to feel psychologically closer to the person. A lingering glance or a forward lean accompanied by a smile can make a person feel connected to the other. The absence of nonverbal cues in email or chat room interactions results in low levels of social presence.

# WHO IS ONLINE AND WHY?

Parks and Roberts (1998) found that the most desirable online relationships center on developing close friendships and finding romance. When seeking interpersonal relationships online, the majority of users interact more often with members of the opposite sex. However, even though men and women use the Internet equally, they use it for different reasons. Boneva and his colleagues (2001) concluded that women spend more time using email to correspond with relatives and close friends.

On the other hand, Scharlott & Christ (1995) found men are more likely to "maximize the number of contacts, presumably to increase their chances of finding someone interested in a physically intimate relationship" (198). Interestingly, women and men achieve different levels of success with their online relationships goals. Women who are looking for friendship achieve their goal thirty-three percent more often than men who are seeking romantic and sexual relationships (Scharlott and Christ 1995). In some instances, individuals may initially use the Internet as a means of establishing friendships, but these relationships eventually transform into something different over time. Consider the following example:

In a FTF conversation, when you see a smile it makes you feel more connected to the other person.

Posted on December 1, 2003

**Margaret wrote:** Wanted to share my internet romance. Back in May of 2001 I went on to an over 40's chat out of curiosity. I was not looking for anybody. I met a man through the chat who also was not on the lookout. I guess in the way I was talking, it caught his eye and he asked if he could e-mail me as a friend. We both stated from the beginning that it was nothing more than friendship. The more we talked, the more things began to change.

He sent me his photo and I sent him mine. He expressed his feelings of love for me and I did the same in return. On September 20th he came to Canada to visit me (he is from the U.S.) and we knew even before the visit we would be attracted to each other. As soon as we met at the airport we knew it! We had such a great time together. He kept telling me how much he loved me, he held my hand constantly as we walked around seeing the sights and the kisses were certainly there as well. On the 23rd he told me that he had to have me and asked me to be his wife. I immediately responded with a yes.

For all you that may think we might be very young people, this is not the case. I'm 42 and he is 51. I work for a police agency and he is in state government. My son and I are now flying down to his state for the American Thanksgiving and to meet his family, friends, and co-workers. He has already started with the immigration papers (which we are truly hoping) will not become a big headache or a long wait. We speak to each other every day either by computer or by telephone expressing our love for each other. In the future, when I have been given permission by immigration to be married, I will then move to the States and we will be married in his home state. I never thought in my wildest dreams that this kind of situation would ever happen to me.

I have heard the negative feedback on internet dating but on the other hand, I've heard more positive coming out of it. I already know—2 girls in my office are successfully internet dating—one with someone in Canada and the other with someone in the U.S. Good luck to everybody who goes this route.

—http://www.internetdatingstories.com/

This example illustrates how rapidly relationships can evolve through CMC as well as the variety of ways that individuals use the Internet. Margaret states that she initially used the Internet because she was "curious," not because she was looking for a mate. She mentions that her online relationship started out as platonic but then quickly transformed into a romantic connection. This example also illustrates the hyperpersonal model of CMC discussed earlier in the chapter.

In addition to sex differences in Internet use, Nie (2001) established a correlation between income and education and the use of the Internet. College graduates are more likely to use the Internet consistently. Furthermore, research indicates that the average age of Internet users is under forty and that these individuals have an average yearly income of $55,000 (Suler 2002). With regard to Internet use among persons of various ethnic and racial backgrounds, research has found that nearly eighty percent of English-speaking Latinos, seventy-four percent of Caucasians, and sixty-one percent of African-Americans use the Internet (Marriott 2006). These demographic statistics support the presence of a *digital divide*, or a gap, between those who have access to the Internet and those who do not. With so many people turning to the Internet as the primary channel for communication and information, the notion of a digital divide is one that demands attention by researchers. The question of "power" becomes an issue as we analyze the accessibility of CMC.

**Digital divide**
A gap between those who have access to the internet and those who do not.

## EFFECTS OF CMC RELATIONSHIPS

The social dynamics and venues created by the Internet generate both opportunities and risks for developing interpersonal relationships (Parks and Floyd 1996). Over the years, our students have shared both success and horror stories about friends, family members, co-workers, or acquaintances who have established romantic relationships and friendships online. Students often recount stories about individuals who travel across the country to meet a "true love," only to find that the person has completely misrepresented him- or herself online. We suspect that the media may also play a role in shaping our students' negative opinions of online relationships. Perhaps the stories of healthy relationships that have developed online are not as newsworthy as those that end in heartache or disappointment. While the media may depict a relatively one-sided view of online relationships, much of the literature on forming online relationships focuses on both positive and negative aspects of communicating online.

## Positive Aspects

An article published in *Time* magazine (Kirn 2000) compared the initiation of online relationships to dating practices of the past. "In many ways this is courtship as it once was, before the advent of the singles bar. There is plenty of conversation but no touching" (73). Communicating online may allow people to gradually build their level of intimacy before they meet, which may result in more meaningful relationships.

Several authors have discussed other positive aspects of using CMC to form interpersonal relationships: less chance of face-to-face rejection, less geographic limitations, less confrontation with unwanted admirers, and more potential relationship prospects (Anderson and Emmers-Sommer 2006; Walther 1993; 1996). Rabin (1999) also feels that there are benefits associated with the use of CMC to establish relationships. Rabin (1999) claims:

> "The risks involved in making an impression in an appearance-obsessed world and the embarrassment of face-to-face rejection are perils that don't affect the cyberflirt… Flirting online frees you from a host of offline pitfalls, including shyness… incompatibility (Poof! Mr./Ms. Wrong is gone just like that!) and geographic limitations (Stuck in a small town? Not any more.)" (2).

Other positive aspects include developing an initial interest without a major emphasis on physical appearance and an increased level of familiarity. Cooper and Sportolari (1997) contend that

> "In FTF [face-to-face] interaction, people make quick judgments based on physical attributes. … People who may have FTF encounters unwittingly keep themselves from intimate relationships by being overly focused upon or critical of their or others' physical appearance are freed up online to develop connections" Furthermore, "frequent contact with others is possible with little inconvenience or cost from the comfort and safety of one's own home" (9).

The concept of the importance of frequent contact supports Hendrick and Hendrick's (1983) contention that individuals who communicate on a more consistent basis tend to develop a stronger attraction to each other.

## Negative Aspects

Studies often describe the physical dangers involved in forming online relationships, but there is an equal amount of danger present during face-to-face interactions (Conley and Bierman 1999). However, there are other negative aspects of forming relationships online.

LACK OF TECHNICAL KNOWLEDGE AND ABSENCE OF SOCIAL CONTEXT CUES. A lack of technical knowledge and the absence of social context cues may impede some individuals from using the Internet to communicate effectively. Rintel and Pittam (1997) contend, "users must not only come to terms with the basics of interaction management vis-à-vis the technical commands necessary to communicate, but also the curtailment of the social context cues that are used in managing interactions and establishing interpersonal relationships" (530–531). In other words, those who choose to communicate via the Internet have to learn not only the technological aspects of interaction, but also how to compensate for the lack of social cues available in electronic messages. If a friend sends you an email, there is some technical knowledge required to access that message. Not only do you have to know how to "log on" to your email, there are probably also passwords and user identification codes that have to be entered in order to access your online mailbox. Once the message is accessed, the next task involves interpreting the emoticons and language that is used to communicate emotions and feelings. Specifically, Parks and Floyd (1996) have asserted, "Relational cues emanating from the physical context are missing, as are nonverbal cues regarding vocal qualities, bodily movements, and physical appearance. Thus, CMC is judged to have a narrower bandwidth and less information richness than face-to-face communication" (81). In essence, there is a new level of knowledge and skill required to effectively communicate online. Unfortunately, some individuals lack online competence. Emails that fail to address the other person by name or that include one-word responses are often perceived as being rude. Given that many email addresses are abbreviations or codes, sending emails without signing your name can also be confusing. After all, how is a receiver supposed to know that js123456@ohiou.edu is Jane Smith if she fails to sign her email? Failure to employ proper online etiquette can result in potential communication breakdowns and misunderstandings.

ANONYMITY. Anonymity when communicating online may also pose problems. Rintel and Pittam (1997) have shared Kiesler, Seigel, and McGuire's (1984) fears that "the increased anonymity [of] CMC leads to uninhibited behavior... by some users to try extreme and (risky) attention-getting strategies to initiate interactions ..." (531). This anonymity or pseudonymity allows individuals to communicate more openly and, in some cases, individuals may feel that they can get away with using exaggerated, deceptive, manipulative, or abusive communication. These risky behaviors "fail to establish new relationships and sometimes result in retaliation rather than interaction" (Rintel and Pittam 1997, 531).

DECEPTIVE BEHAVIOR. Furthermore, online anonymity may lead to an increase in deceptive behavior. Deceptive behaviors include misrepresenting personal attributes, failing to share important personal information such as existing interpersonal relationships with a spouse, an over reliance on an "online" persona, or accelerated intimacy. Greenfield (1999) has discussed the misinformation often shared during online interactions. He has observed:

> There are some estimates that between thirty-three and fifty percent of individuals on the Internet are lying about some aspect of who and what they are. Some people have been found to represent themselves as members of the opposite sex! There is undoubtedly a considerable amount of lying about marital and financial status along with portraying one's personal characteristics as being more desirable than in reality. Everyone online weighs less than the real-time scale indicates! People become actors and actresses, allowing their innermost fantasies to become expressed online (30).

In addition, lying online allows individuals to create a new identity, an online persona. As Cooper and Sportolari (1997) have warned, "rather than using the net as a way to work on inhibited or conflictual aspects of the self, people may instead (consciously or not) use online relating to further split off unintegrated parts of themselves, leading to a compulsive and destructive reliance on their screen personae and relationships" (12). Individuals can create online personas that differ greatly from their real self-presentation. For example, those that want to experience what it is like to be the opposite sex may engage in a practice described as online gender-bending (Slagle 2006). This deceptive practice often involves presenting oneself as the opposite sex in chat rooms or online video games to experience what it is like to be a man or woman. One man interviewed about his gender-bending practices admitted to adopting a female superhero persona named Robotrixie when participating in online games. A female that participates in similar online games stated that she has figured out how to identify males that are engaging in online gender-bending: "The fact that they are scantily clad is a huge clue" and "often the bigger the breasts, the more likely it's a guy" (Slagle 2006).

INTERNET ADDICTION. Although some psychologists believe that excessive reliance on the Internet should not be defined as an addiction because substance abuse is not involved, research has categorized what is considered an excessive amount of Internet use as Internet addiction. According to one study (Young 1998), Internet addiction is characterized by spending six hours or more online at a time, craving online interaction, and feelings of anxiousness and irritation when offline. Furthermore, Young (1998) has contended that Internet addiction can affect an individual's life in many areas, including family and relationships, as it often leads to individuals becoming more involved with their virtual life and less involved with reality.

**ACCELERATED INTIMACY.** If used effectively, CMC can allow a relationship to form gradually. However, Trafford (1982) and Greenfield (1999) have both called attention to a phenomenon they often observe in online relationships known as *coup de foudre* (bolt of lightning), or accelerated intimacy. When comparing individuals that establish relationships online to those that establish their relationships via FTF communication, those establishing relationships online often experience significant increases in the amount of intimate information exchanged. Trafford (1982) and Greenfield (1999) agree that the accelerated amount of intimacy experienced in online relationships may not always benefit individuals or relationships. Most interpersonal researchers agree that it takes a great deal of time and effort to establish trust and intimacy in relationships. Individuals may need time to process information about the relationship partner, observe the relationship partner for consistency in their behaviors, and then determine whether there is the potential for the relationship to move forward.

**➤ Coup de foudre**
State of accelerated intimacy ("love at first sight").

# FORMING SAFE AND MEANINGFUL ONLINE RELATIONSHIPS

Books such as *Putting Your Heart Online* (Capulet 1998), which details the process involved in forming an online relationship, devote pages to developing effective interpersonal relationships online and emphasize that the Internet offers a new framework in which to create meaningful interpersonal relationships. With the emergence of the Internet as a popular social network, there is a need for students of interpersonal communication to examine this form of communication. Thus, we believe that it is important to offer suggestions for forming safe and meaningful relationships online. Two important areas to consider when developing online relationships are time factors and behavioral cues.

## *Time Factors*

Researchers emphasize the importance of taking the necessary time to develop meaningful online relationships (Walther 1992; Rintel and Pittam 1997). Given that many individuals post in-depth personal information on social networking and dating sites, we may think we have achieved intimacy in an online relationship when in fact, it may not be as intimate as we imagine. The information is available—personal likes, dislikes, hopes, and aspirations are posted for all to see. Similar information would typically be revealed only after multiple face-to-face conversations. Ample time for forming CMC relationships and allowing for adequate impression formation is critical.

Walther, Anderson, and Park (1994) applied Walther's (1992) social information processing perspective to analyze the impact of time factors in CMC relationships. This perspective acknowledges that, due to cue limitations of CMC, the medium cannot possibly convey all the task-related information (or the social information) in as little time as multi-channel FTF communication. While the personal information posted in an online profile may cause us to feel like we know a person, it is important to take into consideration that the lack of nonverbal cues may inhibit accurate impression formation. Consider the following example:

> Angela was eagerly anticipating her first face-to-face meeting with Marin. The two had met on Facebook and exchanged emails for the past three weeks. Angela's friends laughed when she said she was "in love," and they pointed out that it wasn't possible to fall in love so quickly. But they just didn't understand. Through their countless emails, they had shared so much information—much more than Angela had ever shared in any of her previous relationships that she developed via FTF interactions. They finally decided to meet in person. From the first awkward hug at the entrance to the coffee shop, Angela began to second-guess things. While they talked, she became annoyed when Marin kept glancing around the room while she was talking, causing Angela to feel as though she really wasn't listening to what she was saying. As the conversation continued, Angela found that she was bothered by the critical tone and negative facial expressions that Marin made when talking about things around campus. At the end of the evening, Angela was crushed—what had happened to the relationship? Things had gone so well when they communicated online, so why did everything fall apart when they finally had the chance to meet?

At the beginning of the example we learn that Angela has been exchanging emails with Marin for three weeks and feels that she may be "in love" with Marin. When Angela says that she has shared more information with Marin online than she has ever shared in her previous FTF relationships, she illustrates the hyperpersonal nature of CMC described earlier in the chapter. This example illustrates the tendency for some individuals to self-disclose at greater depths and at a faster rate in CMC contexts than in FTF contexts. Additionally, this scenario reinforces the importance of spending time with individuals in FTF interactions in order to form more accurate perceptions of their attitudes, beliefs, values and behaviors. Walther, Anderson, and Park (1994) agree that time is an important factor when forming accurate impressions in online relationships. Specifically, they believe that the critical difference between FTF and CMC relationship formation is the rate at which perceived intimacy is achieved. While they acknowledge that we are certainly capable of achieving intimacy in CMC relationships, time is a critical factor.

Based on this research, we encourage students that want to develop relationships online to pay thoughtful attention to time factors. Take time to get to know one another, and recognize the potential value of social cues that are sometimes are only available through a face-to-face meeting. Beebe, Beebe, and Redmond (2002) have asserted, "The key to success [when developing online relationships] is to apply the same skills that you would in a face-to-face relationship" (384). Think about the additional information obtained in a FTF conversation—the tone of voice, nonverbal behaviors, and other cues that offer additional insight about the other person. Just as you would devote a significant amount of time and energy to relationships developed via FTF communication, the same would hold true for relationships developed online.

While we are unable to pinpoint exactly how much time it should take to develop a successful online relationship, we can offer another suggestion related to time. Beware the **coup de foudre**, or being "struck" by the "lightning" pace of a relationship! If you feel that a relationship is moving along too quickly, it probably is.

## *Behavioral Cues*

In addition to considering the time factor, understanding **behavioral cues** is essential when forming online relationships. Ellison, Heino, and Gibbs (2006) conducted a study of the self-presentation strategies, or behaviors, used by online dating participants. Ellison and her colleagues interviewed thirty-four individuals that were currently active on a large online dating site to learn more about how they managed their online impressions. Participants indicated that they often paid close attention to small or minute online cues that they and others sent. For example, one participant described the significance of profiles that were well-written, stating "I just think if they can't spell or… formulate a sentence, I would image that they are not that educated" (Ellison etal. 2006, 10). Another participant commented that she did not want to come across as at all sexual in her profile because she "didn't want to invite someone who thought I was going to go to bed with them [as soon as] I shook their hand" (Ellison etal. 2006, 10). Individuals indicated that they also tried to be brief when responding to potential partners so as not to appear "too desperate for conversation" (Ellison etal. 2006, 10). All of these examples illustrate how individuals monitor behavioral cues to display a certain image online. Individuals must not only understand how to use effective behavioral cues, but also how to assess the behavioral cues of others. When communicating online, there are several strategies to use to maximize effective online communication.

Being honest is the first guideline to follow for effective online communication. Conley and Bierman (1999) contend that honesty is a crucial component of successful online relationships. One should not exaggerate personal attributes and must always be specific about self-attributes and the desired attributes one is looking for in others. Ellison (2006) describes the tendency for people to describe their ideal self, not their actual self, when attempting to find a relationship partner. For example, one woman using online dating services noted that the picture she posted on her profile was from five years ago and that the picture depicted her as a thinner version of her current self (Ellison etal. 2006). Because the picture was dated and depicted her ideal, not actual self, the woman expressed a desire to lose weight so that her online and FTF personas were consistent. This example illustrates the relationship between online behavior, FTF interactions and the potential for relationship development. When individuals are deceptive online about aspects of their appearance, likes, dislikes, or hobbies, they risk being "caught" in a lie once actual FTF interactions occur. Inconsistencies between the ways that individuals present themselves online and in FTF contexts could affect the potential for the relationship to develop further.

Secondly, Swartz (2000) discusses the importance of safety when forming online interpersonal relationships. Specifically, it is important to maintain a degree of anonymity by revealing personal information gradually. He observes, "many times because of loneliness, sexual desire, or desperation we might go against our better judgment" and warns not to "jump headlong into a relationship using a rationalization along the lines of 'you've got to take risks to succeed'" (24).

Moreover, Gwinnell (1998) has emphasized the importance of being very inquisitive during online interactions and has strongly suggested asking the following questions:

1. Are you seeing anyone now?
2. How many online relationships have you had?
3. Why did your last relationship end?
4. How many times have you been married?
5. What would your ex tell me about you?
6. How do you deal with everyday life issues such as cleanliness, religious preference, and use of alcohol and drugs?
7. Is there someone I can contact who can offer his or her personal opinion of you? (78–81). (See also Capulet 1998, 121–127).

While these questions may seem somewhat intrusive, it is important to learn as much as you can about this individual prior to meeting FTF.

In addition to being inquisitive, one must be alert to the possibility of deception. Beebe, Beebe, and Redmond (2002) believe "the detection of deception in face-to-face encounters is aided by the presence of nonverbal cues. However, online such deception is almost as easy as simply typing the words" (389). Thus, one must "be cautious in forming relationships with Internet strangers" (Beebe et al., 2002. 389). Detecting the warning signs of deception is paramount. Swartz (2000) provides one of the most comprehensive discussions of "red flags" for detecting deception. Specifically, he advises one to look for signs of vagueness or non-responsiveness, which may indicate the person is hiding something. Swartz also recommends that individuals pay attention to whether or not the person goes offline or disappears for days or weeks at a time. Consider when the individual seems to be the most available to communicate. If he or she seems to be getting online at odd hours or odd times of the day, this may indicate that the person is concealing something from you. Another warning sign to consider is the individual's tendency to form quick online emotional attachments. Finally, Swartz encourages online users to focus on the other person's knowledge of current or historical events, which may indicate actual age or specific gender information. In the same way that we attempt to identify red flags during initial FTF encounters, we can use these guidelines to monitor the quality of online interactions.

## CHAPTER SUMMARY

An article in *Newsweek* (Levy 1997) describes the surge of consistent Internet use as an "indelible feature of modern life" (52). Those who support forming relationships online also believe that CMC is not necessarily a replacement for face-to-face interactions; rather, CMC can provide an option that allows people to be more selective when searching for interpersonal relationships. However, before using CMC individuals must possess the knowledge, skills, and motivation needed to communicate effectively using this medium. This chapter offered an overview of how the Internet has changed the way we establish relationships with others.

In the past, FTF communication with family and community members was the primary means of networking with others to establish platonic and romantic relationships. Today, individuals can connect with others through CMC and establish romantic or platonic relationships with individuals from all over the world! Of course, there are both benefits and drawbacks associated with CMC. We hope that individuals will adopt the suggestions offered in this chapter for communicating effectively online. By following the experts' guidelines and paying attention to any red flags that may indicate deceptive online behavior, we hope that our students will establish safe and rewarding relationships.

# APPLICATIONS

## Discussion Questions

1. Discuss the different communication channels used to interact with your friends and family. On any given day, which communication channel do you use the most? Explain why.
2. Discuss the pros and cons of using social networking sites such as Myspace and Facebook. Why do you think college students use these sites so often?
3. Do you feel that individuals are more willing to self-disclose private information through computer mediated communication than FTF communication? Why do you feel that this is/is not the case? Support your position with specific examples.
4. How is the *coup de foudre* phenomenon that often results from developing relationships via CMC problematic for individuals? What suggestions could you offer someone that chooses to establish an online romantic relationship?

## KEY WORDS

*Active vs. passive communication activity* Active communication requires involvement between the two or more participants, with prompted questions and answers and implied mutual interest in communication. Passive communication involves less engagement between participants, including potential avoidance of expression in one or both participants.
"The vast majority of our face-to-face interactions require us to be **active** participants in a conversations. Of course, there are times when someone may engage in **passive** communication behaviors, but our physical presence typically requires us to be engaged in an interaction."

*Asynchronous* Involves a time lapse between when a message is received and when a response is made.

*Coup de foudre* State of accelerated intimacy ("love at first sight").

*Detachment* Voluntary or involuntary inability to form attachments or emotional connections.
"Another consequence of reduced social cues is the tendency for **detachment**."

*Digital divide* A gap between those who have access to the internet and those who do not.

*Flaming* Aggressive attacks made against another person.

*Hyperpersonal model of CMC* Online communication that often facilitates relationship development and perceptions of intimacy.

*Informal vs. formal language style* Informal language style is casual and/or intimate, while formal language style adheres to societal and grammatical rules and/or boundaries.

"As a result, our CMC messages are often more **informal** in terms of language style compared to the more elaborate and **formal** nature of FTF messages."

*Media richness theory* Describes the capability of a communication channel to convey a variety of cues.

*Reduced social cues theory* Explains the absence of nonverbal cues in online interactions.

*Social networking* The process of connecting with others to form different types of relationships.

*Social presence theory* Describes the perceived psychological closeness that occurs during a FTF interaction.

*Synchronous* Occurs in real time, or simultaneously.

# REFERENCES

Anderson, A.T., and T.M. Emmers-Sommer. 2006. Predictors of relationship satisfaction in online romantic relationships. *Communication Studies, 57,* 153–172.

Althaus, S.L., and D. Tewksbury. 2000. Patterns of Internet and traditional news media in a networked community. *Political Communication, 17* (1), 21–45.

Adler, R.B., and N. Towne. 2003 *Looking out, looking in.* (10th ed.).Belmont, CA: Wadsworth.

Beebe, S.A., S.J. Beebe, and M.V. Redmond. 2002. *Interpersonal communication: Relating to others.* (3rd ed.). MA: Allyn & Bacon.

Boneva, B., R. Kraut, and D. Frohlich. 2001. Using e-mail for personal relationships: The difference gender makes. *American Behavioral Scientist, 45,* 530–549.

Capulet, N. 1998. *Putting you heart online.* CA: Variable Symbols, Inc.

Cohen, J., and G. Langer. Poll: Rudeness in America, 2006. Retrieved from abcnews. go.com June 6, 2006.

Conley, L., and J. Bierman. 1999. *Meet me online: The #1 practical guide to Internet dating.* NC: Old Mountain Press, Inc.

Cooper, A., and L. Sportolari. 1997. Romance in cyberspace: Understanding online attraction. *Journal of Sex Education & Therapy, 22* (1), 7–14.

Cyber Atlas. 2005. Geographics: Population explosion http://cyberatlas.internet.com/big_picture/geographics/article.

Daft, R.L., and R.H. Lengel. 1984. Information richness: A new approach to managerial behavior and organization design. *Research in Organizational Behavior, 6,* 191–233.

DeGol, T. (Executive Producer). (2003, February 13). *WTAJ Channel 10 News* [Television broadcast]. Altoona, PA.

Ellison, N., R. Heino, and J. Gibbs. 2006. Managing impressions online: Self-presentation processes in the online dating environment. *Journal of Computer-Mediated Communication, 11,* 1–28. Retrieved online June 19, 2007 from *www.blackwell-synergy.com.*

Emmers-Sommer, T.M. 2005. Non-normative relationships: Is there a norm of (non) normativity? *Western Journal of Communication, 69,* 1–4.

Greenfield, D.N. 1999. *Virtual addiction: Help for netheads, cyberfreaks, and those who love them.* CA: New Harbinger Publications.

Gwinnell, E. 1998. *Online seductions: Falling in love with strangers on the internet.* NY: Kodansha America, Inc.

Hian, L.B., S.L. Chuan, T.M.K. Trevor, and B.H. Detenber. 2004. Getting to know you: Exploring the development of relationship intimacy in computer-mediated communication. *Journal of Computer-Mediated Communication, 9,* Retrieved June 24, 2007 from http://www.ascusc.org/jcm/vol9/issue3/detenber.html.

Hendrick, C., and S. Hendrick. 1983. *Liking, loving and relating.* CA: Brooks/Cole.

Jedlicka, D. 1981. Automated go-betweens: Mate selection of tomorrow? *Family Relations, 30,* 373–376.

Johnson, T.L., and B.K. Kaye. 1999. Cruising is believing? Comparing Internet and traditional sources on media credibility measures. *Journalism and Mass Media Quarterly, 75* (12), 325–340.

Kiesler, S., J. Seigel, and T.W. McGuire. 1984. Social and psychological aspects of computer mediated communication. *American Psychologist, 39,* 1123–1134.

Kirn, W. 2000. The love machines. *Time, 155,* 73.

Knapp, M.L., and J.A. Daly (Eds.). 2002. *Handbook of interpersonal communication.* (3rd ed.). CA: Sage.

La Ferle, C., S.M. Edwards, and W.N. Lee. 2000. Teens' use of traditional media and the Internet. *Journal of Advertising Research, 40* (3), 55–66.

Lee, J. 2002. I Think, Therefore IM. *New York Times,* September 19, p.G.1.

Lenhart, A., and M. Madden. 2006a. Teens, Privacy, and Online Social Networks, PEW Internet and American Life Project. http://www.pewinternet.org/report_display.asp?r=211. Accessed May 26, 2007.

———. 2006b. "Online activities and pursuits," PEW Internet and American Life Project. http://www.pewinternet .org/PPF/r/177/report_display.asp. Accessed May 28, 2007.

Lerner Productions. 2003. *Master the basics: Birth of the net.* http:// www. learnthenet.com.

Levy, S. 1996/1997. Breathing is also addictive. *Newsweek,* December/January, 52–53.

Marriott, M. 2006. Digital Divide Closing as Blacks Turn to Internet. *New York Times,* March 31.

Miller, T.E., and P.C. Clemente. The 1997 American internet user survey: Realities beyond the hype. NY: Find/Svp, Inc. [On-line]. Available: http://www.findsvp. com/.

Nie, N.H. 2001. Sociability, interpersonal relations, and the internet: Reconciling conflicting findings. *The American Behavioral Scientist, 45,* 420–435.

Parks, M.R., and K. Floyd. 1996. Making friends in cyberspace. *Journal of Computer Mediated Communication, 46* (1), 80–97.

Parks, M.R., and L.D. Roberts. 1998. 'Making MOOsic' The development of personal relationships on line and a comparison to their off-line counterparts. *Journal of Social and Personal Relationships, 15* (4), 517–537.

Pew Research Center. 2006. Pew Internet and American Life Project. http://www. pewinternet.org

Pratt, L., R.L. Wiseman, M.J. Cody, and P.F. Wendt. 1999. Interrogative strategies and information exchange in computer-mediated communication. *Communication Quarterly, 47* (1), 46–66.

Rabin, S. 1999. *Cyberflirt: How to attract anyone, anywhere on the world wide web.* NY: Penguin Putnam, Inc.

Rintel, S.E., and J. Pittam. 1997. Strangers in a strange land: Interaction management on internet relay chat. *Human Communication Research, 23* (4), 507–534.

Rogers, R.M. 1997. *Looking for love online: How to meet a woman using an online service.* NY: Simon & Schuster Macmillan Co.

Rumbough, T. 2001. The development and maintenance of interpersonal relationships through computer-mediated communication. *Communication Research Reports, 18,* (3), 223–229.

Scharlott, B.W., and W.G. Christ. 1995. Overcoming relationship-initiation barriers: The impact of a computer-dating system on sex role, shyness, and appearance inhibitions. *Computers in Human Behavior, 11* (2), 191–204.

Short, J.A., E. Wiliams, and B. Christie. 1976. *The social psychology of telecommunications.* New York, NY: John Wiley & Sons.

Slagle, M. August 2006. Gender-bending proves popular in online games. Retrieved July 16, 2007 from Hamptonroads.com http://content.hamptonroads.com/ story.cfm?story=109533&ran121532

Sproull, L., and S. Kiesler. 1986. Reducing social context cues: Electronic mail in organizational communication. *Management Science, 32,* 1492–1512.

Swartz, J. 2000. *The complete idiot's guide to online dating and relating.* IN: Que Corporation.

Suler, J. 2002. Internet demographics. In *The Psychology of cyberspace,* www.rider. edu/suler/psycyber/basicfeat.html (article orig. pub.1999).

Trafford, A. 1982. *Crazy time: Surviving divorce.* NY: Bantom Books, Inc.

Tanner, W. 1994. Gender gap in cyberspace. *Newsweek,* May, 52–53.

Walther, J.B. 1992. Interpersonal effects in computer-mediated interaction: A relational perspective. *Communication Reports, 19,* 52–90.

———. 1993. Impression development in computer-mediated interaction. *Western Journal of Communication, 57,* 381–389.

———. 1995. Relational aspects of computer-mediated communication: Experimental observations over time. *Organization Science, 6,* 186–203.

———. 1996. Computer-mediated communication: Interpersonal, intrapersonal, and hyperpersonal interaction. *Communication Research, 19,* 52–90.

Walther, J.B., J.F. Anderson, and D.W. Park. 1994. Interpersonal effects in computer-mediated interaction: A meta-analysis of social and antisocial communication. *Communication Research, 21* (4), 460–487.

Walther, J.B., and J.K. Burgoon. 1992. Relational communication in computer-mediated communication. *Human Communication Research, 19,* 50–88.

Wildermuth, S.M. 2001. Love on the line: Participants' descriptions of computer-mediated close relationships. *Communication Quarterly, 49* (2), 89–96. Belmont, CA: Wadsworth.

Woll, S.B., and Cosby, P.C. (1987). Videodating and other alternatives to traditional methods of relationship initiation. In W.H. Jones and D. Perlman (Eds.), *Advances in Personal Relationships* (Vol. 1, pp. 69–108). Greenwich, CT: JAI Press.

Woll, S.B., and Young, P. (1989). Looking for Mr. or Ms. Right: Self-presentation in videodating. *Journal of Marriage and the Family,* 51(2), 483–488.

Young, K.S. 1998. *Caught in the net.* NY: John Wiley & Sons, Inc.

# COMPUTER-MEDIATED COMMUNICATION

Most of the people in this classroom were born in the Internet Era. You have grown up in the shadow of Facebook, Google, and Twitter. No technology has impacted social relationships as much as the computer and social media.

Your parents and grandparents witnessed the advances of television and the telephone. I am almost embarrassed to admit that the first computer I saw was in 1974, and it occupied an entire room. Mobile phones were as big as a walkie-talkie, and we carried our music around with boom boxes the size of a small suitcase. (They invented dirt just a few years before I was born.)

Now we are all wired. On Facebook, 900 million "friends" coexist, the third largest "nation" on the planet. Students sleep with their phones for fear of missing a message. The pace of change occurs faster than ever, and consumers are forced to upgrade technologies more often just to keep up with the pace of change. The ultimate question is: **How will all this technology impact our human communication?**

College is an incredibly social time. We are surrounded with people our own age and invited to participate in numerous classes, clubs, and activities. Have you seen the movie The *Social Network*? It suggests that Mark Zuckerberg's failure to stay in a relationship or join the right social clubs was his impetus to create Facebook. The social media is a cyberversion of a college campus. Who is in a relationship? What are you doing right now? Are there any pictures? What music are you listening to? What groups have you joined? Questions you might ask when you meet someone new on campus are being answered on their Facebook page. Will social media replace social interaction? Are cyber friends different than human friends? Do we present ourselves the same way online as we do in real life? Is our self-disclosure different?

At this point in the research, there are many more questions than answers. Businesses exploit social media to determine our tastes in products and how to sell products to networks of friends. It is a brave new world with new challenges for our relationships. Now is a good time to stop for a moment and think about the consequences of technology and the future of human relationships. The possibilities sound almost like futuristic science fiction. (Maybe my avatar will meet your avatar in cyberspace some day. The question is, Will it be by our choice or theirs?)

From the outer reaches of cyberspace to the realm of the small group, life's complexities are forcing us into small decision-making collectives. In business or in life, it is rare that anyone has all the answers. To promote a product today, you need a research and development team, a sales staff, a marketing team, lawyers, and a public relations staff. Gone are the days of a solitary inventor introducing her product to the world. Fears of copyright litigation, product safety, and start-up financing costs require a number of specific people with specific talents. Most of us have done group projects in other classes. Did you enjoy them? Traditionally, the answer is 50 percent Yes and 50 percent No. Some enjoy the social nature of the project, the shared labor, the creativity of teamwork; while a few enjoy watching others do all the work. Conversely, others hate the loss of control, the difficulty in scheduling meetings, having to compromise with others, and knowing that some are watching them do all the work while earning the same grade.

Regardless of which camp you fall into, groups are a part of our modern world. We need others to complete complex tasks. Love them or hate them, groups are more popular (and necessary) than ever before. Where there are groups, there must be leaders. The following two chapters explore the function of groups and group leadership. The hope is that a little understanding of how effective groups operate will motivate the "observers" to get more involved and teach the "dominators" a little tolerance.

It is like our earliest lessons in grade school: We need to learn how to work and play well with others. Of course, the consequences of these lessons are job performance and maintenance of social relationships in voluntary organizations. The dollars and common sense of group performance and leadership will impact us all of our public and professional lives.

# CHAPTER 7

## Understanding Groups and Communication: Let's All Work Together

### Chapter Objectives

After reading this chapter, you should be able to:
- Explain what constitutes a group
- Identify multiple types of groups
- Describe how an individual's communication influences groups
- Identify the many factors that affect a group
- Explain how groups work collaboratively to make decisions

PERSONAL: Your family has decided it is time to get the house in order. You have a family meeting and discuss the division of labor. As the tasks are assigned, your siblings begin to argue with one another. Your parents quickly resolve the conflict by telling them to go to their rooms and begin working. You start cleaning your room but can hear your siblings fighting again. Each is claiming that the other is not doing the correct chore. You think it would be best if the family had a meeting where they talked about each person's roles and duties. How do you approach the subject with your family?

PROFESSIONAL: You have just graduated college and have a full-time job that you enjoy. At your job, you have been asked to be part of a new team. Being asked to join this special project at work has produced both excitement and anxiety. As a member of this special task force, you are required to work with others to generate the best possible solution to a problem in the company. You know you need to listen to the ideas of others as well as incorporate your own ideas to ensure that all members of the group contribute to the project. At your first meeting, you realize some of the members of the group don't seem to get along. They are constantly interrupting one another and negating ideas before the entire group has an opportunity to discuss them. You want to talk to the group about this so it doesn't continue. How do you start this discussion?

PUBLIC: You are excited for the school semester to start. That is, until you get to your first class and the professor announces that the class is centered on working in groups. To make matters worse, you do not get to pick the other members of your group. Instead, the professor assigns students to groups. Once you meet with your group, you decide using Facebook would make communicating easier so you "friend" each other and you begin to look at each member's profile photos. As you scan the photos on their Facebook profiles you see pictures that make you think your group members are not serious about school. In fact, some of the pictures that are posted give you the impression that these group members may depend on you to do all the work. You wonder why your group mates would post these types of photos because they create a negative impression. Though you know them from in-person interactions, their online personas do not seem to match who they appear to be in face-to-face interactions. How should you approach this situation to ensure they are willing to work hard to make the group successful?

# CHAPTER OVERVIEW

You likely read the opening examples and said to yourself, "Yes, I can relate" to some of them. Working on class projects, collaborating with coworkers on tasks, and making decisions as a family are all situations that require us to interact effectively in groups. The opening scenarios illustrate the fact that we don't live in isolation and thus, we depend on others.

Poole, Hollingshead, McGrath, Moreland, and Rohrbaugh (2004) argued that individuals "live in groups" (p. 3). Throughout our daily lives a majority of what we do is performed and coordinated with other people. From the time you wake up, you depend on other people—discussing issues with roommates or family members, going to class and working on group projects, and collaborating with colleagues at your workplace—all of these situations require us to communicate with others to accomplish our common goals. It is also safe to say that these people you work with in groups probably do not behave or communicate just like you. In fact, Gastil (1993) argued that differences in individual speaking style are one of the most common problems facing groups. Additionally, Frey and SunWolf (2005) argued that communication is "the medium through which information in groups is shared and processed" (p. 173). In our professional lives, we will spend a majority of the work week working with others. In a survey of how CEOs of major corporations spent their time, of the 55 hours worked, approximately half of that time was spent working with others ("Time Crunch," 2012). In short, our lives are affected in a number of ways by groups.

# GROUPS DEFINED

**Group**
A collection of individuals with a common purpose.

If small groups are an integral part of our lives, how then do we know if we are part of one? At the most basic level, *groups* are a collection of individuals with a common purpose. Burkhalter, Gastil, and Kelshaw (2002) indicated groups need at least three people, that the exact size of the group should be "manageable," and people in the group should be able to "see and hear one another" (p. 400). In today's world, seeing and hearing one another can be accomplished both face-to-face and virtually. In addition to having a collection of individuals, inherent to a group is the idea of mutual influence. The behaviors of one person create changes in others' behaviors. Mutual influence is like a tennis match. Both players in the match respond to the other's actions. Player A hits the ball to player B. Player B's movement is dependent upon what Player A does first. Player B's actions are in response to the previous actions by Player A. Player A then reacts to player B's actions and returns the ball.

Interdependence is like a tennis match as both players respond to the other's actions.

Related to this idea is that of interdependence. Each group member has mutual influence on others because they are dependent upon the others in the group in some way. Think of the group as being like a family. You likely depend on certain people to perform certain functions. For example, one member of the family might make dinner, another takes out the trash, another might tease everyone, yet another member is the one who always checks in on the family. A group follows this model. You expect certain people to do certain things. When one person is not present, the group (just like the family) is different and individuals may need to adjust their behaviors to assume responsibility for the missing behaviors.

Another key component of group life is that of a common purpose or goal. All group members are working together toward the completion of some task. That is, they share in the achievement of a common end state. Without this common goal or purpose, they are simply individuals interacting without an end mission in mind. It is the common purpose or goal that helps to solidify the group and bring individuals together to focus on one project.

# TYPES OF GROUPS

As evidenced by the scenarios at the beginning of this chapter, there are different types of groups. These include the people you work with at school, the church groups to which you belong, the clubs and organizations in which you participate, and the people with whom you work at your jobs. As research suggests, your past group experiences will influence your future group behaviors such as commitment to the group (Forrest & Miller, 2003). That is, if you have had a terrible group experience in the past, it could impact how you work with others in the future. Based on that negative experience, you probably said to yourself, "Never again will I do this!" Thus, your past experiences influence your perception of working in groups in the future.

**Peer group**
Members who consider one another to be equals in terms of abilities, background, age, responsibilities, beliefs, social standing, legal status, or rights.

**Consensus**
State in which all group members must agree.

A team of athletes is considered a purposive group.

Do you enjoy working in groups? When asked this question, students are often divided in their response, with some indicating they like working in groups and others reporting that they despise group assignments. You will be part of a number of different types of groups throughout your life. In some instances, you will have the opportunity to choose to be part of a group while other groups will be forced upon you. While this might sound a little intimidating, understanding the different types of groups and the factors that impact group communication will enhance your effectiveness when working in a group. The following are examples of groups that you are likely to encounter in your personal, professional, and public lives (Figure 7.1). It is important to note that some of these groups are voluntary while others are involuntary. Voluntary groups are those that we self-select to be part of, whereas involuntary groups are those in which group membership is assigned.

A *peer group* is one that is "composed of members who consider one another to be equals, in terms of abilities, background, age, responsibilities, beliefs, social standing, legal status, or rights. Not all group members agree about the equality of all other members at all times, but there is overt *consensus*

© Jamie Roach/Shutterstock.com

that members of the group are primarily equal" (SunWolf, 2008, p. xii). Reflect on the number of peer groups that you have been a member of throughout your life. Most likely, you are part of many peer groups in your own life. Examples of these include a group of friends, a troop of scouts, or a congregation of worshipers.

A *purposive group* is a group "that has a goal" (Poole et al., 2004, p. 6), that is, working toward the completion of some task. You will be a member of numerous purposive groups throughout your professional and public lives. Examples of purposive groups include work project teams, a school board committee that will give a formal presentation to the board of trustees, support groups that raise awareness of a specific cause, or groups at school that work together to complete an assigned project.

*Factional groups* are defined as those "in which members are representatives or delegates from social entities" (Li & Hambrick, 2005, p. 794). That is, individuals from divergent areas of expertise are brought together to work toward the completion of a common goal. Especially prevalent in your professional life, for example, are

YOU IN CLASS

**Purposive group**
A group that is attempting to achieve the completion of a goal.

**Factional group**
When group members are representatives or delegates from other social entities.

FIGURE 7.1

Types of groups.

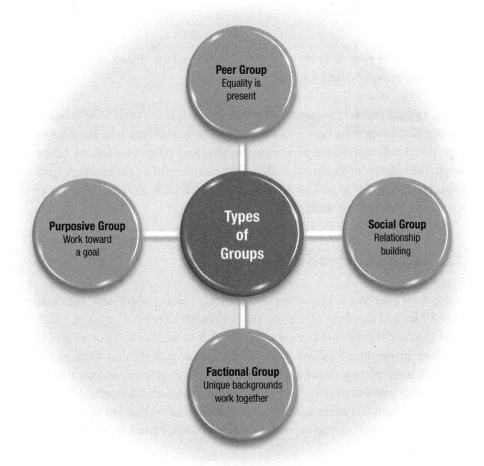

A family is a type of social group.

© szefei/Shutterstock.com

individuals from two different parts of a company (e.g., those in marketing and sales) who combine to find a solution to a problem.

**⫸ Social group**
Collection of individuals focused mostly on relationship-building that gives members a place to develop self-esteem.

Finally, a ***social group*** is a collection of individuals focused mainly on relationship-building that gives members a place to develop self-esteem and have a sense of unity. This is different from a peer group because a social group does not necessarily contain the equality or sameness as shared by members of a peer group. An example of this type of group would be a family or a social club, as these types of groups provide for our need for ***solidarity***.

**⫸ Group solidarity**
The tendency of a group to act as a single unit instead of as a collection of individuals.

# THE NATURE OF GROUPS

**⫸ Dyad**
A collection of only two people.

Groups may take on a life of their own. Individuals collect and blend unique personalities and members of a group travel through a series of stages in which they "come together." Recall that groups work together to achieve a common goal. These stages help group members orient toward the task or goal at hand. Communication that takes place among members of groups can include interpersonal interactions among group members, but the overall group dynamics are inherently different from interpersonal, ***dyadic*** interactions. As a result, special consideration needs to be given to what makes group communication unique from other types of interactions.

Groups develop and "come together" in stages. One popular way to explain this process is by exploring the five stages of group development: forming, storming, norming, performing, and adjourning (Tuckman, 1965; Tuckman & Jensen, 1977). In the *forming stage*, individuals gather together and assemble the group. During this period, members of the group begin orienting to the task, search for a leader, and determine the purpose of the group. Communication tends to focus on polite interactions to ensure we don't "step on others' toes" and small talk to learn more about one another. In the *storming stage*, the group may experience conflict as a result of individuals' emotional responses to completing tasks. Members of the group may have different approaches toward accomplishing the goal, multiple people may want to fulfill the same role (e.g., be the leader), and arguments may ensue about how the group should proceed. It is not uncommon for group members to clash during this period; in fact, this is typically the stage where most of the conflict occurs. Once the group works through the conflicts, they reach the *norming stage*. Group members have calmed the rough seas of storming and determined how best to work with one another. Individuals begin to adopt roles and share ideas with others. Rules are created for interaction and performance. In the *performing stage*, the roles that were adopted in the norming stages become cemented. In essence, the "kinks" have been worked out and the group is able to address both the completion of tasks and the social demands of working with others. In essence, the group becomes a "well-oiled machine." Once the tasks are completed or the goal is accomplished, some groups cease to exist. During the *adjourning stage*, individuals have performed their duties and reached the conclusion of the group experience. During this time, emotional changes such as sadness or excitement as members leave the group may occur. During this stage, there should be critical reflection of individual and others' performance.

**Forming stage**
Initial stage in group development.

**Storming stage**
Second stage of group development, where most conflicts will occur.

**Norming stage**
Third stage of group development in which members create behavioral standards and punishments.

**Performing stage**
Fourth stage in group development in which all members are working toward completion of the group's task.

**Adjourning stage**
Final process of group life that signals the completion of tasks.

To effectively perform groupwork during each of these stages, Hawkins and Fillion (1999) argued that several communication skills are essential. First, they emphasize the importance of effective listening. You have already learned about the listening process in Chapter 5. Remember that listening is a skill that requires effort. Working with others provides a unique opportunity to attend to and comprehend their messages. Additionally, everyone should understand each person's role as part of the larger work group. That is, all members of the group need to know how they "fit" with the others in the group. Building from this idea, Hawkins and Fillion also indicate that all members of the group should contribute actively to the group. Each person should be sure to perform his or her roles and duties. In addition, members should ask questions, use clear and concise language, and convey nonverbal professionalism. By picking the most efficient verbal and nonverbal behaviors, we can be sure that our communicative efforts are easily understood. Efficient verbal communication could entail summarizing each person's responsibilities before concluding a meeting. Nonverbally, it is unlikely that rolling your eyes or raising your voice would be appropriate and well received by others in your group. Given the global world in which we live, it is argued that we also need to devote attention to respecting cultural differences. Simply put, our culture influences our behavior. What is considered professional in one culture might not be regarded the same in another culture. For example, a handshake is a standard greeting of introduction in the United States whereas Chinese cultures may bow or nod instead. When working with diverse individuals, care should be taken to learn about others and attempts made to understand practices.

While somewhat intuitive, these skills are not only necessary for a group to be successful, but they can also be the easiest to forget when working with individuals who are different from us or when conflict emerges. Have you ever worked with a group and someone suggested an outlandish idea? It might have been something you thought was so off the wall that you rolled your eyes or made a facial expression similar to that of disgust. Similarly, when conflict emerges, have you ever lost your temper or perhaps attacked a person and not the idea? While we carefully monitor our verbal response in these situations, we sometimes neglect to consider our nonverbal reactions. Keeping communication concepts such as effective verbal and nonverbal communication and cultural differences in mind, we now look at other factors that impact group life and our ability to be a successful group member.

## Size

The size of a group is important to consider. Scholars seem to agree that the ideal group size is three to seven members to ensure effective communication. Remember, a group is a collection of individuals who influence one another.

Have you ever attended a large dinner party? Perhaps you sat at a table that was so long you could not speak to the people at the far end. We would not consider that a group because your verbal and nonverbal behaviors cannot be effectively interpreted by all of the people at the table. Ultimately, group size should manageable so all individuals in it can consider themselves a part of the group.

## Task versus Social Dimensions within Groups

Once individuals begin to gather and membership in the group is established, two types of communication occur. Communication can focus on the group's task dimension or the social dimension. The *task dimension* is characterized by messages that focus on solving problems, completing a task, or achieving a goal

**Task dimension**
Measures a group's actual progress toward its goals.

This study group is an example of a small group.

(Fujishin, 2001), while the *social dimensions* are those conversations among group members that focus on their relationships and feelings for one another. The social dimension can dictate how individuals approach the task. For example, what if you dislike a member of your group? If that person takes over the group and becomes the leader, you now have to "report" to him and "check in." If you do not like this person, the social dimension—your negative feelings—can affect how you approach the task. You could produce lower quality work, miss deadlines, or avoid communicating with the person, if possible. Thus, both task and social dimensions must be considered when working in groups. It is important for a group to maintain effective relationships in order to accomplish its goals. This does not mean that individuals need to be best friends or even like one another. They do, however, need to establish and manage their social interactions to ensure that they don't derail the group from its purpose.

> **Social dimension**
> Group members' relationships and feelings for each one another.

## Roles

Individuals offer unique contributions to groups through the types of roles they fulfill. One popular definition of *roles* is "that set of common expectations shared by the members about the behavior of an individual" (Bormann, 1969, p. 184). Roles are labels placed on individuals based on their function within a group. These labels have a set of expected behaviors that the individual playing that role or having that label must then perform. Roles can be formal and assigned. However, roles can

> **Roles**
> Labels placed on individuals based on their function within a group.

also be informal and emerge as a result of group interaction. For example, when preparing for the first group meeting, you might know that someone needs to be in charge and create an agenda for the meeting or perhaps send emails to make sure all group members are doing their work. This would be a formal role. Perhaps one group member is self-assigned the role of leader. However, during your interactions with the other group members, it becomes evident that the group needs someone to take notes during meetings because members have difficulty recalling the previous meetings' proceedings. As a result, another group member takes on the role of note-taker. This role would be an informal role because it became evident through interactions among group members that someone needed to provide the function of note-taker. The role of note-taker could be formally elected or appointed through an election process while others can evolve more informally.

Benne and Sheats (1948) proposed a typology of group roles, organizing them into three categories. In a group, your role could be task, relational, or individually focused (Table 7.1).

**Task roles**
Includes all roles that focus on the group's assignment.

*Task roles* focus on the group's assignment. A task role would include an evaluator-critic. This person focuses on setting standards and meeting goals. This individual will question the logic of others when unsure about the accuracy of a proposed idea.

**Relational roles**
Focus on building and maintaining connections among group members.

*Relational roles* focus on building and maintaining connections among group members. A relational role includes that of the harmonizer. This group member produces communication that strives to bring the group members together and achieve cohesiveness. *Individual roles* are those in which individuals focus on self-achievement and not the efforts of the group. An individual role would include that of recognition-seeker. This individual attempts to bring light to his personal accomplishments and will likely take on more work in an attempt to gather more praise. In Table 7.1, many of the common roles within each of the categories are presented along with examples of how these specific roles are enacted in a group setting.

**Individual roles**
When individuals focus on self-achievement and not group efforts.

The roles in Table 7.1 may be present in every group. Task and relational roles are needed and critical to successful group life. Some members of the group need to focus on achieving task completion while others take care of the individuals in the group. Individual roles, however, can prove challenging as they are typically thought of as something that detracts from the group. They focus more on individual achievement rather than the collective achievement of the group.

## TABLE 7.1

Typology of Group Roles

| Type of Role | Description |
|---|---|
| **Task roles** | **Focus on the group's goals and tasks** |
| **Evaluator-critic** | Focuses on setting standards and meeting goals. Questions others' logic when unsure about accuracy |
| **Coordinator** | Focuses communicative efforts on who in the group accomplishes what tasks and when tasks should be done |
| **Opinion-giver** | Expresses opinions and possible interpretations associated with all tasks |
| **Information-seeker** | Collects information related to tasks and completing tasks. |
| **Relational roles** | **Focus on building connections among members** |
| **Encourager** | Offers praise to others and wants to hear others' opinions and ideas |
| **Harmonizer** | Focuses communicative efforts on bringing group members together to achieve cohesiveness |
| **Compromiser** | Avoids conflict and admits any mistakes; works to incorporate all ideas presented |
| **Gatekeeper** | Ensures participation by all group members and that they are listened to and considered during group processes |
| **Individual roles** | **Focus on self-achievement** |
| **Recognition-seeker** | Likes taking on a lot of work because it means he or she will get extra attention because of it |
| **Dominator** | Focuses communicative efforts on being heard; works to control the group and their efforts |
| **Joker** | Uses light-hearted, humorous communication that is often off topic in attempts to be perceived as funny |
| **Withdrawer** | Fails to connect and interact with the group; offers few opinions and may have issues |

>> **Evaluator-critic** Group member who sets standards and meets goals.

>> **Coordinator** Group member that oversees who accomplishes what tasks and when tasks should be done.

>> **Opinion-giver** Group member who expresses opinions and possible interpretations associated with all tasks.

>> **Information-seeker** Group member who collects information related to tasks and completing tasks.

>> **Encourager** Group member who praises others and hears others' opinions and ideas.

>> **Harmonizer** Group member who offers communication focused on achieving cohesion among group members.

>> **Compromiser** Individual who avoids conflict and admits any mistakes in a group.

>> **Gatekeeper** Group member who ensures participation by all group members.

>> **Recognition-seeker** Group member who takes on a lot of work for extra attention.

>> **Dominator** Group member who likes to be heard and works to control the group.

>> **Joker** Group member who uses light-hearted, humorous communication that is often off topic.

>> **Withdrawer** Group member who fails to connect and interact with the group, offers few opinions, and may have issues.

**Task leader**
Focuses group members on completion of assignments.

**Social-emotional leader**
Voice of the group members in terms of the affective orientation to the group.

**Role Theory**
Ways in which individuals enact different social positions (i.e., roles) in their lives.

How are roles typically adopted in groups? Cragan and Wright (1999) suggested that groups should include "leaders" who are in charge of certain aspects of the group when assigning roles. These include a *task leader* who focuses group members on completion of assignments or a *social-emotional leader* who serves as the voice of the group members in terms of the affective orientation to the group. This idea is addressed in more depth in Chapter 9; however, it is important to note that group leaders have roles too.

One theory used to explain and predict roles that individuals perform is *Role Theory*, which concentrates on the ways in which individuals enact different social positions (i.e., roles) in their lives (Biddle, 1979). Role Theory offers five claims. First, individuals create and adopt roles based on their surrounding contexts; that is, the situation is important to consider when determining which roles are needed in the group. For example, if at a school board meeting, it is determined that all happenings should be video recorded, someone will be in charge of technology. Second, roles are commonly associated with individuals in social positions who share a common identity; that is, a role is something that individuals enact when working with others. Inherent to having a role is the idea that others must be present and you are in a group setting. Third, roles are governed by individual awareness of and expectations for each role; that is, how individuals perform a role is based on their knowledge of the role and the ideas of how the role should be enacted. For example, if you are assigned as group motivator, but are unclear of what that entails, such as motivating and reaffirming verbal communication, your ability to perform that role is diminished. Fourth, roles remain because of the consequences and functions associated with them and also due to the fact that roles are often imbedded within a larger social system; that is, groups need roles to be able to function. Roles may change over time, but the idea there is still a role to perform remains. The job duties of the note-taker may shift, but someone needs to record the happenings of the group. Finally, the fifth claim indicates that individuals must be taught the behaviors associated with each role and they must be socialized by others to properly perform a role. There is a learning curve associated with performing the role effectively. In order to play the role of family caregiver, you must first know what that role entails and the essential job functions. For example, a caregiver may be expected to clean the house, prepare meals, and pay bills.

Role Theory assumes that individuals learn the behaviors that correspond with their role. They remain in that role because that role is necessary for proper group functioning. Regardless of the type of role and how one learns the expectations associated with that role, there are some considerations to be made. As you read the list of role types, you probably thought, "I could perform a lot of these

**224**        **CHAPTER 7: Understanding Groups and Communication**

roles." If so, you experience something called *role flexibility*. This occurs when individuals have the ability to play a variety of roles and adapt according to the demands of the situation. In some instances, an individual could alternate between being the note-taker and being the emotional leader, depending on the situation. However, sometimes individuals are required to fill two or more conflicting roles simultaneously. *Role conflict* occurs when you have to perform multiple roles with seemingly contradictory behaviors. If you refer to Table 7.1, you can see by the descriptions that it would be difficult to be both a harmonizer and a dominator. A harmonizer works to bring the group together whereas the dominator is focused solely on advancing his or her position. A harmonizer tends to lighten the mood of the group, whereas a dominator may use communication that detracts from the task. Imagine working with a group of your peers on a class project. As your group works on its tasks, the harmonizer of the group would attempt to bring the group together by highlighting common interests, while the dominator of the group would try to showcase differences of other group members and pull the conversation to focus on these differences. The final consideration is called *role strain*. Have you ever been asked by others in the group to perform a role that you did not necessarily want to do? For example, if you did not want to be the leader of the group, yet the other individuals in the group encouraged you to do so, you may experience role strain. This occurs when an individual is required to assume a new role that he or she is reluctant to perform.

Collectively, there are a number of important and necessary roles that must be filled for groups to work efficiently. Because so many roles are necessary for a group to function, everyone in the group should have an active part in the group.

## *Rules*

Do you remember when your parents told you to clean your room and they stated that if you did not do it, there would be a punishment? Throughout our personal, professional, and public lives, we encounter a number of rules associated with the roles we fulfill. *Group rules* refer to the notion that group members are expected to engage in specific behaviors, and if they do not do so, there are consequences. Rules can be both explicit and implicit. *Explicit rules* are formalized rules that are discussed and sometimes recorded in a document that all group members can access. For example, explicit or formal rules can be considered a company's bylaws or an organization's constitution. These are rules for what should happen in the group. *Implicit rules* are the unspoken expectations that everyone in the group seems to know and adhere to, although they are not formally documented. For example, members of the group understand that being on time for meetings is important.

**Role flexibility**
When individuals possess the ability to play a variety of roles and adapt according to the demands of the situation.

**Role conflict**
When you have to perform multiple roles with seemingly contradictory behaviors.

**Role strain**
When an individual is required to assume a new role that he or she is reluctant to perform.

**Group rules**
Individuals in a group are expected to do certain things, and if they do not do these things, there are consequences.

**Explicit rules**
Formalized rules that are discussed and often documented so that all group members are aware of them.

**Implicit rules**
Unspoken and unwritten expectations that everyone in the group seems to know and adhere to.

The harmonizer of the group works to bring the group together.

© luminaimages/Shutterstock.com

## Norms

Have you ever been part of a group where you were expected to act and behave in a certain way? These expected behaviors are called norms. **Norms** are standardized behaviors across all group members that focus on expected or anticipated behaviors. Homans (1950) argued that norms are behaviors that individuals in the group ought to perform under any circumstance. For example, if you are working in a group that has a treasurer, you would assume the treasurer would have reports of money spent and money paid and that this person could update the group on any financial happenings. These are norms. We expect certain behaviors given particular positions. In a group, your norms will largely be dictated by your group role. For example, if you volunteered to be the secretary during group meetings, you would take notes, ask others to speak loudly so you can record information accurately, and provide the group members with a written recap of the meeting. Norms for behavior can be seen in a variety of situations, and we each have expectations for how others should communicate based on certain factors. Thus, if we expect people to adhere to specific norms for behavior and they do not, it can make group life difficult. Overcoming these difficulties can be accomplished through open communication where all group members share ideas about anticipated behaviors.

**Norms**
Standardized behaviors individuals in the group ought to do under any circumstance.

## Power

**Power** refers to our ability to influence the behavior of others. Exercising power over others is contingent upon there being someone to control. Say you are part

**Power**
Ability to influence others.

of a softball team. Each member of the softball team decides to skip an optional preseason workout. The only person that attends the workout is the team captain. When the team captain arrives and sees no one on the field, who will the team captain be able to influence? That is right—no one. Power typically requires the presence of an interdependent relationship among group members. Thus, individuals are dependent upon one another for the transaction of power. Members of the softball team need to be present in order for someone to enact power.

Five different power bases have been identified (Table 7.2). According to French and Raven (1960), the relationship between at least two people allows for power to be displayed.

As you can see from Table 7.2, some of these types of power are positive, whereas others are negative. You probably like receiving rewards for your behavior or completion of tasks, and it is safe to say you do not enjoy having your work criticized, especially if it occurs in front of others. Additionally, having someone in your group who has a level of expertise, knowledge, or past experience with the topic can also make for a smoother group process because that individual can offer insights others may not know.

**Reward power**
Ability to give out positive benefits or rewards.

**Coercive power**
Ability to give out punishment.

**Referent power**
Individuals' positive regard for and personal identification with the leader.

**Expert power**
Power derived from the knowledge or expertise one has.

**Legitimate power**
Power that is associated with a certain position. Because of his or her position in the group, an individual has a certain right to influence/oversee others' behaviors.

TABLE 7.2

Typology of Power (French & Raven, 1960)

| Type of Power | Description | Example of Power |
|---|---|---|
| Reward power | Refers to the ability to give out positive benefits or rewards | One who ensures all tasks are completed and gives group members tangible goods once the work is done |
| Coercive power | Refers to the ability to give out punishments | One who scolds, reprimands, criticizes, or offers other negative outcomes |
| Referent power | Refers to an individual's positive regard for/personal identification with the leader. Can be manifested in perceptions of similarity or interpersonal affinity. | When others do as they are told because they find the leader likeable and socially attractive |
| Expert power | Refers to the knowledge or expertise one has | When individuals in a group listen to what someone says about a task because of his or her skillful mastery of a topic or expert understanding |
| Legitimate power | Refers to the power that is associated with a certain position. Because of his or her position in the group, an individual has a certain right to influence/oversee others' behaviors. | When a group elects a "leader" (i.e., someone to oversee the completion of tasks), this person is said to have legitimate power because social norms indicate those designated as leaders have the inherent right to exert control or influence |

When we exert power over others, we influence their behavior. In other words, we get them to do what we want. This is called *compliance-gaining*. Wheeless, Barraclough, and Stewart (1983) suggested that compliance-gaining is the implementation of power. You get others to do what you want (compliance-gaining) because you put your power to work. The authors stated, "Compliance is not only the manifestation of exercised power, it is the very reason for the existence of power" (p. 121). Marwell and Schmidt (1967b, pp. 360–361) created a typology of 16 types of compliance-gaining tactics (Table 7.3) or behaviors that can be used to get others to go along with what we want.

TABLE 7.3

Typology of Compliance-Gaining Tactics (Marwell & Schmidt, 1967b)

| Type of Compliance | Description | Example |
|---|---|---|
| Promise | Offering a reward for compliance | "Because we all agreed to the proposed idea, we can leave the meeting early!" |
| Threat | Threatening with punishment | "If we do not agree to a plan, the meeting will last at least another hour." |
| Expertise – positive | Telling others they will comply and be rewarded because that is just how things work | "If you go along with the plan now, you will be rewarded by the company later because the company likes a team player." |
| Expertise – negative | Telling others that, if they do not comply, they will be punished because that is just how things work | "If you fail to agree to the proposed idea, the team will punish you in the future by not listening to your ideas." |
| Liking | Acting friendly and open to get the receiver in a good frame of mind | "I really like your idea and think your insights are valuable. Would you mind supporting my group's proposed plan?" |
| Pregiving | Offering a reward before compliance is gained | "I like your group's ideas and in the future I plan to vote in favor of any of your group's ideas. Will you consider listening to my group's work now?" |
| Aversive stimulation | Engaging in continuous punishment until the recipient of the message gives in | "Like I've told you before, your group's ideas will not be supported by anyone. You need to really consider alternative solutions." |
| Debt | Making others feel indebted; the recipient of the message has to comply because of past favors he or she has received | "Remember when my group helped your group with that large project? The one we had to work extra hours to complete? My group now needs your group's assistance to complete a task." |
| Moral appeal | Telling others they are immoral people if they do not comply | "It is the right thing to help my group; a good person would do it." |

| Self-feeling – positive | Informing the recipients that they will feel better about themselves when they comply | "My group really needs some assistance. I know you will feel better about yourselves if you all agree to help us." |
|---|---|---|
| Self-feeling – negative | Informing the recipients that they will feel worse about themselves for not complying | "If your group does not agree to help us, you will probably feel bad about yourselves when the group fails." |
| Altercasting – positive | Telling others that a "good" person would comply | "A good person, a person of quality, would help the group." |
| Altercasting – negative | Telling others that a "bad" person would not comply | "Only a bad person would not help the group." |
| Altruism | Sharing with others that you need compliance very badly and asking them to "do it for me" | "Please help the group this time. Do it for me, because of our relationship and friendship." |
| Esteem – positive | Informing the recipient of the message that people he or she values will think better of him or her for complying | "Your help is much needed and you will feel good about yourself knowing that you motivated and encouraged this group to achieve its task." |
| Esteem – negative | Informing the recipient of the message that people he or she values will think poorly of him or her for not complying | "Everyone will think poorly of you if you do not go along with what we want." |

You probably read through the list in Table 7.3 and said, "Some of these would never work on me." Existing research on compliance-gaining would agree with you. Not surprisingly, individuals respond more to positive or socially rewarding techniques than negative compliance-gaining strategies (see Marwell & Schmitt, 1967a; Miller, Boster, Roloff, & Seibold, 1977; Williams & Untermeyer, 1988). How you deliver a compliance-gaining message is important as well. Individuals need to be mindful of tone, such as, for example, those who speak too softly are less likely to gain compliance (Remland & Jones, 1994). Overall, when it comes to working in groups and using power to gain compliance, it is best to approach it from a positive angle and not a negative one. The focus should be on creating a smooth road to goal completion.

## Cohesiveness

*Cohesiveness* is defined as an individual's feeling of belonging to a given group. That is, cohesiveness is the extent to which group members feel like they are part of a group. There is a sense of "togetherness" when groups experience cohesion. In groups, cohesiveness, in general, is a positive characteristic. Generally, we want to feel like all members of the group are "in it" and that these members feel good

> ◢ **Cohesiveness**
> General sense of belonging among group members.

about being part of the group. When group members feel cohesive, they participate in group processes such as goal-setting (Brawley, Carron, & Widmeyer, 1993) and experience satisfaction with the group (Tekleab, Quigley, & Tesluk, 2009). Thus, when you experience cohesiveness with members of a group, you feel as though you are working well with others.

You can help others feel like part of the group by listening. Have you ever told someone a story and they interrupted you? Maybe even changed the subject? Have you ever offered a solution that no one took into consideration? When people listen, they do more than hear. As discussed in Chapter 5, hearing refers to having the physical ability to make sense of noise. It means you have the physical capacity necessary to perform the function. Listening goes beyond that. Not only do you hear the noise, but you also interpret and carefully consider the meaning behind the verbal and nonverbal messages. Feeling valued in the group and wanting to remain in the group often comes from being viewed as a competent source of information. This viewpoint is manifested when we listen to others.

## *Productivity*

➤ **Productivity**
The result of task dimension.

➤ **Macro productivity**
Achieving or finishing the group's task.

➤ **Micro productivity**
Smaller tasks and goals that contribute to macro productivity.

➤ **Efficiency**
When group members are maximizing what they do, completing the necessary tasks as correctly as possible.

➤ **Effectiveness**
When a group meets all of its requirements and completes all of its tasks.

When individuals work together well, they are more likely to accomplish their goals. *Productivity* refers to a group's ability to complete tasks that ultimately lead to accomplishing the group's overall mission that brought them together in the first place. Productivity in a group can be considered at both the macro and micro levels. *Macro productivity* is bigger; it is completing the task that brought the group together. *Micro productivity* refers to the smaller activities that contribute to the completion of the overall task. Consider a class project. Your teacher assigns a task—the writing of a research paper that you will submit at the end of the semester. Completing the paper and submitting a final product is macro productivity. The work that you do along the way, including the collection of research and refining ideas, is micro productivity. Micro productivity contributes to macro productivity. If a group cannot focus on what needs to be accomplished, divide work appropriately, and make thoughtful decisions, it is far less likely they will achieve group productivity.

In addition to productivity, groups must work toward efficiency and effectiveness. *Efficiency* means that group members maximize what they do to complete the necessary tasks as correctly as possible. For example, rather than all members of a group trying to tackle each part of a project or task, they might decide to divide the labor among the individuals within the group and work on tasks that fit specific individual skill sets. *Effectiveness* means that the group meets all of its requirements

Efficiency means that group members have determined how to complete tasks in an organized manner.

© MonkeyBusinessImages/Shutterstock.com

and completes all of its tasks. That is, they accomplish what was asked of or assigned to them. Productive groups work toward being efficient and effective.

Overall, productivity in groups is important and can be enhanced in a number of ways. For example, groups can use technology (McFadzean, 1997) to enhance efficiency and effectiveness. For example, if a group has weekly, brief "check-in" meetings, the group may decide to hold these meetings in an online *forum*, rather than in a face-to-face meeting. Group roles (Rambo & Matheson, 2003) can also be used. Consider the nature of roles. Implied in the assignment of roles is that everyone has a portion of work to do, such as the note-taker keeping record of all meetings and decisions, and the leader setting the agenda and determining when work should be completed. A final technique that can be used to create a productive, efficient, and effective group is building *cohesion* among group members (Podsakoff, MacKenzie, & Ahearne, 1997). For example, making sure all group members contribute to ideas, are aware of one another, and can share in the work will make the group perform better.

**Forum**
Form of discussion in which the audience controls the flow of communication.

**Cohesion**
Describes how groups begin to "gel" together as a unit.

## Conflict

Just as we experience conflict in our interpersonal relationships, we are also likely to experience conflict when working in groups. Our personalities, unique communication styles, and different approaches to accomplishing goals may cause us to experience communication issues that need to be resolved. Keep in mind that *conflict* can be both a positive and a negative experience. Recall from our discussion in Chapter 7 that a key element of conflict is that a struggle between individuals has been expressed verbally or nonverbally. Could you experience conflict with a group member if you don't let them know that you disagree or are upset with them? While you may experience the negative emotions, if you haven't made your feelings known to the other person, conflict may not exist.

**Emotional conflict**
Conflict from relationships with others and can include lack of trust, feelings of dislike or animosity, and frustration.

**Task conflict**
Conflict regarding how to best complete the tasks being performed.

There are two types of conflict you may experience while working with others. ***Emotional conflict*** refers to relational differences among group members and can include a lack of trust, feelings of dislike or animosity, and frustration (Evan, 1965). A second type of conflict is called ***task conflict***, which refers to inconsistencies regarding how group members perceive the best way to complete the tasks being performed (Pelled & Adler, 1994).

As the group works toward a deadline or goal, you may become frustrated, experience personality clashes with a group member, or have differing opinions on how best to complete a task. While some conflict is beneficial because it encourages the group to consider alternate viewpoints and solutions, too much conflict can tear a group apart. Consider your own response to conflict when it occurs. Do you shut down, stop working with the group, or yell at others? While you may experience one or more of these reactions, it's not likely that they will help the group accomplish its goal.

**Conflict style**
Our own reaction to conflict.

Each of us has our own reaction to conflict, known as one's ***conflict style***. According to Kuhn and Poole (2000), "An individual's conflict style is a behavioral orientation and general expectation about one's approach to conflict" (p. 559). In Chapter 7 we discussed interpersonal conflict. While conflict in a group setting may be similar to interpersonal conflict, your style or approach to conflict may differ as you add more individuals to the interaction. Working in a group requires us to combine the personalities, opinions, and experiences of group members. Because of the multiple people you interact with in a group setting, you may respond to conflict differently than when you are simply engaging in dyadic or interpersonal communication. Your conflict style dictates the types of behaviors you display to others in the group. Three common responses that individuals apply to conflicts experienced in groups include avoidant, distributive, and integrative strategies (Sillars, Colletti, Parry, & Rogers, 1982). *Avoidant* strategies are used in an attempt to minimize or ignore the conflict. When asked if something is wrong, a group member who is avoidant will likely indicate that everything is fine. *Distributive* strategies require group members to give in to the wishes or ideas of other group members. Members of the group may adopt one solution rather than discussing all viable options. Finally, an *integrative* approach seeks to incorporate the opinions of all members of the group in order to evaluate options and arrive at the best solution.

As you can see from Table 7.4, some conflict styles lend themselves to positive conflict resolution. It is important to deal with conflict situations when they arise in groups. Allowing the conflict to go unresolved may cause relationships within the group to deteriorate and will likely deter the group from accomplishing its goal. Ignoring a conflict does not make it disappear. Identifying potential conflicts and working toward resolution can assist the group in making effective decisions by considering a variety of options or solutions proposed by group members.

TABLE 7.4

Typology of Power (French & Raven, 1960)

| Conflict Style | Description | Example |
|---|---|---|
| Avoidant | Minimize or ignore conflict or move to another issue | When a group member brings up a topic you do not want to address, you change the subject. |
| Distributive | Involves one person giving in to another | A group member continuously argues for one solution until finally everyone in the group gives in and agrees to the solution. |
| Integrative | Individuals work together to find the best or most workable solution | Individuals in the group brainstorm, discuss, and combine ideas in order to achieve the most viable solution. |

# GROUP DECISION MAKING

It seems clear from our previous discussion of groups that group members must work collaboratively to make a decision. However, this collaboration might be one of those things that is easier said than done. When working in a group, have you ever felt like no one listened to your opinion, that your input was of little value to other people, or that your ideas were not taken seriously? If you answered "yes" to any of these, you may not like working in groups. It *can* be challenging to get other people to listen to you. Effective and efficient groups consider the opinions and ideas of all members.

Group decision making requires thoughtful communication and the exchange of information between members (DeSanctis & Gallupe, 1987). This open exchange

The group needs to divide the labor among all members.

© Goodluz/Shutterstock.com

of ideas that contributes to group decision making can include several steps (Kuhn & Poole, 2000):

1. *Be open to alternatives.* All members of the group have important opinions and these should be given thoughtful consideration.
2. *Answer others' objections to alternatives.* When solutions are questioned, it is important to answer any objections or questions that arise.
3. *Blend ideas and work out compromises among alternatives.* Consider integrating suggestions from a variety of group members; the best possible solutions will likely be the result of incorporating a number of ideas.
4. *Coordinate the division of labor.* To make all members of the group feel important, it is paramount to divide the labor. In other words, everyone should have a job.

This process should also consider two key components: subjective outcomes and performance outcomes. Have you ever been part of a group in which a solution was proposed and, even though you may have used proper decision-making techniques, you still did not like or feel comfortable with the decision? McGrath (1984) labeled this feeling a ***subjective outcome***. It can be thought of as a feeling that is associated with the group members' level of satisfaction with the proposed plan. For example, if you are part of a group that is working on a class project and the group uses the previously identified group decision-making behaviors, but you still do not think the agreed-upon decision is the correct one and instead feel disappointed, this is

**Subjective outcomes**
Something that is associated with group members' level of satisfaction with a proposed plan.

a subjective outcome. In addition to feelings associated with the decision, there are also *performance outcomes*. These outcomes focus on productivity and the measurement of goal achievement. Imagine you and a group of others have been asked to improve parking on your campus. During your **brainstorming** sessions, your group's communication focuses on the task; communication is centered on the generation of ideas and questioning those ideas to determine the most appropriate outcome. Once a solution has been selected, it is then implemented and a plan for monitoring its success is also put into place. Through the monitoring of this solution, it is determined that the proposed solution does indeed improve parking on campus. Effective decisions take both subjective and performance outcomes into consideration. In other words, decisions that meet goals and represent something that the group feels positively toward are preferred.

> **Performance outcomes**
> Focus on productivity and measurement of goal achievement.

> **Brainstorming**
> Generation of as many ideas as possible in a criticism-free environment.

# GROUPTHINK

A key consideration to the group decision-making process is the idea of *groupthink*. Have you ever been part of a group where one person suggests an idea and everyone in the group goes along with it? If no one offers other ideas or solutions and the entire group seems to "jump on the bandwagon" and agree to the proposed idea, you may have experienced groupthink. Groupthink occurs when all of the group members go along with an idea without engaging in thoughtful discussion or careful analysis. Janis (1972) argues that groupthink minimizes disagreement or recognition of alternative options. Your group may be experiencing groupthink if:

> **Groupthink**
> Describes a group's tendency to focus on agreement among its members more than the quality of the group's work.

- Group members pressure others to conform to the group's ideas.
- Group members and their ideas are considered stupid or bad if they go against the group, or if members try to negotiate.
- Group members self-censor and fall silent and their silence is considered agreement.
- Group members perceive the group to be invulnerable or "untouchable," that nothing can bring them down, which can result in an overly optimistic perception of ideas.
- Group members discount others' warnings or ideas and do not reconsider their positions.

As you may be thinking, groupthink is largely characterized as a negative group experience. Groupthink has occurred a number of times in our culture. For example, consider the 1986 explosion of the space shuttle *Challenger*. While a flaw in the design of an important part of the spacecraft, an O-ring, officially caused the explosion, there were several instances of groupthink leading up to the takeoff.

For example, some engineers were concerned about the functioning of the O-ring, but these concerns were silenced and not shared with those higher in the chain of command. Other examples of groupthink in our culture include the Bay of Pigs invasion during President John F. Kennedy's tenure and the Nazi control of Germany. In all of these instances, voices of dissent were marginalized and group members failed to consider options. Groups can work to overcome this negative characteristic by working toward the best solutions, considering alternatives, not agreeing too quickly to one idea, and by asking all group members for input.

## CHAPTER SUMMARY

This chapter has defined groups, discussed the nature of groups, and highlighted the communication issues with which groups deal. While you may or may not enjoy working with groups, it is important to remember that it will likely be something you have to do and it can be a better process when thoughtful attention is given to communicative behaviors. It is a process that can be enhanced with clear communication and a discussion of the roles and rules relevant to groupwork. Remaining open to the insights of others, combining these insights, dividing the labor, and maintaining positive relationships will help groups achieve goals efficiently and effectively. Throughout goal completion, it is important to note that groups can experience both task and relational strain. If left unspoken, the strain can interrupt group processes. Open communication in which all group members are able to provide input will ultimately contribute to the most successful group functioning.

Understanding what a group is, the characteristics that compose group life, and how groups work together to make decisions will enhance your success when encountering group work. While depending on others to complete tasks can prove difficult and sometimes uncomfortable, working with others is a necessary part of your professional, public, and personal lives. Once everyone in a group understands how he or she "fits" in the group, it is easier to complete tasks and manage the social aspect of group life. In the next chapter, we continue our discussion of group life and suggest ways to enhance our group communication skills.

## KEY WORDS

*Adjourning stage* Final process of group life that signals the completion of tasks.

*Authoritarian rule* State in which one person decides on behalf of the group.

*Brainstorming* Generation of as many ideas as possible in a criticism-free environment.

*Coercive power* Ability to give out punishment.

*Cohesion* Describes how groups begin to "gel" together as a unit.

*Cohesiveness* General sense of belonging among group members.

*Compliance-gaining* Getting someone to do something you want.

*Compromiser* Individual who avoids conflict and admits any mistakes in a group.

*Conflict* Disruption or breakdown of the communication process among group members.

*Conflict style* Our own reaction to conflict.

*Consensus* State in which all group members must agree.

*Contingency planning* A plan of action that anticipates or takes into account possible future events and/or ramifications.

"Preparing answers to the final question involves the group in **contingency planning**."

*Coordinator* Group member that oversees who accomplishes what tasks and when tasks should be done.

*Deadlock* Sometimes called **gridlock**, a state that arises when a group does not function as a unit but instead fails to progress because its membership gets embroiled in petty disputes, splinters into antagonistic camps, or simply cannot reach a decision.

*Dominator* Group member who likes to be heard and works to control the group.

*Dyad* A collection of only two people.

*Effectiveness* When a group meets all of its requirements and completes all of its tasks.

*Efficiency* When group members are maximizing what they do, completing the necessary tasks as correctly as possible.

*Emotional conflict* Conflict from relationships with others and can include lack of trust, feelings of dislike or animosity, and frustration.

**Encourager** Group member who praises others and hears others' opinions and ideas.

**Evaluator-critic** Group member who sets standards and meets goals.

**Expert power** Power derived from the knowledge or expertise one has.

**Explicit rules** Formalized rules that are discussed and often documented so that all group members are aware of them.

**Factional group** When group members are representatives or delegates from other social entities.

**Forming stage** Initial stage in group development.

**Forum** Form of discussion in which the audience controls the flow of communication.

**Gatekeeper** Group member who ensures participation by all group members.

**Group** A collection of individuals with a common purpose.

**Group rules** Individuals in a group are expected to do certain things, and if they do not do these things, there are consequences.

**Group solidarity** The tendency of a group to act as a single unit instead of as a collection of individuals.

**Groupthink** Describes a group's tendency to focus on agreement among its members more than the quality of the group's work.

**Harmonizer** Group member who offers communication focused on achieving cohesion among group members.

**Implicit rules** Unspoken and unwritten expectations that everyone in the group seems to know and adhere to.

**Individual roles** When individuals focus on self-achievement and not group efforts.

**Information-seeker** Group member who collects information related to tasks and completing tasks.

**Joker** Group member who uses light-hearted, humorous communication that is often off topic.

**Legitimate power** Power that is associated with a certain position. Because of his or her position in the group, an individual has a certain right to influence/oversee others' behaviors.

**Lurkers** Passive observers who do not participate in discussion.

**Macro productivity** Achieving or finishing the group's task.

*Majority rule* Form of decision making in which a group votes on solutions and selects the solution(s) with the most votes.

*Micro productivity* Smaller tasks and goals that contribute to macro productivity.

*Minority report* Report or summary presented by a dissenting group smaller than the majority.

"The main problem is that the minority gets left out unless they present a **minority report**, which explains dissenting views."

*Negative energy* Effect or state in which groups impede individual accomplishments and underperform compared to solo efforts; attitudes become contagious.

*Norming stage* Third stage of group development in which members create behavioral standards and punishments.

*Norms* Standardized behaviors individuals in the group ought to do under any circumstance.

*Opinion-giver* Group member who expresses opinions and possible interpretations associated with all tasks.

*Peer group* Members who consider one another to be equals in terms of abilities, background, age, responsibilities, beliefs, social standing, legal status, or rights.

*Performance outcomes* Focus on productivity and measurement of goal achievement.

*Performing stage* Fourth stage in group development in which all members are working toward completion of the group's task.

*Positive energy* Effect or state in which each group member's enthusiasm, energy, creativity, and dedication amplify the same qualities in other members, taking the group to higher levels of performance.

*Power* Ability to influence others.

*Problem-solving group* A group assembled to complete a specific task and render a decision.

*Productivity* Ability to achieve goals in an efficient matter.

*Productivity* The result of task dimension.

*Purposive group* A group that is attempting to achieve the completion of a goal.

*Recognition-seeker* Group member who takes on a lot of work for extra attention.

*Referent power* An individual's positive regard for and personal identification with the leader.

*Relational roles* Focus on building and maintaining connections among group members.

*Reward power* Ability to give out positive benefits or rewards.

*Role conflict* When you have to perform multiple roles with seemingly contradictory behaviors.

*Role flexibility* When individuals possess the ability to play a variety of roles and adapt according to the demands of the situation.

*Role strain* When an individual is required to assume a new role that he or she is reluctant to perform.

*Role Theory* Ways in which individuals enact different social positions (i.e., roles) in their lives.

*Roles* Labels placed on individuals based on their function within a group.

*Social dimension* Group members' relationships and feelings for each other.

*Social group* Collection of individuals focused mostly on relationship-building that gives members a place to develop self-esteem.

*Social-emotional leader* Voice of the group members in terms of the affective orientation to the group.

*Storming stage* Second stage of group development, where most conflicts will occur.

*Subjective outcomes* Something that is associated with group members' level of satisfaction with a proposed plan.

*Symposium* More formal, prepared, communication.

*Task conflict* Conflict regarding how to best complete the tasks being performed.

*Task dimension* Measures a group's actual progress toward its goals.

*Task leader* Focuses group members on completion of assignments.

*Task roles* Includes all roles that focus on the group's assignment.

*Withdrawer* Group member who fails to connect and interact with the group, offers few opinions, and may have issues.

# REFERENCES

Benne, K. D., & Sheats, P. (1948). Functional roles of group members. *Journal of Social Issues, 4,* 41–49.

Biddle, B. J. (1979). *Role theory: Expectations, identities, and behaviors.* New York: Academic Press.

Bormann, E. G. (1969). *Discussion and group methods: Theory and practice.* New York: Harper & Row.

Brawley, L. R., Carron, A. V., & Widmeyer, W. N. (1993). The influence of the group and its cohesiveness on perceptions of group goal-related variables. *Journal of Sport and Exercise Psychology, 15,* 245–260.

Burkhalter, S., Gastil, J., & Kelshaw, T. (2002). A conceptual definition and theoretical model of public deliberation in small face-to-face groups. *Communication Theory, 12,* 398–422.

Cragan, J. F., & Wright, D. W. (1999). *Communication in small groups: Theory, process, skills* (5th ed.). Belmont, CA: Wadsworth.

DeSanctis, G., & Gallupe, R. B. (1987). A foundation for the study of group decision support systems. *Management Science, 33,* 589–609.

Evan, W. (1965). Conflict and performance in R&D organizations. *Industrial Management Review, 7,* 37–46.

Forrest, K. D., & Miller, R. L. (2003). Not another group project: Why good teachers should care about bad group experiences. *Teaching of Psychology, 30,* 244–246.

French, J. R. P., & Raven, B. (1960). The bases of social power. In D. Cartwright (Ed.), *Studies in social power* (pp. 150–167). Ann Arbor: University of Michigan Press.

Frey, L. R., & SunWolf. (2005). The communication perspective on group life. In S. A. Wheelan (Ed.), *The handbook of group research and practice* (pp. 159–186). Thousand Oaks, CA: Sage.

Fujishin, R. (2001). *Creating effective groups: The art of small group communication.* San Francisco: Arcada.

Gastil, J. (1993). *Democracy in small groups: Participation, decision-making, and communication.* Philadelphia: New Society.

Hawkins, K., & Fillion, B. (1999). Perceived communication skill needs for work groups. *Communication Research Reports, 16,* 167–174.

Homans, G. C. (1950). *The human group.* New York: Harcourt Brace Jovanovich.

Janis, I. L. (1972). *Victims of groupthink.* Boston: Houghton-Mifflin.

Kuhn, T., & Poole, M. S. (2000). Do conflict management styles affect group decision making?: Evidence from a longitudinal field study. *Human Communication Research, 26,* 558–590.

Li, I., &Hambrick, D. C. (2005). Factional groups: A new vantage on demographic faultlines, conflict, and disintegration in work teams'. *Academy of Management Journal, 48,* 794–813.

Lott, A. J., & Lott, B. E. (1965). Group cohesiveness as interpersonal attraction: A review of relationships with antecedent and consequent variables. *Psychological Bulletin, 64,* 259–309.

Marwell, G., & Schmitt, D. R. (1967a). Compliance-gaining behavior: A synthesis and model. *Sociological Quarterly, 8,* 317–328.

Marwell, G., & Schmitt, D. R. (1967b). Dimensions of compliance-gaining behavior: An empirical analysis. *Sociometry, 30,* 350–364.

McFadzean, E. (1997). Improving group productivity with group support systems and creative problem solving techniques. *Creativity and Innovation Management, 6,* 218–225.

McGrath, J. E. (1984). *Groups: Interaction and performance.* Englewood Cliffs, NJ: Prentice-Hall.

Miller, G. R., Boster, F., Roloff, M. E., & Seibold, D. (1977). Compliance-gaining message strategies: A typology and some findings concerning effects of situational differences. *Communication Monographs, 41,* 37–51.

Pelled, L. H., & Adler, P. S. (1994). Antecedents of intergroup conflict in multifunctional product development teams: A conceptual model. *IEEE Transactions on Engineering Management, 41,* 21–28.

Podsakoff, P. M., MacKenzie, S. B., & Ahearne, M. (1997). Moderating effects of goal acceptance on the relationship between group cohesiveness and productivity. *Journal of Applied Psychology, 82,* 974–983.

Poole, M.S., Hollingshead, A. B., McGrath, J. E., Moreland, R. L., & Rohrbaugh, J. (2004). Interdisciplinary perspectives on small groups. *Small Group Research, 35,* 3–16.

Rambo, E., & Matheson, N. (2003). *Enhancing group-work productivity through coordinator roles.* Retrieved from http://jalt-publications.org/archive/proceedings/2003/E059.pdf.

Remland, M. S., & Jones, T. S. (1994). The influence of vocal intensity and touch on compliance gaining. *Journal of Social Psychology, 134,* 89–97.

Sillars, A. L., Colletti, S. F., Parry, D., & Rogers, M. A. (1982). Coding verbal conflict tactics: Nonverbal and verbal correlates of the "avoidance–distributive–integrative" distinction. *Human Communication Research, 9,* 83–95.

SunWolf. (2008). *Peer groups: Expanding our study of small group communication.* Thousand Oaks, CA: Sage.

Tekleab, A. G., Quigley, N. R., & Tesluk, P. E. (2009). A longitudinal study of team conflict, conflict management, cohesion, and team effectiveness. *Group and Organization Management, 34*, 170–205.

Time crunch: Breakdown of CEOs' time in a 55-hour workweek. (2012). *Wall Street Journal*. Retrieved from http://si.wsj.net/public/resources/images/MK-BS273B_CEOTI_NS_20120213203917.jpg

Tuckman, B. W. (1965). Developmental sequence in small groups. *Psychological Bulletin, 63*, 249–272.

Tuckman, B. W., & Jensen, M. A. C. (1977). Stages of small group development: Revisited. *Group and Organization Studies, 2*, 419–427.

Wheeless, L. R., Barraclough, R., & Stewart, R. (1983). Compliance-gaining and power in persuasion. *Communication Yearbook, 7*, 105–145.

Williams, M. L., & Untermeyer, N. K. (1988). Compliance-gaining strategies and communicator role: An analysis of strategy choices and persuasive efficacy. *Communication Research Reports, 5*, 10–18.

# CHAPTER 8

## Enhancing Groups Through Leadership and Group Processes: Who's In Charge?

### Chapter Objectives

After reading this chapter, you should be able to:
- Identify different types of leadership
- Explain the approaches to leadership
- Describe how team-building activities can benefit a group
- Elaborate on why groups should avoid groupthink
- Explain the creative problem-solving process
- Identify key strategies for the improvement of group meetings

From *Communicating in your Personal, Professional, and Public Lives* by Sara Chudnovsky Weintraub, Candice Thomas-Maddox and Kerry Byrnes-Loinette. Copyright ©2015 by Kendall Hunt Publishing Company. Reprinted by permission.

**PERSONAL:** Your are planning a vacation with five of your friends. You and your friends have agreed that you want to travel during the fall and would like to visit a beach. Determining exactly what month and what beach to visit has proven more difficult. The brainstorming of ideas and dates has occurred largely via email with everyone "replying all" when offering opinions. This has proven somewhat convenient because you are able to read everyone's opinions but you are becoming overwhelmed with the amount of emails your friends are sending. No one can seem to agree on when and where to travel. You decide something should be done to take control of the situation. Where should you begin?

**PROFESSIONAL:** At your job, you have been asked to present material to a potential client about a new business solution. After agreeing to present your ideas, you discover that you will be working with four additional people to create and present a single proposal. You meet with your coworkers to discuss ideas and quickly realize that the group members are quite different. While they all have good ideas, two of the members seem to detract from the group discussion by bringing up topics that are not relevant. As the leader of the team, it is your job to refocus the discussion. How should you approach your off-topic group members?

**PUBLIC:** Because of your education and experience, you have been asked by the local library to be part of a project that deals with increasing literacy in the community. At the first meeting, you learn that you will be working with a collection of individuals and will present your plan to improve literacy to the local governing body. During the first several meetings, you notice most of the people in the group seem knowledgeable and share some great ideas. However, no real decisions or plans are made. Instead, at the weekly meetings, the group seems to talk about the same things without making progress. You think to yourself that something has to be done to increase the efficiency in this group. What steps should you take to do this?

## CHAPTER OVERVIEW

As the opening examples illustrate, there are many instances in your life where you may have to be in charge or act as the leader of a group. Whether the situation involves planning a vacation with friends, working with others on a group project at work, or determining how to increase group productivity, working in groups often requires someone to take a leadership position and determine how to best work with others in the group. It is likely that you have either been a leader or been guided by others at some point. Understanding the leadership process and ways to enhance the group experience could make working with others easier. In

Chapter 8, we emphasized the prevalence of groups in your personal, professional, and public lives. Individuals are often required to depend on others to accomplish goals. At times, achieving these goals can prove difficult; however, understanding different communication strategies for leading others will make the process easier. In addition to understanding how to lead a group, this chapter also explores techniques groups can use to improve the group process.

## LEADERSHIP DEFINED

Leadership is a concept that is often difficult to define. Numerous books have been published on the topic and there are multiple approaches to and philosophies about leadership. Communication scholars and theorists have even offered numerous views on leadership. Common definitions of leadership indicate that it includes elements of influence (Cragan & Wright, 1999) and goal accomplishment (Shaw, 1981). *Leadership* can be defined as a process by which individuals influence others' actions and behaviors in order to achieve a goal. The leadership process relies on using communication to affect and motivate group members' behaviors. Leadership is necessary to help group members work well together, motivate them, and help them accomplish the goals of the group.

> **Leadership**
> Process in which individuals influence others' actions and behaviors in order to achieve some goal.

The process of leadership or influencing others' actions is directly connected to communication. Consider being assigned to a group for a class project. As the group begins to form, several people in the group ask what specific tasks need to be accomplished. It appears as though the group members are looking for someone in the group to answer their questions and formulate a plan of action. Having an understanding of the assigned tasks, you begin to answer their questions and determine what the group needs to achieve to be successful. At the next group meeting, the group then looks to you to facilitate the meeting. To engage in leadership and influence behaviors, communication needs to be considered. In fact, various elements regarding leadership and communication have been studied and provide insight into how to enact the process of leadership.

## APPROACHES TO THE STUDY OF LEADERSHIP

There are a number of ways to explore the concept of leadership. Studies can focus on the leader, the members (i.e., others in the group), or the interactions between the leaders and members. While these diverse approaches provide many

A leader guides the group to achieve its goals.

© Stuart Jenner/Shutterstock.com

perspectives for viewing leadership, they adopt inherently different orientations (see Table 8.1). Investigating leadership as something an individual possesses is called the *trait approach*. In this approach, the focus is on the common personality characteristics shared by leaders. The *situational approach* examines how leaders behave or act in a variety of situations and with different individuals. Finally, the *interaction approach* examines leadership from a relational perspective. The focus is on the communication that is exchanged between leaders and members.

**Trait approach**
One way to study leadership; focuses on the characteristics/traits of the leader.

**Situational approach**
One way to study leadership; focuses on the characteristics of the group members and the situation.

**Interaction approach**
One way to study leadership; focuses on communicative exchanges in the leadership process.

## TABLE 8.1

Approaches to the Study of Leadership

| Approaches to Leadership | Description |
|---|---|
| Trait approach | Focuses on the characteristics of the leader |
| Situational approach | Focuses on the specific characteristics of the group, both the leader and followers, to achieve a given task |
| Interaction approach | Focuses on the communicative exchanges of leaders and members |

## Trait Approach

The trait approach, initially developed in the early 20th century, was one of the first perspectives of leadership. Embedded in the trait approach is the idea that "a leader is born, not made." The trait approach argues that there are certain characteristics that all leaders tend to have in common. Initially, trait theories did not make assumptions about whether leadership traits were inherited or learned; rather, they stated that the qualities of leaders are simply different from nonleaders (Kirkpatrick & Locke, 1991). In other words, there are identifiable personality characteristics that leaders possess. Some traits often associated with leadership are intelligence, honesty, dependability, sociability, and communicative competence. Consider how a leader's communication behaviors reflect his or her ability to lead and motivate others. Individuals are deemed intelligent if they can offer appropriate, task-specific information. They appear confident if, while talking to others, their nonverbal cues such as facial expressions and posture appear sturdy. For example, Warren Buffet, Oprah Winfrey, and the late Steve Jobs are all leaders and viewed as competent in their respective industries; individuals who can follow through on a task; provide honest, authentic views; and are perceived as hard-working individuals that other people enjoy being around. While the trait approach is relatively easy to understand because it implies that leaders have certain qualities, there are some limitations to this view of leadership. It is fairly limiting in that it does not take into account the group members or the task; rather, it focuses only on one person and his or her inherent qualities. For example, serving as the leader for a class project you are to complete with your peers is very different than serving as the leader of a group of 6-year-olds. It is likely that your communication would be quite different with your peers versus young children.

Oprah Winfrey has evolved as a leader in the entertainment industry.

© DFree/Shutterstock.com

## Situational Approach

Another approach to the study of leadership accounts for more than just the individual qualities and characteristics of the leader. The situational approach considers the combination of the leader's ability to direct tasks, the relationships between the group members, and the abilities of individual group members as these pertain to accomplishing the tasks (Hersey & Blanchard, 1993). While the leader is perceived as being "in charge," the role of group members is not ignored. Rather, in this approach, members of a group can have considerable influence on both the leader and the leadership process. It is a two-way street: The leader affects and influences the group members and the group members affect and influence the leader. For example, if members appear to be disinterested in completing group tasks, the leader needs to motivate and encourage members in order to instill a desire for the group to achieve its goal. The leader in this group situation would need to highlight additional tasks and continue to push the group members to work. The leader could compliment the work completed by the members, provide suggestions for improvement, or remind the group about progress made.

Blanchard (1985) developed the Situational Leadership II model to highlight four leadership styles based on the characteristics of the leader and the developmental level (i.e., the intelligence and skill level) of the members of the group: directive, supportive, coaching, and delegating (Figure 8.1). The leadership styles are based on two key dimensions: directive communication and supportive communication. A leader's communication can be either high or low in directive and supportive communication. Directive communication is task-focused communication whereas supportive communication focuses on relational aspects of group life. *Directive leadership* is high in directive communication and low in supportive behavior; it is focused on task completion. The leader does not spend much time trying to make others feel comfortable; rather, directions are given regarding what goals need to be accomplished and how they can best be achieved. Little to no feedback is solicited from the group members. The leader "tells" and members are expected to follow. The next style is *supportive leadership*. In this style, the leader is high in supportive communication and low in directive communication. In this style, the leader focuses primarily on relational aspects of the group. They are primarily dedicated to employing behaviors that highlight and develop the skills of the group members. A leader using this style would focus on communication that encourages others, such as complimenting their work or inquiring about how they feel about the task. Another type of leadership style focuses on coaching. The *coaching leadership* style is high in both directive and supportive communication. Leaders who use coaching focus their communication not only on achieving goals but also on meeting the emotional needs of the members. In this approach, the leader asks group members about the progress of the task and solicits their opinions or ideas on how to best fulfill the goal. Ultimately, the leader determines the proper decision for accomplishing goals. The final style of leadership is the delegating approach. The *delegating leadership* style is the opposite of coaching in that leaders

**Directive leadership**
Focuses on task completion.

**Supportive leadership**
Solicits feedback and employs behaviors that will highlight and develop the skills of group members.

**Coaching leader**
Type of leader who uses both highly directive behaviors and highly supportive behaviors; focuses communication on not only achieving goals but also on meeting the followers' emotional needs.

**Delegating leadership**
Offers little advice, input, or social support and control is handed over to the group members.

do not exhibit or provide support or direction; they are low in both supportive and directive behavior. Very little advice or input is offered from the leader. Instead, control is handed over to the group members, and little social support is offered by the leader. If a leader, for example, tells a group that a series of tasks needs to be accomplished but then allows the group to determine how to accomplish the tasks, offers little insight, and neglects the relationships among the group members, the delegating style has been used.

FIGURE 8.1

Blanchard's (1985) Situational Leadership II model.

| High concern for relationship among group | SUPPORTING | COACHING |
|---|---|---|
| Low concern for relationship among group | DELEGATING | DIRECTING |
| | Low concern for task | High concern for task |

Recall that the Situational Leadership II model also included a discussion of the group members in addition to the leadership styles. Called the developmental level, this focuses on the competence level of the group members (which includes ability, knowledge, and skill) and their commitment level (which includes their confidence and motivation). The group members can be classified into four levels: D1, D2, D3, and D4. They are organized by level and range from low competence to high competence. D1 group members have lower levels of task competence, while D4 group members are highly competent in the task. D1 individuals are low in competence and high in commitment. They may not know how to do something but they are excited about the challenge. For example, if you do not know much about repairing cars but your parent asks for your help and you are willing to help and continue the entire project, you would be a D1-level worker. You may not know much about fixing cars but you are willing to help and are committed to doing so.

D2 individuals are those who are competent or knowledgeable on a topic but they possess a low level of commitment. They have started learning about the job but lack the motivation to complete tasks. This could easily occur if you have been working on a task for an extended period of time or have made little progress on your task. For example, if your boss asked you to be part of a group project a year ago, but others in the group failed to meet or finish the work, you may begin to feel a decreased level of commitment.

D3 individuals have moderate to high levels of competence but are uncertain about whether they can accomplish the task themselves. That is, they have the intelligence and

D4 individuals are high in both competence and commitment when working on a task.

© Rawpixel/Shutterstock.com

skills necessary to accomplish the task but lack confidence in their ability to complete the task at hand. You may have felt like this in your personal, professional, or public life. For example, while preparing for an important group presentation at work, you may be knowledgeable about your topic, confident about the content of your speech, and proud of the work that others have done, yet you feel as though the group lacks the skills needed to give an effective group presentation. In this situation, a leader is extremely necessary as he or she needs to instill confidence in the group members.

Lastly, D4 individuals are high in both competence and commitment. These individuals truly have the necessary skills and motivation to achieve their goals. Have you ever felt prepared and excited about a task? Perhaps you are working with others who are equally knowledgeable on the topic and have a strong desire to continue the project until it is concluded. The D4 group member is knowledgeable about the topic and is determined to finish all tasks associated with the project. Ultimately, the development level or skills and commitment of the group member is an important consideration for those working in groups.

In adopting the situational approach and specifically the Situational Leadership II model, characteristics of both the leader and group member become important. Group members may enter the group experience with lower levels of competence, knowledge, and skills. To increase the group members' competence, knowledge, and skills, the leader then adjusts communication behaviors and leadership styles. As the group member gains knowledge and progresses to higher developmental levels, such as D3 and D4, the leader again reassesses and asks him- or herself what communication-based behaviors are best suited for this situation with this particular group. Situational factors influence our ability and desire to complete a task. Leaders must consider the task (e.g., the type, the size) and the people with whom they are working. Answers to these questions help the leader decide if they have D1-level group members and need to use the directive approach, or they have D2-level group members and, as a result, need to use more of a coaching style. If a mixture of levels emerge, the leader needs to assess the overall group qualities and determine what would work best to get the members to achieve group goals.

## Interaction Approach

The third approach to the study of leadership is the **interaction approach**. In this approach, communicative exchanges between leaders and group members are the primary focus. Verbal and nonverbal communication behaviors of all group members are evaluated in promoting optimal group functioning. Some communication styles are better than others when working in groups. *Promotive communication* focuses on messages that contribute to the group's tasks. It includes messages that help the group stay focused. For example, while at a group meeting, if one group member reminds individuals of assigned tasks and completion dates, promotive communication has occurred since the reminder helped the group achieve its goal. On the other hand, *disruptive communication* includes messages that detract group members from accomplishing their goal. Examples of disruptive communication could include asking others about weekend plans, discussing another class, or any other conversation that strays off the topic of the group task. An efficient leader tries to increase promotive communication and minimize disruptive communication. When disruptive communication occurs, a leader needs to refocus the discussion on the team's goal. This could include inquiries about the status of projects and assigning group roles.

Communication scholars embrace the interaction approach because of its focus on the verbal and nonverbal message exchange between individuals. It takes into account that communication is the most important element of group life and that all group members affect the group's proceedings. If you reflect on your own experiences, you probably have worked with well-functioning groups as well as those groups that seemed to accomplish nothing. In these groups, did members ensure that messages were received accurately? Did group members communicate with one another to clarify assignments? Most likely, the groups that functioned the best contained members that were able to communicate about the tasks in such a way that everyone could understand and achieve the established goals.

> **Promotive communication**
> Focuses on messages that contribute to the group's tasks.

> **Disruptive communication**
> Detracts group members from accomplishing their goals.

# STYLES OF LEADERSHIP

As you can see, leadership and communication work together. Your communication behaviors, verbal and nonverbal, are usually reflective of a specific type of leader. Your communication style or the way you interact when working with others mirrors the type of leader you are. For example, if your family needs to achieve a common goal, you may be more interested in learning how everyone is feeling about achieving the goal. Your communication would focus on questions such as "How does that make you feel?" or "Do you feel prepared to accomplish this goal?" However, in a professional setting, your communication behaviors could change. Rather than focusing on individuals' feelings, your message may focus on task achievement. You might ask others when they will finish certain elements of a group project or ask to schedule a meeting. You have a general style of leadership that is manifested through your verbal and nonverbal communication with others. Researchers (see, e.g., Lewin, Lippit, & White, 1939; Mumford, 2006) have identified a number of styles of leadership, including task leader, socioemotional leader, charismatic leader, laissez-faire leader, democratic leader, and authoritarian leader. Each of these is defined in Table 8.2.

## TABLE 8.2

Styles of Leadership

| Leader | Definition |
|---|---|
| Task leader | Focuses on the completion of the group's goals. Pays close attention to deadlines and ensures the group divides labor to achieve a common purpose. |
| Socioemotional leader | Concerned with the relationships among group members. Focuses on issues such as group conflict or individual experiences to ensure individuals can work well together. |
| Charismatic leader | Considered a dynamic individual with prosocial personality traits such as confidence, interpersonal attractiveness, and communication skills. |
| Laissez-faire leader | Prefers to use a nondirective approach. Typically laid-back and has little involvement in group functions. |
| Democratic leader | Consults group members when making decisions. Seeks inputs and listens to others to incorporate multiple ideas and opinions. |
| Authoritarian leader | Related to a task leader, focuses not only on task completion but communication; also addresses how tasks should be completed. |

The leadership styles in Table 8.2 reflect very different approaches to managing group members. As noted above, these styles are manifested through your verbal and nonverbal communication. If, when working with others, your communication focuses on the completion of tasks, you may consider yourself to be a **task leader**. Your verbal communication is centered on specific topics including deadlines, solutions, and brainstorming. Your communication does not stray into superfluous topics; rather, you use promotive communication. As stated previously, promotive communication is centered on the completion of a task. If, when working with others, your communication has instead focused on building relationships and asking group members how they feel about the group experiences, your leadership style can be identified as a **socioemotional leader**. Rather than focus on the division of labor, your communication would center on asking the group members how they feel about their assigned tasks and if they perceive they can accomplish the tasks. It is not uncommon when working with others that both of these types of communication occur from different individuals. For example, if you were brainstorming with a group at your job, the person who summarizes potential ideas and offers additional suggestions could be referred to as the task leader while the person who asks if everyone feels like they can voice their opinions would be labeled the socioemotional leader.

**Task leader**
Type of leader who is primarily concerned with completing the group's goals.

**Socioemotional leader**
Type of leader who is primarily concerned with the relationships among group members.

**Charismatic leader**
Type of leader who has characteristics such as confidence, interpersonal attractiveness, and effective communication skills.

Have you ever been part of a group that was led by someone you just wanted to be around, that you were naturally drawn to? They seemed to have an "it" factor. The **charismatic** leader's communication is very persuasive. Verbally, they may use storytelling as a way to draw the group to them while nonverbally, they attempt to appear confident in their posture and vocal tone. The charismatic leader often describes a bigger vision for the group experience.

**Laissez-faire leader**
Prefers a "hands-off" mentality to leading others.

Yet another type of leader style is the **laissez-faire** style. This style is hands-off. This leader typically engages in less communication with the group and instead takes a back-seat approach. This type of leader will not actively seek to be part of the group, allowing group members to "figure it out on their own." If pressured, the laissez-faire leader can step up and offer insights and motivate the group members.

**Democratic leader**
Actively consults group members before making decisions.

A very different type of leadership is the **democratic** style. The democratic leader actively seeks out and engages with the group. The democratic leader solicits opinions and feedback, and decisions are made as a group effort. The democratic leader may need to make decisions for the group, but it is always couched with the understanding that seeking opinions from the group is top priority. Rather than simply issuing "this is how it is going to be" statements, this leader engages with the group in the decision-making process.

The task leader focuses on the completion of the group's goals.

Finally, the ***authoritarian*** style of leadership is similar to the task leader. This person is focused on achieving goals and tasks but this person dictates and mandates what is to be done in addition to how it is to be done. Essentially, this person "rules with an iron fist." This leader speaks and assumes that others will naturally follow along.

**Authoritarian leader**
Mandates what must be done in a group setting.

As you can see, the leadership styles are directly connected to your verbal and nonverbal communication. In fact, you may have to adjust your verbal and nonverbal communication in order to successfully lead a group. For example, an authoritarian leadership style may not be successful in leading a group of individuals who need motivation and coaxing to follow along. Rather, this type of leader may need to adjust behaviors and offer the group reasons or information about the benefits of a plan of action to get the group to follow it. Similarly, a democratic leadership style may not be successful if the group members are expecting to receive direct orders and assignments about tasks. Asking for others' opinions would not be beneficial. This leader may need to adjust behaviors and become more directive in communication.

To identify your own leadership type, consider the following questions:
1. When I work with others, which is more of a priority? Is it the task or the relationships among group members? If the task is more important, do

I strive to create a plan of action to achieve the goals/tasks? Task leaders focus on tasks and goals whereas socioemotional leaders focus on the relationships formed among members.

2. Do I like to pose questions and attempt to inspire new ideas by using witty banter? If so, you might find yourself to be a charismatic leader.
3. Do I like to gather insights from others and seek opinions before making decisions? If so, you could be a democratic leader.
4. Do I prefer to take a hands-off approach and allow the group to figure out how to work together, only leading if completely necessary? If so, you might find yourself using a laissez-faire style.
5. Do I like telling people exactly how to do each task? If so, you might be using an authoritarian leadership focus.

Ultimately, there is no one way to lead, and your opinion on leadership and your individual style may evolve over time. When determining how to lead, it is appropriate to consider those with whom you are working and to understand that your leadership style may need to change in order to create the best possible working environment given a particular group. The environment will be affected by the relationships among group members. When working with others, there are techniques to enhance group practices. As the leader it will become important to consider how to get the members of the group to work together. We move now into a discussion of how to create positive group experiences.

# TEAM-BUILDING

**⯈ Team-building**
Process that includes gathering cooperation from individuals to achieve a common goal.

In our personal, public, and professional lives, there will be many instances of groupwork. *Team-building* activities contribute to building positive relationships among group members. They are strategies that can enhance your time working with others. These techniques can create and sustain positive relationships, which in turn can enhance the quality of the tasks completed by the group. The strategies listed in Figure 8.3 and outlined here are easy to implement. When you accept a job, you sign a contract. You pledge your commitment to other people in the organization. You agree to show up, do your best work, perform tasks, and help the organization accomplish its goals. The same idea holds true for groupwork. Individuals must make a commitment to one another and the group's tasks in order to have a successful experience. Four strategies that can enhance the effectiveness of teams are establishing common goals, working together, engaging in creative problem solving, and avoiding groupthink.

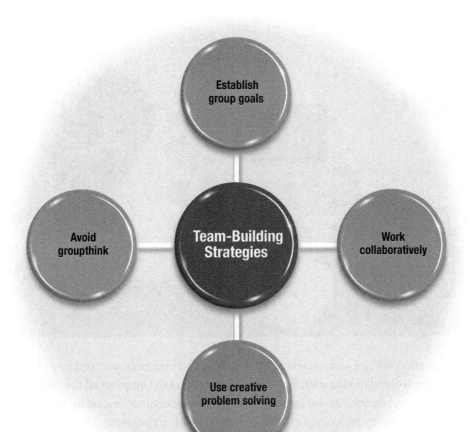

FIGURE 8.3

Team-building
strategies.

## *Establish Group Goals*

Have you ever been part of a group that talked about performance expectations before beginning its work? Rather than immediately starting the project, the group spends time communicating about what each person anticipates will happen while in the group experience. They share ideas about how meetings should occur, discuss how the work should be distributed, and how to best approach the task. This process can be used to openly establish and clarify what each person wants and values. After all, a group is greater than the sum of its parts—each individual has ideas, experiences, and expectations about groupwork. In order to build effective teams, it is important to begin with a discussion of the individual expectations that group members bring to the group experience. Then, it is beneficial to address how each individual's ideas can be summarized and combined with the goals of the other group members in order to identify a game plan for accomplishing the task. When expectations are explicitly communicated, group members become more aware of the perceptions of others and standards of a group experience. This

A social loafer is like someone who sits around on the sofa all day watching TV.

communication can combat social loafing. If you've ever been part of a group where someone seemed to take a back seat and allow others to complete all the work, then you have experienced *social loafing*. Social loafing occurs when an individual fails to invest in group tasks or complete assigned tasks. If, however, all individuals in the group have a working understanding of what others expect, members are more likely to work together.

> **Social loafing**
> Avoiding groupwork and allowing others in the group to perform tasks.

## Work Collaboratively

When students are asked why they do not like working in groups, they frequently complain that all members do not equally contribute to the work of the group. When group members work collaboratively, they try to incorporate all of the people in the group and all ideas and suggestions. Ideas are combined and discussed until the best solution or idea is created. While working with others, have you ever experienced an increase in your productivity simply because others depended on you? Perhaps you even completed extra work. This is the idea behind *social facilitation*. This occurs when the presence of others, that is, working with others, increases the potential to improve our own performance. For example, when working with someone you consider to be "smart" or a "hard worker," you may strive to "keep up" with this person. You may complete tasks ahead of deadlines or volunteer to do extra work for the group due to the influence of the other person.

> **Social facilitation**
> Presence of someone else in the group increases members' performance.

Both social facilitation and social loafing occur in groups and can hinder the collaborative experience. Social facilitators may become so eager to complete goals that they may complete tasks assigned to other individuals in the group. Social loafers may skip meetings or not contribute to the group. Should one of these instances occur, it is best for the group as a whole to discuss how to resolve the situation. Rather than ignore the situation, the group members need to communicate about the experience. Recall from Chapter 8 that one of the stages of group development, norming, was an important component of coming together as a group. It was during this time that group members "normalized" and determined how the group was going to function. Recalling and reexamining how the group decided to function can serve as a reminder for what each member should be doing.

## *Use Creative Problem Solving*

Chances are that you will occasionally experience conflict when working in a group. After all, groups are comprised of individuals with a variety of personalities, different levels of motivation, and perhaps unique goals. No matter what situations the group faces, problem-solving techniques, when implemented, help groups work successfully. When group members work collaboratively to identify solutions, positive outcomes can occur. The following step-by-step process was created by John Dewey (1910) to help group members navigate difficulties. The steps include defining the problem, analyzing it, determining solutions, proposing solutions, evaluating solutions, and selecting a solution.

First, groups must work to define the problem. What is the specific issue the group is facing? To begin the process, it is important to clearly identify and describe the particular problem so that all group members can focus on it. For example, you might have a problem with parking on your campus. By clearly focusing on the problem you can ensure that everyone in the group is working on the same thing.

In the second step, you begin to analyze the problem. What factors contributed to the problem? Determine how long the problem has existed, what caused the problem, and what key elements contribute to the problem. In the previous example, the key problem is the inadequate number of parking spaces for all students, faculty, and staff on campus. The first step in addressing the problem would be to address all the factors that contribute to the problem. For example, your campus could have a large number of students who commute all trying to find parking spaces. There could be multiple sections of courses offered at the same time, thus making the parking lot crowded. Perhaps your campus is land-locked and has no options for expanding or building new parking lots. All of these factors contribute to the parking shortage.

In the third step, you determine guidelines for the best solutions. What are the criteria that will be used to judge all possible solutions? In solving any problem,

FIGURE 8.4

Problem solving process.

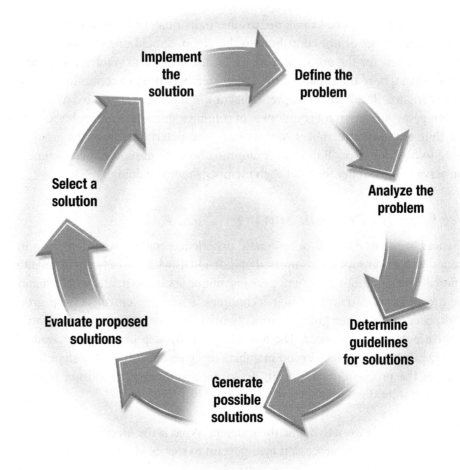

Brainstorming can be an effective way to create solutions.

© wavebreakmedia/Shutterstock.com

there are always parameters to keep in mind. For instance, if you were discussing the parking problem on your campus with individuals on the board of trustees or the president of your school, you may be told that any solution should be affordable as the school does not want to spend a substantial amount of money to fix the problem.

In the fourth step, you and your group propose solutions. What are the possible solutions? *Brainstorming* is a popular technique to help groups generate potential solutions. Although it may sound too simple to be useful, the art of free thinking (and writing it down) can actually help groups see ideas they had not previously considered. The key to successful brainstorming is not just to write some ideas down, but to write *everything* down. No idea should be deemed worthless.

**Brainstorming**
Technique used for generating ideas.

In the fifth step, the group evaluates the proposed solutions. You should assess the advantages and disadvantages of each proposed solution. Using the criteria identified in step three, the team should now evaluate the possible solutions. Recall that the board of trustees prefers a cost-effective solution. Other criteria your group could have considered are the potential for future growth on your campus or plans for expanding public transportation. Using the criteria your group developed, your group evaluates each proposed solution against it.

Step six requires the group to select a solution. You should pick the solution that works best or has the most merit or worth to solve the problem. Your group may decide that requiring all students to pay for parking permits will control the flow of cars and alleviate the parking issue, while also providing a low-cost solution to the problem.

Finally, your group will implement its solution. Decisions are made about how to put the solution into practice. It is important to determine a process for tracking and monitoring the effectiveness of the plan. For example, your group might decide to complete monthly monitoring of the parking, solicit student feedback, and interview administrators about their experiences with the solution after its implementation.

In addition to using Dewey's (1910) problem-solving sequence, additional suggestions that may help the group complete tasks include planning ahead, taking a break from the task or project, reassigning group roles, working toward consensus, and voting with majority rules.

Planning ahead is one of the most useful things a group can do. It is best to map out a game plan and create a schedule of tasks to be completed before the deadline. This provides the group with time to review and revise the work, if necessary, before the due date. Next, removing yourself from the project, even for a short period of time, allows you to think of different ideas to incorporate or ways to improve the problem to be solved. Have you experienced a situation in which you couldn't come up with any alternative solutions? Taking a break may enable you to clear your mind and approach the task from a fresh perspective.

Another idea is to try changing group roles. Oftentimes, individuals adopt ways of thinking that relate to their specific group role. In order to change orientations to a group problem, it can be helpful to switch things up from time to time. Breaking the routine and shifting roles can help group members experience group life in a new way and assist them in replacing habitual behaviors and tired ways of thinking.

Consensus occurs when all members of the group reach the same opinion. Every person is included; ideas are contributed, combined, and built from one another; and everyone has the opportunity to veto an idea. Consider working with a group of peers on a class assignment. The professor has asked you to complete a group assignment but the artifact you submit to the professor at the conclusion of the semester is to be selected by the members of the group. Using consensus principles, each group member is able to share ideas about what the project should be, combine ideas with others, and veto any ideas.

Finally, majority rule might be yet another technique to incorporate when working with others. This occurs when a resolution is voted on and approved by a majority of the group members. For example, if you and your group of six friends are trying to determine what movie to see and vote on which one you would prefer, a majority vote occurs when four of the six friends agree to a movie. Collectively, these tactics can be used to help groups reach thoughtful decisions that are appropriate for the task at hand. Groups should use these types of practices to avoid achieving false agreement.

## *Avoid Groupthink*

In Chapter 8, we introduced the concept of groupthink. You'll recall that groupthink is largely considered a negative occurrence in group life. In situations where everyone in the group seems to "go along" with a proposed idea to get along in the group instead of trying to work toward the best possible solution, consider implementing strategies to steer your team away from the groupthink trap. Some suggested strategies include:

1. *Ask questions.* Sometimes, you may think it is easier to just go along with a solution rather than asking questions to ensure that you completely understand the implications of the group's decision. However, it is

important that all group members work to understand how proposed ideas or solutions fit with the group's overall goals.

2. *It is okay to be skeptical.* Related to the notion of asking questions, it is acceptable to feel skeptical or unsure. Just because everyone else in the group is going along with an idea does not make it correct. If you have doubts about a plan of action, these should be voiced. In voicing these doubts, hopefully the idea and decision can be strengthened.

3. *Openly discuss ideas.* Rather than sharing your ideas with only one or two members of the group, make sure everyone in the group has the opportunity to listen to all ideas. Sharing information with others can help new ideas surface.

It appears that finding the best possible solutions for a task while working with others requires effort and care. Everyone in the group should have a chance to voice his or her experiences and opinions. In sharing those insights, ideas and solutions are enhanced and strengthened. During your meetings with groups, several things can be done to have more efficient meetings.

# ENHANCING THE MEETING PROCESS

Scheduling and coordinating group meetings can be quite difficult. An unproductive group meeting could leave group members feeling unmotivated to work and contribute to negative feelings toward working with others. There are, however, strategies to promote quality, efficient group meetings.

## *Manage Meeting Time*

Time is valuable, and respecting the time of group members is important. The time allocated for group meetings should be carefully managed, perhaps by the leader of the group. The leader of the group could assign one person to serve in the role of timekeeper for the group to ensure that the group remains focused on accomplishing tasks within the specified time constraints. Remaining engaged and focused on group tasks can be challenging. Have you ever attended a meeting where the discussion went "off topic"? Meetings are often sidetracked due to conversations among members or discussions that are unrelated to the group's function. These unwanted discussions have an impact on the overall length of the meeting. In turn, this could affect people's commitment to the group. For example, you may think that being part of a group or a committee isn't important because "nothing gets accomplished" and so you stop attending meetings. Similarly, when members arrive late or leave early and expect time during the next meeting to be devoted to "catching them up" on what they've missed, productivity and commitment to the group diminishes.

## Develop and Adhere to an Agenda

Few things are worse than a group meeting in which individuals feel negative about the group or its processes. An agenda can improve the quality of a meeting. The *agenda* is simply a list of the activities or tasks that need to be accomplished during a particular meeting. It may include what needs to be accomplished at the current meeting and also contain information about upcoming due dates or tasks. Organizing the agenda by specifying the amount of time devoted to each topic of discussion is another helpful way to ensure an effective meeting structure. *Time on task* is how much time the group will spend discussing a given topic. When writing the agenda, place items that require more time at the beginning of the agenda. By doing this, people in the group will feel productive as they move through the agenda items. It is best to tailor the agenda to fit the time allocated to the meeting. If the items that require more time are placed at the beginning of the agenda, and a meeting needs to end early, the important, necessary items have already been addressed. If you know the group will meet for only an hour, there is no need to place superfluous tasks on the agenda. Adjusting

The meeting agenda is a list of items that need to be accomplished.

© Dusit/Shutterstock.com

the agenda to fit the group members and goals is a process that takes refinement during the initial meetings. It is also helpful to get the agenda to the group before meetings. This way, group members are able to prepare thoughts and comments and time is not wasted trying to come up with answers or suggestions. Ultimately, when an agenda contains only the tasks to be addressed, it can help the group members feel as though they actually accomplish their tasks and ultimately can accomplish the group's purpose. This, in turn, could improve the overall quality and effectiveness during the meeting.

## Demonstrating Respect for Others

Consider the following example:

> Your company has noticed that people seem indifferent about coming to work. No one seems overly excited to be there; people rarely come in on time and often are quick to leave. In addition, people do not interact while at work and the overall environment seems very isolated. As a result, your company has recently created a committee to address this issue. The committee was asked to create ways to boost or increase worker morale and propose solutions for improving relationships among workers. At the first meeting, however, the person who was asked to be in charge of the committee and serve as the leader is heard saying, "I hate working with others. Who cares about relationships with other people?"

If you heard this, how would you react? Would you want to continue working on a project with someone who doesn't seem interested? You're probably thinking that the person's language is quite counterproductive to what the group is trying to accomplish. Another tool for enhancing group meetings is demonstrating respect for others. This may be done by the type of language used. Most likely, you were told as a small child to "think before you speak" or "what you say to others matters." These old adages have some utility when working with others. Be sure to use inclusive language to reinforce the collective nature of the group. Terms such as "our project" and "we can accomplish this" help create a sense of cohesiveness.

Groupwork is difficult and you and the others in the group may want to take sides when determining solutions to problems. Nonjudgmental language and questions will demonstrate respect for others and enhance the group experience. Asking questions ensures that everyone is "on the same page." Using statements such as "What I think I hear you saying is ..." is one example of paraphrasing what others have said to make sure that you have understood them correctly. It's important to note that paraphrasing doesn't necessarily mean that you agree with ideas or opinions. Rather, you are attempting to understand someone else's ideas. By doing so, you will make others in the group feel valued. Ask open-ended questions. **Open-ended questions** are those that cannot be answered with a one-word statement. They often start with who, what, why, or how. By using open-ended questions, others are encouraged to share and elaborate in discussing their ideas. When everyone is given a voice, all members feel valuable. If group members feel valued, they are more likely to be committed to accomplishing the group's goal.

In situations where confrontations occur, incorporate "I" statements to explain your perception. Statements such as "I feel frustrated when I feel like nobody is listening to my ideas" show personal ownership of the experience rather than the more accusatory, "You never listen to me."

Another way to demonstrate respect for the group is by arriving on time with all previously assigned tasks completed. If, at a previous meeting, you are given a task to complete, you should be able to report on the status of that task at the next meeting. During your update of the assigned task, your communication should stay focused and not drift into superfluous or unnecessary information.

Ultimately, group meetings can be quite productive. These simple and practical steps can ensure that a meeting achieves its goals and allows everyone an opportunity to express their ideas. By managing time and respecting others' boundaries and ideas, there is a greater chance of having a positive group experience.

# CHAPTER SUMMARY

There are many different approaches to leadership and leading a group. In fact, because of the different types of leaders, being an effective leader who guides group members to completing tasks can appear to be overwhelming. However, it is possible to tailor your leadership style to your particular group and task. This chapter provides tools and suggestions for determining an appropriate leadership style. These tools include considering the group's purpose, members, and potential obstacles. By doing so, you are likely to have a more positive leadership experience and a successful group. Ask yourself this series of questions:

- What is the group's purpose?
- With what type of individuals am I working?
- In what type of environment is the group working?
- What are the potential obstacles in the way of completing the task?
- Am I the best person for a leadership position?

In asking and honestly answering these questions, you have begun to understand the group's dynamics and, as a result, will communicate more efficiently and effectively. Thus, it is important to think carefully about the important components to working in a particular group and tailor your communication accordingly. This will be beneficial in your personal, professional, and public lives. It is beneficial because all members of the group can have a clear understanding of what the tasks and challenges are, everyone can share insights about the group, and you, as the leader, can create messages that guide the group to successful completion of its tasks and goals.

While working with others can be daunting, there are simple strategies that can contribute to its overall effectiveness. It is important to keep in mind that there is no one right way to lead in a group. Oftentimes, you will experience individual differences and preferences for a certain leadership style over others. You must remember that these potential differences should not interfere with the group's overall functioning. If a problem arises, engaging in careful problem solving can efficiently minimize any difficulties. Ultimately, it is best to focus the group by using simple management solutions. With these ideas in mind, you and your group can successfully achieve the group's goals.

## KEY WORDS

*Agenda* List of the activities or tasks that need to be accomplished at the meeting.

*Authoritarian leader* Mandates what must be done in a group setting.

*Brainstorming* Technique used for generating ideas.

*Charismatic leader* Type of leader who has characteristics such as confidence, interpersonal attractiveness, and effective communication skills.

*Coaching leader* Type of leader who uses both highly directive behaviors and highly supportive behaviors; focuses communication on not only achieving goals but also on meeting the followers' emotional needs.

*Delegating leadership* Offers little advice, input, or social support and control is handed over to the group members.

*Democratic leader* Actively consults group members before making decisions.

*Directive leadership* Focuses on task completion.

*Disruptive communication* Detracts group members from accomplishing their goals.

*Interaction approach* One way to study leadership; focuses on communicative exchanges in the leadership process.

*Laissez-faire leader* Prefers a "hands-off" mentality to leading others.

*Leadership* Process in which individuals influence others' actions and behaviors in order to achieve some goal.

*Open-ended questions* Questions that cannot be answered with a one-word statement.

*Promotive communication* Focuses on messages that contribute to the group's tasks.

*Situational approach* One way to study leadership; focuses on the characteristics of the group members and the situation.

*Social facilitation* Presence of someone else in the group increases their performance.

*Social loafing* Avoiding groupwork and allowing others in the group to perform tasks.

*Socioemotional leader* Type of leader who is primarily concerned with the relationships among group members.

*Supportive leadership* Solicits feedback and employs behaviors that will highlight and develop the skills of group members.

*Task leader* Type of leader who is primarily concerned with completing the group's goals.

*Team-building* Process that includes gathering cooperation from individuals to achieve a common goal.

*Time on task* How much time the group will spend discussing a given topic.

*Trait approach* One way to study leadership; focuses on the characteristics/ traits of the leader.

# REFERENCES

Blanchard, K. H. (1985). *SLII: A situational approach to managing people.* Escondido, CA: Blanchard Training and Development.

Cragan, J. F., & Wright, D. W. (1999). *Communication in small groups: Theory, processes, skills* (5th ed.). Belmont, CA: Wadsworth.

Dewey, J. (1910). *How we think.* New York: Dover.

Hersey, P., & Blanchard, K. (1993). *Management of organizational behavior: Utilizing human resources* (6th ed.). Englewood Cliffs, NJ: Prentice Hall.

Kirkpatrick, S. A., & Locke, E. A. (1991). Leadership: Do traits matter? *The Executive, 5,* 48–60.

Lewin, K., Lippit, R. & White, R. K. (1939). Patterns of aggressive behavior in experimentally created social climates. *Journal of Social Psychology, 10,* 271–301.

Mumford, M. D. (2006). *To outstanding leadership: A comparative analysis of charismatic, ideological, and pragmatic leaders.* Mahwah, NJ: Erlbaum.

Shaw, M. E. (1981). *Group dynamics: The psychology of small group behavior.* New York: McGraw-Hill.

# CHAPTER 9

## Mediated Communication: The Channel Matters

## Chapter Objectives

After reading this chapter, you should be able to:
- Define mediated communication
- Distinguish between mass and social media
- Identify strategies for effective communication via mediated channels
- Describe reasons for using mass media and social media
- Discuss the impact of media on relationships
- Identify strategies for improving media use

**PERSONAL:** Your friend tells you about a conflict he recently had with his romantic partner. The conflict is the result of a text message. Your friend told his partner that he wanted to go to the movies this weekend. His partner replied, "Yeah, right, that will totally happen." Your friend was confused and hurt when after the weekend was over, he and his partner never went to the movies. He defends his actions to you and indicates that he was very explicit in what he wanted to happen and felt unclear about why his partner would agree to a movie then never take him. How did the text message cause confusion on the part of both individuals?

**PROFESSIONAL:** At work, you have been asked to be part of a team that includes members from your home office and people from an office overseas. Because of clear geographical differences, in order to have face-to-face communication, the team decides to use Skype for meetings. All meetings are scheduled via email and you need to prepare for the meeting scheduled for next week. During your preparations, what should you consider when using an online system for communication?

**PUBLIC:** You have recently graduated from college and during your transition to adult life, you begin to review your social media profiles on Facebook, Twitter, and Instagram. You realize that some of the information on your profile might not be appropriate for an employer to see. After all, you want to project a professional image. What kinds of information should you delete from your profile?

As the opening examples illustrate, you spend a large portion of your day surrounded by or using mediated communication. It can be useful to accomplish daily tasks and maintain your social life. In fact, this form of communication might be something you rely on so heavily that you cannot imagine living without it. In this chapter, you learn about the various mediated sources we use and consume daily. Specifically, we address the many forms of mediated channels of communication that are available to us, and why we choose to use mediated forms of communication. We also highlight the unique challenges of mediated communication and identify tips to improve and enhance your usage.

# MEDIATED COMMUNICATION DEFINED

You wake up in the morning to your favorite song, which you downloaded from the Internet. As your day begins, you catch up on the news on television then listen to sports talk radio in the car as you drive to work. During the day, you watch YouTube videos, read magazines, and research recipes for dinner. In the evening,

Copyright © by Marketing Charts. Reprinted by permission.

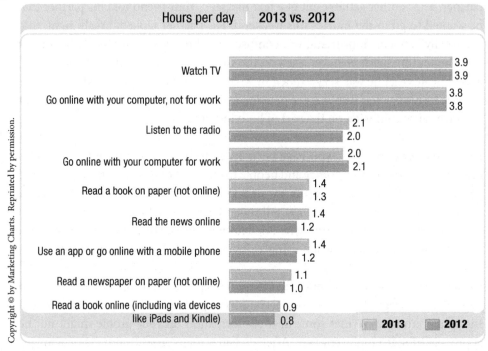

## Americans' Daily Media Consumption

Hours per day | 2013 vs. 2012

| | 2013 | 2012 |
| --- | --- | --- |
| Watch TV | 3.9 | 3.9 |
| Go online with your computer, not for work | 3.8 | 3.8 |
| Listen to the radio | 2.1 | 2.0 |
| Go online with your computer for work | 2.0 | 2.1 |
| Read a book on paper (not online) | 1.4 | 1.3 |
| Read the news online | 1.4 | 1.2 |
| Use an app or go online with a mobile phone | 1.4 | 1.2 |
| Read a newspaper on paper (not online) | 1.1 | 1.0 |
| Read a book online (including via devices like iPads and Kindle) | 0.9 | 0.8 |

you send emails to your family, catch up with a long-distance romantic partner via FaceTime, and spend a few moments reviewing your favorite blog. As a society, we are inundated with mediated forms of communication. Throughout the day, we encounter a wide variety of media. As the chart in Figure 9.1 shows, in 2013 Americans spent over half their day engaged with some form of media.

Not only are you bombarded with mediated forms of communication, but the messages communicated via these channels impact you in a variety of ways. Worsnop (1989) identifies several ways in which media impacts our lives. Specifically, media:

1. Helps us understand the workings of our immediate world. It gives us information about current events, locally, nationally, and internationally.
2. Serves as a source of stories. Media outlets serve as the authors of the stories we consume.
3. Requires us to learn and use critical thinking skills. When turning to the media for information, we should be examining what we consume for accuracy.
4. Defines how we communicate. Media can shape our communication with others by influencing the channels we use for communication and the topics of our conversations.
5. Helps us (mis)understand ourselves and others. It serves as a tool for

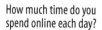
How much time do you spend online each day?

© Spectral-Design/Shutterstock.com

helping us learn more about who we are and who we are not.

6. Explains how things work. Media can provide us with useful insights about the processes of events and gather explanations of how happenings occur.

7. Brings us pleasure. We can turn to media to view videos and articles that bring us joy or help us escape from the mundane routine of life.

Considering the amount of time we spend with media and the multiple types of information and impact it can have on us, it seems crucial to understand the role it plays in our lives. The scope of media and the constant consumption of mediated messages can affect nearly every aspect of our lives.

*Mediated communication* involves individuals utilizing technology as a channel of delivery for a message. Mediated forms of communication include cell phone calls, texts, and emails. Recall from Chapter 1 that mediated communication includes both *mass media* and *social media*. When you watch television and listen to commercials, you are a receiver of mass media communication. "Mass" refers to the large audience that receives the message, and "media" refers to the technological channels used to communicate the message. *Mass media* utilizes technology to send messages to a large number of people. *Social media* are websites used to create an online identity and may include sites such as Facebook or Instagram that build communities of people.

Most mediated communication can be described as *lean communication*. This

> **Mediated communication**
Utilizing technology as the channel of delivery.

> **Mass media**
Utilizing technology to send messages to masses of people with the intent to influence behaviors.

> **Social media**
Websites that allow for individuals to create a profile to build communities.

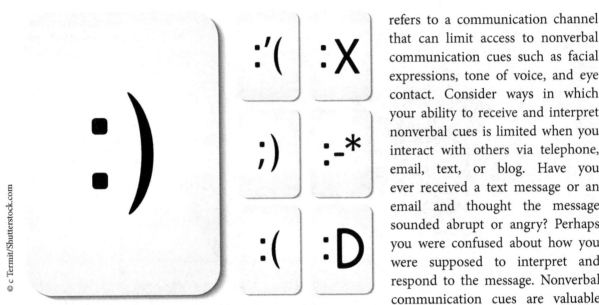

Do you use emoticons in your text messages?

**Lean communication** Communication channels that reduce access to nonverbal communication, such as facial expressions, touch, and eye contact.

refers to a communication channel that can limit access to nonverbal communication cues such as facial expressions, tone of voice, and eye contact. Consider ways in which your ability to receive and interpret nonverbal cues is limited when you interact with others via telephone, email, text, or blog. Have you ever received a text message or an email and thought the message sounded abrupt or angry? Perhaps you were confused about how you were supposed to interpret and respond to the message. Nonverbal communication cues are valuable tools that assist us in understanding the intended meaning behind the message. We depend on both nonverbal and verbal communication in order to understand the intended meaning behind the message, as both dimensions of communication provide insight into how the message is interpreted. Some mediated channels of communication—for example, email or text messaging—reduce access to this nonverbal information. You may use emoticons (such as a smiley face) or acronyms (such as LOL) to help the receiver of the message understand the ways in which the message should be interpreted; however, it can still be difficult to interpret the message accurately.

## DISTINGUISHING TYPES OF MEDIATED COMMUNICATION

At its most basic level, mediated communication involves the use of technology, such as a computer to send an email or a cell phone to call or text someone. However, these are not the only mediated forms of communication. Radio, television, magazines, billboards, and websites all provide us with channels to share messages with others. Communication scholars focus on specific types of mediated communication: mass media and social media. Mass media utilizes technology to send messages to a large number of people. In Table 9.1 you can see there are many types of mass media. Mass media can be useful in terms of shaping ideas, sharing culture, and influencing behaviors. For example, do you remember television shows such as *Friends* and *Jersey Shore*? Each of these shows was popular at one point in

© c Termit/Shutterstock.com

time, and both created social impact. For example, Rachel, a character on *Friends*, had a very popular hairstyle that influenced a number of women to ask their hairstylists for "The Rachel." Characters on *Jersey Shore* had a distinct verbal style and vocabulary. They wore glittery t-shirts designed by Ed Hardy and described not-so-attractive women as "grenades." These t-shirts soon became embraced by our society and their description of unfortunate women became a popular phrase.

TABLE 9.1

Types of Mediated Communication

| Channel | Examples |
|---|---|
| Mediated communication | Email, cell phone calls, and texts |
| Mass media communication | Radio, newspaper, billboards, television, news magazines, Internet |
| Social media communication | Collaborative projects (e.g., Wikipedia), blogs, content communities (e.g., YouTube), social networking sites (e.g., Facebook), virtual game worlds (e.g., World of Warcraft), and virtual social worlds (e.g., Second Life) |

Boyd and Ellison (2008) describe ***social media*** as websites that individuals use to create or portray profiles to a list of users with whom they interact. According to Kaplan and Haenlein (2010) there are a number of types of social media, and examples of these are included in Table 9.1. Each of these social media has a unique focus. ***Collaborative projects*** focus on co-creating information with other individuals. These would include websites such as Wikipedia where individuals can add or delete information. ***Blogs*** are often more personal in nature and can be considered an online journal. They are typically written from a one-person perspective and shed light on any number of topics. Websites that aim to build both personal and professional connections with others are called ***social networking.*** Examples of social networking sites include Facebook, Instagram, and LinkedIn. ***Virtual game worlds*** and

**⇒ Collaborative projects**
Focus on co-creating information with other individuals.

**⇒ Social networking**
Sites that aim to build both personal and professional connections with other individuals.

**⇒ Virtual game worlds**
Online games that include a created reality and encourage the following of rules to play a game.

Virtual game worlds create fictional lives for players.

© Barone Firenze/Shutterstock.com

*virtual social worlds* create fictional lives. Game worlds focus on players following the rules of a game and include games such as *World of Warcraft*. Social worlds provide a space for individuals to create another life and interact with others and include games such as *Second Life*. While participating in virtual game worlds, people wear headsets that allow for verbal interaction with their opponents. Virtual social worlds allow for interaction in the game as characters can interact.

Mediated forms of communication—be it using a phone, playing a game online, or watching your favorite television show—are prevalent in our daily lives. Each form of mediated communication has unique qualities. We first explore mass media communication and then turn our attention to social media. Included in our social media discussion is an examination of texting, calling, and emailing. While distinct from social media, texting, calling, and emailing do aid in relationship initiation, maintenance, and termination. As a result, these channels of communication share many of the same properties as social media.

## MASS MEDIA IN OUR LIVES

Mass media is noteworthy because you have choices and decide what you listen to and watch. It can be used as a tool to influence our interactions with others. A popular television show from 1998 until 2003 was *Dawson's Creek*. Actors on the show included James Van Der Beek and Katie Holmes, and the plot focused on their lives as teenagers. It was a favorite show of one of the authors, and she often watched it with her friends. The next day at school she and her friends would discuss the current week's episode. When other friends would join the group, they were often told the topic and asked to wait until they were finished discussing the show before starting a new topic of conversation. In this way, the television impacted the flow of interaction. It informed the topic of conversation (the topic was the current episode) and who could participate in the discussion (only those who had watched the episode).

Many times we have a choice about what media we consume (e.g., listening to the television at your home or the radio in your car); however, not all mass media consumption is by choice. The billboards you pass while driving are considered mass media, and the content shared on these signs is beyond your control. However, recall the perception process. You do not take in and comprehend every message to which you are exposed; rather, we make careful decisions about what we will be able to recall based on certain criteria. The same can be said of the decision-making process behind mass media consumption. You make careful decisions about the media you put into your life.

## Selecting Media Sources

Suppose you have a favorite television show you never miss. You and your friends may discuss the characters or storyline. Perhaps you find yourselves "taking sides" and having emotional reactions to the characters' experiences (called *parasocial interactions*, an idea that is discussed later in the chapter). Additionally, you may have websites that you frequently visit. For example, for the latest news, you may only check *www.cnn.com*. Your decision to select specific media is often based on the utility of the information, the relevance of the message, or how similar the message is to your existing attitudes, beliefs, and values. Thus, you focus on mass media messages that hold value for you. Once you believe that the message is either helpful or has the potential to be of benefit in the future, you are likely to select it.

One theoretical lens used to understand how individuals use media is the *Uses and Gratifications Theory*. The uses and gratifications approach argues that media are strategically selected in order to meet our personal needs. This theory seeks to understand the relationship individuals have with the media. While it might seem odd to think of yourself as in a relationship with media, you use the media to fulfill personal needs and, in doing so, you are gratified or get something out of it. When selecting media, we may use it before we have a need for information, persuasion, education, or entertainment. Media can also be selected to meet cognitive needs, affective needs, personal integrative needs, social integrative needs, and/or entertainment needs (Katz, Blumler, & Gurevitch, 1974). Each of these needs is described in Table 9.2. Suppose you have had a bad day at work, then you remember that your favorite television show airs that night. Once at home, you eagerly sit in front of the television as your show starts. For the next hour it is as if nothing else matters. You selected a favorite show and are now using it to get away from the bad day you had.

Uses and Gratifications Theory focuses on the audience—that is, it seeks to comprehend why individuals use media in an effort to explain the media choices individuals make and the consequences experienced. The Gratifications Sought and Obtained Scale highlighted in Figure 9.2 (Palmgreen, Weener, & Rayburn, 1980) helps to explain further why people use media and what needs the media fulfills for them.

## TABLE 9.2

Needs Satisfied by the Media (Hamilton, 1998)

| Need | Description | Example |
|------|-------------|---------|
| Cognitive | Seeks information or knowledge | View the nightly news on television to gather information about the world in which you live |
| Affective | Seeks emotional reassurance, positive feelings | Watch sitcoms such as *How I Met Your Mother* because the show contains feel-good messages |
| Personal integrative | Seeks self-esteem support | Read a book about popular interviewing techniques and ways to prepare for an upcoming interview |
| Social integrative | Seeks interaction with others | Log on to your favorite gaming website because it allows you to connect with others |
| Entertainment | Seeks fun and excitement | Meet with friends on a weekly basis to watch *Real Housewives of New Jersey* because you perceive the television show to be full of drama |

## FIGURE 9.2

The Gratifications Sought and Obtained Scale.
Source: Philip Palmgreen, Lawrence A. Wenner, J.D. Rayburn, *Communication Research, Volume 7, Issue 2,* April 1980, pp 161-192, Copyright © 1980 by SAGE Publications. Reprinted by permission of SAGE Publications.

This scale has been used to understand why people watch TV news. Below are 15 reasons people have given. As you read each one, please indicate how much it applies to you. If the reason <u>very definitely applies to you, give it a 5</u>; if it <u>does not apply at all, give it a 1</u>. If it applies somewhere in between, give it a 2, 3, or 4 depending on how much.

1. I watch TV news to keep up with current issues and events. _____
2. I watch TV news so I won't be surprised by higher prices and things like that. _____
3. I watch TV news because you can trust the information they give you. _____
4. I watch TV news to find out what kind of job our government officials are doing. _____
5. I watch TV news to help me make up my mind about the important issues of the day. _____
6. I watch TV news to find out about issues affecting people like myself. _____
7. I watch TV news because it's often entertaining. _____
8. I watch TV news because it's often dramatic. _____
9. I watch TV news because it's often exciting. _____
10. I watch TV news to support my own viewpoints to other people. _____
11. I watch TV news so I can pass the information on to other people. _____
12. I watch TV news to give me interesting things to talk about. _____
13. I watch TV news because the newscasters give a human quality to the news. _____
14. I watch TV news to compare my own ideas to what the commentators say. _____
15. I watch TV news because the reporters are like people I know. _____

Philip Palmgreen, Lawrence A. Wenner, J.D. Rayburn, *Communication Research, Volume 7, Issue 2, April 1980,* pp 161-192, Copyright © 1980 by SAGE Publications. Reprinted by permission of SAGE Publications.

The Gratifications Sought and Obtained Scale assesses several key ideas. The first three questions pertain to general *information-seeking* or the extent to which you attempt to gather information about happenings in the world. Questions 4–6 seek to address your *decisional utility*, or the extent to which media are used to gain information and make informed decisions. Questions 7, 8, and 9 focus on *entertainment* or the extent to which you find media to be a source of pleasurable distraction. Questions 10–12 seek to understand your *interpersonal utility*. That is, do you perceive media to be a source of useful information that can be used in your relationships with other people? The final questions address *parasocial interaction*. These questions assess your perceived interpersonal or relational connections with individuals in the media. Have you ever heard a news report that details someone stalking a celebrity? For the person doing the stalking, in his or her mind a relationship is present with the famous person; the two individuals are connected. This instrument serves as one way to address the various functions media fulfills. By using media, we gather information to discuss with others. This information can assist us in building relationships or serving as a starting place for potentially difficult conversations.

> **Information-seeking**
> Extent to which you attempt to gather information about happenings in the world.
>
> **Decisional utility**
> Extent media is used to gain information and make an informed decision.
>
> **Entertainment**
> Extent to which you find media to be a source of pleasurable distraction.
>
> **Interpersonal utility**
> Extent to which media is perceived to be a source of useful information that can be used in your relationship.

## Retention of Media Info

Given that we are inundated with messages, recalling everything that we've been exposed to on a daily basis would be a daunting task. It would be nearly impossible to remember every message. Humans are limited-capacity processors. This refers to the fact that we can only retain so much information. When studying for a test, for example, have you ever thought there is no possible way you will be able to take in any additional information? It is almost as if your brain is "full." To retain or recall information, we need to perceive the information to have utility. If the information is viewed as being helpful, we can recall it. We also remember information if it is novel or new. When we say to ourselves, "Wow, that is interesting" or "Hmmm, I had no idea," it is likely information that we will be able to recall later. In our interactions with others, you have likely expressed statements such as "Guess what I heard today on television…?" Media informs our discussions and gives us new topics of conversation. This information is helpful for our personal, professional, and public lives. If, for example, you have ever been on a job interview and created a list of topics to discuss as you prepared for the meeting, you may have used something that you heard from mass media.

# FUNCTIONS OF MASS MEDIA

The media fulfills a variety of functions. We look to mass media as a source of information, in addition to fulfilling the needs previously discussed. Katz et al. (1974) argues that we use media "to match one's wits against others, to get information and advice for daily living, to provide a framework for one's day, to prepare oneself culturally for the demands of upward mobility, or to be reassured about the dignity and usefulness of one's role" (p. 20). Mass media provides insight on a variety of topics. From gathering information about current events to understanding how families communicate, we often use mass media to gather information about the world in which we live that we then use to help us form ideas.

## Information Gathering and Idea Formation

Consider the following example. Your friend encourages you to purchase a new car. You are open to suggestions, and your friend is eager to offer advice. She encourages you to buy a Ford. Since you have never driven a Ford, you have no previous knowledge about the company or its vehicles. You begin researching the Ford your friend wants you to purchase. Information is gathered from commercials, the Internet, radio, and television, and you notice that with every mass media message you take in, each has a different opinion of the product. From all of these messages, you begin to form an opinion about the product.

Mass-mediated messages can be a valuable resource for gathering information about the world in which we live. Turning on the television or surfing the Internet for insights about current events is easy. In fact, the media are often the primary source of information when we are gathering information, deciding on purchases, researching information on lawmakers and policies, and seeking entertainment. However, during this consumption, there are some key ideas to consider. According to the Center for Media Literacy (n.d.), all media have five core concepts that individuals should consider that center around authorship, format, audience, content, and purpose (Figure 9.3). First, authorship refers to the idea that all media messages are constructed, created, or produced by someone or some entity. It is important to note who created it as those individuals likely have a vested interest in it. Each person and the company he or she represents have allegiances, alliances, and values that impact what messages are conveyed. Additionally, all messages are created in a particular format, such as advertisements in a magazine, billboards on the highway, or banners that appear on a Web page. These messages are produced for an intended audience. A company, for example, may produce an advertisement for a magazine and the targeted audience is the consumer of the magazine. It is important to note that different people experience the same message differently. As discussed in Chapter 2, our perception may cause each of us to react differently to the same message. Thus, even if we are exposed to the same media, each of us may interpret the messages in very distinct ways. You and your friend could be exposed to the same commercial yet create different impressions of the same content. The content used in the media is influenced by the audience who is being targeted and

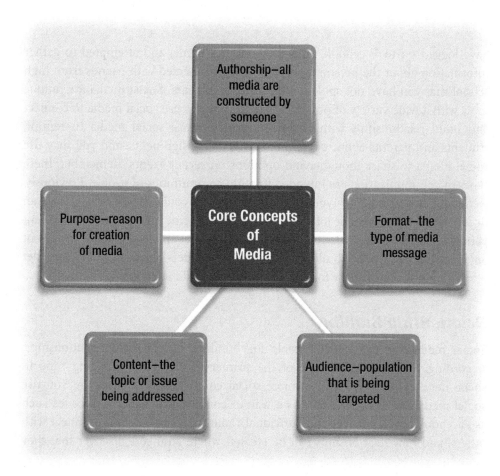

FIGURE 9.3

Core concepts of media.

includes particular language or visuals that are used to grab the viewer's attention and it is important to pay attention to these cues. Finally, purpose refers to the idea that much of mass media is produced for the purposes of gaining attention, power, or profit. These motivations impact how a message is created. It is important to be a thoughtful consumer of mass media and check facts with multiple sources.

Hopefully by now you realize that mass media serves a significant purpose in our lives. It has a noteworthy impact on our beliefs, it informs our language system, and it ultimately impacts our interactions with others. Other forms of media impact and influence our knowledge and interactions too. We now turn our attention to social media.

# SOCIAL MEDIA

Chances are either you or someone you know has used social media to either collect information about someone else or to connect with others. Perhaps you have logged on to Facebook, entered someone's name, and attempted to gather information about the person. Maybe you've reconnected with friends from high school that you have not spoken with for several years. Social media are unique tools with a wide variety of potential uses. Businesses use social media to connect and build relationships with customers, teachers use social media to remind students and parents about upcoming events and assignments, and you may use social media to share thoughts and opinions on recent events. Remember, these types of communication are intended to build communities of people. Previously, we identified a number of types of social media you could choose to use. You can decide what sites to visit or join, and you can also decide how you want to present yourself on these sites. Once you have joined these sites and decided how to present yourself, you will work to build relationships with others. Each social media outlet offers a unique opportunity for us to connect and build relationships with others.

## Relationship Building

Social media can be valuable tools for building or enhancing relationships. According to boyd (2006), one of the primary reasons for investing time in social networking sites is to promote social connections. Chances are you use social media websites primarily as a way to connect with others. Websites such as Facebook have enhanced the individual's ability to connect and reconnect with others, and new relationships can be created where strangers discover that they

Websites such as Facebook have helped people (re)connect with others.

© Twin Design/Shutterstock.com

share a common interest or activity. Quan-Haase and Young (2010) utilized Uses and Gratifications Theory to understand the gratifications individuals experienced when using Facebook versus instant messaging. They found that individuals perceived using Facebook as fun and a shared social activity. That is, if a friend suggested using Facebook, participants in the study were likely to listen to their friends and join the social networking site. Additionally, they found that college students view Facebook as an entertaining networking opportunity. Thus, your social networks play an important role in the types of social media you choose to use, and, because of their influence on your choices, you could gain a larger social network because you may connect with individuals you had not previously connected. While the study above addressed Facebook, there are many different types of social networking sites individuals can choose from when interacting with others. Sites such as Instagram, LinkedIn, and Pinterest are also social networking sites individuals can use to connect with others. According to boyd (2008), there are benefits in using social networking sites. These benefits include:

1. Outlets or opportunities for involvement with the community;
2. Enhancement and growth of individual creativity through sharing of art or music;
3. Growing or developing ideas from the creation of blogs, podcasts, or videos;
4. Expansion of one's online connections; and
5. Fostering of one's individual identity and unique social skills.

While social media can promote the creation of relationships, it too can diminish the quality of a relationship. Consider the following example posted on the website *www.thinkbeforeyousend.com*:

> "My wife was forwarding an e-mail from her father. She had made sarcastic comments about a friend in her email, and prior to forwarding the email, forgot to delete the sarcastic comments. That friend was one of the people who received the forwarded message. This situation seriously strained the friendship."

This example illustrates the concept addressed in Chapter 1: communication cannot be reversed. While this concept is true of all communication, this idea becomes particularly salient to mediated communication because the message is written and recorded. Often the time and date of the message accompany it for later reference. Emails, text messages, or social media posts can be revisited and reread and used as evidence in conversations. Thus, it proves more difficult to deny or change communication and it could, as a result, hurt relationships.

## Networking and Social Movement

Two particularly interesting aspects of social media are its networking and social movement abilities. First, online communities such as LinkedIn and Facebook provide opportunities to network with others. Organizations and companies may turn to social media sites such as LinkedIn when recruiting new employees. People can search sites and locate reputable talent to assist them in projects. Companies can promote their services and build their identities. These online relationships can supplement face-to-face relationships or serve as the primary medium of connection.

Additionally, social media sites can be used as a way to create a social movement. Unze (2010) describes how a 17-year-old boy used Facebook as a way to gather support for a skate park proposal. The plan needed to be approved by the city council. The teen created a Facebook profile describing the cause so users could follow and "like" the information. As a result of the Facebook support generated, the teen had evidence of the impact of the project and funding was eventually allotted for the park. Due to the widespread popularity of social media sites, many celebrities and political candidates have turned to Facebook, Twitter, and Instagram to share their opinions and messages. Consider, for example, President Barack Obama's use of social networking websites during the 2008 election. He tried to connect with voters by turning to websites such as Facebook and Myspace. Previous to this election, this strategy had been less utilized.

Social media sites can be used as a way to create social movement.

© PIXXart/Shutterstock.com

Social media efforts connect individuals and companies alike. Moreover, they can be used strategically as a means of persuasive communication and to gather support for incentives. These powerful tools should be used with caution, however. Social media users should be mindful of what types of information they are disclosing. In fact, websites are dedicated to cautioning people about the uses of social media. For example, Microsoft cautions users to be careful when clicking on links, mindful of whom you allow to be your friend, and selective in deciding what social media websites you use.

# ONLINE IDENTITIES

It is important to keep in mind that when we use social media, we often first create an online identity or person—a public image of ourselves that we share with others. One key concern for communication scholars investigating mediated forms of communication is that of identity or *impression formation*. Scholars refer to the sense-making of others' actions and disposition as impression formation. Typically, through our interactions with others, we form a general impression or idea about the other person's character or qualities and personality (Hancock & Dunham, 2001). For example, after meeting and interacting with someone for the first time, you may think to yourself, "He seemed polite," "I really liked her clothing," or "They seemed a little uncomfortable." All of these are possible impressions that we form of others and that others form of us. Impression formation is a two-way street with us forming impressions of others and others forming impressions of us. If everything you do sends a message, it is important to consider the impressions created by words and photos that are posted online.

**Impression formation**
Sense-making of others' actions and disposition.

Social media profiles enable us to share a variety of information. All of this information is "up for interpretation" by the reader. Impressions are formed based on the information you choose to share. Perhaps you post the lyrics from a country music song and a coworker then invites you to attend a country music concert with her. In reality, you do not enjoy country music, you just appreciated the message behind the lyrics. In this example, we see then that the way you meant to send information, liking a song for meaning, can be interpreted differently, that you actually enjoy country music.

Hancock and Dunham (2001) found that after viewing a person's profile with whom you have no relational history, judgments made are more intense than if the people had met and communicated face-to-face. That is, interacting with a person's online persona (via their profile information) left viewers with stronger attributions and perceptions of the individual. Online representations often fail to incorporate a person's complete or true identity. Because of this, individuals who view your profile can make exaggerated explanations about your personal qualities. They may, for example, stereotype you based on some aspect of your persona. If you disclose online that you enjoy country music, a reader may assume that you are a conservative person too. Thus, individuals should use caution in online forums and work to manage the impressions they can elicit in others.

## Self-Presentation and Decision Making

Perhaps one of the most interesting aspects of social media is the fact that you are in control of the information that you share with others. You decide what material you disclose to others and what information you choose to keep private. Individuals often make careful decisions about what they post for others to see or read. These decisions are called *self-presentation* strategies. As mentioned in Chapter 2, Goffman (1959) describes self-presentation as impression management. Self-presentation strategies are the choices about content (e.g., photos, quotes, or other demographic information) that we make when sharing with others. These choices guide the creation of the online personal profile. Individuals make a conscious effort to control how their audience perceives them. This effort becomes especially heightened in online mediums. In an online format, images are often carefully selected and perhaps even edited to convey physically attractive qualities. Quotes and phrases are chosen to reflect a person's attitudes, and friendships are created and maintained by sharing information about interests and hobbies.

> **Self-presentation**
> Choices about content (photos, quotes, information, etc.) that individuals make when crafting an online profile.

Unfortunately, the anonymity of our online presence results in some instances of deception and dishonesty. The MTV television show *Catfish* follows individuals that have built relationships online. People meet and interact online without physically meeting one another, then television crews share their stories as they meet for the first time. The most notable aspect of the show is that oftentimes the individuals have been talking to a fake persona. Consider, for example, former University of Notre Dame linebacker Manti Te'o. Te'o, who was drafted to play in the National Football League in 2013, was duped into believing a woman he was communicating with and dating online was a real person. The person he thought he was communicating with, however, didn't exist. In fact, an acquaintance of Te'o's admitted to creating the fake profile. When using mediated forms of interaction and building online relationships, it is possible to experience deception, that the creator of the profile may have strategically altered information or photos.

© Michael Tureski/Icon SMI 147/Michael Tureski/Icon SMI/Newscom

While the source or creator of a profile can control the content posted on social media sites, when it is viewed by others, the responses they may acquire cannot be controlled. While you may be able to post a specific photo, you are not able to control how people will perceive that post and respond to it. In fact, individuals can perceive, react, and respond to the same post in a variety of ways. Determining how to respond to others' social media presence is an important component in the decision-making process. Remember that using social media is not just about creating responsible profiles, but it is also deciding how to respond to others' profiles. Shea (1995) crafted rules of etiquette for the Internet to provide guidelines for appropriate online interactions. Her book *Netiquette* summarizes some best practices for Internet use:

*Rule 1:* Remember that there is a human component. There is a real person on the other side of the social network site. Use caution and treat others as you would prefer to be treated.

*Rule 2:* Adhere to the same standards of behavior online that you follow in real life. Most people tend to follow laws and rules. Use an ethical compass to guide your behaviors.

*Rule 3:* Know where you are in cyberspace. Much like the public speaking process, which calls for audience analysis, you too should analyze a website before you begin posting. Standards of conduct vary from website to website.

*Rule 4:* Respect other people's time. Your message is important, but so too is the reader's time. Make sure to create efficient and effective communication.

*Rule 5:* Make yourself look good online. The content and quality of your message will be judged. Take care in the tone, spelling, and grammar of your message.

*Rule 6:* Share your expertise. If you know the answer to another's question, offer your insights.

*Rule 7:* Help keep flame wars under control. Flaming occurs online when individuals attack one another or offer insults. When individuals "flame," they are freely sharing emotions and not "pulling any punches." While flame wars can be entertaining initially, they can lose value quickly.

*Rule 8:* Respect others' privacy. It seems likely that you would not invade someone else's space by examining the contents of a man's wallet or a woman's purse. The same should be true of someone's email.

*Rule 9:* Do not abuse your power. If you have access to another's private information, respect the person and do not read materials.

*Rule 10:* Forgive others' mistakes. All users start somewhere. A lack of experience on websites or blogs could contribute to errors. Give others a break.

Because mediated communication appears to be only increasing in popularity, individuals need to use caution when determining how to convey themselves in online settings. Remember, because you cannot control the reader's perceptions, you should take care to create a thoughtful profile. Esterline (2009) offers guidelines to create positive personal, professional, and public social media identities. These tips can be used when creating your online identity, specifically when creating a profile online and subsequently updating the profile information.

*Tip 1: Status updates.* Do not update your status with information an employer may not want to know.

*Tip 2: Photos.* Post photos with caution. Avoid posting photos that compromise your image.

*Tip 3: Groups and applications.* Avoid joining groups, fan pages, and applications that are not relevant to your field.

As you can see from the above list, a number of considerations should be taken when creating an online profile. Online personas should reflect carefully thought-out and planned communication. In many instances the positive connections you form online can "spill over" or be continued in face-to-face relationships. For example, you may post a status or an article that other people enjoy reading and can discuss in face-to-face interactions.

# THE IMPACT OF SOCIAL MEDIA ON FACE-TO-FACE RELATIONSHIPS

Given the nature and prevalence of social media, it makes sense that it would impact your face-to-face relationships. You can probably recall a time when social media helped you learn information about someone that caused you to feel emotionally close to the person. Perhaps you discovered new information that you had not known previously. Just as social media may be useful in forming relationships, it may also be helpful in maintaining existing relationships and promoting feelings of closeness and relational satisfaction. However, some also indicate that social media can be used as a replacement for face-to-face interactions and contribute negatively to relationships.

Lickerman (2010) argues that the overuse of social media may serve to isolate a person. Data suggests that we spend approximately 16 minutes out of every hour engaged in online social media sites (Finn, 2013). This isolation takes time away from face-to-face interactions and may diminish the quality of a relationship. The author argues for using a balance of mediated and face-to-face communication. Thus, not all interactions should occur on social media channels. Face-to-face communication does allow for important elements of nonverbal communication, such as the use of touch, that social media does not allow. Consider, for example, asking your relationship partner to marry you. You may determine that face-to-

What elements of nonverbal communication do you get from face-to-face interaction that social media does not allow?

© Rob Marmion/Shutterstock.com

face communication is better for this communicative exchange because it allows you to hear your partner's response.

Kearsley (1998) recommends the following rules for communicating via mediated channels. These recommendations will likely be useful when communicating professionally, personally, and publicly. These tips are useful when sending email communications, building websites, or using chat functions, all of which are part of the relationship-building function of social media sites. First, being brief is likely best. All messages, files, and photos should have focus. For example, do you have a friend that updates his or her Facebook status multiple times a day? What impression does that create in your mind? Over-posting could be perceived negatively. It could make someone think that you do not have anything better to do with your time or that you are scattered and cannot decide on one status you like. Also, remember these are public domains. Think carefully about what you write. If, for example, in an email you indicated to a coworker that you do not like a policy that your boss is enforcing and your coworker forwards the message to your boss, this communicative act cannot be undone. Always assume that anything you post could be made public. Additionally, remember to be kind. There is no need to make social network sites a negative place where people attack one another. Presenting different opinions and discussing issues is very different from attacking someone's character and competence. Finally, you should provide structure in your messages. When you send an email, for example, take a moment to create a subject line or description that your receiver will not only understand but that will help orient him or her to the purpose/context of the information.

Hopefully, throughout this chapter, you have been thinking about your own social media use. Social media can be a helpful tool in building relationships and it provides us with a unique method of communication with its own strengths and weaknesses. Much like mass media, we get to make decisions regarding our social media use. Because we are in control of the content, it is important to select content that is representative of us as individuals and creates a positive impression on our receivers.

## CHAPTER SUMMARY

Mass media and social media provide us with opportunities for including information-gathering, entertainment, and relationship creation and maintenance. There are many strategies for successfully using mass and social media in your personal, professional, and public lives such as using caution with photos and posts. Ultimately, you need to make careful decisions about the types of media you consume. Each mass media outlet comes with its own biases and viewpoints. It is important to consider these when determining how to use the messages you receive. Social media, in all its forms, can contribute to relationships. It allows us to initiate contact to build relationships, maintain the status of those relationships, and diminish relationships and quality. Ultimately, we need to remember to be cautious in our online personas, as communication in this format can leave a lasting record. Remember, once something is posted, it cannot be undone.

## KEY WORDS

*Blog* Online journal.

*Collaborative projects* Focus on co-creating information with other individuals.

*Decisional utility* Extent media is used to gain information and make an informed decision.

*Entertainment* Extent to which you find media to be a source of pleasurable distraction.

*Impression formation* Sense-making of others' actions and disposition.

*Information-seeking* Extent to which you attempt to gather information about happenings in the world.

*Interpersonal utility* Extent to which media is perceived to be a source of useful information that can be used in your relationship.

*Lean communication* Communication channels that reduce access to nonverbal communication, such as facial expressions, touch, and eye contact.

*Mass media* Utilizing technology to send messages to masses of people with the intent to influence behaviors.

*Mediated communication* Utilizing technology as the channel of delivery.

*Parasocial interaction* Your perceptions of connections to individuals in the media.

*Self-presentation* Choices about content (photos, quotes, information, etc.) that individuals make when crafting an online profile.

*Social media* Websites that allow for individuals to create a profile to build communities.

*Social networking* Sites that aim to build both personal and professional connections with other individuals.

*Uses and Gratifications Theory* Theoretical lens through which relationships individuals have with media is understood.

*Virtual game worlds* Online games that include a created reality and encourage the following of rules to play a game.

*Virtual social worlds* Provide a space for individuals to create another life and interact with others and include games such as Second Life.

# REFERENCES

boyd, d. m. (2006, December). Friends, Friendsters, and MySpace top 8: Writing community into being on social network sites. *First Monday*. Retrieved from http://131.193.153.231/www/issues/issue11_12/boyd/index.html.

boyd, d. m. (2008). *Taken out of context: American teen sociality in networked publics*. Retrieved from www.danah.org/papers/TakenOutOfContext.pdf.

boyd, d. m., & Ellison, N. B. (2008). Social network sites: Definition, history, and scholarship. *Journal of Computer-Mediated Communication, 13*, 210–230.

Center for Media Literacy. (n.d.). *CML's five key questions and core concepts of media literacy for deconstruction*. Retrieved from www.medialit.org.

Esterline, R. M. (2009). *8 tips to building and maintaining a professional online image*. Retrieved from http://bizzywomen.com/2009/8-tips-to-building-and-maintaining-a-professional-online-image/.

Finn, G. (2013, April). *Study: 27% of time online in the U.S. is spent on social networking*. Retrieved from http://marketingland.com/study-27-of-time-online-in-the-us-is-spent-on-social-networking-40269.

Goffman, E. (1959). *The presentation of self in everyday life*. New York: Doubleday.

Hamilton, N. T. (1998). Uses and gratifications. *Theories of Persuasive Communication and Consumer Decision Making*. Retrieved from http://www.ciadvertising.org/studies/student/98_fall/theory/hamilton/leckenby/theory/elements.htm.

Hancock, J., & Dunham, P. (2001). Impression formation in computer-mediated communication revisited: An analysis of the breadth and intensity of impressions. *Communication Research, 28*, 325–347.

Kaplan, A. M., & Haenlein, M. (2010). Users of the world unite!: The challenges and opportunities of social media. *Business Horizons, 53*, 59–58.

Katz, E., Blumler, J., & Gurevitch, M. (1974). Utilization of mass communication by the individual. In J. Blumler & E. Katz (Eds.), *The uses of mass communication: Current perspectives on gratifications research* (pp. 19–34). Beverly Hills, CA: Sage.

Kearsley, G. (1998). *A guide to online education*. Retrieved from http://home.sprynet.com/~gkearsley/online.htm#rules.

Lickerman, A. (2010). The effect of technology on relationships. *Psychology Today*. Retrieved from www.psychologytoday.com/blog/happiness-in-world/201006/the-effect-technology-relationships.

Palmgreen, P., Weener, L. A., & Rayburn, J. D. II. (1980). Relations between gratifications sought and obtained: A study of television news. *Communication Research, 7*, 161–192.

Quan-Haase, A., & Young, A. (2010). Uses and gratifications of social media: A comparison of Facebook and instant messaging. *Bulletin of Science, Technology and Society, 30*, 350–361.

Shea, V. (1995). *Netiquette*. San Francisco: Albion.

Temkin Group. (April, 2013). *American's daily media consumption, 2012 vs. 2013*. Retrieved from http://trends.e-strategyblog.com/2013/04/04/americans-daily-media-consumption/10074.

Unze, D. (2010, March). Facebook helps spark movements. *USA Today*. Retrieved from www.usatoday.com/news/nation/2010-03-25-facebook_N.htm.

Worsnop, C. M. (1989). *Media literacy through critical thinking: Teacher materials*. Retrieved from http://depts.washington.edu/nwmedia/sections/nw_center/curriculum_docs/teach_combine.pdf.

# CHAPTER 10

## Public Speaking in Our Lives: Beginning the Process

## Chapter Objectives

After reading this chapter, you should be able to:
- Identify some of the challenges public speakers face
- Characterize the various types public speeches typically given
- Explain the purposes of each type of speech
- Provide an overview of the public speaking process

**PERSONAL:** You've been best friends since middle school. Throughout high school, you played on the same teams, had the same group of friends, and were in many of the same classes together. Although you went to different colleges, you stayed in contact with each other. Upon graduation, you settled in different cities and chose different career paths but still remained close friends. Now, your friend is getting married and has asked you to be in the wedding party. You are thrilled and honored, but you also realize you will be giving a toast at the reception. Although you are nervous, you want to give a toast that honors your friend. Where do you begin?

**PROFESSIONAL:** For the past 3 months, you've been working on a huge project at your company. Your supervisor asks you to present your findings to the board of directors at next month's meeting. You have a great deal of material to cover, but with a full agenda for the meeting you will have only 15 minutes to convey 3 months of work. Although you are accustomed to speaking to members of your own department, this speaking situation is a complete departure for you. How will you organize so much information into a 15-minute presentation?

**PUBLIC:** The local school district has submitted their budget for the next fiscal year and it is well over the original estimate your city council felt was appropriate. As chair of your city's parent–teacher organization, you strongly believe in the need for the additional funds requested by the school system. The city council has invited citizens to attend a special meeting to express their opinions on the issue. Although you have never been called upon to address the council before, you want to represent the needs of the students and faculty in the system as best you can. Where do you start?

# CHAPTER OVERVIEW

Whether it is making a toast at your best friend's wedding, sharing the results of your work on a project, or speaking to support an issue in your community, you may be called upon to speak publicly for personal, professional, or public reasons. There are many potential scenarios in which people find themselves speaking in public. Perhaps you are an officer of a club or organization and you need to facilitate a meeting. You may be working on a project that will benefit your community and need to speak to another group to elicit their help on the project. Maybe you are presenting the results of a project to your class or representing your company and making a presentation to a potential client. Whether you are speaking to a small group of people or a large audience, there are certain elements that enable public speakers to be more effective when delivering presentations. These elements center on the preparation for and delivery of one's message. This chapter focuses on the challenges public speakers face and the common types and purposes of public speeches. In addition, we provide an overview of the public speaking process.

# THE CHALLENGES OF PUBLIC SPEAKING

As you learned in Chapter 1, it is considered public speaking when one person communicates to an audience. During a public speech, typically one person speaks and the audience listens. In most public speaking situations, while the speaker is presenting, the audience responds primarily through nonverbal cues. Once the presentation is over, a question-and-answer period often allows for verbal interaction between the speaker and the audience. This process may present some challenges for many public speakers. For example, speakers may feel anxious and try to avoid public speaking altogether. Other challenges include establishing and maintaining credibility as well as being an ethical speaker. These are the challenges that we discuss in the following pages.

## *Anxiety*

Public speakers face many challenges highlighted in Figure 10.1. One prominent challenge that speakers encounter is the anxiety they may experience. Dwyer and Davidson (2012) found speaking in public was "selected more often as a common fear than any other fear, including death" (p. 99). Communication researchers have studied communication apprehension for more than 40 years as a real phenomenon that affects some speakers (McCroskey, 1977, 2004, 2005; McCroskey, Andersen, Richmond, & Wheeless, 1981; McCroskey & Beatty, 1999, 2000). Chapter 1 defined *communication apprehension* as the fear, nervousness, or anxiety we experience when faced with real or imagined interactions. Typically, we consider there to be four forms of communication apprehension. They are trait-like communication apprehension, audience-based communication apprehension, situational communication apprehension, and context-based communication apprehension. If you have *trait-like communication apprehension*, you will experience anxiety in most speaking situations. Thus, whether you are speaking one on one, to a small group, or to a large audience, you will experience communication apprehension. *Audience-based communication apprehension* occurs when you are anxious when speaking to a particular audience or receiver. Thus, you may not experience apprehension when speaking with a group of peers in a class or with your colleagues at work, but you may become apprehensive when speaking to the board of directors of your company or in front of a group of strangers.

➤ **Communication apprehension**
The fear, nervousness, or anxiety we experience when faced with real or imagined interactions.

➤ **Trait-like communication apprehension**
Fear of public speaking (e.g., one-on-one, to a small group, or to a large audience).

➤ **Audience-based communication apprehension**
Fear of public speaking with a specific audience (e.g., you may not be apprehensive when you are speaking with your peers in a course but apprehensive when you are speaking to the board of directors of your company).

Most public speakers feel some level of nervousness.

© Africa Studio/Shutterstock.com

If you are normally confident meeting with your supervisor but nervous to meet with your supervisor to ask for a raise, or if you are comfortable speaking with a particular teacher but are nervous about asking this teacher for an extension on an assignment, you may be experiencing *situational communication apprehension*. This type of apprehension is based on a specific occurrence. Finally, if you are anxious about public speaking but do not have any problems communicating in small groups or in other settings, you are experiencing *context-based communication apprehension*.

Certainly, some level of communication apprehension, anxiety, or stage fright is normal for most public speakers. Some physical symptoms of communication apprehension include trembling hands, a dry "cotton" mouth, butterflies in the stomach, or a racing heart. Although you may perceive that these symptoms are obvious to the audience, typically they are not, and there are ways to mask them. For example, you may want to sip on water to alleviate the feeling of a dry mouth, place your hands down by your sides if you feel they are shaking, or take some deep breaths to relax and help you slow down a racing heart. In addition to the physical symptoms associated with communication anxiety, speakers also experience emotional or psychological symptoms. Being unable to sleep the night before a speech or having your thoughts preoccupied by the speech days before you're scheduled to present are examples of psychological manifestations of anxiety.

➤ **Situational communication apprehension**
Fear of public speaking based on a specific occurrence (e.g., you are nervous about meeting with your supervisor to ask for a raise or your town's planning board to ask for a variance).

➤ **Context-based communication apprehension**
Fear of speaking only in one setting (e.g., fear of speaking in public but not in other settings such as in small groups).

The good news is that for most individuals, anxiety can often be reduced through careful preparation and extensive practice. Usually, the more time you spend researching your topic, developing your speech, and practicing your delivery, the more comfortable you will be with the material. As a result, you will enhance your ability to convey your topic in an interesting and understandable manner. In addition to practice and preparation, many speakers create their own techniques to reduce anxiety. For example, some speakers use breathing exercises to calm their nerves. Breathing in slowly while counting to three and then exhaling slowly for three counts is a technique some speakers use to relax before approaching the podium. Other speakers may use positive visualization before getting up to speak in front of an audience. In this case, they visualize the audience engaged in the topic and giving positive feedback. Still other speakers use positive self-talk to reduce anxiety. These speakers internalize thoughts such as "I can do this," "I am well prepared," or "I have a lot of material that the audience will find interesting and relevant."

While speech anxiety is often considered a barrier that must be overcome, there are some benefits to this type of nervousness. Apprehension has been compared to an athlete "getting psyched" to play a game. By channeling the butterflies associated with public speaking, our anxiety may actually make us more effective speakers. When channeled appropriately, nervousness can actually lead to a more energized delivery. While we may feel we are the only ones with this type of anxiety, it is a common occurrence. Many public figures including actors have speech anxiety. For example, in 2006, when Reese Witherspoon won the Oscar for Best Actress in the movie *Walk the Line*, she said she actually hoped they would *not* call her name because "…the idea of having to give a speech in front of everyone in the world" terrified her. Likewise, Harrison Ford called public speaking "a mixed bag of terror and anxiety" (Bailey, 2008). Overall, despite the fact that many public speakers face some form of communication anxiety, usually, the more public speaking one does and the more one prepares and practices, the more comfortable one becomes.

## *Credibility*

**Credibility**
Extent to which a speaker is trustworthy, knowledgeable, and well prepared.

The ability to achieve credibility is another challenge public speakers encounter. *Credibility* is the degree to which an audience believes and trusts a speaker. As speakers, we want our audience to perceive us as credible sources on our given topics. The more credible an audience perceives a speaker to be, the more likely it is that audiences will listen to and believe the speaker. Do you listen more carefully to some public speakers than others? Do you believe certain people more than others? If you answered yes to these questions, you are like most people. The truth is, we do listen to people differently and this is partially influenced by their credibility. For example, you would listen and trust the advice of a doctor versus a friend regarding how to treat a medical concern. The doctor's medical training and experience increases the doctor's credibility.

How do we achieve credibility? First, speakers can build their credibility by putting in the effort and time to carefully and competently prepare for a speaking occasion. Thus, *competence* is a key factor in credibility. If you are a competent public speaker, you are knowledgeable about your topic. You may have gained this knowledge through your education or through your professional or personal experiences. For example, a person may be perceived as a competent public speaker on the subject of French culture. This may be true because he has undergraduate and graduate degrees in French. He may also be viewed as a competent public speaker on the subject because he has taught French for several years or because he has lived and studied in France.

Another way speakers gain or lose credibility is through their perceived character. *Character* is an audience's perception of a speaker as trustworthy, sincere, and likable (Booth-Butterfield & Gutowski, 1993). Thus, if an audience likes a speaker and believes she is genuine and has the audience's best interests at heart, they are more likely to perceive the speaker as credible.

Something else to consider is that credibility can vary by speaker or by audience. You may be perceived as credible when speaking about one specific topic, but not on others. For example, your communication professor is credible when speaking about communication, but would your teacher have as much credibility if he or she spoke on electrical engineering? Likewise, credibility may vary because of the audience. One audience may view a speaker as very credible while another audience may believe the same speaker lacks credibility. For example, if you present a speech on the threat of global warming to an audience who also believes in global warming, they will be more likely to perceive you as credible. However, if the audience does not believe in global warming, they may discount whatever you say about the subject as well as your credibility. In addition, in one audience, you may be perceived as competent because you know more about the topic than your audience. With a different audience, one that perhaps has the same knowledge level as you, your competence may be perceived differently. For example, if someone is taking a introductory course in astronomy, your instructor is an expert in the subject. When your instructor goes to a convention with other professors of astronomy and scientists, the level of competence may be perceived differently.

When an audience perceives that you know your topic, your credibility increases.

© Africa Studio/Shutterstock.com

For most speakers, credibility is gained over time. In your public speaking course, everyone will start with a "credibility quotient" that will either go up or down after each speech. One way to achieve credibility in a public speaking situation is through careful preparation and practice. When an audience perceives that you have devoted time researching, organizing, and practicing a speech, your quotient will go up. On the other hand, if an audience feels that you have not spent adequate time carefully preparing and practicing your speech or presentation, your quotient will decrease.

Overall, achieving credibility is a challenge for public speakers but is attainable through knowledge of the subject, careful preparation, practice, and the sincerity of the speaker.

## Ethics

**Ethical public speaking**
Speaking that demonstrates respect for one's audience, honesty, use of reliable and valid sources, and responsibility for everything that is said and/or done during a speech.

A final challenge that public speakers must address relates to ethics. *Ethical public speaking* involves the demonstration of respect for one's audience; honesty; use of reliable and valid sources; and accountability for the information shared during a speech. Public speakers have a number of ethical responsibilities.

First, speakers must always give credit where credit is due. It is important to cite all sources consulted for a speech. Examples of unethical practices include purchasing speeches from Internet sites or copying sections of a speech and using it without citing the original source. When using direct quotes from other sources, be sure to give credit where it's due and cite the original source. Not only is this an ethical practice, but it also demonstrates to your audience that you have thoroughly researched your topic.

Speakers also have an ethical responsibility to use appropriate and non-offensive language. Profanity or language that would insult anyone based on that person's race, ethnicity, age, gender, religion, or sexual orientation should not be used.

Third, although we are afforded freedom of speech by the First Amendment of the U.S. Constitution, speakers should not abuse this protection. It would be unethical, for example, for public speakers to give information they know is false, to slander another person, or to say something that would damage the audience's civil rights. While there are speakers who distort the truth or make offensive comments yet remain legally protected by the First Amendment, this does not necessarily mean they are ethical speakers.

Fourth, speakers should never do anything during the speech that would intentionally insult or embarrass the audience. For example, pictures or YouTube clips that would not be appropriate for public consumption should not be used in a public speech. Respect should be shown for audiences. This is ensured by maintaining honesty, avoiding plagiarism, using reliable and valid sources, and demonstrating responsibility for all that a speaker says and/or does during a speech.

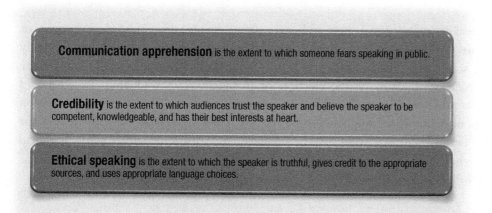

**Communication apprehension** is the extent to which someone fears speaking in public.

**Credibility** is the extent to which audiences trust the speaker and believe the speaker to be competent, knowledgeable, and has their best interests at heart.

**Ethical speaking** is the extent to which the speaker is truthful, gives credit to the appropriate sources, and uses appropriate language choices.

FIGURE 10.1

The challenges of public speaking.

Overall, public speakers face many challenges. Some people may be reticent to speak in public while others may be unwilling to speak in certain situations. Issues of credibility and ethics also provide challenges for some public speakers. Understanding yourself as a public speaker and the challenges you face speaking in public is the first step to becoming a competent speaker. As you go through the rest of this chapter, it is important to keep these potential challenges in mind in order to address them as you prepare the speeches you will deliver in your personal, professional, and public lives.

# THREE TYPES OF PUBLIC SPEECHES

Speaking to inform, speaking to persuade, and speaking for special occasions are three common types of public speaking and are the focus of this section of the chapter. As each speech type is discussed, we examine when you would most likely use each type and some examples are provided as well.

## *Informative Speeches*

**Informative speaking**
Type of speech used to help an audience become aware of or better understand a topic.

*Informative speaking* involves the presentation of ideas and support to enhance an audience's knowledge and understanding of the topic. The primary goal is to share new information with the audience, not to change their attitudes or behaviors on the topic. Informative speeches provide the audience with insight that is unbiased and objective. Speakers increase an audience's knowledge and/or understanding of a topic by providing facts, examples, quotes by those informed about the topic, and other types of supporting material. If the audience possesses prior knowledge about the topic, then speakers may need to provide additional facts or data or provide a fresh perspective on the topic.

Speakers may inform their audiences about events, processes, ideas, people, or objects (Figure 10.2). An event may be something that has happened recently or something that occurred in history. For example, a speaker may focus on the *Challenger* disaster or the election of President Barack Obama. Events could also relate to someone's cultural background. Someone might share information about cultural wedding rituals or rites of passage such as a quinceañera or a bar or bat mitzvah. An event may be related to a professional sports team or a local celebration. For example, a speaker might inform the audience of the history of the World Series or Bunker Hill Day celebrated in Boston.

A speaker may also inform an audience about a process. Demonstration speeches are a type of informative speech where a process is explained to help an audience understand steps or procedures. Examples of demonstration speeches that explain a process may include how to bake a cake, prepare a résumé, or edit a film.

Ideas, concepts, or theories may also be topics for informative speeches. Topics in this category are generally more abstract in nature, so the challenge is to present something that is abstract in a way that the audience is able to understand. Examples may include speeches about global warming, media literacy, or stem cell transplants.

People are another common subject for informative speeches. Perhaps you have a favorite singer, author, or actor whose life you could explore. There may be an artist whose work you have always admired or someone in history who has made a difference in the world. People from sports figures to political figures to religious and cultural figures can all serve as topics for informative speeches.

Finally, informative speeches can focus on objects. These are things that have a physical existence. Hybrid cars or the latest iPhone are examples of objects that could be topics for informative speeches. In addition, places are also considered in this category. For example, famous examples of architecture such as the Eiffel Tower in France or the Prado Museum in Spain are examples of objects that could become informative speech topics.

While the topics mentioned above primarily relate to speaking within an academic setting, informative speeches are also relevant in professional contexts. In your work

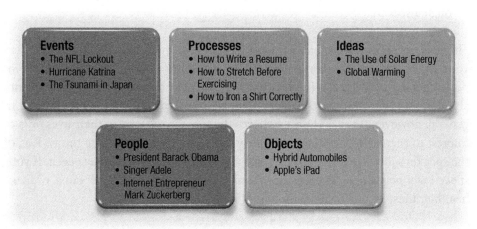

**FIGURE 10.2**

Topics for informative speeches.

In your work setting, you may be asked to present new information to colleagues.

© Monkey Business Images/Shutterstock.com

setting, you may be asked to explain a new computerized process your organization will use to track expenses, explain a new product to potential clients, or present orientation information to new employees.

Likewise, if you are part of a community group or work within your local or state government, you may be asked to speak on a variety of topics. For example, if your town is celebrating a milestone event, implementing a recycling program, or honoring a citizen, you might be asked to share information or offer an explanation through a speech.

The goals of informative speaking are to gain and maintain audience interest in your topic, help the audience understand the information, and assist them in remembering your speech (Figure 10.3). In the next chapter, you will learn more about the specific strategies speakers use to gain and maintain audience interest. In general, however, if the audience believes the topic is relevant to their lives or is of interest to them, they will be more likely to listen to what you have to say. Part of the speaker's job is to show an audience *why* they should listen to a speech. If your speech will help them do better in school, secure the job of their dreams, or live a healthier lifestyle, they will be more motivated to listen to you.

The second goal of informative speaking is to say things in such a way that your audience understands your ideas. In part, this is accomplished by using clear and descriptive language. Understanding who your audience is will help you select the language you need to use in your speech. If you are informing an audience that has little technical knowledge about how to increase the memory on their computer, it would be confusing to use terminology such as "gigabytes," "RAM," and "virtual memory." Instead, you would need to clearly define any technical words and relate these words to concepts the audience understands. Consider the fact that if a doctor tells you that you have otitis media, you might be much more upset than if the doctor says that you have an ear infection. Clarity of language makes all the difference in your audience's ability to achieve common understanding.

The third goal of informative speaking is to present your speech in such a way that your audience will remember what you said long after you have finished your speech. In addition to using clear and descriptive language, this is also accomplished by the support material you select and the manner in which you organize your speech. Various forms of support material are discussed in the next chapter. In general, if you present a variety of support materials, tailor the forms of support to the audience's knowledge and attitude toward the topic, and use support that is verbally and visually memorable, you will help your audience recall your message. In addition, presenting information in an organized fashion will help the audience recognize the main ideas of a speech. This, in turn, will help them remember the speech. Understanding the goals of informative speaking will also help you select the strategies you use to help you achieve those goals.

FIGURE 10.3

The three goals of informative speeches.

© Maxim Blinkov/Shutterstock.com

Visual aids can help to reinforce what you say in your presentation.

**Strategies**
Techniques speakers use to engage their audience and to keep the audience focused.

There are several *strategies* public speakers use to help them inform their audiences. Strategies are techniques speakers use to engage their audience and to keep the audience focused. Since audiences are more likely to listen to a speech if they believe your topic is relevant to them, one useful strategy is to show them how your topic will help them or is somehow meaningful to them. For example, you will be implementing a new billing system and you plan to explain it to the employees who will be using it. Your presentation will show them how it will work as well as the reasons why it will help them do their jobs more effectively. Because your presentation is relevant to them, they will be more likely to listen to you. Overall, as stated earlier, if you can show how your topic can help them do better at work or in school, get the job they want, or live a better life, they will be more likely to listen to you.

Another strategy informative public speakers use is to reinforce what they are saying verbally with visual support. The old adage, "A picture is worth a thousand words" is very true in public speaking. A chart, graph, diagram, picture, or any other visual means of support can help to summarize, clarify, and reinforce what you have said verbally. For example, you have summarized the growth in one of your divisions over the past 5 years and have created a chart so your audience may see this visually as you discuss it. Helping an audience "see" what you are "saying" will help increase their understanding of your material. The forms of visual support are discussed more specifically in the next chapter.

A third strategy public speakers use is to repeat their key points. Repetition helps maintain an audience's attention while helping them remember your main ideas. Thus, if a speaker says, "There are three types of …." and then explains each type and repeats the three types again, audiences are more likely to follow the speaker's points.

Another useful strategy is to provide a new or different perspective on a topic about which an audience is already knowledgeable. If an audience feels like they have "heard it all before," they are less likely to listen to the speaker. If, on the other hand, the speaker takes a different approach to a topic, the audience is more likely to engage in listening.

If an audience knows little or nothing about a topic, the focus of the informative speech might be to define the topic. For example, you might define the term *robotics* in a speech or what it means to play an "RPG" or "role-playing game." You might also define the "4 C's" of selecting a diamond (i.e., cut, clarity, carat, and color). If you are informing your audience about a process, you could use an explanation. For example, you might explain how furniture is refinished or artwork is restored. You might explain how certain events in history led up to a particular war or event.

You may also inform an audience by demonstrating your topic. By demonstrating how to salsa dance, shoot the perfect foul shot, stretch before working out, or do a favorite craft, you can inform your audience in a very visual and practical manner. Using definitions, explanations, or demonstrations in your informative speeches will help to increase an audience's understanding and knowledge of a topic.

To summarize, there are many types of informative speeches that you will encounter in your life. In general, the goals of informative speaking and the strategies you use are similar whether you are speaking in your personal, professional, or public life. If your main purpose is to help an audience become more aware of a subject or have a better understanding of it, it is considered an informative speech. If, on the other hand, you are taking a stand on an issue, trying to get an audience to believe the same way you do, or asking an audience to take action regarding something, you will be speaking to persuade.

## Persuasive Speeches

**Persuasive speaking** is focused on three primary goals: changing an audience's existing belief, reinforcing a belief or attitude, or motivating an audience to take action or behave in a desired way (Figure 10.4). Examples of persuasive speech topics designed to change existing beliefs or attitudes may include current or controversial issues such as advocating legislation prohibiting texting while driving or the legalization of euthanasia. At times, the speaker and the audience may hold similar beliefs or attitudes. In that case, the goal of the persuasive speech may be to reinforce attitudes rather than change them. For example, while an audience may believe that exercising one's right to vote is important, many individuals may not vote on a regular basis. A persuasive speech about the importance of voting may reinforce their existing belief.

If the goal of the persuasive speech is to motivate the audience to action, a speaker will need to present data and arguments to influence and inspire others. For example, you might want to persuade the audience to sign up to become organ donors, volunteer for Habitat for Humanity, or exercise on a regular basis.

**Persuasive speaking**
Type of speech used to change an audience's existing belief, to reinforce their existing belief, or to get an audience to take action regarding the topic.

FIGURE 10.4

The goals of persuasive speeches.

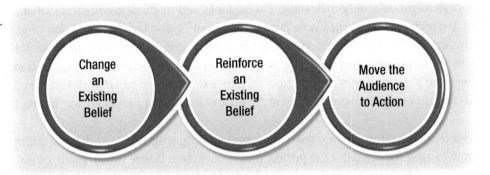

Persuasive speaking opportunities are commonplace. You may persuade others to join a community group to which you belong, donate time to help rebuild a playground, or persuade a local school committee to accept a proposal. In a corporate setting, you may use persuasion to gain new clients, secure the endorsement of a board of directors to expand a company, or sell your company's goods or services. Likewise, you are a constant consumer of persuasion in your personal, professional, and public lives. Politicians try to gain your support, salespeople attempt to have you purchase their product, heads of companies try to secure support for a company merger and persuasion is the means by which they attempt to accomplish their goal.

> **Aristotle**
> Ancient Greek philosopher and scientist.

> **Ethos**
> In communication, a speaker or writer's appeal to the ethics of the listener or reader by way of communicating character in argument.

While persuasion is everywhere in our personal, professional, and public lives, the roots of persuasion date back thousands of years and much of what we know about persuasion can be credited to *Aristotle*. Aristotle believed in using "all of the available means" to persuade an audience. These include ethos, pathos, and logos (Table 10.1). *Ethos*, as you may surmise just by looking at the word, focuses on the ethics of the speaker. If an audience is to believe what the speaker is saying and be persuaded by the speaker, they must trust the source. How does a speaker gain the audience's trust and become viewed as a credible source? As mentioned earlier in the chapter, some of this credibility is based on the source's background, experiences, and/or education, while some is based on the audience's perception that the speaker has its best interests at heart. Ethos is also influenced by a source who has thoroughly researched a topic, is organized, and who has rehearsed and is prepared to speak.

*Pathos* is the use of emotion to persuade. Generally speaking, we are more likely to listen to and be persuaded by speakers who are passionate about a topic. The difference between a speaker who seems not to care about the topic and one who speaks with passion about a topic will certainly influence an audience to be persuaded or not be persuaded by the speaker. Martin Luther King, Jr. spoke with passion when he delivered his famous "I Have a Dream" speech. Jim Valvano, the former head basketball coach at North Carolina State University, also spoke passionately in 1993 when he was presented with the Arthur Ashe Courage Award. His acceptance speech, titled "Don't Ever Give Up," was given roughly 8 weeks before he died of cancer. These individuals, like many others, showed the strength of their emotions and convictions about their beliefs. On the other hand, sadly, there are speakers who rely only on pathos to the exclusion of research and credibility and that can pose a danger for those listening to the speaker. As a consumer of persuasion, make certain that you listen for more than impassioned rhetoric and identify the logic and reasoning behind a speaker's arguments.

The third "means of persuasion" in Aristotle's system is *logos*, or the speaker's use of evidence and reasoning to persuade the audience. The most effective arguments are based on strong evidence and logical reasoning. Evidence includes facts, statistics, definitions, expert opinions, and examples. Reasoning draws conclusions based on the evidence. Speakers may use *inductive reasoning* and provide relevant facts and examples before drawing a conclusion based on these facts. With *deductive reasoning*, the speaker begins with a general statement called a major premise. This is followed by a specific statement called a minor premise that connects to the major premise. From this, a conclusion is drawn based on the major premise and the minor premise. In persuasive speaking, it is important to select examples that are most representative of the point you are trying to make, not the exceptions to the rule. Evidence needs to be valid and reliable and sufficient to support your ideas.

Not all speakers, however, use a logical approach when persuading others. Unfortunately, some speakers may use a tactic known as a fallacy. A *fallacy* is faulty or false reasoning and this should be avoided. There are several types of fallacies; however, only a few examples are provided here. For example, if a speaker uses only a few examples yet draws a general conclusion from those limited examples, the speaker may be relying on what is known as a *hasty generalization*. Thus, if a researcher interviews three college students and discovers none of them exercise on a regular basis, it would be incorrect to conclude that college students in general do not exercise. Another type of fallacy is what is known as the *bandwagon* or ad *populum* fallacy. With this type of faulty reasoning, one indicates that something is true because a number of people have said so—not necessarily because there is clear evidence of its truth. Advertisers have often used the claim that "everyone"

## Pathos
In communication, a speaker or writer's appeal to the emotions of the listener or reader by way of creating an emotional response to a situation or argument.

## Logos
In communication, a speaker or writer's appeal to the logic of the listener or reader by use or reason in argument.

## Inductive reasoning
Type of reasoning that provides strong and sufficient facts and examples and then draws a conclusion based on these facts.

## Deductive reasoning
Type of reasoning that begins with a general statement, is supported by specific support, and then draws a conclusion.

## Fallacy
Faulty or false reasoning.

## Hasty generalization
Type of faulty logic when the speaker uses only a few examples yet draws a general conclusion from those limited examples.

## Bandwagon fallacy
Type of faulty reasoning used when one indicates that something is true because a number of people have said it is true, not necessarily because there is clear evidence of its truth.

**Ad hominem**
Type of faulty reasoning used when a speaker attacks or criticizes a person, rather than the arguments provided or the issue itself.

will benefit from their product or tell children not to be the "only one not to have" a particular toy or game. A third type of fallacy is known as *ad hominem*, which means "to the man." If a speaker attacks or criticizes a person, rather than the arguments provided or the issue itself, the *ad hominem* fallacy is being used. In political debates, candidates often try to diminish the credibility of their opponents by using this type of faulty logic. Again, these are only a few examples of fallacies or the use of faulty logic.

TABLE 10.1

Aristotle's Means of Persuasion

| Appeal | Definition | Example |
|---|---|---|
| Ethos | The ethics of the speaker | Based on the speaker's expertise, competence, genuineness, trustworthiness, or charisma |
| Pathos | The use of emotion to persuade an audience | Based on the speaker's ability to evoke emotions such as fear, anger, pride, or happiness |
| Logos | The use of sound logic and reasoning to persuade an audience | Based on the speaker's use of examples, statistics, and other forms of reliable information as well as a well-thought-out way of organizing and presenting the evidence |

**Questions of fact**
Type of question or claim that may be proven true or false.

Persuasive speeches typically involve the use of claims: fact, value, and policy. *Questions of fact* are those claims that can be proven true or false. Suppose a speaker tries to prove whether the SAT is a true indicator of a student's ability to do well in college. Documented evidence and statistics examining the correlation between SAT scores and college graduation rates may provide facts to support this claim.

**Questions of value**
Type of question or claim that has to do with someone's ideas of right and wrong or good or bad.

When persuasion focuses on an individual's idea of what is considered right or wrong, *questions of value* are being asked. These may be based on a person's religious or philosophical beliefs. Speeches designed to persuade an audience about airline security procedures, abortion, or sex education are rooted in individual beliefs or values. Depending on the audience's existing beliefs, you will need to organize your speech accordingly.

**Questions of policy**
Type of question or claim that focuses on actions or changes that should or should not be made by governing bodies.

*Questions of policy* focus on formalized actions or changes that should or should not be implemented by institutions or organizations. A speech designed to persuade an audience that a single-gender institution should go co-ed involves a question of policy designed to persuade an audience to alter an existing policy on gender segregation.

Your approach to persuasion will depend on the attitude the audience has regarding your persuasive proposition. If the audience is already in favor of your proposition, or at least largely in favor of it, you will create your speech based on that knowledge. Needless to say, persuasion is easier to obtain in this scenario. Thus, if you believe in mandatory seatbelt laws and your audience does as well, you will design a speech that reinforces their and your already existing belief. You would not need to spend a great deal of time in your speech presenting the arguments in favor of mandatory seatbelt laws. Instead, you would construct your speech so the audience will take action regarding the law by voting for it or asking their legislator to vote for it.

On the other hand, if your audience is against your persuasive proposition, you will have a more challenging time persuading them to believe as you do. Although you may not persuade them in one speech, if you are able to at least get them to listen to your arguments for or against something, you will have accomplished a great deal. In this instance, you may want to provide information that will help them consider an alternative viewpoint.

There are also times when an audience has no opinion about the subject of your speech. This may happen when the audience is unaware of your persuasive topic or has little knowledge about it. They may also know about the topic but have not yet formed an opinion about it. There are also those who know about the topic and simply choose to remain neutral about it.

There are times when you will address an audience whose members have more than one perspective on your persuasive proposition. In this case, you will need to carefully word your speech so that you do not antagonize those who are against your topic, encourage those in favor to take action, and try to move those who have no opinion on the topic to your viewpoint. This is not an easy task, to say the least.

Overall, it is important to remember that audiences are more likely to listen to and be persuaded by speakers who they trust, by evidence and reasoning they view as relevant and strong, and by speakers who speak with passion and conviction. Relying on Aristotle's "available means of persuasion" will help a speaker change an existing belief, reinforce an existing belief, or move an audience to action.

## Special Occasion Speeches

The third and final type of speech covered in this chapter is known as *special occasion speeches*. These types of public speech occur frequently in our lives. Special occasion speeches are used to mark distinctive events in our lives. They are given to honor someone or some occasion and to reflect on the importance of that

> ➤ **Special occasion speeches**
> Speeches that cover a broad range of settings, circumstances, and occasions and usually acknowledge, celebrate, honor, or remember someone or something.

The wedding toast's purpose is to wish the couple a long and happy life together.

© Sergey Ryzhov/Shutterstock.com

person or occasion in our lives. There are many different types of special occasion speeches. We cover 11 of these in the following pages.

One of the most popular types of public speeches that may occur in our personal, professional, or public lives is the toast. The chapter started by mentioning one of the most common toasts—the wedding *toast*. Whether the toast is given by the best man, the maid of honor, the father of the bride, or any other person close to the couple, it usually focuses on the characteristics of the people who have just gotten married and why they are perfect for each other. Often, the speaker provides brief anecdotes or humorous stories about one or both of the couple. Finally, the person giving the toast wishes the couple a long and happy life together. You may have heard a toast at a wedding or even given one. If this is the case, hopefully it was brief. In more than one case, wedding toasts have gone on and on and, like most other types of special occasion speeches we discuss, they are meant to be "short, sweet, and to the point."

*Speeches of introduction* are presented to highlight the accomplishments or present the credentials of a speaker before he or she begins a presentation. This type of speech helps build a rapport between the speaker and the audience and motivates the audience to listen to the speaker. If your company has invited a consultant to discuss organizational motivation or a PTO group has asked a well-known

**► Toast**
Speech given to congratulate a person or people on an achievement or a special occasion.

**► Introduction speech**
Brief speech given to introduce and welcome a speaker and to build a rapport between the speaker and the audience as well as motivate the audience to listen to the speaker.

educator to discuss the prevention of bullying, a representative of the group should introduce the speaker to provide the audience with the speaker's credentials and a brief overview of the topic to be discussed. A speech of introduction can be used strategically to enhance the source's credibility. If you are asked to provide a speech of introduction, your remarks should be relatively brief to avoid taking time away from the person who is delivering the presentation.

The *welcome speech* is designed to formally recognize and greet an audience to an event. Unlike the context for the speech of introduction, the welcome speech involves only the speaker presenting the welcome and is not followed by another speaker. When a convention is held in a city, the mayor or another local representative may greet attendees in a speech of welcome.

Another example of a special occasion speech is the ***commencement speech***, in which a speaker is invited to represent graduates during a ceremony. Some commencement speakers are selected based on their academic achievements, while others are invited to address graduates with words of inspiration and encouragement. The essence of the commencement speech is to highlight accomplishments and provide a vision for the future.

***Anniversary speeches*** are another type of special occasion speaking. Speeches of this type are meant to remind an audience of a person, event, or holiday that is

**Welcome speech**
Speech to formally recognize and greet a person or a group who is visiting, for example, a school, a convention, a special event, or a city.

**Commencement speech**
Type of speech often given at a graduation to review what has been accomplished and provide a vision for the future.

**Anniversary speech**
Type of special occasion speech used to remind an audience of a person, event, or holiday that is being commemorated.

The commencement speech offers words of inspiration and encouragement.

© hxdbzxy/Shutterstock.com

**Dedication speech**
Type of special occasion speech given that speaks about the significance of an occasion (e.g., a building being named for a particular person).

**Tribute speech**
Special occasion speech designed to praise someone (e.g., living or in the case of a eulogy, someone who has passed away).

**Eulogy**
Speech of praise for someone who has passed away.

**Presenting an award**
Type of special occasion speech that outlines the purpose, history, and/or the significance of the award; the criteria used to determine the awardee; and the relevant achievements of the recipient and how these accomplishments satisfied the criteria employed to determine who would receive the award.

**Accepting an award**
Special occasion speech by the person receiving an award that recognizes the importance of the award and expresses his or her appreciation to those who are giving the award; acknowledges those who helped the recipient achieve this recognition and, if there were other nominees, acknowledges them as well.

being commemorated. Speeches that celebrate our country's independence, the life of Martin Luther King, Jr., or the anniversary of the establishment of a city or town are all examples of anniversary speeches.

*Dedication speeches* are another type of special occasion speech. This type of speech is given when a building or a playground, for example, is being named for an individual. Colleges frequently name buildings to honor donors, past presidents, or others who have made significant contributions to the college. When the dedication is made, someone speaks on the significance of the occasion and why the building is being named for this particular person or persons.

*Tribute speeches* are another frequent type of special occasion speech. This type of speech is designed to praise someone. You might be asked to speak about a teacher who is being honored or a co-worker who is leaving the company or retiring. With speeches of tribute, your goal is to emphasize the accomplishments and attributes of the individual and underscore the importance of these to the audience.

Another form of tribute speech is a *eulogy*. This is a speech of praise for someone who has passed away. It is not an easy speech for someone to write or to present. It is usually given by someone close to the person who has passed away. Although it addresses the characteristics of the deceased and is usually serious in nature, some humor may be interspersed within the eulogy to demonstrate the human side of the individual being eulogized. Caution should be taken as not all in the audience will react in similar ways to humorous attempts. Some individuals may find incorporating this type of material highly inappropriate while others in the audience will find the humor a much-needed relief. Ultimately, the intent of the eulogy is to provide comfort to the mourners and help them remember the traits of the deceased that they most cherished.

*Presenting an award* or, if you are lucky enough, *accepting an award* are two additional types of special occasion speeches. In a school setting, you could be an officer of a student group that gives an annual award or you could be the student receiving the award. In a professional organization or a civic group, you could also be the one asked to present an award to someone or, again, you might be the recipient. No matter what the setting, presenting and/or accepting awards are common occurrences in a person's personal, professional, or public life. If you are the one presenting an award, you would first outline the purpose, history, and/or the significance of the award and the criteria used to determine the awardee. Next, you would outline the relevant achievements of the recipient and how these accomplishments satisfied the criteria employed to determine who would receive the award.

We have all heard acceptance speeches at the Academy Awards, the Country Music Awards, or one of the many other televised award shows. While we know they often differ in length (despite the best efforts of the production staff), they generally follow the same format. First, the person receiving the award recognizes the importance of the award and then expresses his or her appreciation to those who are giving the award. The awardee should also acknowledge those who helped the recipient achieve this recognition. If there were other nominees, it is also considerate to acknowledge them as well.

Speeches as you leave or enter an office are also considered types of special occasion speeches. When someone enters office, it is typical to give an ***inaugural address***. Certainly, we see this type of speech when the president of the United States is sworn into office. The goals of this type of speech are to outline the key issues the newly elected officer hopes to address while in office, to look toward the future, and to thank his or her predecessor. Inaugural addresses may also be given by newly appointed presidents of colleges or universities, corporations, community organizations, and civic groups. Likewise, when someone leaves an office, it is usually a time to reflect on what has been accomplished, to thank those who helped accomplish what was done, to outline what still needs to be accomplished, and to congratulate the next individual taking office.

> **Inaugural address**
> Special occasion speech given when someone takes office or begins a new position that outlines the key issues to address while in that position, looks toward the future, and thanks his or her predecessor.

Informative, persuasive, and special occasion speeches are three types of speeches you will likely encounter throughout your personal, professional, and public lives. One point to remember is that these types of speeches are not mutually exclusive. For example, even though the intended objective of a speaker may be to persuade, he may also inform an audience by sharing new information. As we begin to prepare a speech, we go through several steps before actually delivering it. These steps include selecting a topic, defining your purpose, analyzing the audience, conducting research, organizing your speech, and practicing the speech. In addition, the process also includes delivering the speech and reflecting on the speech, including the audience's reaction to it. Each of these steps is discussed in the next section.

## AN OVERVIEW OF THE PUBLIC SPEAKING PROCESS

Understanding the process of developing a public speech (Figure 10.5) is important as you begin to prepare any type of presentation. By adhering to the steps of this process, you will enhance your success as a public speaker.

FIGURE 10.5

The public speaking process.

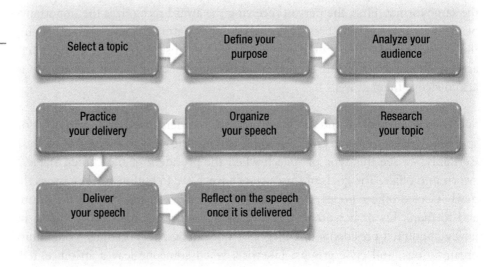

## Select Your Topic

The first step involves selecting a speech topic. In a classroom situation, you may be provided with parameters such as the purpose of the speech (e.g., to inform or to persuade) and perhaps some suggested topics. Beyond the classroom, you may be asked to speak about something in your area of expertise or a concern. For example, in your professional career you may speak on the current financial status of your department or provide an outline of the new marketing plan for an upcoming product launch. In your public life, you may be asked to deliver a committee report that has investigated potential sustainability solutions at a city council meeting.

Regardless of the speaking context, one of the most crucial steps in the public speaking process is to select a topic. If you are allowed to choose your own topic, the first step is to brainstorm possible topic ideas. You may do this simply by thinking of and jotting down ideas for intriguing topics about which you either have current knowledge or are curious to learn more. For example, consider events, processes, ideas, people, and objects when identifying a topic for an informative speech. If you're having difficulty brainstorming ideas, read a newspaper or browse the Internet to help identify potential topics. As you begin to formulate your topic, consider how to approach the topic and how you can make it interesting and relevant to your audience.

Three key considerations should be made with topic selection: the level of interest generated, the scope of the topic, and supporting sources of information. A topic should be of interest to both you and to your audience. If you are interested in the topic, you will devote the time and effort it takes to thoroughly research the topic, select the best support material, and practice delivering it. In addition, your interest will enhance your speech delivery. The topic should also be of interest to the audience. Knowing your audience will help you select a topic that will be interesting and relevant to them.

In addition, the topic must be focused enough to meet the time limitations for your presentation. In both academic and professional settings you will be expected to adhere to time guidelines for your speech to ensure that the class or meeting stays on schedule. A topic cannot be so broad that it cannot be clearly discussed within the allotted time frame. For example, while you may be passionate about the topic of sustainability, you will need to narrow your discussion of the topic to fit the time limit you have been given for your presentation. Generally speaking, it is much better for a public speaker to cover fewer main ideas with more depth than to try to cover too many broad ideas without adequately explaining each idea.

Finally, it is also important to select a topic that can be supported through research that extends beyond the speaker. Even when you are knowledgeable about the subject, it is vital to explore what others have to say about the topic. Citing this research during your speech will potentially enhance your credibility as a speaker, since audiences want to know that speakers are well prepared and can share information that goes beyond their own opinions.

## *Define Your Purpose*

Once you have selected a topic, the next step in the process is writing a clear and focused statement of your speech purpose. The ***general purpose*** indicates whether the speech goal is to inform, persuade, or present a speech for a special occasion. A ***specific purpose*** statement is generally one sentence that provides an overview of the speech objective or the key points of the speech. The goal of the specific purpose statement is to focus on what you want your audience to know or do by the end of your speech. For example, your specific purpose might be "to inform the audience about the types of stem cells that exist and two ways in which they are currently being used to treat diseases." Another specific purpose could be "to persuade the audience to donate blood at the upcoming blood drive at the college." Although brief, this type of statement will help guide the next steps in the speech-building process.

**General purpose**
Provides the broad goal for your speech (e.g., to inform, persuade, or entertain).

**Specific purpose**
Clear and concise statement indicating what you want your audience to know, do, or believe by the end of your speech.

A demographic analysis takes into account the audience's characteristics so you can refine your topic.

© Monkey Business Images/Shutterstock.com

**Audience analysis**
Gaining knowledge about the audience such as their demographic information, their attitudes, their level of knowledge of the topic, the speech environment, and the occasion for the speech in order to best prepare the speech.

**Demographic analysis**
Type of audience analysis that takes into account the characteristics of the audience including the audience's gender, age, race, ethnicity, and level of education.

**Attitudinal analysis**
Type of audience analysis that considers the audience's position on a particular topic (e.g., for, against, or no opinion).

## Analyze Your Audience

Once the topic is selected, and your purpose is clear, it is important to analyze the audience. There are many strategies to *audience analysis*, and the more information you have about your audience, the more effective you will be at creating a speech that they will understand and remember. One method used in the audience analysis process is called a *demographic analysis*. This type of analysis takes into account the characteristics of the audience. Look around your classroom and identify characteristics about your classmates. Demographic features include the audience's gender, age, race, ethnicity, and level of education. When you have a strong understanding of the demographics of the audience, you may find that you need to refine your choice of speech topic. For example, an audience consisting of 18- to 23-year-old college students would probably have a general understanding of what Facebook is and how it works. Instead, you might want to focus on how organizations are using this type of social media to understand marketing trends among college students. Knowing this type of information helps the speaker select appropriate support material for the speech and identify the best way to approach the topic.

Another type of analysis is an *attitudinal analysis*. Securing information about an audience's attitude toward the topic before you begin to research and write a speech is important. A speaker will need to approach a topic differently depending on whether the audience is in favor of the topic, against it, or has no opinion. For example, if a public forum is presented in a particular town and the audience is already in favor of recycling, the speaker will not need to spend time focusing on the benefits of recycling in general and can concentrate on how a recycling program can be instituted in that particular town. On the other hand, if the speaker does not know what the audience's attitude toward the subject is, the speaker should try to ascertain this information by circulating a brief survey prior to creating a speech or by speaking with the person who invited you to find out the audience's likely attitudes toward your topic.

Finally, the speaker must be aware of the occasion and the environment in which the speech will be presented. This is known as a *situational analysis*. Is the occasion formal or informal? Does it commemorate something specific or honor a person's accomplishments? Is it a solemn or light-hearted occasion? Understanding the environment will also help the speaker to construct a more effective speech. Environmental elements including the time of day at which the speech will be given, the room where it will be delivered, and the size of the audience are all important pieces of information. For example, how receptive do you think an audience would be to a formal and lengthy presentation in an organizational setting on a Friday at 4:00 P.M.? What things would you do to maintain the audience's interest? How should the room be set up for your presentation (e.g., theater or auditorium style, conference or boardroom style)?

> **Situational analysis**
> Type of audience analysis that takes into account the occasion of the speaking event as well as the time, place, and size of the audience.

Overall, gathering demographic, attitudinal, and situational information about an audience is an important step in the speech preparation process. The more information you have about an audience, the more likely you will be to construct an effective speech.

## Research the Topic

Once a speaker understands the audience, the next part of the speech development process involves researching the topic. A variety of resources are available through the library and the Internet that make finding the best support material for a topic and a given audience relatively simple. Databases, websites, books, and interviews are all potential sources of support for a speech. It is the speaker's responsibility to ensure that the material selected is valid and reliable. Thus, you will want to consider factors such as who authored the article and when it was published, as well as the source of the article to determine if it is a trustworthy and useful source. In addition, you will want to cite the source of information in the speech. Most schools maintain a variety of library databases available for student use. These

Databases, websites, books, and interviews are all potential sources of support for a speech.

© Ammentorp Photography/Shutterstock.com

can be helpful for your research because they provide access to a wide range of periodicals and scholarly journal articles.

When using the Internet to search for information, exercise caution when using commercial sites (*.com*) because they may be biased since their goal is to "sell" something. Education sites (*.edu*) are usually reliable, but be careful and check who posted the material as well as the purpose for which it was posted. You may also find chapters from books and magazines as well as interviews useful as you gather information for your speech.

As a speaker, you will want to find a variety of sources as well as different forms of support. In general, facts and statistics, definitions, examples, quotes by authorities, stories, and illustrations as well as visual presentations are all types of support a speaker looks for and incorporates into a speech. These are discussed further in the next chapter. Conducting research on the topic will also help you focus your topic and help you refine the key points you want to discuss in your speech.

## *Organize the Speech*

Once you have conducted your research and consulted a variety of sources, the next step for the speaker is to organize the material in a manner that will help the audience understand and process the topic and the information presented. It is important to note there are several ways to organize a speech and all relate to your purpose. The most common patterns include chronological, spatial, cause–effect, problem–solution, and topical order. These organizational strategies are discussed in more detail in Chapter 11.

## Practice Your Delivery

Once the speech is organized, the next crucial step in the process involves practicing your presentation. While this is discussed in more depth in Chapter 12, it is important to note that the more you practice a speech, the more comfortable you will be while presenting it. Obviously, the more comfort the speaker has with the topic, how it is organized, and the support material for it, the less anxiety a speaker will experience when presenting it to the audience. Maximizing your preparation and practice is one clear way to minimize your stress when delivering your speech.

## Deliver Your Speech

While this is also discussed in more depth in Chapter 12, delivering your speech is an important part of the preparation process. All of the previous steps in the process will have brought you to this moment and the more time and effort you put into those earlier steps, the more effectively you can present your speech. While you are delivering your speech, you should be aware of the audience's nonverbal feedback. This will let you know if the audience understands and is engaged in what you are saying. Knowing this information will allow you to make any adjustments while you are speaking to assist the audience to receive your message effectively.

## Reflect

Once the speech is presented, a public speaker's work is not done. Just as you need to analyze your audience before and during the speech construction process, and just as you should analyze your audience while delivering the speech through the feedback you receive from them, it is just as important to reflect on the speech and how the audience responded to it after it is delivered. Thus, after every presentation or public speaking event, the speaker should reflect on the speech to determine what worked, what did not work, and how things could be improved upon for the next speech. By becoming a reflective speaker, you will learn through self-analysis and improve with each new speaking opportunity.

Overall, careful preparation and practice of any speech will provide the speaker with more confidence while delivering the speech and will increase the chance that the audience will become engaged in the speech and will remain so.

# CHAPTER SUMMARY

In this chapter, we discussed the challenges of public speaking, the types of public speaking, and a brief overview of the process of public speaking. Some of the challenges a public speaker faces include communication anxiety, establishing credibility, and ethical considerations. In your personal, professional, or public lives, you will likely experience the opportunity to give a variety of speeches. To enhance your effectiveness, you must carefully consider all of the steps that are involved in the speech process.

The public speaking process entails selecting the topic, analyzing the audience, finding good support material for the topic, organizing the speech, practicing the speech, delivering the speech, and then reflecting on the strengths of the speech as well as what could have been done to improve the speech. When public speakers go through the process step by step, there is a greater chance they will be effective. As we began this chapter, we provided examples of speeches that occur in our personal, professional, and public lives. Although you may not yet be comfortable with the idea that public speaking will be a part of your life now and will continue to be a part of your life in the future, for most people, it will be. Understanding the challenges, the types of public speaking, and the process public speakers go through to help them become effective will help you as you encounter public speaking in your personal, professional, and public lives.

## KEY WORDS

*Accepting an award* Special occasion speech by the person receiving an award that recognizes the importance of the award and expresses his or her appreciation to those who are giving the award; acknowledges those who helped the recipient achieve this recognition and, if there were other nominees, acknowledges them as well.

*Ad hominem* Type of faulty reasoning used when a speaker attacks or criticizes a person, rather than the arguments provided or the issue itself.

*Anniversary speech* Type of special occasion speech used to remind an audience of a person, event, or holiday that is being commemorated.

*Areas of speaker analysis* The speaker, the audience, the occasion.

*Aristotle* Ancient Greek philosopher and scientist.

*Attitudinal analysis* Type of audience analysis that considers the audience's position on a particular topic (e.g., for, against, or no opinion).

*Audience analysis* Gaining knowledge about the audience such as their demographic information, their attitudes, their level of knowledge of the topic, the speech environment, and the occasion for the speech in order to best prepare the speech.

*Audience-based communication apprehension* Fear of public speaking with a specific audience (e.g., you may not be apprehensive when you are speaking with your peers in a course but apprehensive when you are speaking to the board of directors of your company).

*Bandwagon fallacy* Type of faulty reasoning used when one indicates that something is true because a number of people have said it is true, not necessarily because there is clear evidence of its truth.

*Commencement speech* Type of speech often given at a graduation to review what has been accomplished and provide a vision for the future.

*Communication apprehension* The fear, nervousness, or anxiety we experience when faced with real or imagined interactions.

*Context-based communication apprehension* Fear of speaking only in one setting (e.g., fear of speaking in public but not in other settings such as in small groups).

*Credibility* Extent to which a speaker is trustworthy, knowledgeable, and well prepared.

*Dedication speech* Type of special occasion speech given that speaks about the significance of an occasion (e.g., a building being named for a particular person).

*Deductive reasoning* Type of reasoning that begins with a general statement, is supported by specific support, and then draws a conclusion.

*Demographic analysis* Type of audience analysis that takes into account the characteristics of the audience including the audience's gender, age, race, ethnicity, and level of education.

*Ethical public speaking* Speaking that demonstrates respect for one's audience, honesty, use of reliable and valid sources, and responsibility for everything that is said and/or done during a speech.

*Ethos* In communication, a speaker or writer's appeal to the ethics of the listener or reader by way of communicating character in argument.

*Eulogy* Speech of praise for someone who has passed away.

*Fallacy* Faulty or false reasoning.

*General purpose* Provides the broad goal for your speech (e.g., to inform, persuade, or entertain).

*Hasty generalization* Type of faulty logic when the speaker uses only a few examples yet draws a general conclusion from those limited examples.

***Inaugural address*** Special occasion speech given when someone takes office or begins a new position that outlines the key issues to address while in that position, looks toward the future, and thanks his or her predecessor.

***Inductive reasoning*** Type of reasoning that provides strong and sufficient facts and examples and then draws a conclusion based on these facts.

***Informative speaking*** Type of speech used to help an audience become aware of or better understand a topic.

***Introduction speech*** Brief speech given to introduce and welcome a speaker and to build a rapport between the speaker and the audience as well as motivate the audience to listen to the speaker.

***Logos*** In communication, a speaker or writer's appeal to the logic of the listener or reader by use or reason in argument.

***Pathos*** In communication, a speaker or writer's appeal to the emotions of the listener or reader by way of creating an emotional response to a situation or argument.

***Persuasive speaking*** Type of speech used to change an audience's existing belief, to reinforce their existing belief, or to get an audience to take action regarding the topic.

***Presenting an award*** Type of special occasion speech that outlines the purpose, history, and/or the significance of the award; the criteria used to determine the awardee; and the relevant achievements of the recipient and how these accomplishments satisfied the criteria employed to determine who would receive the award.

***Questions of fact*** Type of question or claim that may be proven true or false.

***Questions of policy*** Type of question or claim that focuses on actions or changes that should or should not be made by governing bodies.

***Questions of value*** Type of question or claim that has to do with someone's ideas of right and wrong or good or bad.

***Situational analysis*** Type of audience analysis that takes into account the occasion of the speaking event as well as the time, place, and size of the audience.

***Situational communication apprehension*** Fear of public speaking based on a specific occurrence (e.g., you are nervous about meeting with your supervisor to ask for a raise or your town's planning board to ask for a variance).

***Special occasion speeches*** Speeches that cover a broad range of settings, circumstances, and occasions and usually acknowledge, celebrate, honor, or remember someone or something.

***Specific purpose*** Clear and concise statement indicating what you want your audience to know, do, or believe by the end of your speech.

**Strategies** Techniques speakers use to engage their audience and to keep the audience focused.

**The Rhetoric** Aristotle's work on the art of persuasion in communication.

**Toast** Speech given to congratulate a person or people on an achievement or a special occasion.

**Trait-like communication apprehension** Fear of public speaking (e.g., one-on-one, to a small group, or to a large audience).

**Tribute speech** Special occasion speech designed to praise someone (e.g., living or in the case of a eulogy, someone who has passed away).

**Welcome speech** Speech to formally recognize and greet a person or a group who is visiting, for example, a school, a convention, a special event, or a city.

# REFERENCES

Bailey, E. (2008). Celebrities with anxiety: Harrison Ford: Fear of public speaking, *Health Guide*. Retrieved from http://www.healthcentral.com/anxiety/c/22705/36519/celebrities-public/

Booth-Butterfield, S., & Gutowski, C. (1993). Message modality and source credibility can interact to affect argument processing. *Communication Quarterly, 41*, 77–89.

Dwyer, K. K., & Davidson, M. M. (2012). Is public speaking really more feared than death? *Communication Research Report, 29*(2), 99–107.

McCroskey, J. C. (1977). Oral communication apprehension: A review of recent theory and research. *Human Communication Research, 4*, 78–96.

McCroskey, J. C. (2004). A primer of stage fright. *Review of Communication, 4*, 86–87.

McCroskey, J. C. (2005). Motives and communibiology's texts: Whose motives? *Communication Theory, 15*, 468–474.

McCroskey, J. C., Andersen, J. F., Richmond, V. P., & Wheeless, L. R. (1981). Communication apprehension of elementary and secondary students and teachers. *Communication Education, 30*, 122–132.

McCroskey, J. C., & Beatty, M.J. (1999). Communication apprehension. In J. C. McCroskey, J. A. Daly, M. M. Martin, & M. J. Beatty (Eds.), *Communication and personality: Trait perspectives* (pp. 215–232). Cresskill, NJ: Hampton Press.

McCroskey, J. C., & Beatty, M. J. (2000). The communibiological perspective: Implications for communication in instruction. *Communication Education, 49*, 1–6.

Sellnow, D. D. (2005). *Confident public speaking* (2nd ed.). Belmont, CA: Thomson Wadsworth.

# CHAPTER 11

## Preparing Public Speeches: Taking the Next Steps

## Chapter Objectives

After reading this chapter, you should be able to:
- Define the elements of the introduction, the body, and the conclusion
- Identify the types of organizational patterns public speakers can use
- Explain three different strategies for outlining a speech
- Prepare appropriate presentational aids for a public speech
- Identify key considerations for appropriate language use in public speeches

**PERSONAL:** You have been assigned an informative speech for your public speaking class. It took you a while but you have now selected a topic and you have done a considerable amount of research on it. You feel like you have narrowed the topic down enough so that it will be workable given the time limit provided by your instructor. You have a strong sense of your audience's interests since you have gotten to know many of your classmates. You feel confident that your audience will be interested in your topic. Now what?

**PROFESSIONAL:** You have been asked to discuss a new product with clients. Since you were involved in the development of the product, you feel very comfortable speaking about it. In addition, you have done a lot of research on comparable products in the field. In your presentation, you would like to include information about the development of the product, its advantages, and comparable product information. In addition, you also have to address any client questions. You have been given 15 minutes to accomplish all of these goals. Where do you go from here?

**PUBLIC:** You work for the Department of Environmental Protection. The department has sent you to a small town to present a new initiative that urges towns (and cities) to turn former landfills into solar or wind energy farms. The town has been selected as one of the sites where the state would like to see this happen. You have been asked to speak about the concept and to persuade the town to consider implementing this program. You know you will be speaking to an audience that contains residents who favor the project, those who do not favor the project, and those who have no opinion. Where do you begin?

# CHAPTER OVERVIEW

No matter what type of speech you will be giving, once you know your topic, have analyzed your audience, and conducted preliminary research, the next step is to actually prepare your speech. This chapter discusses the key components found in every type of speech and how speeches are organized and prepared. In addition, the chapter focuses on various ways to outline a speech to ensure you have sufficient support for each main idea and that it is appropriately placed in your speech. Furthermore, the importance and use of presentational aids are explained and some of the techniques to ensure the appropriate use of language in public speaking are shared. Because public speaking occurs in your personal, professional, and public lives, possessing the tools to research, organize, and develop public speeches will increase the likelihood of your success when you speak in public.

# THE THREE PARTS OF ANY SPEECH DEFINED

No matter how long or short, a speech always contains the same three parts: the introduction, the body, and the conclusion. Each part of a speech serves a particular purpose. In addition, connecting your material within and between main ideas are transitions that help guide the audience from one point to the next. All of these elements are discussed in the next section.

## *Introduction*

**Introduction**
Gains the audience's attention, clearly states the topic, and previews the main points to be discussed.

The first part of any speech is the introduction. The goals of the *introduction* are to gain the audience's attention, indicate the topic and purpose of the speech, and provide a preview of the intended organization. During the introduction, the speaker should also work to establish credibility and build a rapport with the audience. Gaining the audience's attention is important. If you are not able to do this within the opening moments of your speech, the audience may decide to tune you out and tune into their favorite daydream. There are several strategies that can be used to get your audience to become interested in your speech (Figure 11.1). Some speakers begin the speech with a rhetorical question. The purpose of this type of question is to entice the audience to consider your topic. Usually, it is intended to stimulate thought, and not to encourage a discussion between the speaker and the audience. Some examples of rhetorical questions include:

- How many of you have ever wondered what it would be like to experience a totally new culture where you didn't know anyone and didn't even speak the same language as everyone around you?
- What would you do if you could change the course of someone's life just by giving 3 hours of your time a week?
- Can you imagine living in a city where you are in constant fear of your life, where it is not even safe for children to play outside, or where you might lose loved one after loved one or friend after friend due to violence?
- Have you ever said something to someone at some point and wished it could be taken back?

Other speakers begin with a joke or a humorous story. Grice and Skinner (2013) stated, "The use of humor can be one of a speaker's most effective attention-getting strategies. Getting the audience to laugh with you makes them alert and relaxed" (p. 171). Not everyone is successful at using this strategy. If a speaker tells a joke, it must be a joke that would not offend anyone, and it must be relevant to the speech topic. The same may be said about a humorous story. The speaker must make certain that he or she can move from the joke or humorous story to the speech topic seamlessly and that the connection between the humorous joke or story and the topic is clear. Humor, when used appropriately and effectively, can set a light-hearted tone for the speech; however, it should be noted that what is funny to one person is not funny to all and caution should be used when crafting humorous messages.

Other speakers gain an audience's attention through the use of a direct quote that is relevant to the speech topic. Quotes can include a quote from literature, quotes by individuals from the present or past, or quotes by experts on a particular topic. Examples of literary quotes include Shakespeare's "To thine own self be true" from *Hamlet* or "It is a far far better thing I do today..." from the Dickens classic *A Tale of Two Cities*. We may also use quotes by those in the present or past to gain the attention of our audience. For example, John F. Kennedy's "Ask not what your country can do for you, ask what you can do for your country" is a memorable quote from his inauguration speech that is still relevant in today's world. Authorities are often considered experts due to their training or their education. Thus, a quote by an authority on child abuse may help gain an audience's attention, especially if the authority has studied this topic extensively. Authorities may also become experts because they have firsthand experience with a topic. For example, beginning your speech with a quote by someone who has endured child abuse would be an effective strategy to gain the audience's attention.

Statistics are one type of evidence people use to support a point.

© lightpoet/Shutterstock.com

Speakers may also use facts, figures, or statistics to gain an audience's attention. These can help provide evidence for the audience about the prevalence or importance of an issue. If an audience realizes that 8 out of 10 individuals will face a health scare before they are 30 years old or that 80% of all college-age individuals will not graduate in 4 years, it enables them to focus on the speech topic.

Similarly, many times your audience may be unaware of a particular topic. If this is the case, speakers may gain the audience's attention by beginning with a definition. Suppose your audience has never heard of Tax Form 1098-T? This is the form issued by colleges showing the amount students are "billed for qualified tuition and related expenses" that may qualify them for deductions on their tax returns. You would want to define this term before you begin to discuss it with the audience.

Examples are also used to gain an audience's attention. These include factual or hypothetical examples. Factual examples are drawn from real life. They include actual cases or incidents speakers have personally experienced, or those they have identified through research or stories shared by others. Factual examples help gain an audience's attention because they demonstrate the reality of your topic. For example, if you were persuading the audience to sign up to be organ donors, you could tell them a story about a friend who needed a heart transplant and describe the emotional details experienced as he prepared for, and then waited to receive, his heart. An example like this provides the audience with an illustration of the need to register for organ donation. Other examples may be conceivable, but not have actually occurred. These are hypothetical examples and involve asking the audience

FIGURE 11.1

Attention-getting strategies.

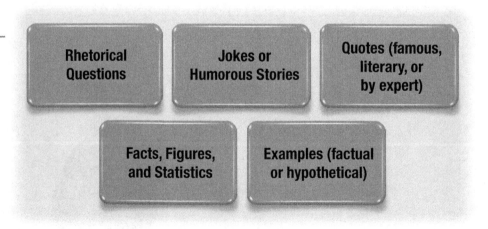

to "Picture this" or "Imagine that this happened to you." These hypothetical examples place audiences in possible, plausible scenarios and help them connect with the topic to be discussed.

Whatever attention-getting strategy is used to gain an audience's attention, it should be well thought out, help introduce the topic, and engage the audience in the speech. It should also be influenced by the purpose of the speech, the audience to whom you are presenting, and the impression you want to create.

In addition to gaining the audience's attention in the introduction, the speaker must also reveal the purpose of the speech. As mentioned in Chapter 10, three common general purposes of speeches are to inform, to persuade, or to speak on a special occasion. The specific purpose can be compared to a thesis statement. The specific purpose should clearly indicate the primary focus of the speech and should be succinct. Usually, one concise sentence indicating the goal of your speech is sufficient. Examples of speech purposes may include to inform the audience about the three primary changes to their financial aid agreements or to explain the four elements to consider when selecting a diamond ring.

Following the purpose statement, a preview of the main ideas that will be discussed is presented. This is similar to the "preview of coming attractions" one sees before the main feature begins at a movie theater. A preview gives the audience a glimpse into the highlights of the speech. It is important because it provides the audience with cues to help them listen more effectively to the speech. If an audience knows that the speaker will discuss the causes, the effects, and the treatments of a particular disease, they will be able to follow the speech more accurately.

Additional elements to be addressed in the speech introduction include connecting with one's audience and establishing yourself as a credible source on the topic. When speakers build rapport with an audience, they try to demonstrate that the topic is relevant to the audience and that they have the audience's best interests at heart. If audiences believe they will derive some personal, educational, or professional benefit from listening to a particular speech, they are more likely to pay attention. Thus, if you show your audience that they can improve their cardiovascular health, learn how to manage their time more efficiently, create a more effective résumé, or learn a more effective way to track sales, they are more likely to listen to your speech. Likewise, audiences are more likely to listen to speakers they trust. If audiences believe you are a credible source as a result of your education, experiences, and/or your careful research on a subject, they will also be more likely to attend to your speech.

FIGURE 11.2

Important elements of
the introduction.

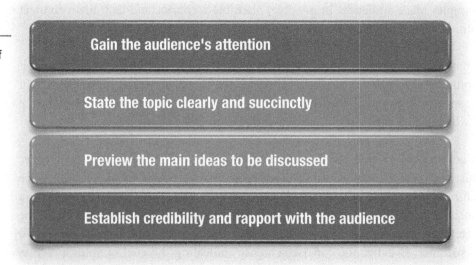

Achieving a positive first impression with the audience is a critical element in public speaking. During the introduction the speaker gains the audience's attention, states the specific purpose of the speech, previews the main ideas that will be addressed in the speech, and lets the audience know they can trust what you are saying and that you have their best interests at heart (Figure 11.2). If your introduction contains all of these elements, you will help your audience prepare effectively for the next part of your speech.

## Body

**➤ Body**
The heart of the speech; its purpose is to state each main idea and support each idea fully.

The second part of any speech is the *body*, which constitutes the major portion of a speech. The purpose of the body is to state the main ideas and provide backing for each one. It is important to clearly articulate each main idea and then support each one with sufficient evidence. Gathering the support for your main ideas is crucial to the overall success of your speech. In today's world, it is relatively easy to gather support for speeches. Your school's library probably provides students with access to a variety of databases. Some of these databases may include:

- *Academic Search Complete* is a comprehensive scholarly, multidisciplinary, and full-text database that contains more than 8,500 full-text periodicals, including more than 7,300 peer-reviewed journals.
- *Communication & Mass Media Complete* provides research particularly related to communication and mass media. This database has coverage of more than 770 titles including full text for over 450 journals.

- *LexisNexis Academic Universe* contains full texts for about 5,000 public and commercial business, legal, newspaper, and media sources.
- *Medline* contains studies of medical issues.
- *PsycINFO*, from the American Psychological Association, is a resource for abstracts of scholarly journal articles, book chapters, books, and dissertations.

While databases are a great resource for locating support for the main points of a speech, there are a variety of other options that can also be used. Depending on the topic, you may consult newspapers, magazines, and government publications to provide the support for the ideas in your speech. Interviewing those who have expertise related to your topic or searching relevant websites may also be helpful. It is beneficial to consult a variety of sources to support your speech. However, it is important to carefully consider the credibility of the sources you select to support your points. Knowing where and how to gather evidence is important. Next, we discuss the types of information that is used to support your main ideas.

Through your research, you will find various types of information that can be used to support the main ideas of the speech. These include using facts and statistics, examples, definitions, and quotes. First, you may provide evidence by citing verifiable facts or statistics. Knowing how many people are affected by a phenomenon on a daily basis emphasizes the significance of an issue. Consider the following example:

> According to the American Automobile Association (AAA), distracted driving contributes to as many as 8,000 crashes every day. In addition, more than 1 million people have died in car crashes over the past 25 years in the United States, with 33,788 lives lost in 2010 alone. (AAA Foundation for Traffic Safety, 2010)

These facts show the extent of this issue; however, facts may also show the rarity of occurrence. Consider this example:

> According to the Progeria Research Foundation (2014), "Progeria is a rare, fatal genetic condition characterized by an appearance of accelerated aging in children. . . . It affects approximately 1 in 4–8 million newborns. There are an estimated 200–250 children living with Progeria worldwide at any one time."

Whether your support shows how extensive or rare something is, facts and statistics are useful forms of proof. When using this type of support, it is important to give credit to the source of the facts or statistics during your speech and to confirm the credibility of sources.

Examples are another type of support and are often used to help clarify something that seems abstract. Speakers use examples to explain things in real terms. Thus, if you are trying to support the idea that people who exercise can facilitate the weight loss process, providing an example of someone for whom that strategy has worked will help support that idea. You may provide statistics on the extent of homelessness; however, if you describe the experiences of someone who is homeless, it may have a greater impact on your audience since it puts a human face on the issue. When discussing techniques to gain an audience's attention, we indicated that examples may be actual or hypothetical in nature. This is also true for examples used to support an idea. If using hypothetical examples, however, they must reflect something that may not have happened but that *could* happen. Thus, when using an example, be sure that it is reasonable, relevant to the point you are trying to make, and detail-oriented to provide a clear and vivid picture in the minds of the audience.

Definitions are another form of support used by speakers. Consider a speaker who is delivering a presentation that is focused on a specific industry or specialization. Words and concepts must be clearly defined for those with no expertise or understanding of the topic in order to understand the point the speaker is making. Examples of topics that may need to be defined could include presentations discussing IPOs (initial public offerings) or the new IRS regulations for spousal liability. Providing a clear definition for difficult terminology not widely known can help the audience understand your ideas.

Quotes by authorities are another way to support the main ideas of a speech. As mentioned previously, authorities are those who are considered knowledgeable about a subject because they have studied it, have gained valuable work experience connected to it, or they have experienced it. If, for example, you are speaking to your audience about the benefits of study-abroad programs, you certainly may obtain quotes from those who have studied this topic area; however, perhaps even more compelling evidence may be the quotes of those who have participated in study-abroad programs themselves. Once you provide a quote, it is also helpful to explain the quote and make the connection to your idea. Going beyond just providing the quote will help the audience truly understand its meaning and intent.

It is important to go beyond simply stating the main ideas in a speech and take the next step to provide ample support for each of these ideas. To enhance the credibility of your ideas, go beyond simply stating what you think and provide support through facts or statistics, examples, definitions, and quotes. Keep in mind that evidence must be accurate, obtained from reliable sources, relevant, current (when that is important), and appropriately selected for the particular audience you are addressing. Researching and selecting the best evidence is a speaker's ethical obligation. In addition, it is important to vary the types of support you provide to your audience. Imagine if a speaker spouted statistic after statistic or quote after quote. After a while, the audience would most likely turn their attention elsewhere. As baseball coaches tell their pitchers, it is important to "mix your pitches." By doing so, the batter never goes on "auto pilot" and must stay alert and focused. Varying your forms of support for each idea will help an audience stay focused.

## Conclusion

After providing the audience with the main ideas of your presentation, the final task is to bring the speech to a close. The purposes of the *conclusion* are to review the key points or ideas you have discussed and to leave your audience with something to remember or consider further. The conclusion may issue a challenge to your audience in order to motivate them to take action. Just as there are several techniques to gain your audience's attention in the introduction, there are several ways you may conclude your speech so they remember what you said. Provide a succinct, memorable summary of the main ideas of your speech by using short, simple statements to refocus and summarize your speech. Just as you might state in the preview section of your introduction, "Today, I will be informing you about the causes, effects, and common treatments for …" you can say, "In summary, I have discussed the causes, effects, and common treatments for …" Your summary can

**➤ Conclusion**
Summarizes or reviews the main points presented in the speech and leaves the audience with a final unifying thought.

There are several ways to end your speech so that the audience remembers what you said.

go one step further to briefly clarify and restate the content of your speech. Thus, instead of just noting you have discussed "causes" in your speech, you can state something like, "As I indicated in my speech, there are three main causes of … and these occur most often in men and women between the ages of 20 and 24 …" This will help reinforce key points in your speech.

Following the brief review of the speech's main ideas, leave your audience with something to consider or do. This can be considered the attention-getter in reverse. There are many techniques you might use to accomplish this goal. The same strategies that can be used to gain attention in the introduction can be used to reinforce an idea in the conclusion and leave a memorable impression. Use facts or statistics, rhetorical questions, quotes by authorities, or examples. Rephrase your attention-getting technique. For example, if you started your speech by asking your audience to "imagine you are sitting on a beach…" your conclusion could be "so remember, the next time you are on a beach…" The goal is to motivate the audience to continue thinking about your topic long after you have completed your speech. If they do, it is likely that they will give further consideration to your topic, accept a challenge you presented, or be motivated to take action. A strong conclusion will help guarantee the audience remembers your ideas and information.

## *Transitions*

You have likely written a paper for one of your classes that used words or phrases to connect or link ideas together. Transitions are the final element in any speech. *Transitions* help the listeners make connections and move smoothly from one point to the next. They signal that the speaker is moving from one idea to the next or from one type of support to the next. If you are moving from one major idea to the next, you may guide your audience to the new idea by stating, "Now that I have discussed the causes of …, I will explain the effects of …" This simple statement will alert an audience that you have completed the discussion of one main idea and are now moving on to the next main idea.

**Transitions**
Words or phrases that help listeners move smoothly from one point to the next; signal to the audience that the speaker is moving from one idea to the next or from one type of support to another.

Although transitions may be used to let the audience know you are moving from one point to the next, they may also be used to indicate the next idea is similar, different, or more important than the previous one. For example, if you say, "Just like the first principle of persuasive speaking, the second principle …" it will let the audience know that the first idea is similar to the second one. If you say, "In contrast to my first point …" it alerts your audience to the fact that the next idea is different from the first. Finally, statements such as, "Even more important than my first two ideas is …" lets the audience know that this idea is more significant than the preceding ones.

Transitions are also used within a discussion of a main idea. If speakers provide one form of support for an idea and are about to provide another, they may use words and phrases such as "Also," "In addition," and "Furthermore," to let the audience know more evidence is forthcoming. When speakers are completing an idea, phrases and words such as "In summary," "In conclusion," "Thus," or "Therefore" alert the audience that they are preparing to transition to the next idea.

In summary, regardless of the overall length of a speech, it always contains an introduction designed to capture the audience's attention, states the purpose of the speech, and previews the key points that will be discussed. In addition, the body of the speech clearly states the main ideas and provides support for each of them. The final part of the speech, the conclusion, provides a summary of the key points that were discussed and creates the final audience impression. Throughout each section of the speech, transitions are used to guide the audience from one idea to the next and to help them maintain their attention. As you prepare your own speeches, be sure to include each of these key elements.

## ORGANIZING YOUR SPEECH

Now that you are aware of the main parts of a speech, this section emphasizes the specific ways in which speeches are organized.  A well-organized speech will help

A well-organized speaker greatly helps an audience understand the concepts of the speech.

© VladKol/Shutterstock.com

an audience understand and remember your ideas. If you have ever tried to listen to a speaker but simply could not follow what they were saying, it may be due to a lack of organization on the speaker's part. Recalling the "causes, effects, and common treatments" example stated earlier, if the speaker randomly spoke about a cause, then a treatment, then another cause, then an effect, and so on, the audience would most likely have a difficult time following and remembering the ideas presented by the speaker. In this section, we present organizational patterns that are most used in public speaking. We then focus on some organizational patterns more often connected to persuasive speeches. These patterns of organization are typically used when organizing the body of the speech.

## Common Organizational Patterns for Speeches

**➤ Chronological order**
A pattern of organization particularly useful when you are trying to describe the order in which something occurs or occurred; used to explain a process, discuss historical events, or talk about someone's life. Also known as *time order*.

One common pattern of organization used in speeches is *chronological order* or time order. This pattern is particularly useful when you are explaining a process, discussing historical events, or describing the highlights of someone's life. When the order in which something occurs is important, this is an appropriate organizational strategy to use. Imagine if you were trying to explain your life to someone and first described your life at age 5, then at age 25, before explaining age 10, and then age 20. Your audience would not get a clear sense of the order of your life experiences over the years. Likewise, if you were trying to discuss the career of a famous musician, going back and forth from that person's early career to his later career and then back to discuss his midcareer, it is likely that your audience would find it difficult to follow the career progression.

When trying to explain a process, the order in which you undertake the process will have an impact on the steps involved and the subsequent product. Suppose you are explaining how to make chocolate chip cookies. The order in which you present the instructions is important. If you instruct your audience to cream the butter and the sugar and then add the flour before telling them to add the eggs, the final product may not turn out as expected. If you state that they should bake the cookies and then add the chocolate chips, the final product would not be chocolate chip cookies as we know them. Thus, when the order of events or a process is important, chronological or time organization is an effective organizational strategy to use.

**➤ Geographical order**
An organizational pattern used when you want to show how the various parts relate to each other and to the whole. Also known as *spatial order*.

Another common pattern of organization is *geographical order* or spatial order. If the goal of the speech is to illustrate how various parts relate to each other or to the whole, this is an appropriate organizational pattern. There is a song that says, "The hip bone's connected to the thigh bone and the thigh bone's connected to the knee bone ..." When showing the spatial relationship between the various parts, consider this organizational pattern. For example, you could use a geographical order to describe your school's campus. In this case, you would select a starting point (e.g., "When you enter the main gates of the campus …") and describe each building to the next building by describing its geographical location or proximity to the next.

A third pattern of organization is *cause–effect order*. With this pattern, events or occurrences that have resulted in a particular outcome are identified. For example, you might provide evidence for the different events that led to the closure of a business, an increase in the joblessness rate, or a decline in the economy. Public speakers may provide support for the various causes that led to a particular effect or outcome. They may also start with the effect and then trace the causes of it. When speakers want to show the connection between certain events that have caused a particular event or set of events, they often use this pattern.

**Cause–effect order**
Uncovering events that have resulted in a particular outcome. Speakers may also use the reverse order and begin by speaking about the effects and then go back and trace the causes.

The *topical pattern* is another strategy used in organizing a speech. This pattern takes a broad topic and breaks it down into subtopics or parts. Suppose you were asked to present a speech on the topic of pollution. Since the topic is broad, it could be organized to discuss the various types of pollution, such as noise pollution, water pollution, and air pollution. Another way to organize subtopics of pollution might include discussing the types of pollution, recent legislation that helps prevent pollution, the role of the average citizen in reducing pollution, and the future impact of pollution on our country. Thus, with the topical pattern, you organize your speech into categories and support each category with evidence.

**Topical pattern**
In this pattern, you divide your speech into categories and support each category with evidence.

*Problem–solution* is an organizational pattern also used by speakers. This pattern examines a particular problem and then offers a potential solution to the problem. Providing information on the nature, the extent, and the origins of the problem helps the audience understand the solution that you propose to solve the problem. This pattern is based on John Dewey's (1933) reflective thinking process, discussed in Chapter 9. The process employs a step-by-step process to solving a problem. The steps are (1) identifying and defining the problem, (2) analyzing the problem, (3) determining the criteria for finding a solution to the problem, (4) generating possible solutions to the problem, (5) selecting the best solution to the problem, and (6) implementing the chosen solution. The problem–solution pattern can be used in informative speaking but is also used in speeches to persuade.

**Problem–solution**
Pattern that examines a particular problem and then offers a potential solution to the problem; based on John Dewey's reflective thinking process.

## Common Organizational Patterns for Persuasive Speeches

In this section, we discuss patterns often used to organize persuasive speeches. One organizational strategy used exclusively in persuasive speeches is *Monroe's motivated sequence* (Monroe, 1935). With this pattern of organization, the goal is

**Monroe's motivated sequence**
Most often used in persuasive speaking, with this type of organizational strategy, the speaker gains the audience's attention, shows there is a need (or a need for change), provides a solution that satisfies the need, visualizes the benefits of the stated change, and moves the audience to action.

to guide the audience through five steps: *attention*, *need*, *satisfaction*, *visualization*, and *action*. In the first step, ensure that the audience is interested in your topic. This is similar to gaining the audience's attention in the introduction of the speech. Engage them in your speech topic. The next step involves establishing a need or explaining why they need to listen to your message, why it is somehow relevant to their lives, or why there is a need for change. The third step is the satisfaction step. In this portion of the speech, you propose a solution and explain how it will solve or help remedy the problem. Visualization is the fourth step of Monroe's motivated sequence. In this step, ask your audience to "picture this." Provide them with the benefits that will be derived if your solution is adopted. The final step in this organizational pattern is the action step. This involves clearly stating what you want your audience to do or believe and then motivating them to take action and accept your persuasive proposition. For example, if you were persuading the audience to exercise more, you might get the audience's attention by providing statistics about the general lack of fitness among college-age students; offer a rationale for why the audience needs to exercise more; specify a solution to help the audience develop an exercise program; demonstrate how it can be incorporated easily into their lives; discuss the benefits they will derive; and, finally, challenge them to begin to exercise more.

**Comparative advantage pattern**
A speech organization often used in persuasive speaking, it demonstrates to the audience that accepting the speaker's persuasive proposition has more benefits than other possible propositions that others may be advocating.

The *comparative advantage pattern* organizes information in a way to help the audience see that accepting the persuasive proposition is more beneficial than other possible options that others may be advocating. In the business world, salespeople use this strategy when a customer is considering their product against a competitor's product. Likewise, a salesperson may explain how the product she represents will present greater benefits (e.g., cost, efficiency, ease of use) than the product the customer is currently using. For example, if your company is building a new facility and is considering two sites for the building, the project manager might compare the advantages of each site and advocate for why one of the sites would be most advantageous to the company.

**Statement of reasons pattern**
In this pattern, each of the speaker's main points provides a reason why the proposal should (or should not) be supported.

A final organizational strategy used in persuasive speaking is known as the *statement of reasons pattern*. In this pattern, each of the speaker's main points provides a reason why a proposal should (or should not) be supported. For example, if you are speaking to persuade an audience that music education should not be eliminated in public schools, you would provide several reasons and corresponding evidence to support that proposal. Each main idea would include a reason to keep musical education in the schools. Examples of reasons might include improved learning in all subject areas, enhanced student creativity, and the development of a lifelong appreciation of music. Support for each of these reasons would take the form of statistics, quotes by authorities, and examples.

There are a variety of patterns used to organize speeches. Some are particularly useful in speeches to inform and others are better suited for persuasive speeches. Keep in mind that often, as you research, a natural organizational pattern will emerge that is appropriate for your speech's purpose. In addition, there are times when more than one organizational pattern may be integrated into a speech. For example, if you are discussing a recent trip across the country, you would most likely use the geographical or spatial pattern; however, you may also describe your journey chronologically.

Understanding the various types of organizational patterns that may be used in the body of your speech will help you focus and develop your main ideas. The next step involves organizing your ideas into an outline to help you prepare to deliver your speech.

# OUTLINING YOUR SPEECH

An *outline* is a tool that speakers use to organize their main ideas and support material into a coherent speech. There are various types of outlines available to you when you write a speech. These include word, phrase, and sentence outlines. A word outline, as the name suggests, is very brief. Main ideas and support are limited to single words. The phrase outline provides slightly more detail while the sentence outline contains the most information of the three general types. The type of outline you choose depends on the nature of your speech, your familiarity with the subject and supporting material, the length of your speech, and the type and size of your audience. Each type is discussed in more detail shortly, but first let's consider the general advantages of using an outline when speaking. There are many benefits to using an outline. First, an outline helps a speaker to maintain eye contact with the audience. When you have an outline, the material is blocked out and it is easy to see the main points and subpoints for each idea. Thus, if you are on the first main idea and you have

**Outline**
Tool that speakers use to organize their main ideas and support material into a coherent speech.

An outline helps a speaker maintain eye contact with the audience.

© hxdbzxy/Shutterstock.com

given two forms of support for it, it is much easier to find your place (or not lose your place) if you have spoken directly to your audience. In addition, an outline is a great way to ensure that you have organized your speech effectively. At a glance, you can make sure that each subpoint belongs with the appropriate main idea. If it does not, it is easy to move each element to its appropriate location in the speech. Third, an outline is a great practice tool because it visually differentiates between main points and subpoints. Fourth, an outline helps the speaker maintain focus and avoid getting "off track" during a speech. If you are the type of speaker who tends to go off on tangents when speaking, an outline will remind you of the main ideas and the sequence in which you want to make them. Finally, an outline is useful should you need to edit a speech while you are speaking. Suppose you have three main ideas in the body of your speech and four forms of support for each idea. It is easy for you to visually see how many subpoints should accompany each main idea. For example, if you indicated in the introduction that you will discuss three main ideas, you can glance at your outline and confirm the number and order of the main ideas. If you have four subpoints for each main idea and time is limited, the outline will enable you to quickly eliminate a subpoint without losing your place or needing to eliminate one of your main points to accommodate the time limitation.

An outline is an important tool in the speech preparation process. As stated earlier, there are different types of outlines, and the one you choose is dependent on factors such as your familiarity with the topic and the supporting ideas. If you are less familiar with the topic or if you have several quotes, statistics, or other material that you need to quote directly, your outline is more likely to be prepared as a sentence outline.

**Word outline**
Type of outline that contains only key words to help the speaker remember the sequence in which main points should be discussed. Because of its brevity, it is most useful when the speaker is very comfortable with the speaking situation and knows the material in the speech exceptionally well.

The first type of outline is the *word outline*. This is often used by speakers when they are very familiar with the material. If you are very sure of all of the material you want to cover, you could use a word outline. This contains the least amount of information, but for speakers who know their material well and are comfortable presenting it to the audience, this type of outline serves as a way to capture the sequence of ideas the speaker wants to cover. For example, a word outline addressing the three parts of a speech might include only the following:

I. Introduction
II. Body
III. Conclusion

If you look back at the material previously discussed on the three parts of a speech, you probably now realize how much may be said about each of these areas. You would need to be very familiar with your supporting material in order to use this type of outline.

You could even broaden your outline further to guide you more specifically by indicating how you want to approach each area. In that case, your word outline would look like the following:

I.    Introduction
    A.    Purposes
    B.    Techniques
II.   Body
    A.    Purposes
    B.    Techniques
III.  Conclusion
    A.    Purposes
    B.    Techniques

The second type of outline is the *phrase outline*. This type of outline contains key phrases to help the speaker move from point to point. It expands on the word outline but is still relatively brief. Similar to the word outline, it helps the speaker avoid reading from the outline since most of the speech content is not on the actual outline. Thus, if you use a phrase outline, it might look like this:

I.    Introduction = first section of speech
    A.    Three purposes
        1.    Get audience's attention
        2.    State purpose/topic
        3.    Preview key points
    B.    Several techniques to gain attention
        1.    Tell a joke
        2.    Provide a definition
        3.    Ask a rhetorical question
        4.    Provide an example

**Phrase outline**
Type of outline that contains key phrases to help the speaker move from point to point. It expands on the word outline but is still relatively brief. It does help the speaker avoid reading from the outline since most of the speech content is not on this type of outline.

Without going into each section, it is easy to see how the phrase outline gives you more information but is still brief.

When you are less familiar with the topic and its evidence, a *sentence outline*, also known as a full-content outline, is appropriate. This is a very detailed outline containing most of what the speaker will say during the speech. It is very useful for organizing a speech and for practicing it as well. Some speakers use it during their speech, while others use it only to formulate and practice the speech. Once a speaker is comfortable with the speech, the outline may be converted to a phrase outline. Changing to a phrase outline can help a speaker maintain eye contact with the audience. Using the same example as above, a sentence outline might look like the following:

**Sentence outline**
Very detailed outline containing most of what the speaker will say during the speech. It is very useful for organizing a speech and for practicing it as well. Also called a full-content outline.

I.   The first part of any speech is the introduction.
   A.   There are three purposes of the introduction.
      1.   The first purpose of the introduction is to gain the audience's attention.
         a.   Often, the degree to which you get an audience's attention in the first 30 seconds to 1 minute is the degree to which you will maintain their attention over the course of the speech.
         b.   Your goal is to captivate your audience and show them why they should listen to you.
      2.   The second purpose of the introduction is to state the topic and purpose of the speech.
         a.   Letting your audience know what your topic and purpose are helps them get ready to listen to you.
         b.   It also lets them know if you are informing or persuading them and the perspective you will be presenting.
      3.   The third purpose of the introduction is to preview the key points you will discuss in your speech.
         a.   The preview helps the audience understand what your organizational strategy will be.
         b.   This will help your audience listen more effectively and know when you are moving from one point to the next.

Clearly, there are great differences among the three types of outlines. Again, the type you use should be based on your knowledge of a topic as well as your comfort with public speaking. The less dependent you are on an outline, the more conversational you will be while delivering your speech. The type of outline you use may also be determined by your instructor. Overall, an outline is an excellent organizational tool to help you prepare to speak in public.

# DEVELOPING PRESENTATIONAL AIDS

*Presentational aids* are audio and/or visual types of support that help the speaker emphasize, clarify, or summarize an idea. They should never overshadow or overpower the speaker or the message. Presentational aids are simply that—aids that provide support for the speaker's points. When misused, they may actually detract from the speech, confuse the listener, or cause the audience to become distracted.

**Presentational aids**
Charts, bar graphs, pictures, diagrams, models, the actual object, and even the speaker him- or herself are considered to be visual aids. Audio aids include recordings of music, famous speeches, interviews, or even sounds from nature. Audio-visual aids include clips from movies, instructional DVDs, or anything that combines both sound and sight. They are all used to clarify, highlight, or summarize a speaker's ideas

Therefore, it is important to know the types of audio and/or visual aids you may want to use in your speech as well as when to use and how to prepare them.

There are a variety of types of visual aids. Charts, bar graphs, pictures, diagrams, models or replicas; the actual object under discussion; and even the speaker him- or herself may be useful visual aids. Audio aids can include recordings of music, famous speeches, interviews, or even sounds from nature. Audio-visual aids include clips from movies, instructional DVDs, or anything that combines both sound and sight.

© Maxim Blinkov/Shutterstock.com

## Visual Aids

Visual aids may take many forms. For example, *charts* provide a visual display for information contained in your speech. They may help explain how things relate to each other or the sequence something goes through as it is processed. One common example is an organizational chart where each person's position in the organization and that position's relationship to the other positions in the organization are shown visually. Another common example of a chart is a *pie chart* (sometimes called a *pie graph*), which shows what amount of the total each individual "slice" of the pie contributes. Finally, *flow charts* are also commonly used by public speakers. They illustrate the sequence in which the steps of a process occur.

*Bar graphs* are another type of visual aid and are often used to translate statistical comparisons and relationships into visual representations. It is easier for audiences to understand the relationships among different numbers when they can see these comparisons visually. A bar graph, for example, could show enrollment trends over the last 5 years or compare how males and females scored on several different components of a standardized test.

Visual aids should support a speaker's message.

**Charts**
Visual display for information contained in a speech; help explain how things relate to each other or the sequence something goes through as it is processed.

**Bar graphs**
A type of visual aid often used to translate statistical comparisons and relationships into visual representations.

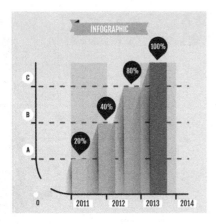

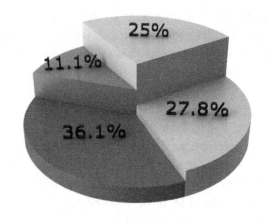

Bar graph                                                    Pie chart

**➤ Pictures and diagrams**
Provide helpful visual images to augment a speaker's description of something.

*Pictures and diagrams* also provide helpful visual images to augment the speaker's description. For example, if you are speaking about the various sights to see while in the city of Boston, pictures of these attractions would be useful to help the audience visualize what you are discussing. Likewise, if you are trying to explain the parts of a motor and the relationships among those parts, you might use a diagram to help the listeners better understand your material.

**➤ Model**
Replica of an object used as a visual aid.

A *model* is a replica of an object and this can also be a useful visual aid. When explaining the circulatory system, it would be useful to have a scaled model or replica to show the audience while discussing the various elements of the system and its processes. In some instances, you would need a model or replica because the actual object would not be accessible or it might be too large or too small to be useful in a public speaking situation. However, there are times when the actual object may be used during a public speech. For example, science teachers have shown a healthy lung and a diseased lung to demonstrate the dangers of smoking to their students. Finally, the *speaker* may serve as a visual aid. If you are showing an audience how to stretch before or after exercising, you may describe the process and actually demonstrate it to the audience so they can actually see the stretches as you describe them. If you are explaining how to do a backhand stroke in tennis, you would become a visual aid if you were to swing a tennis racket as you describe the proper technique.

## Audio and Audio-Visual Aids

Audio and/or audio-visual aids may also be helpful in public speeches. If you are speaking about a singer whose work has contributed to a particular genre of music, you may want to play a clip of that artist's work to provide an example of her style of music. If you are comparing two styles of music, you may want to give an example of each style to help the audience understand the differences between them.

Audio-visual aids in the form of clips from movies or television, for example, are also useful tools for public speaking. The Internet serves as a great resource for a wide variety of audio-visual aids. For example, if you are doing a speech on texting while driving, you may want to search YouTube for an example of a public service announcement, interview, or news report that could help you demonstrate the dangers of texting while driving.

## Strategies for Using Presentational Aids

Deciding when, as well as how, to use presentational aids is an important piece of the speech preparation process. As stated earlier, presentational aids are used to emphasize, clarify, or summarize ideas. They can help you maintain the audience's attention, make the material you present more memorable, provide additional support to your ideas, make your speeches more interesting, and simplify difficult material, making it more understandable and less complex. There are several guidelines for their use. First, presentational aids of any type should not be overused and should always be relevant to the ideas you are conveying. Second, they should always be well prepared. Computer-generated presentational aids can be very professional but care should be given to the choice of fonts, colors used, and the size of the graphic so that audiences can easily see and understand each slide. Third, if you are using video or audio clips, you need to be careful about their length since they are usually incorporated into the amount of time you are given to speak. If not used carefully, they can overshadow a speech or the speaker. When using this type of presentational aid, it is best to use clips that are no longer than 30 seconds to 1 minute in length. In addition, be sure not to use clips longer than 10% of your total speaking time. Thus, if you are speaking for 10 minutes, you would not want to devote 5 minutes of your time to audio or video clips. Since most students today are knowledgeable about producing electronic presentational aids and are comfortable with the technology, and since these aids are readily available, they may help public speakers become more effective in conveying their ideas.

# WORD CHOICE

When developing a speech, *word choice*, or the language you use, is important to consider. There are a variety of factors to think about when selecting the right words to express ideas in a speech. The first consideration should be your audience.

Would you use the same word choice to discuss solar energy with a group of second graders as you would use when speaking to a group of engineers attending an energy convention? It's not likely. Matching your word choice to your audience's age, education level, and experience with your topic is essential to planning an effective speech. If your audience is familiar with technical language or jargon, you can incorporate it in the presentation. However, if they know little or nothing about your topic, the use of jargon would not be appropriate. Poor word selection often results in an audience becoming distracted and not listening to the message.

A second factor to consider is the use of clear and descriptive language. Concrete language provides the audience with a clear understanding of your topic. For example, if you were to reference "my car" when presenting a speech on automobile repair, unless your audience knows what type of car you drive, they may each perceive a different make and model of car. If, on the other hand, you reference your "2002 Volvo S80 sedan," they would receive a much clearer image of your car. As you develop your speech, choose concrete and descriptive words that will help paint a clear picture for your audience.

Use of appropriate language is important for any audience.

© val lawless/Shutterstock.com

When making language choices, use words that are not ostentatious. Some speakers like to enhance perceptions of credibility by using words that are grandiose or imposing. Audiences are usually not impressed by this tactic and, in fact, may lose interest in the speech and the speaker. When speakers use this type of language, audiences often perceive them as condescending or trying to appear of higher status.

It is important to choose language that is ethical. As discussed in Chapter 10, refrain from using language that degrades or offends others based on their gender, race, cultural background, sexual orientation, or religion. Similarly, it is best to use gender-neutral language. Referring, for example, to *firefighters* and *police officers* instead of *firemen* and *policemen* will help alleviate stereotypes. Public speakers have many ethical obligations to their audiences and being conscious of the ethical use of language is very important.

Finally, public speakers should avoid using slang. Although you may be speaking in a college classroom, the use of appropriate language remains important. The use of slang may not be understood by the entire audience and it may offend some people. Keeping all of these things in mind when developing your speeches will help you be an effective public speaker.

# CHAPTER SUMMARY

In this chapter, we have discussed many considerations when preparing speeches. First, regardless of the length of a speech, it always includes an introduction, body, and conclusion. The goal of the introduction is to capture the audience's attention, state the topic to be discussed, and provide a preview of the key ideas that will be presented in the speech. Transitions should be incorporated throughout the speech to guide the audience from one main idea to the next. Internal transitions are also useful signposts to indicate the direction and flow of the speech. Examples of these include phrases such as "In addition," "For example," "Furthermore," or "Finally." Ensuring that your speech contains all of these components will enhance your effectiveness as a public speaker.

In addition to ensuring that all parts of the speech are included, patterns of organization are important to consider. Organizational patterns help you divide a topic into its main ideas and this, in turn, helps you to fit your research into its appropriate and logical place within the speech. Commonly used patterns of organization include chronological, spatial or geographical, cause–effect, topical and problem–solution organization. Additional patterns of organization are frequently used in persuasive speaking include Monroe's motivated sequence, the comparative advantage pattern, and the statement of reasons pattern. Understanding and using organizational patterns will help you with the next phase of speech preparation, which involves preparing an outline of your speech.

There are three main types of outlines to assist speakers in their preparation. These include word, phrase, and full-content or sentence outlines. Choosing the type of outline depends on your familiarity with the topic and the requirements provided by your instructor if you are preparing your speech for a classroom setting. In general, full-content or sentence outlines are helpful to create because they help ensure there is enough support for each idea and that each form of support is appropriately placed under a particular main idea.

Presentation aids provide speakers with a way to emphasize, clarify, or summarize an idea. Given the technology available in today's world, presentation aids can be easily created and incorporated into public speeches. However, they should never be used just for the sake of using them. Aids should only be used when they help the speaker make a point. When overused or poorly prepared, they may actually detract from the speaker's effectiveness.

Finally, selecting words that are concrete and descriptive will help your audience understand your message. In addition, it is important to avoid using language your audience may not understand, slang, or language that would offend. Using appropriate and clear word choice will have a positive impact on the overall quality of your speech.

In conclusion, there are many things to keep in mind when preparing a public speech. The more time a public speaker dedicates to the preparation phase of the process, the more likely that the speaker will be effective and accomplish the goal of the presentation. In the next chapter, practicing and delivering public speeches are discussed.

**Bar graphs** A type of visual aid often used to translate statistical comparisons and relationships into visual representations.

**Body** The heart of the speech; its purpose is to state each main idea and support each idea fully.

**Cause–effect order** Uncovering events that have resulted in a particular outcome. Speakers may also use the reverse order and begin by speaking about the effects and then go back and trace the causes.

**Charts** Visual display for information contained in a speech; help explain how things relate to each other or the sequence something goes through as it is processed.

**Chronological order** A pattern of organization particularly useful when you are trying to describe the order in which something occurs or occurred; used to explain a process, discuss historical events, or talk about someone's life. Also known as *time order*.

**Comparative advantage pattern** A speech organization often used in persuasive speaking, it demonstrates to the audience that accepting the speaker's persuasive proposition has more benefits than other possible propositions that others may be advocating.

**Conclusion** Summarizes or reviews the main points presented in the speech and leaves the audience with a final unifying thought.

**Geographical order** An organizational pattern used when you want to show how the various parts relate to each other and to the whole. Also known as *spatial order*.

**Introduction** Gains the audience's attention, clearly states the topic, and previews the main points to be discussed.

**Model** Replica of an object used as a visual aid.

**Monroe's motivated sequence** Most often used in persuasive speaking, with this type of organizational strategy, the speaker gains the audience's attention, shows there is a need (or a need for change), provides a solution that satisfies the need, visualizes the benefits of the stated change, and moves the audience to action.

**Outline** Tool that speakers use to organize their main ideas and support material into a coherent speech.

**Phrase outline** Type of outline that contains key phrases to help the speaker move from point to point. It expands on the word outline but is still relatively brief. It does help the speaker avoid reading from the outline since most of the speech content is not on this type of outline.

**Pictures and diagrams** Provide helpful visual images to augment a speaker's description of something.

**Presentational aids** Charts, bar graphs, pictures, diagrams, models, the actual object, and even the speaker him- or herself are considered to be visual aids. Audio aids include recordings of music, famous speeches, interviews, or even sounds from nature. Audio-visual aids include clips from movies, instructional DVDs, or anything that combines both sound and sight. They are all used to clarify, highlight, or summarize a speaker's ideas.

**Problem–solution order** Pattern that examines a particular problem and then offers a potential solution to the problem; based on John Dewey's reflective thinking process.

**Sentence outline** Very detailed outline containing most of what the speaker will say during the speech. It is very useful for organizing a speech and for practicing it as well. Also called a *full-content outline.*

**Statement of reasons pattern** In this pattern, each of the speaker's main points provides a reason why the proposal should (or should not) be supported.

**Topical pattern** In this pattern, you divide your speech into categories and support each category with evidence.

**Transitions** Words or phrases that help listeners move smoothly from one point to the next; signal to the audience that the speaker is moving from one idea to the next or from one type of support to another.

**Word outline** Type of outline that contains only key words to help the speaker remember the sequence in which main points should be discussed. Because of its brevity, it is most useful when the speaker is very comfortable with the speaking situation and knows the material in the speech exceptionally well.

# REFERENCES

AAA Foundation for Traffic Safety. (2010). *2010 Traffic Safety Culture Index*. Retrieved from www.aaafoundation.org/pdf/2010TSCIndexFinalReport.pdf.

Dewey, J. (1933). *How we think*. Boston: D. C. Heath.

Grice, G. L., & Skinner, J. F. (2013). *Mastering public speaking* (8th ed.). Boston: Pearson.

Monroe, A. H. (1935). *Principles and types of speech*. Chicago: Scott Foresman.

Progeria Research Foundation. (2014). *Progeria 101 FAQ*. Retrieved from www.progeriaresearch.org/progeria_101.html.

# COM 101 SPEECH DEMOGRAPHICS

| | | |
|---|---|---|
| **Gender** | M | F |

| | | |
|---|---|---|
| **Age** | 17 or below | 18 |
| | 19 | 20 |
| | 21 | 22 or older |

**Which do you use most often?** (Rank order with 1 being most often and 6 being least often.)

_____ Twitter          _____ Instagram

_____ Snap Chat          _____ Facebook

_____ Tumblr          _____ Other (specify) _____

| **Major** | CAS | Physical Sciences | COE | Early |
|---|---|---|---|---|
| | | Arts | | Middle |
| | | Humanities | | High School |
| | | Social Sciences | | Intervention |
| | COBE | Management/Entrepreneurship | CONHS | Nursing |
| | | Marketing/Hospitality/Fashion | | Health Sciences |
| | | Finance/Economics | | Accounting/IS |
| | | Sport Management | | Fashion Merchandising |
| | | Undecided | | Postsecondary |

| | | |
|---|---|---|
| **Do you consider yourself** | Athletic or Not athletic? | Artistic or Not Artistic? |
| **Are you on an** | AU/High School Athletic team? | Do you play an intramural sport? |

| **Hometown size** | under 500 | 500–2000 | |
|---|---|---|---|
| | 2000–5000 | 5000–10,000 | |
| | 10,000–30,000 | 30,000–50,000 | |
| | 50,000–100,000 | over 100,000 | |

| **Graduating class** | under 50 | 50–100 | |
|---|---|---|---|
| | 100–200 | 200–500 | over 500 |

| **Outside Job?** | Part-time | Full-time | None |
|---|---|---|---|
| | On campus | Off-campus | |

# COM 101 PEER CRITIQUE SHEET

Name _____ Topic _____

Was the *topic* clear?

Was the *organization* clear?

Was the *support* clear/adequate?

Was *audience adaptation* clear?

Was *delivery* clear?

List two things you liked            List two suggestions

_____

_____


Name _____ Topic _____

Was the *topic* clear?

Was the *organization* clear?

Was the *support* clear/adequate?

Was *audience adaptation* clear?

Was *delivery* clear?

List two things you liked            List two suggestions

_____

_____

# COM 101 PEER CRITIQUE SHEET

Name _____     Topic _____

Was the *topic* clear?

Was the *organization* clear?

Was the *support* clear/adequate?

Was *audience adaptation* clear?

Was *delivery* clear?

List two things you liked                List two suggestions

_____

_____


Name _____     Topic _____

Was the *topic* clear?

Was the *organization* clear?

Was the *support* clear/adequate?

Was *audience adaptation* clear?

Was *delivery* clear?

List two things you liked                List two suggestions

_____

_____

# COM 101 PEER CRITIQUE SHEET

Name _____ Topic _____

Was the *topic* clear?

Was the *organization* clear?

Was the *support* clear/adequate?

Was *audience adaptation* clear?

Was *delivery* clear?

List two things you liked         List two suggestions

_____

_____


Name _____ Topic _____

Was the *topic* clear?

Was the *organization* clear?

Was the *support* clear/adequate?

Was *audience adaptation* clear?

Was *delivery* clear?

List two things you liked         List two suggestions

_____

_____

# COM 101 SPEECH PRESENTATIONS

**Requirements** for the Informative Speech assignment:

TOPIC:

Time limit:

Number of sources:

You will be judged on the following criteria:

**Content**

Introduction/beginning

Organization

Transitions

Conclusion

Source citation during speech

Overall content (captivating or not)

Other:_____

**Physical Control**

Body (head, arms/gestures, feet/legs)

Eye contact

Formal attire

**Vocal Control**

Pauses/pace

Projection/enthusiasm

Emotion/variation in delivery

**Typed outline due** _____
- Include citations within text of outline in APA format
- Include complete citations in APA format at end of outline

# COM 101 EXERCISE
# SPEECH RESEARCH ACTIVITY

Name _____ Speech Topic _____

List three possible outside sources. Include the title, author, and type of source.

Title                                        Author                                        Source Type

_____

_____

_____

List three pieces of supporting material you could choose from the above sources. Identify which category of supporting material they fall under.

Supporting Material                                                              Category

_____

_____

_____

# COM 101 SPEECH CRITIQUE SHEET

Name _____     Topic _____

**Introduction**

Attention

Credibility

Topic

Listening Reason

Preview

**Body**

Organization

Support

Audience Adaptation

Language Use

Transitions

Sources cited (4)

1. _____

2. _____

3. _____

4. _____

**Conclusion**

    Review

    Closure

**Delivery**

    Eye contact

    Note card use

    Volume

    Rate/articulation

    Vocal variety/emphasis

    Posture

    Gestures

    Extra movements

    Visual Aids

**Time**

# COM 101 HUMAN COMMUNICATION
# TOPIC EXPLORATION ACTIVITY

Find a partner and talk through the following areas. I will give you about 5–10 minutes for each person's topic. Talk through all the areas for one person's topic first. I will tell you when it is time to switch to the other person.

1.  Tell your partner a little bit about your speech topic. Be sure to say whether you plan to do informative or persuasive. (If you haven't decided, pick something you might be speaking about.)

2.  Ask your partner these three questions about your topic:

    • How much do you know about my topic?

    • How do you feel about my topic? (positive/negative)

    • How interested are you in my topic?

3.  Have your partner ask you two questions about your topic.

4.  Ask your partner to give you feedback about the kind of information they would find interesting/helpful in understanding your topic. If you are doing persuasion, ask them what they think would make your case most convincing.

Be prepared to share with the class two things you learned about your topic that may be useful as you plan your upcoming speech.

# COM 101 EXERCISE
# SPEECH TOPIC ACTIVITY

1.  Think of one possible topic you could give a speech on for this class.

2.  Find a partner and tell each other a little bit about your topics.

3.  Have each person ask two questions about the other person's topic.

4.  Ask your partner these three questions about your topic

    •   How much do you know about my topic?

    •   How do you feel about my topic? (positive/negative)

    •   How interested are you in my topic?

# COM 101 TIPS FOR USING VISUAL AIDS IN YOUR SPEECH

Sometimes it is easier to forget about visual aids than prepare them. It's hard enough work writing your speech, let alone having to produce a multimedia extravaganza to push home your point—right?

Maybe some speeches don't require visual aids, such as wedding speeches or toasts. However, for a lot of speeches, using visual aids will not only enhance your presentation, but will also help you to remember key points and keep you and your audience focused. Visual aids, or "props," can be as small or large as you want. They can vary in their simplicity or complexity. How much a part of your speech they are used for—it's up to you.

Here are some tips for successful use of visual aids in your presentation:

1. Props should be visually stimulating and supportive of the topic you are speaking on.
2. If using pictures on your slides, fill up the whole screen with the illustration.
3. Don't pack the slide with wordy paragraphs and information. Break your data into bullet points.
4. Ask the organizers what visual aids are available for your presentation. Ensure everything is present and working before you begin your speech.
5. Make sure every audience member can see the visual aids.
6. When you use the visual aid, ensure the audience is focused on it. After you have made each point, remove the visual and refocus the audience on you.
7. If you have trouble remembering your speech, use your visual aids as memory joggers.
8. Visual aids aren't only overheads and slides. They can be noisemakers, costumes, and tricks. Visual aids can be used to induce a laugh, stimulate the audience, or make a passionate point. Select your "alternative props" with care.
9. When you reveal your visual aid, make sure you continue speaking to the audience, not to the prop.
10. Handouts are also considered visual aids. Determine the correct time to distribute them. You want your audience to focus on your words, not to read and discuss elements of the handout during your speech.

**Why should I use visual aids?**

Visual aids support your argument and increase audience understanding of the main points the mind better remembers picture information rather than word information. A visual presentation will enhance your credibility, and it may even help you with your nerves. If you have a visual aid to focus on rather than your shaking hands, your fears will be forgotten as you take the audience through the points on the screen.

**\*\*\* Practice using your visual aids well before the day of your presentation. \*\*\***

# COM 101 SPEECH EXPLORATION ACTIVITY

Name _____    Speech Topic _____

Possible Main Points

_____

_____

_____

Why should we listen to you? How do you know about it?


Why should we be interested? How does it connect to us?


Possible Outside Sources

# COM 101 GROUP PROJECT PARTICIPATION FORM

Name _____

Topic _____

Key: 2 = Excellent; 1 = Average; 0 = Poor            Do not evaluate yourself.

|  | Name | Name | Name | Name | Name | Name |
|---|---|---|---|---|---|---|
| Participated frequently and effectively during the project development |  |  |  |  |  |  |
| Encouraged others to participate |  |  |  |  |  |  |
| Carried out individual assignments promptly |  |  |  |  |  |  |
| Contributed to the understanding of the group project |  |  |  |  |  |  |
| Avoided unnecessary conflict with group members |  |  |  |  |  |  |
| Helped keep group meetings on track |  |  |  |  |  |  |
| Appeared committed to group's goals by attending every meeting and being prepared every time |  |  |  |  |  |  |
| Had a good attitude about the project |  |  |  |  |  |  |
| Contributed to the effectiveness of the final presentation |  |  |  |  |  |  |
| Overall, this member was valuable to the group |  |  |  |  |  |  |
| Totals |  |  |  |  |  |  |

# COM 101 EXERCISE
# PRESTIGE OF OCCUPATION WORKSHEET

As a group, reach a consensus about the prestige of the following occupations. Use discussion to rank these occupations from 1 to 14. Focus more on your top/bottom 5 first and then fill in the middle if there is time.

_____ Firefighter               _____ Air Traffic Controller

_____ Farmer                    _____ Journalist

_____ Doctor                    _____ Television Star

_____ Police Officer            _____ Nurse

_____ Teacher                   _____ Construction Worker

_____ Garbage Collector         _____ Truck Driver

_____ Physical Therapist        _____ Computer Consultant

# COM 101 EXERCISE
## SURVIVAL

It is around 10 a.m. in mid-July, and your plane has crash landed in the desert somewhere in Arizona. The twin-engine plane has completely burned, with only the frame remaining. You and the other four passengers are uninjured. Before the crash, the pilot was unable to notify any airport of the plane's position. However, based on what the pilot said, you are approximately 80 miles south of the interstate. The immediate area is flat and barren, and the temperature usually reaches 110–130°F. You are dressed in a short-sleeved-shirt, shorts, and tennis shoes. Before the plane caught fire, you and the other four passengers were able to salvage 15 items. These items are:

| | | | |
|---|---|---|---|
| _____ | 2 quarts of water | _____ | two pair of sunglasses |
| _____ | plastic raincoat | _____ | 1 quart of water per person |
| _____ | flashlight | _____ | book entitled _Edible Animals of the Desert_ |
| _____ | cosmetic mirror | _____ | bottle of 100 salt tablets |
| _____ | magnetic compass | _____ | compress kit with gauze |
| _____ | jackknife | _____ | sectional air map for the area |
| _____ | one jacket per person | _____ | loaded .45 caliber pistol |
| _____ | red and white parachute | | |

Rank these items in the order of their importance for your survival, starting with 1 for the most important and 15 for the least important.

# COM 101 COMMUNICATION CONTEXTS EXERCISE

Discuss the impact of each variable below on the following communication events.

1. Having a social drink with a friend

2. Studying in the library with classmates

3. Meeting with a professor after 5 p.m.

4. Texting your friend in California

5. Talking on the phone with your mom/dad

**Contextual Variables**

| | |
|---|---|
| Time of day | Touch |
| Smells/scent | Time of year |
| Weather | Relationship history with other person |
| Other people present | Your mood/their mood |
| Distractions | Cultural differences |
| Location | Internal noise |
| Clothing/accessories | Furniture arrangement |
| Physical distance | Power/status influences |

# COM 101 FIRST IMPRESSIONS EXERCISE

A. Choose a partner for this assignment that you did not know prior to this class meeting. Without talking and basing your ideas solely on your observations this far, answer the following questions about your partner. You may tell your partner your first name only. Do not discuss the questions with your partner until all statements have been completed.

1. My partner's middle name is _____.

2. My partner's major is _____.

3. My partner's favorite food is _____.

4. My partner's favorite movie is _____.

5. My partner's favorite car is _____.

B. After completing these statements, discuss your answers and find out how accurate your impressions were.

C. Working as a team, answer these questions about your professor.

**Discussion questions:**

How accurate were you?

What did you base your answers on?

      Main-stream cultural assumptions?

      Specific people you know that remind you of your partner?

      Yourself?

Did you stereotype your partner? If so, in what ways?

Was your stereotype accurate?

# COM 101 WHO WILL GET THE KIDNEY

You have been hired as the kidney transplant coordinator for Summit County. On this day, you have eight patients who have been admitted to the Akron City Hospital for a kidney transplant. Unfortunately, there are only three kidneys available. Your task is to select the three recipients from the list of eight patients.

Patient #1: Joy Wise, age 27. Joy is married and has six children who range in age from 2 to 10 years old. Her husband, Louis, owns a small automotive repair business in downtown Stow, OH.

Patient #2: Peter Gafferty, age 31. Peter is a health care analyst for a pharmaceutical corporation. He is a former Rhodes Scholar with a Ph.D. in physics. He has never been married and serves as the primary caretaker for his mother who has Alzheimer's disease.

Patient #3: Mario Santini, age 46. Mario is an ex-convict, having been convicted of tax evasion, and served seven years in a federal penitentiary. It is rumored that Mario is a member of a prominent Mafia family based in New Jersey. He is responsible for his two nephews, ages 6 and 9, whose parents were tragically killed by a drunk driver two years ago.

Patient #4: John Lappelton, age 9. John has an IQ of 160, but is severely mentally disturbed after having witnessed an accident that killed his grandmother. He hasn't spoken in two years.

Patient #5: Christy Aune, age 27. Christy is an instructor at a local community college, working on her Master's degree in Communication Studies. She is married to Don, who refuses to work and spends his time playing guitar in local bands. Christy and Don are approximately $25,000 in debt.

Patient #6: Chance Thomas, age 35. Chance is a bachelor. He spends most of his free time hanging out at BW3's pub playing Trivia with his friends and has no long-term plans for his life. He works as a clerk for the Ohio State Police.

Patient #7: Reverend Jacoby, age 53. Reverend Jacoby spends a lot of time arranging missions to help the people of inner city Cleveland. He is an alcoholic.

Patient #8: Justin Mathias, age 22. Justin is a student at Ashland University and works 30 hours a week as a bartender to pay for his education.

# COM 101 ACTIVITY

**Listening and Hearing**

You just listened to a message presented in class. Answer the following questions about the information in the message:

1. What was the overall meaning of the message?

2. What words do you believe helped deliver the intended message?

3. Why did these words stand out to you as projecting the meaning of the message?

4. What do each of these words mean?

_____

_____

_____

_____

_____

_____

_____

_____

_____

_____

_____

_____

_____

_____

_____

_____

_____

_____

_____

Break into two groups, males and females. Answer each of these questions again as a group. Were your answers the same as above? Were there any differences in the response of your classmates based on gender? Do men and women, in general, focus on different content in messages? Do men and women, in general, hear and/or listen to messages differently?

_____

_____

_____

_____

_____

_____

_____

_____

_____

_____

_____

_____

_____

_____

_____

_____

_____

_____

_____

_____

_____

Dr. Dariela Rodriguez

# COM 101 ACTIVITY
# THE LUNCH TIME REALIZATION

Take a trip to the Eagle's Nest or Convo and watch how individuals interact with each other. Watch how they approach friends and strangers. How do they greet their friends? How do they greet strangers? Do they approach males differently than they approach females? Do they speak differently with students versus faculty or staff? How do you know this based on what they say or do?

_____

_____

_____

_____

_____

_____

_____

Engage with at least three individuals you do not know. Is verbal communication necessary when first approaching strangers (i.e., introducing yourself, saying hello), or can you simply sit down at their table and be able to engage with the individual without an introduction? What nonverbal behaviors can you use/did you use to make the interaction less awkward?

_____

_____

_____

_____

_____

_____

_____

_____

Dr. Dariela Rodriguez

# COM 101
# NONVERBAL VIDEO EXAMPLES

**What meanings did you see expressed through:**

Kinesics (body movement/gestures)

Facial expressions

Eye contact (or avoidance)

Haptics (touch)

Physical Appearance (gender, skin color, size)

Artifacts (clothing and accessories)

Proxemics (space)

Territory

Chronemics (time)

Paralanguage (rate, volume, pitch)

Silence

**Discussion questions:**

How does nonverbal express cultural and sub-cultural differences?

How do contradictions between verbal and nonverbal come out?

What does nonverbal tell you about people's relationships?

What do reactions tell you about expectations and rules?

# COM 101 HUMAN COMMUNICATION
# PERSONAL NARRATIVE GRADING RUBRIC

Name _____

|  | Excellent (1 pt) | Needs some work (½ pt) | Weak or Missing (0 pt) |
|---|---|---|---|
| **Introduction**<br><br>___/2 pt | Interesting beginning, (not "Hi, my name is") Nice impact | Not much that really grabbed our attention. More energy needed | Awkward opening Plan for a solid beginning. |
| **Organization**<br><br>___/4 pt | Order was clear and easy to follow | Mostly clear, but some areas needed more organization | Topics shifted making organization difficult to follow |
| **Content/ supporting details**<br><br>___/4 pt | Fun and interesting facts give. Created a memorable image. | Some interesting facts, more/less depth needed. | Not much depth or detail included. |
| **Conclusion**<br><br>___/2 pt | Interesting ending (not "that's my speech") Nice impact | Some closure, but still a bit awkward at the end. | Abrupt ending. No real closure |
| **Eye contact**<br><br>___/3 pt | Excellent throughout the speech | Came and went from time to time | Not much direct eye contact used. |
| **Vocal clarity, volume**<br><br>___/2 pt | Strong and interesting | Dropped a bit at times | Low, hard to hear |
| **Conversational tone/style**<br><br>___/2 pt | Slow, clear, and precise | Need to slow/speed up | Very difficult to follow |
| **Use of body movement**<br><br>___/2 pt | Enhanced ideas and helped explain content | Some movements to enhance, but more can occur | Not much in terms of adding movement to enhance the speech. |
| **Distracting body movement**<br><br>___/2 pt | No distractions. Very poised and professional | Some distractions in a places. | Many distracting movements that pull attention away from the story. |
| **Time requirement**<br><br>___/2 pt | Perfectly timed | Off by less than 30 sec. | Off by more than 30 sec. |

**TOTAL_____/25 points**

# COM 101 HUMAN COMMUNICATION
# SELF-INTRODUCTION GRADING RUBRIC

Name _____

| | Excellent (1 pt) | Needs some work (½ pt) | Weak or Missing (0 pt) |
|---|---|---|---|
| **Introduction**<br><br>___/1 pt | Interesting beginning, (not "Hi, my name is") Nice impact | Not much that really grabbed our attention. More energy needed | Awkward opening Plan for a solid beginning. |
| **Organization**<br><br>___/1 pt | Order was clear and easy to follow | Mostly clear, but some areas needed more organization | Topics shifted making organization difficult to follow |
| **Content/supporting details**<br><br>___/1 pt | Fun and interesting facts give. Created a memorable image. | Some interesting facts, more/less depth needed. | Not much depth or detail included. |
| **Conclusion**<br><br>___/1 pt | Interesting ending (not "that's my speech") Nice impact | Some closure, but still a bit awkward at the end. | Abrupt ending. No real closure |
| **Eye contact**<br><br>___/1 pt | Excellent throughout the speech | Came and went from time to time | Not much direct eye contact used. |
| **Note cards/reading**<br><br>___/1 pt | None or excellent use | Some reading of notes | Lots of reading of notes |
| **Vocal clarity, volume, and rate**<br><br>___/1 pt | Strong and interesting | Dropped a bit at times | Low, hard to hear |
| **Conversational tone/style**<br><br>___/1 pt | Slow, clear, and precise | Need to slow/speed up | Very difficult to follow |
| **Use of body movement**<br><br>___/1 pt | Enhanced ideas and did not distract us. | Some distracting movements | Many distracting movements |
| **Time requirement**<br>___/1 pt | Perfectly timed | Off by less than 30 sec. | Off by more than 30 sec. |

TOTAL_____/10 points

# INFORMATIVE/PERSUASIVE SPEECH RUBRIC

Name: _____

Topic: _____

| Content | Excellent | Right Idea, but Needs Work | Weak | NOTES |
|---|---|---|---|---|
| **Purpose/ Topic Choice Audience Analysis**<br><br>_____ 5 pts. | Topic Appropriate for Purpose Subject Appropriate for audience Topic narrowed to fit time limit | Topic Loosely Fits Purpose Not clear how Subject Fits Audience Topic needed to be narrowed/expanded to fit time limit (less than 1 minute over/under) | Topic Doesn't Fit Purpose Subject Inappropriate for Audience Topic needed to be narrowed/expanded to fit time limit (more than 1 minute over/under) | |
| **Introduction**<br><br>_____ 10 pts. | Good attention-getter Topic/thesis clear Clear credibility Clear preview | Attention-getter needs work Topic/thesis could be clearer More credibility needed Clearer preview needed | No Attention-Getter Topic/thesis Unclear No importance established No credibility established No clear preview of main points | |
| **Body and Transitions**<br><br>_____ 20 pts. | Clear organizational pattern Transition Easy to Follow | Work on organizational pattern Reorganize or chunk some of your information so it is easier to follow and remember and/or give us stronger cues. | Poor organization Difficult to Follow | |
| **Support/Explanation of Ideas**<br><br>_____ 20 pts. | Good Depth Good Development of Major Idea Information Supported Purpose Statement Good use of logos, pathos, and ethos (persuasion) | More Depth Needed / Narrow Topic Information loosely supported Purpose Statement Some use of logos, pathos, and ethos (persuasion) Work on Development of Ideas | Very Broad Ideas Lack Substance Information didn't support Purpose Not much use of logos, pathos, or ethos (persuasion) | |
| **Sources**<br><br>_____ 10 pts | All THREE sources used All Credible/Quality sources Sources cited clearly | Some sources used Some credibility issues Some sources not clearly cited | No sources used No Sources cited | |
| **Conclusion**<br><br>_____ 5 pts. | Emphasized your main point(s) Good use of closure | Conclusion a somewhat abrupt Work on summary Audience Questioned if you were finished | Just Stopped Conclusion a Very Abrupt Little or No Summary | |

| Content | Excellent | Right Idea, but Needs Work | Weak | NOTES |
|---|---|---|---|---|
| **Delivery** | | | | |
| **Eye Contact**<br><br>_____ 10 pts | Good Eye Contact<br>Use notes as Cues,<br>not Crutches<br>Eye contact was excel-<br>lent in all areas of the<br>room. | Rely less on your notes<br>Make better use of eye<br>contact to all parts of<br>the room. | Significant reading<br>from notes<br>Little Eye Contact | |
| **Vocal Rate,<br>Pitch, Pauses<br>and Volume**<br><br>_____ 5 pts. | Good Volume Easy<br>to Hear<br>Excellent Rate for<br>Effective Pace<br>Pitch, and pauses<br>Used Well<br>Good Variety of Tones | Volume needs work<br>Rate of speech<br>needs work<br>Use vocal variety to<br>enhance your message | Volume very<br>problematic<br>Rate problematics,<br>hurts clarity<br>No Vocal variety to<br>your message | |
| **Vocal Quality<br>Articulation &<br>Pronunciation**<br><br>_____ 5 pts. | Your voice was conver-<br>sational<br>Articulation and pro-<br>nunciation were clear.<br>Used Voice to Enhance<br>your Message | Voice needs to be more<br>conversational<br>Articulation and<br>pronunciation unclear.<br>Mumbled Some<br>Some Distractive Verbal<br>Tones (um, um, and,<br>and) | Voice Not Conversa-<br>tional<br>Speak Clearly<br>Articulation and<br>pronunciation<br>Mumbled Some<br>Numerous Distractive<br>Verbal Tones (um, um,<br>and, and). | |
| **Nonverbal<br>Posture/<br>Gestures**<br><br>_____ 5 pts. | You looked comfortable<br>Natural using your<br>hands, body, and facial<br>expressions<br>NO Distractive Move-<br>ments | You looked fairly<br>comfortable<br>Work on Natural using<br>your hands, body, and<br>facial expressions<br>Some Distractive<br>Movements | Very Stiff<br>Work on Natural using<br>your hands, body, and<br>facial expressions<br>Significant Distractive<br>Movements | |
| **Preparedness,<br>Composure,<br>and Polish**<br><br>_____ 5 pts | Appeared well prepared<br>Demonstrated excellent<br>confidence<br>Polished Presentation | Evidence of preparation<br>but needs work<br>Demonstrated some<br>confidence<br>Work on Polishing<br>Presentation | Evidence of little<br>preparation<br>Need to demonstrate<br>confidence<br>Presentation<br>pretty rough | |
| _____ | **TOTAL 100 POINTS<br>POSSIBLE** | **Assigned time:<br>5-7 Minutes** | **Your Time:<br>Minutes** | |

CPSIA information can be obtained
at www.ICGtesting.com
Printed in the USA
LVOW02s2306240817
546175LV00004B/25/P